SECOND
THOUGHTS

To Mary Ruane,
a much treasured and loved source
of second thoughts and knowledge.
To Lina Cerulo, for convincing the men in the family
that "girls" deserved a college education too.

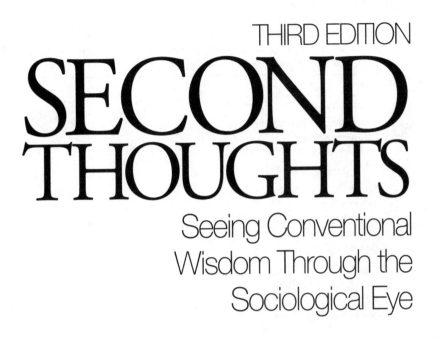

THIRD EDITION

SECOND THOUGHTS

Seeing Conventional Wisdom Through the Sociological Eye

JANET M. RUANE
Montclair State University

KAREN A. CERULO
Rutgers University

PINE FORGE PRESS
An Imprint of Sage Publications, Inc.
Thousand Oaks • London • New Delhi

For information:

Pine Forge Press
A Sage Publications Company
2455 Teller Road
Thousand Oaks, California 91320
E-mail: order@sagepub.com

Sage Publications Ltd.
1 Oliver's Yard
55 City Road
London EC1Y 1SP
United Kingdom

Sage Publications India Pvt. Ltd.
B-42, Panchsheel Enclave
Post Box 4109
New Delhi 110 017 India

Printed in the United States of America on acid-free paper.

Library of Congress Cataloging-in-Publication Data

Ruane, Janet M., 1954-
Second thoughts : seeing conventional wisdom through the sociological eye / Janet M. Ruane and Karen A. Cerulo.— 3rd ed.
    p. cm.
Includes bibliographical references and index.
ISBN 0-7619-8824-6 (pbk.)
    1. Sociology. 2. Sociology—Quotations, maxims, etc. 3. Maxims. I. Cerulo, Karen A. II. Title.
HM585.R867 2004 301—dc22   2003025173

04   05   06   07   08   09   10   9   8   7   6   5   4   3   2   1

Acquiring Editor:	Jerry Westby
Editorial Assistant:	Vonessa Vondera
Project Editor:	Claudia A. Hoffman
Copy Editor:	Carla Freeman
Typesetter:	C&M Digitals (P) Ltd.
Indexer:	Molly Hall
Cover Designer:	Michelle Lee Kenny

About the Authors

Janet M. Ruane (Ph.D. Rutgers University) is Associate Professor of Sociology at Montclair State University. She has served as her department's Coordinator of Undergraduate Advising and as the Advisor of the Graduate Program in Applied Sociology. Professor Ruane's research interests include formal and informal social control mechanisms, domestic violence, media and technology, research methods, and applied sociology. She is the author of *Essentials of Research Methods* (Blackwell) and has contributed articles to several journals, including *Sociological Inquiry, Law and Policy, Communication Research, Sociological Focus, The Journal of Applied Sociology, Science As Culture, Simulation and Games,* and *The Virginia Review of Sociology.* Over the years, Professor Ruane has gained considerable classroom experience, teaching both introductory and advanced-level sociology courses as well as graduate courses in applied sociology.

Karen A. Cerulo (Ph.D. Princeton University) is Professor of Sociology at Rutgers University. Her research interests include culture and cognition, symbolic communication, media and technology, and comparative historical studies. Professor Cerulo's articles appear in a wide variety of journals, including the *American Sociological Review, Contemporary Sociology, Poetics, Social Forces, Sociological Forum, Sociological Inquiry, Communication Research,* and annuals such as the *Annual Review of Sociology* and *Research in Political Sociology.* She is the author of three books: *Identity Designs: The Sights and Sounds of a Nation,* a work that won the ASA Culture Section's award for the best book of 1996 (The Rose Book Series of the ASA, Rutgers University Press); *Deciphering Violence: The Cognitive Order of Right and Wrong* (Routledge); and *What's the Worst That Could Happen?* (forthcoming, University of Chicago Press). She also has edited a collection entitled *Culture in Mind: Toward a Sociology of Culture and Cognition* (Routledge). Professor Cerulo's teaching experience includes the Rutgers University Award for Distinguished Contributions to Undergraduate Education.

Contents

> In this introduction, we discuss the roots of conventional wisdom. We
> also contrast such knowledge with that acquired via the sociological
> perspective. In this way, we introduce students to a sociological mode
> of thinking.

Concepts Defined and Applied
Conventional wisdom; social patterns; social context; cultural value;
self-fulfilling prophecy; sociological imagination.

> Americans like to "run the numbers." No matter what the realm—
> sports, business, politics, or entertainment—numbers often provide
> the bottom line. Why is our faith in numbers so strong? Conventional
> wisdom tells us that numbers don't lie. Is such wisdom accurate? Can
> we take confidence in the "realities" claimed by national polls, social
> scientific surveys, and other quantitative studies? In this essay, we
> note several important elements to consider in establishing the
> "truth" of numbers.

Or is it? This essay reviews the conditions under which stress can
prove beneficial in one's everyday activities. In so doing, we highlight
the importance of considering social context in assessing social
behaviors.

Concepts Defined and Applied
Social structure; social location; social context; chronic stress; social
support network; Gemeinschaft; Gesellschaft; task-oriented stress; role
conflict; social strain.

Growing old—no one looks forward to it. Yet, this essay illustrates
that our worst fears about growing old may be largely unfounded,
simply products of a "master status" for which we have been
inadequately prepared.

Concepts Defined and Applied
Emotional regulation; master status; anticipatory socialization;
macro-level analysis; social context; age structure.

This essay examines social relations in the United States, exploring
in particular the characterization of contemporary Americans as
increasingly isolated, disconnected, and dangerously individualistic.
Here, we argue that social relations in the United States are more
multifaceted than conventional wisdom suggests, a result of the
complex interplay of social structure and culture.

Concepts Defined and Applied
Individualism; social relations; relational polyphony; pluralism;
bilateral relations; communalism; communities of talk; linear models;
culture; cultural construction; diffuse instability.

This essay explores the power in a name, highlighting the central role of symbols and labels in the construction of identity.

Concepts Defined and Applied
Symbols; identity; impression management; boundary construction; postmodern theory; labeling theory; secondary deviance.

This essay documents the social advantages enjoyed by physically attractive individuals—tall, slim, and beautiful or handsome women and men. We also discuss the powerful role physical attractiveness can play in the construction of self-identity.

Concepts Defined and Applied
Cultural inconsistency; self-fulfilling prophecy; cultural capital; social status; identity; socialization; appearance norms; primary socialization; rituals; looking-glass self.

Stratification 99

If so, our garbage collectors are worth more than our teachers, and baseball players are worth more than those searching for a cure to AIDS. This essay addresses the inconsistencies often found between what we pay for work and the value we place on it.

Concepts Defined and Applied
Income; Davis-Moore thesis; functional analysis; conflict theory; wealth; power; occupational prestige; occupational prestige scale; stratification system.

This essay documents the impact of income on issues of mortality and life chances. Money, with all its alleged downfalls, can still mean the difference between life and death.

Concepts Defined and Applied
Mortality rate; socioeconomic status; infant mortality; life expectancy; negative life events; life chances; functional analysis.

There's no social ill that the law can't fix . . . or at least that is what many Americans believe. In this essay, we review various social functions of the law. We also consider whether or not we are overly dependent on this tool of formal social control.

Concepts Defined and Applied
Social control; norms; informal social control; formal social control; social engineering; moral entrepreneurs; civil lawsuits; class action suits; tolerance.

. . . except, of course, when reporting your income, revealing your age, sparing the feelings of another—the list can go on and on. In this essay, we explore the conditions under which lying is viewed as normal. In so doing, we use lying as a case study that aptly demonstrates both the pervasiveness and the relative nature of deviance.

Concepts Defined and Applied
Norms; deviance; deviant lies; normal lies; techniques of neutralization; social scripts; primary deviance; secondary deviance.

Social Institutions: Marriage And Family

Mom, dad, and the kids—is this the unit on which American social life is built? This essay documents the history of family in America, showing that the nuclear family is a relatively recent phenomenon and one that soon may be replaced by other forms of family. In addition, the stability of the nuclear family is explored in light of idyllic stereotypes.

Concepts Defined and Applied
Macro-level analysis; nuclear family; extended family.

High divorce rates, couples living together, the need for "space," fear of commitment—have such trends doomed the institution of marriage? Here, we discuss research suggesting that the practice of marriage is alive and well despite conventional wisdom to the contrary. We also note the historical "popularity" of divorce in America and speculate on why such a trend marks our culture.

Social Institutions: Education

> Conventional wisdom tells us that educating the masses will bring
> equal opportunities to people of all races, ethnicities, and genders. In
> this essay, we explore the truth of this claim and review the progress
> we have made in bringing a quality education to all.

Concepts Defined and Applied
> Intergenerational upward mobility; structural functionalism; literacy;
> conflict theory; socialization; tracking; self-fulfilling prophecy.

Preface

It is not uncommon for those assigned to teach entry-level sociology courses to experience some trepidation, even dread, about the teaching task ahead. In many ways, intro to sociology is a "tough sell." Some students perceive the discipline as nothing more than a "re-hash" of the obvious; it speaks to everyday life, something many students believe they already know and understand. Other students confuse sociology courses with disciplines such as psychology or social work; they take our courses hoping to "figure out the opposite sex," learn to better "work the system," or overcome their personal problems with regard to deviant behavior or family relations. To muddy the waters even more, many intro students are likely to be in our courses not because of some desire to learn sociology but because the courses satisfy a general education requirement. Taking all of these factors into account, sociology instructors can face substantial resistance. Getting students to "adjust" their visions of the world so as to incorporate the sociological eye is no small feat.

Despite these challenges, it remains essential to achieve success in entry-level sociology courses. From an instrumental point of view, the discipline recruits future sociologists from these courses, thus mandating a sound foundation. Furthermore, departments may gain significant institutional resources by keeping intro course enrollments up. Intellectual concerns also contribute to the importance of entry-level courses. Many sociology instructors believe that intro courses offer a guaranteed "dividend" for the student: The sociological vision represents an essential tool for understanding and surviving our increasingly complex social world. Thus, intro courses provide instructors with a valuable opportunity to plant and nurture the sociological imagination in each new cohort of college students. Thought of in this way, failing the intro student can carry long-term social costs.

Second Thoughts offers a "tried and true" approach to successfully nurturing sociological thinking in the newcomer. The book provides a vehicle with which to initiate dialogue; it allows instructors to meet their students on "common ground." Each chapter in this book begins with a shared idea—a conventional wisdom that both instructors and students have encountered by virtue of being consumers of popular culture. Once this common footing is established, *Second Thoughts* introduces relevant sociological concepts and theories that "mesh" with each conventional wisdom. Sociological ideas and perspective are used to explain, qualify, and sometimes debunk conventional wisdom.

At the conclusion of each chapter, we provide a vehicle by which students can apply their new sociological knowledge beyond the classroom. We have incorporated a set of exercises linked to the subject matter covered in the chapter. The exercises, too, are grounded in the familiar. We encourage students to turn to everyday, common resources for some firsthand learning experiences.

Our own classroom experiences prove the "familiar" a "user-friendly" place to jump-start discussion, thus laying the foundation for critical thinking and informed analysis. In the classroom, we also have found the "familiar" to be a useful tool with which to delineate the sociological vision. This book attempts to pass along some of the fruits of our own learning. In pushing beyond the familiar, *Second Thoughts* also exposes students to the sociological advantage. At minimum, readers will accrue the benefits that come from taking time to give conventional ideas some important "second thoughts."

Acknowledgments

There are, of course, a number of people who have contributed to this book. First and foremost, we would both like to acknowledge the students encountered in the many sociology courses taught at SUNY Stony Brook, Rutgers University, and Montclair State University. These students challenged us to make the sociological imagination a meaningful and desirable option on students' learning agendas. Thanks also go to our two research assistants Tilak Jani (a wonderful Rutgers undergrad) and Jennifer Hemler (an extremely talented graduate student at Rutgers). Their inquisitiveness and tenacity brought great improvements to this edition of *Second Thoughts*. Thanks also to our friend Maureen Gorman, a patient and skilled reference librarian who always meets our information needs with a better-than-excellent effort. We are grateful to these reviewers for their careful readings and productive suggestions on various drafts of the manuscript: Hugh F. Lena, Providence College; Jay Howard, Indiana University/Purdue University; Ted Paul McNeilsmith, Adams State University; Sara L. Crawley, University of New Orleans; and Tom "Paul" Semm, San Diego State University.

Thanks also go to our wonderfully supportive editor, Jerry Westby, and to the solid support staff at Pine Forge, including Vonessa Vondera, Claudia Hoffman, and Carla Freeman. Several colleagues—Deborah Carr, Peter Freund, Allan Horwitz, Laura Kramer, Sarah Rosenfield—deserve our thanks for offering feedback, suggestions, and helpful citations used in the writing of this manuscript. We would also like to thank several friends and family members (Mary Agnes, Anne, Jay, Sam, Joan, and Jane) for consistently asking about "the book" and/or planning a book celebration, thereby indirectly prodding us to stick with the program.

Introduction

THE SOCIOLOGICAL PERSPECTIVE

Introduction

The Sociological Perspective

In this introduction, we discuss the roots of conventional wisdom. We also contrast such knowledge with that acquired via the sociological perspective. In this way, we introduce students to a sociological mode of thinking.

Conventional wisdom is a part of our everyday lives. We are exposed to its lessons from early childhood, and we encounter its teachings until the day we die. Who among us was not taught, for example, to "be fearful of strangers" or that "beauty is only skin deep"? Similarly, we have all learned that "stress is bad for our well-being" and that "adult life is simply incomplete without children."

Conventional wisdom comes to us in many forms. We encounter it via folk adages, "old wives' tales," traditions, and political or religious rhetoric. We find it in advice columns, cultural truisms, and the tenets of "common sense." **Conventional wisdom** refers to that body of assertions and beliefs that is generally recognized as part of a culture's "common knowledge." These cultural lessons are many, and they cannot be taken lightly. They are central to American society, and they are frequently the source of our beliefs, attitudes, and behaviors.

To be sure, conventional wisdom often contains elements of truth. As such, it constitutes a starting point for knowledge (Mathisen 1989; Ruane 2004). Consider, for example, the well-known truism: "Actions speak louder than words." Many laboratory studies indeed have shown that those assessing an individual who says one thing but does another are influenced more strongly by the individual's actions (Amabile and Kabat 1982; Bryan and Walbek 1970; Ekman and Frank 1993; Ekman et al. 1991; Van Overwalle 1997). Similarly, a long line of research supports the adage that warns, "Marry in haste, repent at leisure." When we define *haste* as "marrying too young or marrying too quickly," we find that those who "marry in haste" report less satisfaction over the course of the marriage and experience higher divorce rates than those who make a later or a slower decision (Furstenburg 1979; Glenn and

Supancic 1984; Grover, Russell, and Schumm 1985; Kitson et al. 1985; Martin and Bumpass 1989; National Marriage Project 2003).

Complete faith in conventional wisdom, however, can be risky. Social patterns and behaviors frequently contradict the wisdoms we embrace. Many studies show, for instance, that adages encouraging the "fear of strangers" often are misguided; most crimes of personal violence are perpetrated by those we know (see Essay 14). Similarly, research documents that beauty may be merely "skin deep," but its importance cannot be underestimated. Physically attractive individuals fare better than those of more average appearance in almost all areas of social interaction (see Essay 9). Many studies suggest that stress is not always "bad for one's well-being"; it can sometimes be productive for human beings (see Essay 5). And despite all of the accolades to the presence of children in our lives, research shows that many adults report their highest levels of lifetime happiness take place *before* they have children or *after* their children leave home (see Essay 3).

Second Thoughts: Seeing Conventional Wisdom Through the Sociological Eye addresses the gaps that exist between conventional wisdom and social life. The book reviews several popular conventional wisdoms, noting the instances in which such adages cannot be taken at face value. Each of the following essays uses social research to expose the gray area that is too often ignored by the bottom-line nature of conventional wisdom. In so doing, *Second Thoughts* demonstrates that social reality is generally much more involved and complex than these cultural truisms imply. The book suggests that reviewing conventional wisdom with a sociological eye can lead to a more complete, detailed understanding of social life.

When Conventional Wisdom Isn't Enough

Although there may well be a kernel of truth to much of conventional wisdom, too often these adages present an incomplete picture. Why is this the case? The answer stems, in part, from the source of most conventional wisdom.

Much of the conventional wisdom we embrace originates from a particular individual's personal experiences, observations, or reflections. Often such adages emerge from a highly specific circumstance; they are designed to address a particular need or event as experienced by a certain social group at a specific place or historical moment. For example, consider this well known adage: "There's a sucker born every minute!" P.T. Barnum coined this now-familiar phrase. But recall Barnum's personal circumstance—he was one of the most famous circus masters in history. When one considers Barnum's unique history, both the source and the limits of his wisdom become clear.

Now consider this maxim: "Don't switch horses in midstream." Abraham Lincoln originated this quote. (His actual words were: "It is not best to swap horses when crossing streams.") But note that Lincoln's frequently cited advice actually represents the political rhetoric of a historical moment. Lincoln coined the phrase as a kind of campaign slogan when seeking reelection to the United States presidency.

Finally, consider the famous quotation: "Good fences make good neighbors." Robert Frost forwarded this thought in his 1914 poem, "Mending Wall." Contrary to popular belief, however, Frost never intended to promote social separatism—quite the opposite. In "Mending Wall," Frost criticized the character who uttered the adage, writing, "He will not go behind his father's saying"—in other words, the character will not break with tradition. In so doing, Frost suggested that the wisdom linking good fences to good neighbors was that of *another* generation in a *former* time; it was not wisdom for *all* time.

Each of these examples shares a common thread. In each case, conventional wisdom was born of a particular experience or a specific social situation. The wisdom took root and grew as it resonated with other people who faced similar events and circumstances. Yet each of these examples also illustrates an inherent weakness of conventional wisdom. The "truth" revealed by such wisdom is tied to the particular circumstances of every maxim's origin. This characteristic can make conventional wisdom a precarious source of generalized knowledge. Because such wisdom is individualistic or situation-specific information, it may not carry the general applications that most people assume of it.

For the sociologist, reliable knowledge mandates that we move beyond individualistic or circumstantial information. Sociologists contend that there is more to the story than any one person's life or the lives of one's associates reveal.

Can one safely conclude that my experiences with an aging parent or my neighbors' experiences in raising their four-year-old will provide others with sufficient knowledge for handling the events of their lives? It is difficult to say. If these experiences are atypical, the wisdom they provide will offer little in the way of general conclusions regarding the treatment of elderly parents or four-year-olds. The wisdom will fail to transcend one individual's personal world. Similarly, wisdom born of experience may or may not transcend various social contexts. The maxim "Delay is the best remedy for anger" may prove fruitful in a variety of social sites: romance, work, friendship, parenting. Yet the adage that instructs you to "keep your cards close to the vest" may lead to success on the job but spell failure for a personal relationship.

Although your life may convince you that "birds of a feather flock together," my experience may reveal that "opposites attract." One situation may convince you that "haste makes waste," although another may convince you to "strike while the iron is hot." To be sure, experientially based or situation-specific information offers us knowledge, but that knowledge presents a fragmented, and thus incomplete, picture of the broader social world.

Relying on individualistic, circumstantial information can prove especially problematic when pursuing information regarding broad social patterns. Consider for a moment the ways in which one's geographic location might influence a person's estimate of general population patterns. The life experiences of Maine residents might lead them to conclude that 97% of the U.S. population is white. Such an estimate would greatly exaggerate the racial homogeneity of the nation. In contrast, the experiences of Californians might lead them to estimate that only 60% of the U.S. population is white, a vast underestimation of population homogeneity. Based on experience, Californians would have no trouble believing that Hispanics are now the largest minority in the United States. Yet the experiences of those in Alabama or Louisiana or Washington, D.C., would identify Blacks, not Hispanics, as the largest minority group. On the basis of experience, residents of Alaska or Wyoming would never guess that the United States averages 81 inhabitants per square mile. Alaska averages one inhabitant per square mile, while Wyoming averages 5. And experience might leave residents of Kentucky or Mississippi baffled by Californians' or New Yorkers' concerns over the number of foreign-born individuals entering the nation and settling in their states. Less than 1% of Kentucky's and Mississippi's state populations are foreign-born, whereas 26% of California's population and 12% of New York's population hail from other nations (U.S. Census Bureau 2002, Tables 22, 19, 9).

The point we are trying to make here is really quite simple. Accurate knowledge about society requires us to move beyond the limitations of experientially based conventional wisdom. That leap represents one of the most compelling features of sociology. Sociologists are interested in social patterns. **Social patterns** are general trends that can be seen only when we force ourselves to stand back and look beyond any one, two, or three cases. In essence, sociologists search for the "big picture": the view that emerges when many individual stories are aggregated into a whole.

The sociologist's emphasis on patterns does not necessarily mean that she or he is never interested in personal stories and experiences. Rather, sociology's strength lies in its ability to place or situate individual stories in a social context. **Social context** refers to the broad social and historical circumstances surrounding an act or an event. Once the sociologist discovers the general trends within a particular group or society, she or he is in a better position to assess the relative meaning of any one individual's personal experiences. General patterns must be documented before we can assess one's personal experiences as typical or as exceptional.

Obstacles to the Sociological Vision

Approached in this way, the task of sociology sounds straightforward and even appealing. The discipline encourages us to move beyond the personal and adopt a broader social vision—a vision that promises to improve the accuracy of our knowledge. With such gains at stake, why do so many approach the sociological vision with skepticism or confusion?

Certain obstacles can make it difficult to adopt a sociological view of the world. For example, the sociological vision contrasts with Americans' long-standing cultural value of individualism. A **cultural value** is a general sentiment regarding what is good or bad, right or wrong, desirable or undesirable. In the United States, we like to think of ourselves as special and unique individuals. We view ourselves as "masters of our own fates." Thus, the notion that our behaviors follow patterns or are the product of social forces is at odds with an individualistic mentality. To illustrate this point, consider our typical reactions to a serious and growing problem in the U.S. today: obesity.

Our individualistic mentality encourages us to see obesity as a problem of the person, an issue involving one's self-control or self-restraint: Thus, individuals are overweight because of their personal eating habits, their lack of exercise, their laziness or their emotional baggage. Contrast such thinking with the sociological perspective. A sociological view of obesity encourages us to push beyond the individual; it forces us to look at obesity in light of broader social patterns and contexts. In analyzing obesity, for example, a sociologist would consider the following facts: More than 60% of Americans are overweight; children are the most at-risk age group; the poor and working poor are more likely to be overweight than other economic groups; and our obesity epidemic is a relatively recent phenomenon, largely a product of the last 30 years. The sociological perspective urges us to "connect the dots" between these facts. In doing so, we discover some important social patterns and social structural sources of the American obesity problem. For instance, when one adopts the sociological perspective, it becomes easier to see that changes in farm, trade, and economic policies during the past few decades have contributed to our national bulk problem. During the 1970s, secretary of agriculture Earl Butz pushed for significant changes in the production, pricing, importing, and exporting of grains and oils, which helped bring down the cost of food for consumers. In the same period, discoveries and innovations in food science and manufacturing led to major reductions in food production costs. But as we are now learning, these changes came on the back of high-fructose sweeteners with questionable health properties and unexpected metabolic costs. Adopting a sociological perspective also helps us discover that Americans' attitudes toward food have changed considerably. During the past three decades, our growing enamorment with snack foods, fast foods, and super-sizes have put more and more "between meals" and "away from home" calories into consumers' stomachs. And school budget cuts, changes in physical education curricula, and increasing hours of television viewing all mean that more and more of the calories we consume stay with us (Critser 2003). With the sociological vision, we can appreciate that our obesity problem is not just one of individual control. Rather, obesity is the product of larger developments in politics, food production, marketing, and lifestyles.

Cultural values, such as those that champion individual control, are not the only obstacle to the sociological perspective. Adopting the sociological vision also can be hindered by our general preference for "certain" rather than "probable" answers. The study of large-scale patterns commits sociologists to predictions that are based on odds or probabilities. In other words, sociologists can identify outcomes that individuals from particular groups and places, or in particular circumstances, are likely to face. However, they cannot predict *the* definitive outcome for any *one* individual. In a culture that favors definitive answers for specific cases (usually, our own), this feature ensures a certain amount of resistance to the sociological approach. Indeed, sociology instructors often note a familiar complaint among newcomers to the field: If sociology can't predict what will happen to *me,* then what good is it?

Developing a sociological vision also can be undermined by the dynamic quality of social existence. Social reality is not static—it changes constantly. So just when we think we know the patterns, new patterns may be emerging. In addition, the very act of examining social phenomena can inevitably influence the entity we are studying. (If you need a concrete example of this, think about how sensitive the stock market is to people's ideas about the economy.) Such dynamics mean that sociologists' work, in a sense, is never done. Furthermore, the conclusions they reach must often remain tentative and open to change. Unlike a physics formula or a mathematical proof, sociological knowledge is rarely final. That dynamic quality often leaves the onlooker questioning its legitimacy.

Another obstacle facing the sociological viewpoint is doubt about the value of *socially* informed knowledge. As conventional wisdom indicates, many people trust only their own personal experiences to teach them about the world, arguing that such knowledge works for them. And, in a certain sense, sociologists must concede the point. Often, it does *appear* as if personal experience is more relevant, or truer, than sociological knowledge. Consider the fact that as thinking human beings, we have some capacity to create our own social reality. If we think people are not trustworthy, for example, we won't trust them, and we certainly won't give them the chance to prove us wrong. This course of action, no matter how ill conceived, serves to substantiate our own life experiences and to validate our own personally informed knowledge. In clinging to such a stance, we create a self-fulfilling prophecy. A **self-fulfilling prophecy** is a phenomenon whereby that which we believe to be true, in some sense, becomes true for us. In this way, self-fulfilling prophecies make personal experience seem like the clear victor over social knowledge.

Finally, the sociological viewpoint often is ignored by those who believe they already possess sociological expertise. One of the earliest figures in American sociology, William Graham Sumner, noted the tendency of people to think they know sociology by virtue of living in societies. "Being there" affords the opportunity to make social observations, and, arguably, social observations are the ingredients of which sociology is made. Thus, "being there" mistakenly is deemed by many as sufficient for generating social knowledge and sociological insights. As our previous discussion indicates, however, personal experience is *not* the same as the sociological perspective.

If you consider all of these obstacles, you will better understand why the sociological vision is not more readily pursued or adopted by all. It requires effort to move beyond our personal views or experiences and develop what C. Wright Mills called "the sociological imagination." **Sociological imagination** refers to the ability to see and evaluate the personal realm in light of the broader social/cultural and historical arenas.

Why Read This Book?

By introducing this broader picture of reality, *Second Thoughts* encourages readers to step back and sharpen their analytic focus on the familiar. The essays that follow highlight the complex reality of modern-day society—a complexity often missed when we restrict our knowledge to personal experience and the common knowledge or popular assumptions born of those experiences.

Second Thoughts also introduces readers to many concepts central to sociology. In this way, the book can serve as an initiation into the ways in which sociologists frame the world around them. For those who find their sociological eye activated, we provide some of the tools needed for additional research. Each essay concludes with several suggested readings that elaborate on key concepts and ideas introduced in the essay. Furthermore, each essay includes several reliable sources from which facts and figures were derived.

Readers may also find that some of the information presented here moves them beyond curiosity and toward action. To assist such individuals, we close many chapters with the names and URLs of organizations where individuals might further pursue their interests. These listings are not meant as publicity for any body or any cause. Rather, we offer them as preliminary leads, starting blocks for those who feel directed toward change.

In moving through the text, it will become clear that we have organized *Second Thoughts* according to topics typically covered in introductory-level courses. Those who wish to consider broader applications of this material should consult the "concepts covered" sections in the table of contents. These lists suggest a variety of issues for which one might use a specific conventional wisdom to "jump-start" critical thinking and discussion.

In Closing

When we open our eyes and carefully examine the world around us, we must concede that the realities of social life often run contrary to our stock of common knowledge. In the pages that follow, we aim to highlight some of these contradictions and, in so doing, to demonstrate that reviewing conventional wisdom with a sociological eye can provide a valuable "correction" to our vision of the world around us.

Learning More About It

To learn more about developing a sociological vision, see Peter Berger's classic book *Invitation to Sociology* (New York: Anchor, 1963). C. Wright Mills also provides a brilliant theoretical treatise on this subject in *The Sociological Imagination* (London: Oxford, 1959). A more recent and very readable treatment of these issues is offered by Earl Babbie in *What Is Society?: Reflections on Freedom, Order, and Change* (Thousand Oaks, CA: Pine Forge, 1994).

William Sumner's definition of the field can be found in his essay, "Sociology," in *Social Darwinism: Selected Essays of William Graham Sumner* (pp. 9–29; Englewood Cliffs, NJ: Prentice Hall, 1963).

A compelling and humanistic introduction to sociology and its core concepts is offered in Lewis Coser's classic work *Sociology Through Literature: An Introductory Reader* (Englewood Cliffs, NJ: Prentice Hall, 1963).

For a more thorough and very engaging discussion of America's obesity problem, read Greg Critser's *Fat Land: How Americans Became the Fattest People in the World* (Boston: Houghton Mifflin, 2003)

Public Agenda Online is a nonpartisan organization that offers users a chance to access public opinion studies on major social issues. The site also provides educational materials on various policy issues. You will find *Public Agenda Online* at: <http://www.publicagenda.org/aboutpa/aboutpa.htm.>

Exercises

1. Think about the social arrangements of your life—that is, your family relations, your neighborhood, your school, and work experiences. If your knowledge of the world were restricted to just these arenas, identify five important facts that you would fail to know.

2. The media give us one view of our social world. Select one week's worth of prime-time TV programs and use them to learn about U.S. society. Put together coding sheets that will allow you to collect basic data on all the program characters you encounter; that is, record each character's age, education, ethnicity, family status, family size, gender, occupational level, race, residence patterns, and so on. Tabulate summary statistics from your data. For example, determine the percentage of characters that are male and female, the average education level, and so on. Obtain a national or world almanac from your local or university library and compare the data you obtain via TV with comparable real-life demographics for the U.S. population. What can you conclude about the media's picture of American society? How did your particular selections of prime-time programming bias or influence your data?

Methods

Essay 1

Conventional Wisdom Tells Us ... Numbers Don't Lie

Americans like to "run the numbers." No matter what the realm—sports, business, politics, or entertainment—numbers often provide the bottom line. Why is our faith in numbers so strong? Conventional wisdom tells us that numbers don't lie. Is such wisdom accurate? Can we take confidence in the "realities" claimed by national polls, social scientific surveys, and other quantitative studies? In this essay, we note several important elements to consider in establishing the "truth" of numbers.

Numbers are everywhere. Indeed, in today's world it is virtually impossible to avoid statistical calculations, data sets, measurements, and projections. We judge the quality of our athletes by their "numbers"—their hits, their home runs, their stolen bases. We use numbers to gauge our financial futures. The Dow is up; the NASDAQ falls. Such numbers drive our investment decisions. The percentages gathered in public opinion polls guide both policymakers and citizen voters in making critical political judgments, and numbers form the cornerstone of research models in fields as diverse as education, medicine, the social sciences, and quantum physics.

Numbers, data, and statistics: Why is our commitment to these entities so strong? Many believe that numbers provide us with precision and objectivity. With numbers, we count rather than guesstimate; we measure rather than suppose; we capture reality rather than assume it. Armed with an empirical blueprint of the day's occurrences, many believe that we move one step closer to seeing the way things *really* are. In essence, many believe that numbers provide us with truth (Babbie 2003; Best 2001; Healey 2002).

Is this conventional wisdom about numbers accurate? Is it true that numbers don't lie? Can we be confident in the "realities" presented by national polls, social scientific surveys, and other quantitative studies?

To be sure, some of the numbers we see and read may indeed provide us with accurate pictures of the world. Yet the "truth" of numbers cannot be taken for granted. Before one can feel comfortable with the conclusions drawn from any body of data, one must consider several research-related factors. As we find ourselves increasingly bombarded with more and more numbers, we would do well to take a little extra time to review certain aspects of every study's design. By posing certain key questions in evaluating numerical findings, one can better gauge the veracity of any statistical claim.

In assessing the truth of numbers, one must first raise the question: *Exactly whom do the numbers in question represent?* This concern focuses our attention on issues of sampling.

Social researchers generally wish to draw conclusions about groups of people or things. For example, a researcher may wish to learn something about all women in the United States, or about first graders enrolled in New Jersey's public schools, or about Asian Americans living in Los Angeles. Similarly, a researcher may be interested in the content of *Time* magazine covers published from 1975 to 2000; he/she may wish to study the characters appearing in second-grade readers published in 1950 versus those published in 2000. Such groups of interest constitute what researchers call a population. A **population** is a collection of individuals, institutions, events, or objects about which one wishes to generalize or describe.

While social scientists are interested in populations, constraints such as time and money make it difficult, if not impossible, to study an entire population. Consequently, researchers often work with a **sample**, that is, a portion of the population. When selecting a sample, ideally, researchers strive to select a **representative sample**. A representative sample refers to a group that mirrors the characteristics of the larger population of interest. With a representative sample, a researcher can make accurate inferences about a large population while working with a small, manageable group.

Representative samples are critical to the truthfulness of numbers. If researchers use nonrepresentative samples to make inferences or generalizations about a population, their conclusions may be misleading or erroneous. The following example helps to illustrate the problem. Suppose that you wish to study dating habits among the students at your college. In particular, you are interested in the ways in which students meet potential partners. To research the issue, you choose a campus dorm and interview the first 20 people who leave the dorm one Thursday evening. Based on the answers offered by your 20 subjects, can you draw conclusions about the college population at large? Unfortunately, the answer is no. Because you took no steps to ensure that your sample was representative, your 20 subjects will provide only a limited picture of overall college dating practices. For example, if your subjects were members of a coed dorm, then their experiences could differ significantly from those of non-coed dorm residents. The fact that you are interviewing people *leaving* the dorm on a Thursday night may also prove significant. Those residents who choose to stay in for the night may exhibit very different dating patterns from those who leave the dorm. Similarly, the dating experiences of your 20 dorm residents may differ quite dramatically from the experiences of students commuting to your college from home or from an off-campus residence. By drawing a sample of college students based on convenience, you failed to represent the general character of the entire student body systematically. Therefore, the data you collect will tell us something about the 20 individuals who live in a particular dorm. However, the numbers generated from these 20 interviews cannot provide a useful picture of overall student dating practices.

Attention to sampling represents a first step in determining the "truthfulness" of numbers. However, if we wish to confirm the veracity of data, we must ask other questions as well. For example, "*How were a researcher's numbers collected?*" A researcher's data collection methods and measurement instruments will tell us much about the ultimate value of her/his research conclusions.

Consider, for example, the area of public opinion research. In today's world, there is scarcely a day when some dimension of public opinion is absent from the news. Public opinion reports typically result from a data collection method known as survey research. **Survey research** involves the administration of a carefully designed set of questions; the questions are posed during a face-to-face interview, a telephone interview, or via a written or an online questionnaire.

If survey researchers construct their questions thoughtfully and subjects answer those questions honestly, then surveys should provide us with an accurate picture of the world, right? Maybe, but maybe not. Questionnaire design presents social scientists with one of the most difficult and challenging tasks of research. Because of this, even the most experienced researchers can fall prey to design problems that may inadvertently influence the accuracy of their numbers.

For example, recent research convincingly shows that the ordering of survey questions can dramatically affect respondents' answers to the questions they are asked. In other words, a subject's exposure to one question on an interview schedule can influence her/his interpretations and responses to subsequent survey questions. Keeping this phenomenon in mind, imagine a survey designed to solicit likability ratings for various public figures. In such a survey, a subject's rating for one individual—say, Hillary Clinton—will vary significantly depending on where and when Mrs. Clinton is presented for evaluation. Hillary Clinton may prove quite likable if she is rated immediately following congressional colleagues such as Trent Lott or Tom DeLay. However, she may not fare as well if rated immediately following other first ladies such as Jacqueline Kennedy or Barbara Bush. In essence, the "numbers" on Hillary Clinton are strongly tied to the instrument by which her likability is gauged. In survey research, the *series* of individuals considered by a respondent can make an impact on a respondent's perception of any one person (Cerulo 1998; Meyers and Crull 1994; Nardi 2003; Tanur 1992).

The ordering of survey questions can lead to other important effects as well. Methodology experts such as Earl Babbie note that the ordering of survey questions can sometimes alter a respondent's perception of current events. Such effects must be considered in evaluating the "truth" of numbers. Suppose, for example, that a survey researcher questions a respondent regarding the dangers of violent crime. Following several questions on this topic, imagine that the researcher then asks the respondent a seemingly unrelated question: "What do you believe to be the single greatest threat to public stability?" Under these conditions, it is highly likely that the respondent will nominate violent crime more often than any other social problem. Why? The researcher's initial questions on violent crime can unintentionally focus the respondent on a specific set of concerns. By directing the respondent's attentions toward one particular subject, the researcher can inadvertently blind the respondent to other areas of consideration (Babbie 2001; Nardi 2003).

The ordering of questions represents one important element of data collection, but in judging the veracity of survey numbers, it is also critical to consider the specific questions that generated the numbers. All too often, critical information is lost in the reporting of survey results. For example, responses can be generalized in ways that misrepresent the questions posed in a survey. Similarly, answers to different questions may be reported and used to suggest changes in public attitudes. Thus, to correctly interpret the actual information that survey numbers provide, we must carefully trace survey data to its original source.

The following example helps to illustrate the importance of tracing survey data to its source. In the early 1990s, the American Jewish Committee commissioned the Roper organization to survey Americans' attitudes on the Holocaust. One of the questions posed in the Roper survey read as follows: "Does it seem possible or does it seem impossible to you that the Nazi extermination of the Jews never happened?" Twenty-two percent of Roper's respondents answered that it was possible that the extermination never happened. (Roper was working with a representative sample of American adults.) Many Jewish leaders were stunned by the survey's results. The numbers suggested that approximately 1 in 5 Americans were terribly misinformed about the Holocaust. Researchers were surprised by these results as well. Hence, they decided to redo the survey. Again, researchers questioned a representative sample of American adults. This time, however, they posed the Holocaust question in a slightly different way. Respondents were asked: "Do you believe that the Holocaust: (a) definitely happened, (b) probably happened, (c) may have happened, (d) probably did not happen, (e) definitely did not happen." In the second survey, only 2.9% of those questioned said that the Holocaust "definitely" or "probably" did not happen (Kifner 1994:A12; Ruane 2004).

What happened here? Did Americans dramatically change their position on the Holocaust between the first and second surveys? On the surface, it may seem that way, but by tracing the data to its source, we can comfortably eliminate that possibility. The shift in Americans' attitudes toward the Holocaust is connected to the change in the researchers' survey questions. In the first survey, researchers posed a confusing question to respondents: "Does it seem possible or does it seem impossible to you that the Nazi extermination of the Jews never happened?" Consider the poor wording of this question. Choosing the seemingly positive response "possible" resulted in respondents expressing a negative view on the authenticity of the Holocaust. In essence, a poorly designed question resulted in a flawed measurement of attitudes. In the second survey, the Holocaust question was more clearly worded. Thus, the second survey produced very different results. Moreover, the clarity of the second survey question suggests that its results are a more accurate representation of American attitudes.

The Holocaust example highlights some other important benefits of tracing data to its source. In checking the source, we verify the quality of the data collection process. For example, examining a survey's original question allows us to assess the validity of a researcher's measurement tools. A **valid measure** is one that accurately captures or measures the concept or property of interest to the researcher. Examining a survey's original question also provides some sense of a measure's reliability. A **reliable measure** proves consistent and stable from one use to the next. The greater the validity and reliability of a researcher's measures, the greater the confidence we can have in the data generated.

Tracing data to its source represents an important step in determining the veracity of numbers. However, in reviewing numbers, it is equally important to consider the issues behind the questions as well. When we review a single study or when we compare the findings from two or more studies, it is important to ask: *What did the researcher hope to measure, and how did she/he operationalize that concept?* **Operationalization** refers to the way in which a researcher defines and measures the concept or problem of interest. Without a full understanding of a researcher's operationalizations, those reviewing a study's findings may misinterpret the researcher's intentions. Under such circumstances, a researcher's conclusions can be inadvertently applied to issues beyond the scope of her/his study. Similarly, when a researcher's operationalizations are misunderstood, projects addressing different concepts may be mistakenly compared, creating conflict and confusion.

For example, in Essay 13, you will read about two important studies of criminal activity: the FBI *Uniform Crime Reports* and the *National Crime Victimization Survey*. Both studies represent highly reputable data analysis projects. Both studies address the annual incidence of crime in the United States. Yet each study presents completely different estimates of crime. For example, while the *Uniform Crime Reports* estimate approximately 504 violent crimes per every 100,000 Americans (U.S. Department of Justice 2002), the *National Crime Victimization Survey* estimates 2,470 violent crimes per every 100,000 Americans—nearly five times the number recorded by the FBI (U.S. Department of Justice 2001b)!

Which report presents the "true" number of crimes? If we failed to note the ways in which each study operationalizes crime, we would probably conclude that one set of numbers is in error. But by examining each study's operationalizations, we learn that the numbers in both reports are credible. The *Uniform Crime Reports* are based on crimes reported to the police. Thus, to be counted in the FBI's statistics, a crime must be known to and officially recorded by some police agency. In contrast, estimates forwarded in the *National Crime Victimization Survey* are based on the self-reports of a nationally representative sample. Note that crimes self-reported by victims may be completely unknown to the police. Furthermore, a violent crime's classification in the *National Crime Victimization Survey* remains solely in the hands of the "victim." Thus, in some cases, a victim's report of a "crime" may not meet the normal standards of the law.

When we consider the very different ways in which these two studies measure violent crime, it becomes easy to understand the discrepancy between the two data sources. The FBI statistics capture "official crime" as reported by the police. In contrast, the *National Crime Victimization Survey* offers "unofficial crime" as reported by ordinary citizens. In essence, each study presents a different operationalization of crime. Each study provides us with different dimensions of violent crime in the United States.

Whom do research numbers represent? How did the researcher collect his or her numbers? How were concepts operationalized? All of these questions should be posed by those assessing the veracity of data. But a complete assessment of data requires one additional question as well: *Who is conducting the research?* Most researchers strive to remain value-free when conducting their work. A **value-free** researcher is one who keeps her/his personal values and beliefs out of the collection and interpretation of data. In some cases, certain ideologies or self-interests can color the nature of a project. For example, should one believe numbers that document cigarettes' effects on health if one learns that the study generating such numbers is funded by a major tobacco company? Similarly, can one feel comfortable with data that suggest racial differences in IQ if one knows that the researcher presenting such conclusions is an avowed White Supremacist? The motives and interests of those executing or sponsoring a study must be carefully considered before one can determine the "truth" behind the numbers.

It is important to note that even the best of researchers—scholars trying to maintain a value-free stance—can unintentionally allow certain biases to color their interpretations of data. Researchers are, after all, social beings. They carry with them certain cultural assumptions and understandings. When executing research, these assumptions and understandings can unknowingly influence that which falls within a researcher's "viewfinder." Anthropologists have been especially effective at uncovering situations in which a researcher's vision is unintentionally distorted. How does such a thing happen?

Imagine a researcher who is interested in studying modes of interpersonal, nonverbal communication. She/he observes and records such exchanges among both American and non-American dyads (a dyad is a group of two). Now suppose that in observing interactions among non-American dyads, the researcher notes several instances in which one member of the dyad sticks out her/his tongue at the other member. Within American culture, such a gesture generally suggests teasing and mockery. Some researchers would allow this American standard to guide their interpretation of these non-American observations. But were the researcher to impose the "American" meaning on interpretations of *all* tongue-sticking incidents, she/he would forward data that was biased by ethnocentrism. **Ethnocentrism** is a tendency to view one's own cultural experience as a universal standard. When ethnocentrism intrudes on research, one's data can present a completely false picture. Consider the fact that sticking out one's tongue in South China, for example, is a sign of deep embarrassment. Among inhabitants of the Caroline Islands, the gesture is used to frighten demons away. In New Caledonia, sticking out one's tongue at another carries a wish for wisdom and vigor. And in India, the gesture is a sign of incredible rage.

As data consumers, we should make a reasonable effort to learn the cultural background of the researcher. We may also wish to explore the researchers' efforts at overcoming their own biases, for if we remain unaware of a researcher's cultural "blinders," we can fall prey to the same misinterpretations made by the professional observer.

In this essay, we have provided much instruction; we have issued many warnings. In light of this stance, you may feel completely doubtful of the conventional wisdom on numbers. How can numbers ever be trusted? But keep in mind that as a research project unfolds, a careful researcher is asking the very same questions posed in this essay. A careful scholar is attending to the veracity of data even as they are produced. When one couples a careful researcher with an astute data consumer, the product can be a set of numbers that sheds much light on aspects of the social world.

Learning More About It

Janet Ruane offers an engaging and very readable discussion of good methodological technique in *Essentials of Research Methods* (Malden, MA: Blackwell, 2004).

Earl Babbie ponders the problems of doing research in *Observing Ourselves: Essays in Social Research* (Prospect Heights, IL: Waveland Press, 1998).

The Gallup organization offers some firsthand insight into selecting a representative sample, formulating questions, and so on. Visit their Web site at <http://www.gallup.com> and click on the link for the "Gallup Polls."

Nora Cate Schaeffer and Stanley Presser instruct us on good questionnaire design in "The Science of Asking Questions," *Annual Review of Sociology* 29: 65–88, 2003.

Joel Best provides a fascinating guide to thinking critically about numbers and spotting "bad" statistics in *Damned Lies and Statistics* (Berkeley: University of California Press, 2001).

Jane Miller discusses the ins and outs of reporting statistics in *Writing About Numbers: Effective Presentation of Quantitative Information* (Chicago: University of Chicago Press, 2004).

Exercises

1. Earlier in this essay, we described a study exploring dating patterns of college students. The essay presented the "wrong way" to draw a sample for such a project. Briefly describe one possible method for drawing a better, more representative sample of a college student community.

2. Consult a sociology dictionary for a definition of *alienation*. Then, visit the Web site for the *General Social Survey* (GSS; <http://www.icpsr.umich.edu/gss/home.htm>) and find the questions used on the GSS to measure alienation. (Once you've accessed the GSS home-page, click on Site Map, then Subject Index, and then Alienation.) Assess the adequacy of the GSS questions relative to your working definition of alienation.

Culture

Essay 2

Conventional Wisdom Tells Us . . . Winning Is Everything

Conventional wisdom suggests that competition and achievement go hand in hand. In this essay, however, we highlight the many studies that show the benefits of cooperation over competition. In so doing, we review American cultural values, strategies of action, and the connection of these elements to both positive and negative outcomes.

Think back to the last Little League, soccer, or professional hockey game you attended. Note the number of stores and businesses that celebrate the "salesperson of the week." Consider the megadollars spent or the "hardball" tactics used by most recent contenders for national political office. And who can forget the thrill of victory and the agony of defeat as read on the faces of the most recent World Series, Super Bowl, or Olympic contenders?

These snapshots of American life remind us that competition is central to our culture. As children, we are taught to play hard and fight to win. As adults, we learn to value winning. We equate winning with the most talented or the "best man," and we regularly remind ourselves that "nice guys finish last." In the United States (as well as in most capitalist societies), the emphasis is on beating one's opponent and being the one "on top," the "king of the hill," the one left standing after a "fair fight."

The conventional wisdom on competition represents a **cultural value**. A cultural value is a shared sentiment regarding what is good or bad, right or wrong, desirable or undesirable. In the United States, competition is a positive cultural value (Aronson 1980; Donald 2001; Hunt 2000; Stinchcombe 1997:13–15). Yet despite our commitment to healthy competition, research shows that the practice may not always be in our best interest. A growing literature suggests that in many areas of social life, cooperation leads to more profitable outcomes than does competition.

Social psychologists David and Roger Johnson reviewed nearly 200 studies on human performance. The results of their research indicate that cooperation promotes higher individual achievement, higher group productivity, better problem solving, and more effective learning than do competitive strategies of interaction. These same studies show that the more cooperative people are, the better their performance. Thus, when group members periodically take the time to review their efforts while executing a task or attempting to solve a problem—that is, when group members reflect on their actions, ensure the equal distribution of responsibility, and protect open communication channels—the benefits afforded by cooperative strategies often increase (Johnson and Johnson 1989; 2002. Also see Alper, Tjosvold, and Law 2000; Bendor and Swistak 1997; De Dreu, Weingart, and Kwon 2000; Jensen, Johnson, and Johnson 2002; Kohn 1986; Wilkinson and Young 2002).

The success of cooperation stems from the strategies of action that it stimulates. **Strategies of action** are the means and methods social actors use to achieve goals and fulfill needs. Research indicates that the cooperative stance allows individuals to engage in more sophisticated and advanced thinking and reasoning than that which typically occurs in competitive environments. Social psychologists refer to these sophisticated thinking strategies as *higher-level reasoning* and *metacognitive strategies*.

Why do cooperative environments enable sophisticated thinking? Research suggests that interaction within cooperative settings typically evolves according to a process that sociologists refer to as a dialectic. A **dialectic** is a process by which contradictions and their solutions lead participants to more advanced thought. The dialectic process consists of three steps. In Step 1, *thesis*, the group experiences conflict. Here, members propose different ideas, opinions, theories, and information regarding the task or problem at hand. This conflict or disequilibrium sparks Step 2, *antithesis*. In antithesis, members actively search for more information and additional views, thus maximizing their knowledge about the task or problem they face. When the search is complete, the group begins Step 3, *synthesis*. Synthesis is a period in which group members reorganize and reconceptualize their conclusions in a way that merges the best thinking of all members (De Dreu et al., 2000; Glassman 2000; Johnson and Johnson 1989, 2002; Malley, Beck, and Adorno 2001; Wichman 1970).

In addition to bettering group and individual performance, cooperation—according to more than 180 studies—enhances the quality of interpersonal relationships. Friends, workers, and intimates who cooperate rather than compete with one another report feeling greater levels of acceptance from their colleagues and partners. As a result, cooperators become more caring and committed to their relationships. Furthermore, those involved in cooperative relationships report higher self-esteem and less psychological illness than those who compete with their friends, colleagues, and partners. Indeed, competitiveness has been repeatedly linked to psychological pathology (Combs 1992; Finlinson, Austin, and Pfister 2000; Johnson and Johnson 1989, 2002; Kohn 1986; Wilson 2000).

Some studies also link cooperation to diminished feelings of prejudice. **Prejudice** refers to the prejudgment of individuals on the basis of their group memberships. For example, individuals who cooperate with those whom they previously had stigmatized or negatively stereotyped report an increased liking toward such individuals. In contrast, individuals placed in competitive situations with members of a previously stigmatized group report a greater dislike for their competitors. On the basis of such studies, many researchers suggest that interracial, interethnic, and intergender cooperative tasks should become a regular "orientation" strategy in workplaces, schools, civic groups, and neighborhood organizations. Many believe that such cooperation "exercises" could help to reduce prejudice and bigotry in the sites of our daily interactions (Aronson and Cope 1968; Aronson and Thibodeau 1992; Holtz and Miller 2001; Jehn and Shah 1997; Johnson and Johnson 2000; McConahay 1981; Rabois and Haaga 2002; Slavin and Madden 1979; Vanman, Paul, and Ito 1997).

If cooperation leads to so many benefits, why do social actors continue to choose the competitive stance? The persistence of competition is a good example of the power of cultural values and the ways in which cultural values can promote a phenomenon sociologists refer to as **culture against people**. Culture works against people when the beliefs, values, or norms of a society lead to destructive or harmful patterns of behavior. When it comes to the value of competition, the culture-against-people phenomenon couldn't be any stronger. Indeed, research conducted over the past several decades suggests that even when individuals are made fully aware that they have more to gain by cooperating with others than by competing with them, they often continue to adopt competitive strategies of action (Deustch and Krauss 1960; Houston et al. 2000; Kelley and Stahelski 1970; Miceli 1992; Minas et al. 1960; Schopler et al. 1993; Schultz and Pruitt 1978; Van Avermaet et al. 1999).

In one experiment, for example, a college professor told his students that they were participating in an investment research project for the *Wall Street Journal*. The project consisted of several simple exercises. In each exercise, students in the class would be asked to write a number, either 1 or 0, on a slip of paper. Before casting their votes, students were informed that the number of "1" votes cast by class members would determine a financial "payoff" for each student. The professor explained that each exercise was designed such that a unanimous class vote of 1 would maximize every class member's payment as well as the total class "pot." The class was also instructed that a single 0 vote could increase *one* voter's payoff, but such split votes would always result in a smaller payment for the remaining class members, as well as a smaller payment for the class overall.

Here is a concrete example of the payoff schedule. If 30 people wrote the number 1, a total of $36.00 would be evenly divided by the class—$1.30 for each class member. But if 29 people chose 1 and one person chose 0, only $35.30 would be paid to the class. The one individual who voted 0 would be paid $1.66; the 29 students who voted 1 would each receive only $1.16. Now, consider a situation in which 10 students choose the number 0 and 20 choose the number 1. Here, the class would divide only $29.00. Students choosing 0 would each receive $1.30, but those choosing 1 would receive only $.80. (The professor provided students with a breakdown of all possible payoffs before the class voting began.)

The professor took several votes in his class, allowing class members to debate strategies before each vote. Yet even when the entire class recognized and agreed that a unanimous 1 vote would be the fairest and most lucrative strategy overall, several class members continued to vote 0 in an effort to maximize their own individual gain (Bishop 1986).

Similar results have emerged from experiments conducted in laboratory settings. The Prisoner's Dilemma, for example, is an experimental game designed to test an individual's preference for cooperative versus competitive strategies. The game is based on a hypothetical problem faced by two suspects and a district attorney, all gathered in a police station. The district attorney believes that both suspects have committed a crime but has no proof connecting the suspects to the crime. Thus, he separates the two, telling each prisoner that he has two alternatives: confess to committing the crime in question, or not confess. Prisoners are told that if neither confesses, both will be convicted of only a minor offense and receive only a minor punishment (1 year incarceration). If both confess, each will be convicted of a major crime and face fairly severe penalties (10 years in prison). If only one of the prisoners confesses, the confessor will receive full immunity, while the nonconfessor will receive the maximum penalty allowed by law (15 years in prison).

The Prisoner's Dilemma is designed to encourage cooperation. Clearly, silence on the part of both prisoners maximizes the favorable chances of each one. Yet in experimental trials, prisoners repeatedly favor competition. When faced with both the cooperative and competitive options, players consciously choose confession—the strategy that offers them the potential to maximize their own gain. In other words, players choose to compete even when such a strategy proves riskier than cooperation (Houston et al. 2000; Kollock 1998; Schopler et al. 1993; Rapoport 1960; Van Avermaet et al. 1999).

The *Wall Street Journal* experiment (devised by three economists, Charles Plott, Mark Isaac, and James Walker), the Prisoner's Dilemma, and other similar games and experiments all illustrate the way in which our cultural value of competition can work against people. These examples suggest that even when a goal can be realized best via a common effort, significant numbers of individuals will *espouse* cooperation but *act* in a competitive way. Significant numbers of individuals will act to maximize their own gain rather than to act in the best interest of the group as a whole—even if that maximization proves risky and the payoff uncertain.

Can we overcome the allure of competition? Are there any circumstances that motivate individuals to choose the cooperative path? For decades, experimental work has suggested that those faced with some type of external threat will abandon their competitive stance and ban together with others in cooperative strategies of defense or protection (Blake and Moulton 1979; Deustch and Krauss 1960; Dion 1979; Lanzetta 1955; Sherif 1966; Sherif et al. 1961; Wilder and Shapiro 1984). Recently, these findings have been replicated in real world settings, particularly in studies devoted to the aftermath of natural disasters or terrorist attacks (Halbert 2002; Heeren 1999; Turkel 2002). Equally exciting is a growing line of research that examines the role of cooperation in capitalism. For centuries, economists have argued that competition is essential to a sustainable, dynamic economy. However, a number of current studies suggest that locally, nationally, or globally, the healthiest economies are those that find a balance between competition and cooperation within institutional structures (Amodeo 2001; Brandendenburger & Nalebuff 1996; Deutsch 2000; Moore 1997; Wisman 2000). Thus, in the final analysis, working together may be the most profitable strategy of all.

Learning More About It

Those interested in a thorough examination of the conditions which foster cooperation and/or in learning how to promote cooperation should consult Robert Axelrod's *The Evolution of Cooperation* (New York: Basic Books, 1984) or *The Complexity of Cooperation* (Princeton: Princeton University Press, 1997).

The notion of "culture against people" stems from a line of work that includes Philip Slater's *The Pursuit of Loneliness: American Culture at the Breaking Point* (Boston: Beacon Press, 1970); Richard Sennett's *The Fall of Public Man* (New York: Knopf, 1977); and Robert Bellah and colleagues' *Habits of the Heart: Individualism and Commitment in American Life* (Berkeley: University of California Press, 1985).

Several interesting articles linking cooperation to successful economies can be found in *The Handbook of Conflict Resolution: Theory and Practice,* edited by Morton Deutsch (San Francisco: Jossey-Bass, 2000).

A good review of cooperation and competition as exercised by children can be found in Jacques F. Richard and colleagues' "Cooperation and Competition," in *Blackwell Handbook of Child Social Development,* edited by P. K. Smith and C. H. Hart, pp. 515–532 (Malden, MA: Blackwell Publishers, 2002).

The following organizations can help you learn more about cooperation:

Cooperative Learning Center
60 Peik Hall, University of Minnesota, Minneapolis, MN 55455
(612) 624–7031; Web site: <http://www.co-operation.org>

Future Problem-Solving Program (Fosters creative thinking in problem-solving efforts)
2028 Regency Road, Lexington, KY 40503–2309
(800) 256–1499; Web site: <http:/www.fpsp.org>

Grace Contrino Abrams Peace Education Foundation
2627 Biscayne Blvd., Miami, FL 33137
1–800–749–8838; Web Site: <http://www.peaceeducation.com>

Institute on Global Conflict and Cooperation
9500 Gilman Drive, La Jolla, CA 92093–0518
(619) 534–3352; Web site: <http://www.ciaonet.org/wps/sites/igcc.html>

Up With People (Builds understanding and cooperation among those of different cultures through a special educational program)
P.O. Box 425, Broomfield, CO 80038–0425
(303) 460–7100; Web site: <http://www.upwithpeople.org>

Exercises

1. To determine the cultural importance of competition, try the following "experiment." Solicit several friends and/or relatives to join you in some traditionally competitive activity, such as basketball, bowling, cards, or tennis. Vary the conditions of play with each individual you choose. For example, use normal game rules with some of your "subjects"; tell others that you don't want to play for points or keep score. Note the different reactions, if any, to the different conditions of play. Does playing without keeping score affect the willingness of some to participate? Affect the quality of interaction? Do you note any effects of gender or age in the reactions you observe?

2. Explore the significance of competition for college grading. Prepare a serious proposal that testing be conducted under conditions of cooperation rather than competition. (Cooperative conditions might include group testing, open discussion during the exam, or adjustment in grade calculation methods such that each student's grade is an average of her or his actual performance as well as the performance of the best and worst students in the class.) Conduct a limited survey of your colleagues. Do they support or reject such a proposal? What reasons do they offer for their position? Is their reasoning consistent with American values on competition? On cooperation?

Essay 3

Conventional Wisdom Tells Us ... Children Are Our Most Precious Commodity

We frequently hear it said: Children are our future. They are our most valuable resource. Here, we present research suggesting otherwise. Children may be the most overlooked, the most neglected segment of the population despite current talk of family values and the future of American youth.

Children—who doesn't love them? In the United States, we refer to children as "our nation's future." Our conventional wisdom celebrates them as society's most precious commodity. National opinion polls repeatedly document that Americans consider children one of life's true rewards. Indeed, couples who want children but cannot have them are assured the sympathies and support of their fellow members of society. In contrast, couples who don't want children frequently find themselves an object of contempt or suspicion.

Much of today's political rhetoric is fueled by the cultural value America places on children. Citizens and elected officials are urged to "Act now" in the long-term interest of the nation's youth. Politicians vow to cut today's spending and spare our children and grand-children a troubled and debt-laden tomorrow. Many advocate curbing social security and Medicare costs so as to protect benefits for future generations. Such prescriptions underscore the importance of children in our youth-oriented society.

Threats to our children can mobilize American sentiments in a way that few other issues can. Consider some landmark moments of the past two decades that joined American citizens in public outrage: the bombing of a federal building in Oklahoma City; school shootings in Arkansas, California, Kentucky, Mississippi, Tennessee, Oregon, Pennsylvania, and, of course, Littleton, Colorado; the Amber Hagerman kidnapping, which inspired the creation of the Amber Alert system; or the murder and rape of Megan Kanka, which resulted in Megan's Law. In such instances, public outrage was fueled in large measure by the fact that these acts threatened and/or took the lives of so many children.

Can we take the pro-child rhetoric of conventional wisdom at face value? How do our pro-child sentiments compare with the behavioral realities of America's children?

A review of worldwide infant mortality rates offers one perspective on the matter. **Infant mortality rates** gauge the number of deaths per 1,000 live births for children under one year of age. Such statistics represent a commonly consulted measure, or social indicator, of a society's behavior toward its children. **Social indicators** are quantitative measures or indices of social phenomena.

Despite the pro-child sentiments of American culture, the United States trails many other nations in the fight against infant mortality. To be sure, infant deaths typically are highest within less developed nations of the world community, such as Afghanistan, Angola, Ethiopia, or Iraq. Yet the U.S. infant mortality rate of 7 is comparable to that found in Cuba, Malaysia, and Slovakia—nations with far less wealth or international power than the United States (see Figure 3.1). A variety of other major (and minor) industrial nations, such as Sweden, Switzerland, Iceland, France, Japan, the Netherlands, Germany, Spain, and Australia have been more effective than the United States in fighting infant deaths. Indeed, the U.S. infant mortality rate is higher than the summary rate (6) for all industrialized countries (UNICEF 2002).

Child inoculation rates are another informative measure of a society's behavior toward its children. Using this gauge, the United States again has a rather dubious record. As we entered the new millennium, 20% of two-year-olds failed to have the full series of childhood vaccinations (Children's Defense Fund 2003). And while recent UNICEF data indicates that 91% of one-year-olds in the United States are fully immunized against polio, that figure is comparable to the rates found in far less developed nations, such as Trinidad and Tobago (90%), Botswana (92%), and El Salvador (92%).

Finally, when it comes to the health and well-being of America's most precious commodity, one set of statistics may prove most noteworthy of all: In the United States, homicide is the second leading cause of death for those 15 to 24 years of age and the fourth leading cause of death for those 1 to 14 years of age (Centers for Disease Control and Prevention 2002). Indeed, in the United States, gunfire kills a child or teen every three hours (Children's Defense Fund 2002a).

These facts and figures on the physical well-being of children in America unveil glaring discrepancies between what we say and what we do with regard to children. However, the discrepancies extend well beyond the realm of health and mortality. For although conventional wisdom celebrates the child, the reality is that millions of American children confront

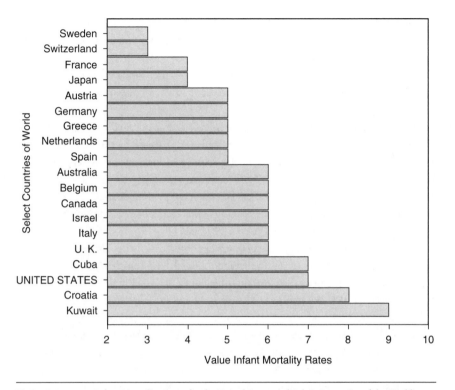

Figure 3.1   Infant Mortality Rates for the United States and Select Countries of the World
(Number of deaths of children under one year of age per 1,000 live births)

SOURCE: UNICEF Child Mortality Statistics, 2000 http://www.childinfo.org/cmr/revis/dbl.htm.

poverty and the many ills that go with it throughout their childhood. In 2001, just over 16% of American children were living in poverty (Children's Defense Fund 2002b). Indeed, for children of every single age—newborn to 18 years—poverty rates were higher than the 11.7 rate for the population at large (U.S. Census Bureau 2002a). It is worth noting that the U.S. child poverty rate is considerably higher than the rate in many other modern industrialized nations. For example, Canada's rate is 9.6, Britain's is 8.4, France's is 2.9, and Sweden's child poverty rate is 1.3 (Madrick 2002). Thus, the United States, a leader among industrialized nations with reference to billionaires, millionaires, gross domestic product, and defense expenditures, is 17th in terms of efforts made to lift children out of poverty (Children's Defense Fund 2002a).

To fully understand the plight of our nation's children, consider this image. In a "group portrait" of the poor in the United States, more than one-third of the faces would belong to children (Weinberg 2001). And while recent welfare-to-work reforms may have cut the welfare rolls, the reforms have also cut the number of services and benefits to families and children (National Coalition for the Homeless 2002). The resulting conditions are staggering. Over 9 million children—almost one in eight—have no health insurance. One in six children are born to mothers who did not receive any prenatal care in the first trimester (Children's Defense Fund 2002a). Children in poverty are eight times more likely than other children to have recently gone hungry. Poor children also suffer in school; they have lower math and reading scores than their wealthier counterparts; they are twice as likely to repeat a grade in school, three-and-a-half times more likely to be school dropouts, and only half as likely to finish a four-year college (Children's Defense Fund 2002a). For many children, poverty goes hand in hand with homelessness; nationally, about 40% of the homeless population are children. Furthermore, families with young children are among the fastest-growing segments of the homeless population (National Coalition for the Homeless 2002). These conditions have prompted at least one writer to observe that child poverty is one of our country's most stunning failures (Madrick 2002).

Even among children who have a roof over their heads, life is not always easy. National surveys suggest rates of physical and sexual child abuse that are completely inconsistent with America's pro-child rhetoric. The U.S. Department of Health and Human Services estimates that just over 900,000 children were victims of abuse and neglect in 2001, while 1,300 children died of abuse and neglect. This figure represents a victimization rate of 12.4 per 1,000 children, a slight increase over the 2000 rate. While it may be hard to fathom mistreating helpless babies and infants, note that it is the *youngest* children who are the most vulnerable to deadly abuse. Children under one year old account for nearly 41% of fatalities; those less than six years of age account for 84.5% of child fatalities (National Clearinghouse on Child Abuse and Neglect Information 2003).

America's pro-child adages also ring hollow in homes broken by divorce. Nearly 40% of the children in mother-only families (a typical product of divorce) currently live in poverty. Contrast this with the fact that only 8% of children in married families are poor (Children's Defense Fund 2002b; Fields 2003). The high poverty rate for children in single-mother families is in part due to "deadbeat dads": one in four of these children do not receive any child support (Children's Defense Fund 2002c). Indeed, the poverty rate for families that do not receive any child support (35.7%) is more than twice the rate for families that receive the support owed (15.2%) (Children's Defense Fund 2002c). The Federal Office of Child Support estimates that as of 2002, $92.3 billion in accumulated overdue support was owed to nearly 20 million children in the United States (Association for Children for the Enforcement of Support 2003).

American schools—another central institution in children's lives—also show evidence of problems that nullify conventional wisdom's pro-child rhetoric. An American child today has many reasons to dread going to school. In 1999, 13% of 12- to 18-year-old students were the targets of hate speech; 36% were targets of hate graffiti. But the problem goes far beyond words. In 1999, students 12 to 18 years old were victims of 2.5 million crimes at school: 186,000 of these incidents were crimes of violence. Furthermore, 17% of 12- to 18-year-old students reported the presence of street gangs in their schools. It is no wonder, then, that 1.1 million of these students avoided certain areas in their schools for fear of their safety. When we examine American high schools, the problems seem even worse. In 1999, 7% of high school students reported carrying a weapon to school. And nearly a third of high school students reported being offered or sold illegal drugs on school property (Kaufman, Alt, and Chapman 2001).

Our schools appear to fail our children with regard to academic achievement as well. Since the early days of the American space program, many have voiced concern regarding the performance levels of American schoolchildren. These concerns are well-grounded. Seventy-one percent of fourth grade students are below reading proficiency levels, and 75% are below math proficiency levels (Children's Defense Fund 2002a). A second wave of a comprehensive study of international education found that students in 14 other nations outperformed U.S. eighth-grade students in math and science (National Center for Education Statistics 2003a). One in three American students is behind at least one grade in school. About 10% of 16- to 19-year-olds are high school dropouts (AmeriStat 2003a). And in the United States, graduating from high school is itself no guarantee of educational achievement. On average, a high school degree enables one to function at a 2 (out of a high of 5) level of literacy (National Institute for Literacy 2002).

These everyday patterns suggest that in America, although we may idealize childhood (especially in our memories), the reality for today's children is often anything but ideal. Indeed, despite our pro-child stance, many children find childhood too difficult to endure. The suicide rate among American youth increased by 240% from the early 1950s to the late 1970s. Suicide is the third leading cause of death for 10- to 24-year-olds (Centers for Disease Control and Prevention 2002). On an average day in the United States, five children or teens will take their own lives (Children's Defense Fund 2002a).

What meaning can we draw from the discrepancies between conventional wisdom's view of children and the way children actually are treated? Are we simply a nation of hypocrites? We gain some perspective on the issue when we consider a distinction sociologists draw between ideal culture and real culture. **Ideal culture** comprises the values, beliefs, and norms each society claims as central to its modus operandi. In other words, ideal culture has to do with aspirations, the ends or goals of our behaviors. In contrast, real culture refers to those values, beliefs, and norms we actually execute or practice. Thus, **real culture** has to do with behaviors or the means to a society's ends.

Your own life experiences have surely taught you that humans have a remarkable capacity to be inconsistent: We can say one thing and do another. In fact, Americans have a cultural prescription reflecting this capacity: "Do as I say, not as I do." When sociologists examine the fit between ideal and real culture, they are exploring the "Say one thing, do another" phenomenon as it occurs at the social level.

For a society to achieve perfect agreement between its ideal and real cultures, it must achieve *both* consensus on goals and agreement regarding the appropriate methods for achieving those goals. That is, ideal and real cultures are in balance only when a society is free of contradiction between what it says and what it does. If a society cannot synchronize its goals and behaviors, then it experiences a condition sociologists refer to as cultural inconsistency. **Cultural inconsistency** depicts a situation in which actual behaviors contradict cultural goals. Cultural inconsistency indicates an imbalance between ideal and real cultures.

Why do cultural inconsistencies emerge in a society? Conflict theorists offer one possible answer. **Conflict theorists** analyze social organization and social interactions by attending to the differential resources controlled by different sectors of a society. These theorists suggest that the inability to balance ideal and real cultures has much to do with the broader issues of power and social policy. **Power** is the ability of groups and/or individuals to get what they want even in the face of resistance. **Social policies** are officially adopted plans of action.

In American society, social policies often guide social behaviors, or what we are referring to as real culture. Yet social policies rarely emerge from general population consensus; they are rarely directed toward ideal culture. Rather, such prescriptions inevitably are influenced by the actions and relative power of various sectors of the population: special interest groups, political action committees, lobbyists, and so on.

By definition, special interest groups promote or advance the cause of certain segments of the population, such as the New Christian Right, senior citizens, tobacco manufacturers, or trial lawyers. Thus, these groups are unduly responsive to the interests of the few—and necessarily ignore the broader interests of the larger population. Special interest groups vie to prescribe social policy. Ultimately, then, social policy generally reflects the particularized goals of groups sufficiently powerful to influence it.

Lacking control of economic resources or access to the political ballot denies children, as a collective, the typical tools of power. Furthermore, age works against the self-serving collective actions of children. Children are dependents; they must rely on adults to act as their advocates. As a result, the interests and rights of children always will be weighed against those of parents, families, and society at large. The child's voice always will be rendered via an intermediary's perspective.

The drawbacks of the child's indirect political presence is aptly illustrated when we review efforts to combat child abuse in the United States. History reveals a parade of policies consistent with child advocates' views and beliefs regarding the best interests of children. For example, child advocates of the early 1800s believed that abused and neglected children were at risk of delinquency; such advocates saw abused children as threats to society. As a result, social and reform policies of the period demanded the institutionalization of abused children. Protecting society was deemed "action in the best interest of the child." In the early 1900s, the newly emerging professions of social work and clinical psychology argued that promoting and protecting intact families would best serve the interests of children. Such policy recommendations remanded abused children to the very sites of their mistreatment (Pfohl 1977).

In the current era, many child advocates continue to cling to the family protection theme. The Family Research Council, for example, is an advisory group that has worked for the past 20 years to promote traditional family values. This group rejects any efforts to view children and their rights as an issue separate from the context of the family; they are dedicated to the primacy of paternal authority (Gusdek 1998). The Family Research Council's position, as well as those of other groups before them, makes the political plight of children clear. Without the ability to organize and lobby solely on their own behalf, children will always be one critical step removed from the social policy process—and the gap between the ideal and real cultures that frame childhood in America will continue to exist.

Given the cultural inconsistency that exists in American society's stance toward children, isn't it hypocritical to continue to espouse the ideals we hold? Should an honorable society promote ends it cannot meet?

Sociologically speaking, there are several important reasons to maintain the concept of an ideal culture even when society fails to practice what it preaches. First, a gap between goals and behaviors—that is, a gap between ideal and real cultures—does not diminish the value of a society's ideals. We can honestly place a high value on children even though our behaviors may fall short of the ideal. Ideals, goals, and values are aspirations and, as such, they are frequently not achieved.

Second, changing ideal culture to fit a society's actual practices might indeed bring an end to cultural inconsistency. However, such a change would not alter an important fact: Children literally are the future of any group or society. For a society to survive, individuals must be persuaded to reproduce themselves. In preindustrial days, economic necessity was an attractive incentive for reproduction. Children furnished valuable labor power to colonial families. Children were valuable sources of family income in the early days of industrialization as well. In the industrialization era, children regularly took their places alongside older workers in factories and sweatshops (LeVine and White 1992; Zelizer 1985).

Today, the economic incentives attached to childbearing have changed dramatically. Children are no longer regarded as valuable labor power or income sources for families. Furthermore, the cost of having and raising children in our society has risen dramatically over the years. The U.S. Department of Agriculture estimates that the expense of raising one child is close to $170,000 for the lowest-income families, just over $230,000 for middle-income families and over $335,000 for the highest-income families! These lifetime expense estimates do *not* include the cost of a college education. Parents who agree to assist with college costs must be prepared to spend tens of thousands of dollars more to cover college tuition and room and board (Lino 2002).

Changes in lifestyles and priorities, education, and career commitments render the decision to have children more problematic today than at earlier points in America's history. Individuals no longer automatically equate children with personal fulfillment and happiness. Surveys reveal that many married adults report that their highest levels of marital satisfaction occurred *before* they had children or *after* their children left home. Research also shows that the only people who are consistently happier than nonparents are "empty nesters" (Dalphonse 1997). The economic and personal costs of child rearing may account for the steady decrease in average family size during the past century. The latest census figures put the average family size at 3.14 (Simmons and O'Neill 2001). Furthermore, surveys indicate that Americans no longer fantasize about "having a house full of children." Rather, trend analysis for the last several years reveals that more and more Americans are citing "two" as the ideal number of children (General Social Survey 2000).

Delayed childbearing also accounts for part of the decline in average family size. Women in the United States are waiting longer to marry (Fields and Casper 2001) and to have children, and such delays ultimately translate into fewer total births (AmeriStat 2003b; McFalls 1992). In addition, increases in education levels, career aspirations, satisfaction with present life situations, and more reliable birth control all appear to be making it easier for some couples to remain childless (Bennett, Bloom, and Craig 1992; Dalphonse 1997; Wu and MacNeill 2002). In 2000, 43% of women of childbearing age were childless. Among those women who were nearing the end of their childbearing years (40–44), 19% remained childless; this percentage is nearly double the 1980 figure (Bachu and O'Connell 2001). A growing trend toward singlehood among the young and middle-aged further complicates overall U.S. fertility patterns. Since 1970, there has been a steady increase in the percentage of males and females who have never married: In 2000, 31% of males and 25% of females 15 years and older fell into the "never-married" category. When we consider all of these changes and trends, it isn't too surprising to see that in 2000, only 24% of all U.S. households embodied the traditional nuclear family, that is, married couples with children under age 18 (Fields and Casper 2001).

Any society interested in its own survival must keep a watchful eye on such developments. In 2002, the U.S. birth rate reached its lowest level since birth records were first kept in the early 1900s: 13.9 births per 1,000 persons, a decline of 17% since 1990 (Zitner 2003)! With this drop, the United States ceased being the only industrialized country with fertility above replacement level and joined the growing ranks of countries with below-replacement-level fertility: China, Japan, most of Europe, and many countries of South and Southeast Asia (Haaga 2003; Haub 2003). **Replacement level fertility** is the level needed for a population to continually renew itself without growing. Currently, replacement level fertility is about 2.1 children per woman. In 2001, the U.S. total fertility rate was 2.03. Some suspect that the sluggish U.S. economy will further reduce our birth rate and bring us closer to the "zero population growth" plight of other industrialized countries of the world (Haub 2003). Many population experts regard lower birthrates as foreshadowing dangerous population decline. In general, low fertility produces shrinking labor forces. Declining birth rates also mean that the burden of supporting the social programs for a nation's aging and retiring population will fall on fewer and fewer shoulders. And the longer low fertility rates exist, the harder it becomes to reverse population declines (McDonald 2001; Zitner 2003). Somewhat ironically, then, nations with increasingly geriatric populations can ill afford record low birthrates—the older a population, the greater its stake in achieving higher birth rates. Viewed in this light, maintaining an ideal culture that values children makes good sense, even when we sometimes fail to practice what we preach. Placing a high premium on children is one important way to ensure that individuals continue to make a financial investment in children. By doing so, they provide the critical raw material for societal survival.

American conventional wisdom on children seems at odds with our behaviors and actions. But this cultural inconsistency is not likely to disappear soon. Indeed, even if the costs of having and raising children continue to increase and the structures of our families continue to change, pro-child rhetoric may grow even stronger in the United States in the days ahead.

Learning More About It

Readers will find a very engaging review of the past two centuries of family life in Stephanie Coontz's *The Way We Never Were: American Families and the Nostalgia Trap* (New York: Basic, 2000). For a very readable view on the present-day American Family, see Coontz's *The Way We Really Are: Coming to Terms With America's Changing Families* (Reprint Edition) (New York: Basic Books 1998).

Viviana Zelizer offers a fascinating historical review on the social value of children in *Pricing the Priceless Child* (New York: Basic Books, 1985).

For an interesting perspective on historical responses to child abuse in the United States, see Stephen J. Pfohl's "The Discovery of Child Abuse," *Social Problems*, 24(3), 310–323, 1977. Murray Straus (with Denise Donnelly) offers a thorough review of corporal punishment and its effects on children in *Beating the Devil Out of Them: Corporal Punishment in American Families and Its Effects on Children* (New Brunswick: Transaction Publishers, 2001)

For a comprehensive review of family violence that offers an integrated theoretical explanation (sociology, psychology, and biology) see Mignon, Larson, and Holmes's *Family Abuse: Consequences, Theories, and Responses* (Boston: Allyn & Bacon, 2002).

For a discussion on the discrepancy between goals and the paths we choose to achieve them, see Merton's classic 1938 work, "Social Structure and Anomie," *American Sociological Review*, 3, 672–682.

The following organizations and sites can help you learn more about children in society:

The Administration for Children and Families
Web site: <http://www.acf.dhhs.gov/>

Children's Defense Fund
25 E St. NW, Washington, DC 20001
(800) CDF-1200 Web site: <http://www.childrensdefense.org/>

Directory of Children's Issues on the World Wide Web site: <http://www.childrennow. org/links.html>

To learn more about children's rights and how nations fare in honoring these rights, consult UNICEF's *The State of the World's Children: 2001 Early Childhood:* <http://www. unicef.org/sowc01/>

The Children's Welfare League of America offers online national and state fact sheets on the status of America's children at: <http://www.cwla.org/advocacy>. Scroll down the page and follow the links for the "National" or the "State" sheets.

If you are interested in the quality of life for children in other countries of the world go to the *Population Connection's* "Kid-Friendly Countries Report Card" at: <http://www. populationconnection.org/kidfriendlycountries/index.htm>

Exercises

1. Take a look at the age statistics in Figure 3.2. Pay particular attention to the relative size of the various age groups and the corresponding implications for population trends over

Age and Gender Distribution of the U.S Population, 1999 and 2025

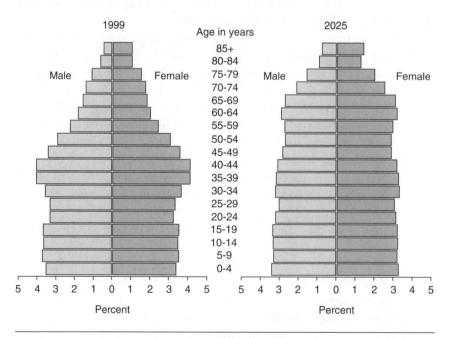

Figure 3.2   Age and Gender Distribution of the U.S. Population, 1999 and 2025

the next 25 years. What does the graph suggest is a likely development with regard to our pro-child culture?

2. Select three family TV programs whose cast of characters includes children. Monitor the content of the programs for a two- to three-week period, noting program incidents and themes. On the basis of your observations, do the programs emphasize ideal or real culture in their portrayal of children in our society? What factors can you offer that might account for your findings?

Social Structure

Essay 4

Conventional Wisdom
Tells Us ... Love Knows No Reason

In this essay, we explore various social statuses—age, education, gender, income, race, religion—noting the ways in which these factors can guide something as seemingly individualistic as Cupid's arrow.

L ove: that invigorating, addictive sensation, the emotional roller-coaster ride that signals the wonder of being human. Conventional wisdom locates love in the world of passion; adages describe it as an experience that can make us irrational, impetuous, and often oblivious to the real-life events that surround us. There is nothing logical about love. Love bows to emotion, not reason.

The conventional wisdom on love is not easily shaken. One might even say it stands shoulder to shoulder with the laws of the land! For example, in 1974, the National Science Foundation awarded an $84,000 grant for a social *scientific* investigation into the experience of love. But upon hearing of the grant, then Senator William Proxmire blasted the investment from the floor of the U.S. Senate, saying:

> I'm against this, not only because no one—not even the National Science Foundation—can argue that falling in love is a science; not only because I'm sure that even if they spend 84 million or 84 billion they wouldn't get an answer that anyone would believe. I'm also against it because I don't want the answer! (quoted in Harris 1978).

Is conventional wisdom accurate when it comes to love? Is the fall into love strictly an emotional journey? Does Cupid's arrow defy reason or direction and truly strike us senseless?

Despite romantic visions, research indicates that the experience of falling in love is much more logical than we might like to admit. Although Cupid's arrow may contain the magic that joins two hearts, Cupid's aim appears to be highly selective, and heavily influenced by the social status of his targets. **Social status** refers to the position or location of an individual with reference to characteristics such as age, education, gender, income, race, and religion. Consider the love-and-marriage game. Our choices for the "love of my life" generally occur along highly predictable lines (Gardyn 2002; Kalmijn 1991, 1994, 1998; Kalmijn and Flap 2001; McPherson, Smith-Lovin, and Cook 2001). Indeed, these choices are guided by "rules" that sociologists refer to as norms of homogamy. **Norms of homogamy** encourage interaction between individuals occupying similar social statuses.

Research shows that the large majority of Americans fall in love and marry mates within three years of their own age (U.S. Census Bureau 2000a). Furthermore, the look of love seems routinely reserved for those of like races, religions, and classes. For example, less than 6% of all U.S. marriages are interracial, and only about a quarter of American marriages occur between people of different religions (Bisin, Topa, and Verdier 2002; Gardyn 2002; U.S. Census Bureau 2002, Table 47). Approximately 60% of all American marriages unite people of the same social class, and 95% of all U.S. marriages join people who are no more than one socioeconomic class apart (Gardyn 2002; Holman, Larson, and Olsen 2001; Hout 1982; Simon 1987).

Cupid's arrow also is typically reserved for those with similar educational backgrounds, similar intelligence levels, and similar physical appearance. And, apparently, Cupid's flights are amazingly short. Research documents a 50/50 chance that individuals will marry people who live within walking distance of their homes or their jobs (Gardyn 2002; Mulford et al. 1998; Sprecher and Regan 2002).

When it comes to love and marriage, research suggests that "birds of a feather seem to flock together," while "opposites rarely attract." Star-crossed lovers may exist in principle, but in practice the stars of love are likely to be carefully charted by social forces—and thus glitter in the eyes of a social peer. Such patterns lead sociologists to characterize both romantic love and marriage as endogamous phenomena. **Endogamy** is a practice restricted by shared group membership; it is an "in-group" phenomenon. What explains the endogamous nature of love? Endogamy generally results from a societal wish to maintain group and class boundaries. In some cases, these boundaries are formally stated. Certain religious groups, for example, strongly urge their members toward intrafaith marriages. Similarly, traditional caste systems generally prohibit marriage between individuals of different castes. In other settings, however, boundary maintenance occurs via more informal channels, where certain key social players may quietly enforce endogamy in love and marriage.

In U.S. society, parents and peers often play the role of enforcer. It is not uncommon for family and friends to threaten, cajole, wheedle, and even bribe individuals in the direction of a "suitable" mate. Suitability generally translates into a partnership based on similar social profiles. Thus, the "American way" of marriage places the most personal decisions of one's life—falling in love and getting married—under "group control." This subtle control serves as a vehicle by which endogamy can be maintained.

Like romantic love, the development and expression of platonic love or friendship is also heavily influenced by the social location of its participants. Research shows that friendship formation is largely a product of one's daily interaction patterns rather than of chance or "good chemistry."

Friendships tend to develop with the people we see most often—those with whom we work, those enrolled in the same classes, or members of our churches, health clubs, and so on. Similarly, friendships tend to form among those who are in close geographic proximity to us, as opposed to those who are farther away—that is, the people in the same apartment complex or those who live in the same neighborhood as we do (Carley and Krackhardt 1996; Festinger, Schacter, and Back 1950; McPherson et al. 2001; Monge and Kirste 1980).

Like romantic love, the platonic love of friendship grows best out of similarity. We tend to build the strongest friendships with those who hold attitudes similar to our own. We also tend to connect with those who share our physical and social characteristics—appearance, income, education level, race, and so on. In the case of friendship, familiarity breeds attraction rather than contempt (Adams and Allan 1998; Allan 1998a; Diamond and Dube 2002; McPherson et al. 2001).

Interestingly, our feelings about friendship—the way we define and express it—differ in systematic ways on the basis of our socioeconomic status. **Socioeconomic status** refers to a particular social location—one defined with reference to education, occupation, and financial resources. Studies show, for example, that working-class Americans conceive of friendship as an exchange of goods and services. Gifts and favors come to indicate the strength of a friendship bond. In contrast, material exchange is absent from middle-class definitions of friendship. Middle-class individuals frequently view friendship as an emotional or intellectual exchange; they may also conceive of friendship simply as the sharing of leisure activities.

The "faces" of our friends also differ by social class. Thus, if you are a member of America's working class, your friends are highly likely to be relatives—siblings, cousins, parents, and so on. In contrast, middle-class individuals prefer nonblood relations for friends. Furthermore, among working-class people, friendships are overwhelmingly same sex, whereas middle-class people are more open to cross-gender friendships. Finally, if you are from America's working class, your friendships are likely to be local. Thus, working-class friends interact, on average, once a week or more. In contrast, middle-class individuals have as many long-distance friendships as they do local ones. Because middle-class life in America often involves high levels of geographic mobility, members of the middle class are more likely than their working-class counterparts to maintain friendships after individuals move out of the immediate geographic area. This distance factor carries a downside, however. Middle-class friends generally report less frequent contact than their working-class counterparts (Allan 1989, 1998b; Bleiszner and Adams 1992; Elles 1993; Fischer 1982; Gouldner and Strong 1987; Liebler and Sandefur 2002; Rawlins 1992; Walker 1995).

The patterned nature of love also emerges in matters of self-love, or what social scientists refer to as self-esteem. **Self-esteem** refers to the personal judgments individuals make regarding their own self-worth. Like romantic and platonic love, love of self appears quite systematically tied to an individual's social situation.

On the level of experience, for example, many studies show that one's self-esteem is directly tied to the love expressed toward that individual by her or his significant others. Not surprisingly, when significant others give positive feedback, self-esteem increases. Conversely, consistently negative feedback from significant others lowers self-esteem (Amato and Fowler 2002; Dolgin and Minowa 1997; Mruk 1999; Voss, Markiewicz, and Doyle 1999). Similarly, the character of one's social or work environment clearly influences an individual's self-esteem. Those who are situated among optimistic people in positive, upbeat environments have been shown repeatedly to enjoy better self-esteem than those who find themselves in negative environments with depressed or disgruntled colleagues (Cross and Vick 2001; Mruk 1999; Ross and Broh 2000). Finally, various social attributes can influence levels of self-love or self-esteem, with members of upper classes and racial majority groups routinely faring better than the poor or those in racial minorities (Coopersmith 1967; De Cremer 2001; Felson and Reed 1986, 1987; Gergen 1971; Keefe and Berndt 1996; Mruk 1999).

Romantic love, platonic love, self-love—when findings from these areas are considered together, we must concede that love, in its various forms, is a highly structured phenomenon. There is much rhyme and reason regarding how we find it, define it, experience it, and express it. And that logic is tied to aspects of our social backgrounds and our social locations. Knowing this, we might do better to trade our notions of the irrational heart for knowledge of the social organization of the heart. Indeed, the study of love reminds us that even the most personal of experiences can succumb to the systematic influence of the social.

Learning More About It

For informative and very readable studies on romantic coupling in America, see *The Mating Game: A Primer on Love, Sex, and Marriage* by Pamela C. Regan (Thousand Oaks: Sage Publications, 2002) or *Talk of Love: How Culture Matters* by Ann Swidler (Chicago: University of Chicago Press, 2001). For a recent review of literature on the social similarities of lovers and friends, see "Birds of a Feather," an article by Miller McPherson, Lynn Smith-Lovin, and James M. Cook, in K.S. Cook and J. Hagan (Eds.), *Annual Review of Sociology* 27: 415–444.

For a firsthand view of online coupling, visit <http://www.lovingyou.com> The site provides a library of love stories, poetry, cards, and dedications. One will also find advice, chat groups, and a host of romantic-oriented links.

For an interesting and still timely look at the social aspects of friendship, see Rubin's *Just Friends: The Role of Friendship in Our Lives* (New York: HarperCollins, 1993). More recently, sociologists have paid special attention to adolescent friendships and the effects of friendship cliques on adolescent identity. For a fascinating study on the topic, consult Patricia and Peter Adler's *Peer Power: Preadolescent Culture and Identity* (New Brunswick, NJ: Rutgers University Press, 1998).

Most sociological work on self-esteem is steeped in the writings of Charles Horton Cooley. His classic works include *Human Nature and Social Order* (New York: Scribner, 1902) and *Social Organization* (New York: Charles Scribner, 1909). A very readable review of recent research on self-esteem can be found in Chris Mruk's book *Self-Esteem: Research, Theory, and Practice* (New York: Springer, 1999).

Exercises

1. Identify the top three traits you desire in a friend. Do these traits correspond to the friendship trends cited here for (a) your social class of origin or (b) the social class to which you aspire? Now, repeat the exercise, this time considering the top three traits that you desire in a spouse. Do your answers suggest the influence of homogamy?

2. Using yourself (if appropriate) and your married friends as case studies, discuss how the rules of homogamy either apply or do not apply in these individuals' selections of marriage partners. Collect similar information about your parents, aunts, and uncles, and compare it with what you found about yourself and your friends. Do you see any important generational changes in the rules for marital homogamy? Are there rule variations that can be linked to class or educational factors?

Essay 5

Conventional Wisdom Tells Us ...
Stress Is Bad for Your Well-Being

Or is it? This essay reviews the conditions under which stress can prove beneficial in one's everyday activities. In so doing, we highlight the importance of considering social context in assessing social behaviors.

Stress has become a regular feature of modern-day existence. Finding a parking space at the mall, hooking up a new computer, navigating the university's new automated registration system, returning your last online purchase—in today's fast-paced, high-tech environment, stress can weave its way into even the most routine tasks.

Modernization and technological advancement have stress-related costs. To be sure, these phenomena make possible amazing strides, including increased life spans, greater geographic mobility, and heightened industrial and agricultural productivity. Yet these changes also actively alter a society's social structure. **Social structure** refers to the organization of a society—the ways in which social statuses, resources, power, and mechanisms of control combine to form a framework of operations.

Thus, for many, a society's "amazing strides" may translate into commuter marriages, single parenthood, long widowhoods, or "downsized" work environments—conditions often associated with increased stress. In addition, such advances may expand the ranks of the poor, trigger rapid population growth, and increase competition for resources. Such structural changes can increase the day-to-day stress experienced by those in certain social locations. **Social location** is an individual's total collection of social statuses; it pinpoints an individual's social position by simultaneously considering age, education, gender, income, race, and so on.

49

The pervasiveness of stress makes it important to weigh conventional wisdom's dire warnings on the subject. Will the benefits of modernization ultimately cost us our physical, mental, or emotional health? Just what toll does stress take on our overall well-being?

The links between stress and well-being are complex because the effects of stress vary by social context (Cockerham 2004:72–93; Iwata and Suzuki 1997; Jacobson 1989; Lennon 1989; Pearlin 1989; Pearlin and Skaff 1996). **Social context** refers to the broad social and historical circumstances surrounding an act or an event. For example, consider the links between stress and health. Many studies link stress to serious physical problems: cancer, heart disease, mental illness, and emotional depression. Research also suggests that stress can trigger increases in smoking, drinking, drug use, and other hazardous behaviors (American Heart Association 2003a; Pearlin et al. 1981; Ross and Huber 1985; Stenson 2003; Wheaton 1983). However, these negative effects are largely confined to contexts in which stress is chronic. **Chronic stress** refers to the relatively enduring problems, conflicts, and threats that individuals face on a daily basis. Most researchers agree that chronic stress contexts, such as persistent financial woes, a bad marriage, sites of crime, violence, overcrowding, or even noise, are harmful to our well-being. In contrast, sporadic, short-term stress generally proves less detrimental to well-being (American Psychological Association 1997; Aneshensel 1992; House et al. 1986; Pearlin 1989; Suinn 2001).

Now consider the stress generated by certain life events—retirement, children leaving home, the death of a spouse, and so on. Conventional wisdom suggests that such events can be the most stressful experiences of our lives. Again, however, research reveals that the stress associated with these life events varies with the social context in which the event occurs. For example, retirement actually has been shown to alleviate stress if one is leaving an unpleasant or difficult job. Similarly, when a child leaves home, stress actually decreases for those parents who perceived their family relationships to be troubled or strained. To determine the level of stress associated with any life event, one must explore the circumstances and activities that precede and/or accompany the event; one must assess the life event within its proper social context (Aneshensel 1992; Burton 1998; Jacobson 1989; Lennon 1989; Martin and Svebak 2001; Mirowsky and Ross 1989; Pearlin 1989; Simon 1997; Simon and Marcussen 1999; Thoits 1983; Wheaton 1982).

In assessing the conventional wisdom on stress, it also is important to note that the negative effects of stress are not inevitable. Research documents several coping mechanisms that can temper or even cancel the negative impact of stress on one's well-being. For example, individuals who enjoy strong social support networks often are protected from the harmful consequences of stress. A **social support network** consists of family, friends, agencies, and resources—entities that actively assist individuals in coping with adverse or unexpected events. Studies document, for instance, that widows and widowers who have close friends or confidants report much less stress from the death of a spouse than individuals who lack such support. Similarly, the stress of divorce appears greatly diminished for those with close friends, confidants, or new romantic interests. And research on children shows that increased parental contact can mitigate the stress experienced by children when families are forced to geographically relocate (Cockerham 2004; Davison, Pennebaker, and Dickerson 2000; Hagan, MacMillan, and Wheaton 1996; Horowitz et al. 2001; House et al. 1986; Kessler, Price, and Wortman 1985; Lin, Ye, and Ensel 1999; Mui 2001; Schutt, Medchede, and Rierdan 1994; Thoits 1995; Treharne, Lyons, and Tupling 2001; Wheaton 1982, 1990).

Certain resources also can influence the experience of stress. Research indicates that relaxation techniques can buffer individuals from the negative impact of stress. Similarly, problem-solving strategies or strategies that can physically or mentally distance one from the site of stress can help mitigate its harmful effects. Research also indicates significant stress reduction among optimists or those who learn to deemphasize the negative aspects of a stress-producing role. And those who perceive some level of personal control over their environment experience less stress than those who feel little or no control (Affleck, Tennen, and Apter 2000; Chan 2002; Danner, Snowden, and Friesen 2001; Frazier et al. 2000; Gianokos 2000; Pham, Taylor, and Seeman 2001; Simon 1997; Thoits 1994, 1995).

Coping mechanisms can offer protection from stress. However, some contend that modern lifestyles may make it difficult for individuals to put these "safeguards" into effect. For example, the geographic mobility that characterizes modern society may place friends and family out of one's immediate reach. Similarly, increased access to information may create a mental overload that eats away at one's relaxation time, and technological advancements that allow one to merge work and home sites may make mental distancing strategies difficult to execute (Hochschild 1997; Nippert-Eng 1996; Pearson 1993; Philipson 2002; Robinson 2003).

The successful enactment of coping mechanisms may be largely related to the kinds of social relationships that characterize one's social environment. Ferdinand Tonnies (1855–1936) analyzed such relationships using two distinct categories: Gemeinschaft and Gesellschaft. **Gemeinschaft** refers to an environment in which social relationships are based on ties of friendship and kinship. **Gesellschaft** refers to an environment in which social relationships are formal, impersonal, and often initiated for specialized or instrumental purposes. Modern social environments, with their emphasis on privacy and individuality, reflect the Gesellschaft environment. As such, the social resources from which coping mechanisms develop may not be readily available to modern women and men.

Are there contexts in which stress positively influences our well-being? Social psychologists have demonstrated that task-oriented stress often can lead to visibly productive consequences. **Task-oriented stress** refers to short-term stress that accompanies particular assignments or settings. Individuals who report feeling completely comfortable or relaxed during the execution of certain mental tasks remember and absorb less information than those who experience moderate levels of task-oriented stress. Indeed, moderate levels of task-oriented stress have been linked to enhanced memory of facts and skills and increased learning ability—important attributes in our postindustrial, knowledge-based society. This suggests that the nervous tingles you experience in studying for the law boards, your driving test, or a public speaking engagement may serve you better than a lackadaisical stance

(Bryan 1996; Ellis 1972; Mughal, Walsh, and Wilding 1996; Memorial Hospital 2000; U.S. Department of the Army 2003). Social psychologists have also demonstrated that stress can promote self-improvement. This is because stressful events encourage (or force) individuals to acquire new skills, reevaluate their positions, and reconsider their priorities. In this way, stress may serve as a catalyst for personal growth (Calhoun and Tedeschi 2001; Tennen and Affleck 1999).

Studies also show that stress can work *through* other physiological or psychological states to produce quite unexpected, and quite positive, behavioral outcomes. For example, when stress leads to a state of emotional arousal such as anxiety or fear, stressed individuals are more likely to befriend or bond with others. (This may explain why your student colleagues always seem more approachable on the day of a big exam.) Furthermore, when stress leads to anxiety or fear, stressed individuals demonstrate a greater tendency to like and interact with people whom they usually dislike or around whom they typically feel uncomfortable. This "benefit" extends to people who differ from the stressed individual in terms of race, socioeconomic status, and personality. In light of these findings, some researchers contend that under the right circumstances, stress may aid the cause of achieving interracial, inter-generational, or interclass affiliations (Kulik and Mahler 1990; Kulik, Mahler, and Moore 1996; Latané and Glass 1968; Olbrich 1986; Schachter 1959).

It is interesting to note that stress that proves detrimental to the well-being of individuals sometimes may prove productive for societies at large. Consider one such example in the area of chronic stress. Chronic stress can emerge from a particular type of long-term situation, a condition sociologists refer to as role conflict. **Role conflict** occurs when social members occupy two or more social positions that carry opposing demands. Military chaplains, working parents, and student teachers all provide examples of potentially conflicting role combinations. Roles that carry opposing demands create a tug-of-war within individuals—a persistent strain characteristic of chronic stress.

Although role conflict can take its toll on an individual's well-being, it sometimes proves the source of positive social change. For example, when role conflict is routinized by changing cultural or economic demands, the resulting stress can actually trigger needed social restructuring. Routinized role conflict can lead societies to institute changes that positively alter the playing field of social interaction. For example, the conflict and stress that emerged from the working-parent role combination served to revolutionize America's work environment. Methods such as flex-time, in-house day care, and work-at-home options—originally antidotes to the stress of role conflict—are now a productive dimension of work in the United States.

We can take this analysis of the positive consequences of stress one step further. The phenomenon of stress need not be confined to individual-level inquiries; societies as a whole also can experience stress. Sociologists refer to this type of stress as social strain. **Social strain** develops when a social event or trend disrupts the equilibrium of a society's social structure. For example, an economic depression may generate social strain by forcing increases in unemployment and exacerbating poverty. In essence, the depression event disrupts expected patterns of resource distribution. Similarly, a large increase in a society's birthrate may place strain on various social institutions. Schools, hospitals, or prisons may suddenly be presented with more clients than they were designed to serve.

Sociologists such as Talcott Parsons ([1951] 1964) or Lewis Coser (1956), although coming from different perspectives, both suggested that social strain creates an opportunity for societal change and growth. (Note that Coser refers to the phenomenon of strain as "social conflict.") With their writings, both Parsons and Coser established a view of society that continues to guide contemporary social thinkers. Social strain is important because it disrupts the status quo. Thus, it can force societies to work at reestablishing smooth operations. For example, the strain placed on the U.S. stratification system by the civil rights movement of the 1950s and 1960s resulted in positive strides toward racial and ethnic equality in America. Similarly, consider the growing demands U.S. entitlement programs currently place on the nation's economic system. Many credit such strain with prompting much-needed public discourse on major budget reforms.

Is stress harmful to our well-being? Taken as a whole, current research on stress paints a less dismal picture than that promoted by conventional wisdom. To be sure, stress is frequently harmful, and it is rarely a pleasant experience. Yet its consequences do not necessarily jeopardize personal health and happiness. In fact, when one views stress in context, or at the level of societies at large, it sometimes proves a useful social resource.

Learning More About It

For a good summary of current findings and controversies within the social science literature on stress, see Carol Aneshensel's 1992 review article "Social Stress: Theory and Research," *Annual Review of Sociology* 18: 15–38; Peggy Thoits's 1995 article "Stress, Coping, and Social Support Processes: Where Are We? What Next?" *Journal of Health and Social Behavior* 36(extra issue): 53–79; or William C. Cockerham's chapter "Social Stress," in his book *Medical Sociology* (9th edition, Upper Saddle River, NJ: Prentice Hall, 2004).

Several interesting experiments document the positive consequences of stress for individuals. Schachter's *The Psychology of Affiliation* (Stanford, CA: Stanford University Press, 1959) represents a classic among such studies.

Stress and conflict within social systems is wonderfully addressed in Lewis Coser's classic, yet still relevant, theoretical treatise, *The Functions of Social Conflict* (Glencoe, IL: Free Press, 1956).

Want to learn something about the history of stress in the marketplace and its "commerce" value? Visit *Stress.inc* at <http://stress.jrn.columbia.edu/> for information, quizzes, and amusing tidbits on the subject.

The following organizations can help you to learn more about stress:

The American Institute of Stress
124 Park Ave., Yonkers, NY 10703
(914) 963–1200; Web site: <http://www.stress.org>

National Mental Health Association
2001 North Beauregard Street, 12th Floor, Alexandria, VA 22311
(703) 684–7722; Web site: <http://www.nmha.org>

Exercises

1. Research suggests that stress can increase an individual's likelihood of affiliating with others. Can stress function in a similar way at the societal level? To test the hypothesis that social stress increases social solidarity, see if periods of economic recession or a nation's involvement in a major war are associated with any indicators of increased group cohesion. Using a source like the *Information Please Almanac,* track membership rates in five national organizations for years before and after the economic recession of the 1970s or World War II.

2. Compare two-weeks' worth of "Letters to the Editor" *prior* to the September 11, 2001, terrorist attacks in America; the declaration of war on Iraq in 2003; or a well-publicized murder or accident in your hometown—with two-weeks' worth of "Letters to the Editor" *after* such an event. Analyze the content of letter writers' remarks concerning their personal feelings and reactions to these events. What does your analysis show regarding the social consequences of stress?

Essay 6

Conventional Wisdom Tells Us . . . The "Golden Years" Are Tarnished Years

Growing old—no one looks forward to it. Yet this essay illustrates that our worst fears about growing old may be largely unfounded, simply products of a "master status" for which we have been inadequately prepared.

Aging is a curious phenomenon. When we are young, we can't wait to be older—or at least old enough to drive, get a good job, and make our own decisions. When we finally reach adulthood, many of us continue to yearn for a later stage in life, a time when we can begin to capitalize on the lessons of youth, a time when we can enjoy the fruits of our labors. Retirement looks like a pretty good deal from the vantage point of youth. Indeed, three-quarters of Americans 45 years old and over feel that retirement will be a very satisfying period in their life (American Association of Retired Persons [AARP] 2003a).

Eventually, however, there comes a time when the benefits of aging seem less clear-cut. We begin to view age as a liability, perhaps even as a thing to be feared. For many, the dread comes with the appearance of their first gray hairs (Graham 2002). The conventional wisdom on aging seems to support this negative stance. We are warned never to "trust anyone over 30." Those in their forties and fifties frequently are characterized as "over the hill." This perception is no doubt helped along by children and adolescents who see their parents as "old fogies." But it is also aided by the law (the Age Discrimination in Employment Act protects employees aged 40 and over from age discrimination); by organizations like AARP, which opens its membership ranks to those 50 and older; and by the Census Bureau, which defines "older Americans" as age 55 and over (U.S. Census Bureau 2000)! Advanced age becomes a liability for many practices and occupations: After all, "You can't teach an old dog new tricks," and retiring can earn one the image of "being put out to pasture."

Despite early desires to "be older," many Americans ultimately develop a rather negative view of growing old. Many Americans picture old age as a time of loneliness, vulnerability, and sickness; a time of stubborn resistance to change and lack of productivity (Administration on Aging 2001). There is a widespread perception today that the aging of America, especially the aging of the "baby boomers," poses a social and economic problem. Are such images accurate? Is conventional wisdom's negative stance on growing old justified? Research suggests that the "negative press" on aging is not fully supported by the facts. In reviewing several studies on the elderly, one finds many inconsistencies between the public perceptions versus the social realities of old age in America.

Consider, for instance, the image of old age as a lonely, isolated existence. It is true that the elderly make up a relatively large portion of single-occupant households in the United States, but only 30% of the elderly live alone. (That's 7-million-plus women and more than 2 million men). The large majority of older persons live with their spouses or others (Administration on Aging 2002a; U.S. Census Bureau 2002, Table 39). For those elderly who do live alone, such living arrangements seem to reflect a personal preference rather than a forced choice. Most elderly Americans report wanting to remain in their own homes for as long as possible—in fact, 82% of those 65 and older think it is somewhat to very likely that they will be able to stay in their current homes for the rest of their lives (AARP 2003a). To be sure, the elderly value their independence. Over two-thirds of older parents with children over 34 years old report *not* wanting to live with their children *even if they were to need assistance and care* (*Health and Medicine Work* 2002). An AARP report finds that even the older disabled express a strong preference for living independently in their own homes (AARP 2003b). Indeed, only about 6% of America's elderly ultimately share living arrangements with their children or other relatives (Administration on Aging 1997).

In addition to living arrangements, several other behavioral patterns contradict the loneliness stereotype. Senior citizens regularly report active companionship in a variety of settings, not the least of which is the family. In 1995, 92% of those aged 70 and older reported having contact with family, and 88% reported contact with friends and neighbors (Federal Interagency Forum on Aging-Related Statistics 2000). Adult children and their parents live in close proximity to each other and visit and talk frequently (Lye 1996). One national study found that more than half of adult children live within an hour's drive of parents; 70% have weekly contact with their mothers; 20% have daily contact (Lawton, Silverstein, and Bengtson 1994). Sixty percent of males aged 65 and older and 69% of females aged 65 and over report that they "love" spending time with families (AARP 2001). In fact, a recently noted trend is the return of the "whole" family vacation—family traveling with and staying with family. In 2002, 35% of grandparents joined their grandchildren on a family trip (Mencimer 2002).

Two-thirds of those aged 45 and older think that they will be able to rely on family and friends for help as they get older (AARP 2003a). In general, research finds that parents and adult children do have a high sense of mutual normative obligation (Johnson 2000; Rossi and Rossi 1990; Umberson 1996). Caregiving for the elderly is clearly a family affair. Indeed, studies show that two-thirds or more of the help received by the elderly is provided by family (Health, Retirement, and Aging Study 1998; Administration on Aging 2002b). Of the single elderly, about half report receiving "time help" (i.e., regular companionship) from their children, and many elderly parents return the favor: Single grandmothers provide an average of 20 hours of child care a week (Health, Retirement, and Aging Study 1998). Indeed, since 1990, there has been a huge increase in grandparent-headed households. Over 10% of grandparents raise a grandchild for six months or longer (Coleman and Pandya 2002). Over 5% of American children live in households maintained by a grandparent (Casper and Bryson 1998). Such findings and developments would all suggest that loneliness is not a necessary companion of old age.

Loneliness is only one of the misconceptions about old age. Public perceptions also paint the elderly as frequent victims of violent crime. Yet violent crime against the elderly has declined drastically over the past 25 years. In fact, age and violent victimization are inversely related—as age goes up, crime victimization goes down. Those between the ages of 50 and 64, for example, are three times more likely to be victims of violent crime than those over the age of 65; individuals between the ages of 25 and 49 are more than seven times more likely to become violent crime victims. And note that when the elderly are victims of crime, they are likely to be victims of property crime rather than violent crime. (U.S. Department of Justice 2000). Yet, the "crime myth" that surrounds old age is not without its consequences; the myth generates a great deal of anxiety among the elderly, especially the disabled elderly. Among persons 65 and older with disabilities, the *perception* that crime is a serious problem in their neighborhoods has nearly doubled between 1984 and 1999 (AARP 2003b).

Public perceptions also suggest that old age is a time of poverty. Until the 1970s, the elderly were more likely than any other age group to live in poverty: 25% of those over the age of 65 were classified as poor. In contrast, the poverty rate for the population at large was only 13%. But changes in the social security system—in particular, changes linking benefits to cost-of-living increases—have helped reduce the percentage of elderly living in poverty. Today the poverty rate for those over 65 years of age hovers around 10%. Thus, current poverty rates for the elderly are below the national poverty rate of 12.4% (Administration on Aging 2002a; Mather 2002).

Images of physical and mental deterioration also pervade public perceptions of old age. To be sure, age does result in some changes on the physical front. The most frequently occurring chronic conditions are (in order) arthritis, hypertension, hearing impairment, and heart disease (Administration on Aging 2002a). Yet it is important to note that *health,* not disease, is the norm for the elderly—even for those over 75! Approximately three in four of those in the 65 to 74 age bracket consider their health to be good, very good, or excellent; two in three of those 75 and over report the same (National Center for Health Statistics 2002a). Between the mid-1980s and 1995, older Americans reported improvement in their ability to walk a quarter mile, climb stairs, and reach up and over their heads (Federal Interagency Forum on

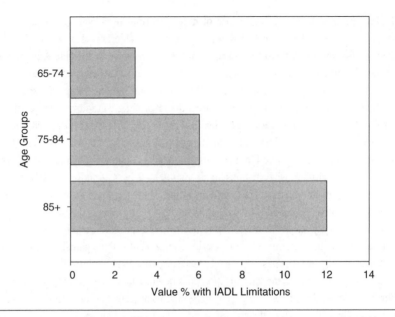

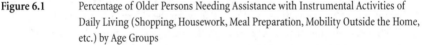

Figure 6.1   Percentage of Older Persons Needing Assistance with Instrumental Activities of Daily Living (Shopping, Housework, Meal Preparation, Mobility Outside the Home, etc.) by Age Groups

SOURCE: AARP (2003b).

Aging-Related Statistics 2000). Between 1984 and 1999, there was a significant drop in the number of elderly reporting IADLs (limitations in instrumental activities of daily living) that is, the ability to go shopping, prepare meals, do housework, and otherwise manage one's affairs independently. Overall, rates of chronic disability for all elderly age categories have also declined since the mid-1980s (AARP 2003b). The elderly's desire for independence and their general good health help explain another important fact: Only 4.5% of the 65+ population live in nursing homes. While the percentage of nursing home residents does increase with age, it is still the case that only 18.2% of those 85 and older are relegated to nursing home care (Administration on Aging 2002a). Figure 6.1 attests to the continued physical independence of elderly Americans.

In terms of mental health, the elderly fare quite well. Most elderly enjoy good mental health—the mental health problems that do arise are *not* part of the normal aging process per se (Administration on Aging 2001). For many major mental disorders (depression, bipolar, and panic disorders), the average age of onset is in *early adulthood* (National Institute of Mental Health [NIMH] 2001). Moderate to severe memory loss affects only 5% of those 65 to 69, 10% of those 70 to 74, and still only about a third of those aged 85 and over (Federal Interagency Forum on Aging-Related Statistics 2000). And although

Alzheimer's disease is frequently associated with old age, it afflicts only 3% of those aged 65 to 74 (National Mental Health Association 2003). Overall, aging appears to bring an elusive mental benefit: The elderly, even with the changes associated with aging, remain highly satisfied with their lives. **Emotional regulation,** or the ability to maintain a positive affect, improves with age. Older individuals have a better ability to solve emotionally charged problems and report greater contentment with life (Carstensen et al. 2000; Charles, Mather, and Carstensen 2003; Stern and Carstensen 2000). Surely some elderly must already know what research is confirming: A positive attitude toward aging is one of the things that keeps us going (Levy et al. 2002).

The facts about old age in America seem to contradict "common knowledge." Why do such misconceptions exist? The concept of a master status may provide one flash of insight in the matter. A **master status** refers to a single social status that overpowers all other social positions occupied by an individual. A master status directs the way in which others see, define, and relate to an individual.

Master statuses are powerful identity tools because they carry with them a set of qualities or characteristics that they impose on those who occupy the status. For example, those who occupy the master status of doctor are assumed to be knowledgeable, wealthy, rational, and usually white and male. Similarly, those who occupy the master status of mother are presumed to be caring, nurturing, stable, and female.

In short, a master status and the traits and characteristics that accompany it have a tremendous capacity to influence what others "see" or assume to be true in their social interactions. Thus, although I can look at a doctor and see that she is not a male, the story doesn't end there. Expectations that stem from the master status "doctor" might nonetheless continue to influence my interaction with my doctor. I may question whether or not she possesses other key traits of the master status, such as knowledge or rationality. I may doubt her ability to diagnose.

During two periods in our lives, childhood and our senior years, age serves as a master status. In childhood, the master status of age is equated with qualities such as dependency, unbounded energy, innocence, inquisitiveness, irresponsibility, and the ability to be uninhibited. As senior citizens, the master status of age is associated with characteristics such as dependency, frailty, loneliness, stubbornness, and the lack of creativity.

In essence, age becomes a master status early and late in life due to a lack of competition. We begin to accumulate statuses more powerful than age only as we move out of childhood and through adolescence, young adulthood, and our middle-aged years. During life's middle stages, we embark on careers, take spouses, raise children, join clubs and associations, become homeowners, and pursue leisure-time or self-fulfilling interests. During life's middle stages, occupational and family statuses typically assume the master status position.

In our later years, we exit many of our occupational and family statuses. Children leave home, people retire, spouses die, and homes are sold. When such status losses occur, age and the characteristics associated with it once again return to the forefront of our identities.

Misconceptions about our golden years may also result from a lack of anticipatory socialization. **Anticipatory socialization** refers to socialization that prepares a person to assume a role in the future. Consider the fact that as children, we "play" at being mommies and daddies, teachers, and fire fighters. As we move through the early stages of our lives, anticipatory socialization provides a road map to the statuses of young adulthood and the middle years. High school and college put us through the paces via internships, apprenticeships, and occupational training. We receive on-the-job instruction when we are initiated to the workforce. Such preparation is simply not given to the tasks involved in senior citizenship. At no time in our lives are we schooled in the physiological changes and social realities that surround retirement, widowhood, or other events of old age.

This lack of anticipatory socialization should not surprise us. Preparing for old age would be inconsistent with typical American values and practices. We are an action- and production-oriented society. We generally don't prepare for doing less. As a society, we don't encourage role playing for *any* statuses that carry negative traits and characteristics, such as being old, criminal, terminally ill, widowed, and so on.

Switching our focus to a macro-level analysis provides additional insight regarding the misconceptions on aging. A **macro-level analysis** focuses on broad, large-scale social patterns as they exist across contexts or through time. Consider aging as a historical phenomenon. Old age in America is a relatively new event. In the first census, in 1790, less than 2% of the U.S. population was 65 or older; the median age was 16. (Historians suggest that these statistics probably characterized the population from the early 1600s to the early 1800s; see Fischer 1977.) Thus, old age was an uncommon event in preindustrial America. Those of the period could not reasonably expect to live into old age. Indeed, individuals who did reach old age were regarded as exceptional and often were afforded great respect. Life-earned experience and knowledge were valuable commodities in a preindustrial society (Fischer 1977).

The youthful age structure of early America meant the absence of retirement. Preindustrial societies consisted of home-based, labor-intensive enterprises. Thus, the ability to produce, not age itself, was the relevant factor for working. Prior to the 20th century, most Americans worked until they died.

With the rise of modern society and industrialization, this pattern changed. The skills, experience, and knowledge of older workers did not resonate with the demands and innovations of factory work. Younger and inexperienced (that is, cheaper) workers were the better economic choice for employers. Such changes in the knowledge and economic base of American society had a profound impact on social and cultural views on aging (Watson and Maxwell 1977). With this shift, old age ceased to be exalted, and a youth-oriented society and culture began to develop.

The youth mentality of the industrial age is clearly articulated in one of the 20th century's most influential pieces of legislation: the Social Security Act of 1935. This act can be credited with setting the "old-age" cutoff at 65. (Note that older workers lobbied for a higher age cutoff and younger workers lobbied for a lower age cutoff at the time of the act's passage.)

Furthermore, the act legally mandated that older workers must make way for younger ones. The directive has been successful. Only about 13% of older Americans are still in the workforce (Administration on Aging 2002a).

The forced retirement instituted by the Social Security Act contributed to the negative image of old age. Retirement signifies both a social (occupational) and an economic "loss." Despite the reality of social security benefits, the elderly as a whole have less income than all other age groups except 15- to 24-year-olds (U.S. Census Bureau 2002, Table 664). In 2001, the median income for the 65+ age group was $14,152 (Administration on Aging 2002a). When one couples these losses with the natural physiological and social changes that accompany aging (increasing risk of chronic diseases, some vision and hearing impairment, relinquishment of parental and spousal roles, and so on), it becomes easier to understand the development of old age's negative image.

Before leaving this discussion, it is important to note that the analysis of old age in America must be qualified with reference to social context. **Social context** refers to the broad social and historical circumstances surrounding an act or an event. Those in certain social circumstances can find the aging experience to be a greater hardship than do others. For example, although poverty among the elderly *as a whole* has diminished over the past 30 years, some segments of that population still experience high poverty rates.

Elderly women, elderly minority members, and, in particular, elderly Hispanic women living alone continue to suffer rates of poverty that exceed the national average (Administration on Aging 2002a) (See Figure 6.2.) Similarly, *overall,* the elderly experience

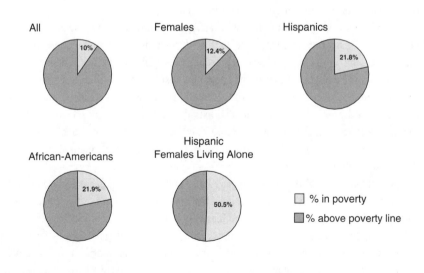

Figure 6.2   Poverty Among Various Segments of Elderly Population—U.S., 2000–2001
SOURCE: U.S. Department of Health and Human Services (2002a).

high rates of emotional calm or peace of mind. However, such rates can vary widely among subgroups of the elderly population. For instance, while older black females have suicide rates well below the national average, white men over 85 years of age have the highest suicide rate of any age group (National Institute of Mental Health 2003). Between 1980 and 1998, the suicide rate for men 80 to 84 years of age increased by 17%, from 43.5 to 52 per 100,000 (National Center for Injury Prevention and Control 2002). These high rates have been attributed to the difficulty older males experience in coping with the trauma presented by the loss of a spouse. Thus, elderly divorced or widowed men are nearly 3 times more likely than married men to commit suicide, and more than 17 times more likely than married women in the same age bracket to commit suicide (National Center for Injury Prevention and Control 2002).

Despite the multiple sources for our misconceptions on aging, all of our views on the matter may soon undergo significant revision. The changing age structure of the U.S. population helps to explain such a shift. **Age structure** refers to the distribution that results from dividing a population according to socially defined, age-based categories: childhood, adolescence, young adulthood, middle age, and old age.

Since the early 1900s, the median age in America has risen steadily; so, too, has the proportion of our population that is 65 or older. Today, approximately 12% of the population is over 65. With the aging of baby boomers, these numbers will increase significantly. By 2030, the elderly should comprise about 20% of the population; by 2050, more than one-fifth of the population will be over 65 (Administration on Aging 2002a). Furthermore, the 80+ age group is the fastest-growing cohort in the United States and the world (Shalala 2003). (See Figure 6.3.) Such fundamental changes to the age structure of our society will produce major consequences for both the image and the reality of old age.

The 65+ age group has the highest voter registration and turnout rates of any age group (U.S. Census Bureau 2002, Table 393). With such high civic-mindedness and with their increasing numbers, the elderly represent a powerful voting block. The elderly also benefit from the lobbying efforts of the largest interest group in politics today: the AARP (Cockerham 1997). Through its Web site, the AARP regularly offers its members a primer on Capitol Hill proceedings. The site also lists the daily and weekly schedules of both the U.S. Senate and the House of Representatives. Such organizational efforts are credited with increasing the political impact of elderly Americans (Button and Rosenbaum 1990).

The political clout of the elderly already has resulted in a significant reduction in the percentage of elderly living in poverty. Such clout also has figured in positive changes with regard to medical care (via Medicare) and lifestyles of the elderly (tax breaks for people over 65). Indeed, the voting power of the old and "near-old" has helped make social security and some of its related assistance programs the "third rail" of American politics. To be sure, social security is *the* major source of income for the elderly—it is received by 91% of older persons and provides at least half of the total income for the majority (65%) of recipients (Social

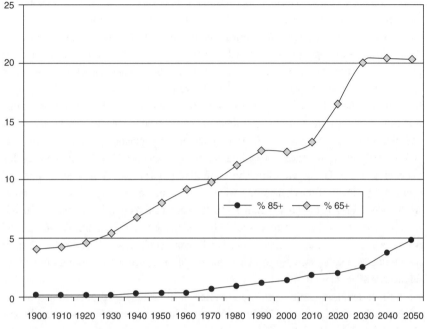

Figure 6.3   Older Population by Age: 1900–2050—Percentage 65+ and 85+

SOURCE: U.S. Administration on Aging, Based on 2000 Census Bureau data. (http://www.aoa.gov/aoa/ STATS/AgePop2050.html)

U.S. Bureau of the Census. Data for 1900 to 1940, 1960, and 1980 shown in 1980 Census of Population, PC80-B1, General Population Characteristics, Tables 42 and 45; Data for 1990 from 1990 Census of Population and Housing, Series CPH-L-74, Modified and Actual Age, Sex, Race, and Hispanic Origin Data. The 2000 data is from the 2000 Census. The figures for 2010 to 2050 are from NP-D1-A Census Projections issued January 13, 2000.

Security Online 2003). Social security benefits have been credited with saving about half of the elderly from the clutches of poverty (Center on Budget and Policy Priorities 1998). As the size and political power of the elderly continues to grow through the aging of the baby boomers, we should expect to see significant "corrections" in our social views of old age in America. Indeed, we may be seeing signs of the change already. There is a new phenomenon being noted by students of pop culture: "eldercool." It seems that the twenty-something crowd are particularly apt to grant celebrity status to older individuals who are "cool" enough to speak their own minds and be their own authentic selves: Muhammad Ali, Clint Eastwood, Bob Barker (that's right, come on down), and Donald Rumsfield are but a few of the cool oldies (Dudley 2003).

Are the golden years tarnished? Research suggests not. We have used several sociological tools—master status, anticipatory socialization, macrohistorical analysis, and contextual analysis—to understand the discrepancy between the myths and realities of aging.

However, the story on aging in America is hardly complete. Perhaps more than any other social phenomenon, aging is an extremely dynamic process. Given recent and continuing population changes, it is more and more difficult to talk about a single elderly population. On any number of fronts (health, social, financial), we need to differentiate the "young-old" (65–75) from the "old" (75–85) and the "old-old" (85+). It is, for instance, the last group that is increasing at the fastest rate. In 2000, there were over 50,000 Americans aged 100 or older (Administration on Aging 2002a). Consider that current population estimates for the year 2050 place life expectancy near 100 (Administration on Aging 1996). Such a shift means that many of us will be facing futures in which one-third of our lives will be spent in "old" and "old-old" age. Think of the changes this will bring to family, economic, and social relations. As the elderly age into (and beyond) their 80s, their adult children will face greater demands for (and conflicts over) elder care (Posner 1995). Today, the average caregiver is a 46-year-old woman who is married and employed outside the home (Coleman and Pandya 2002). In the near future, a possible scenario will be a "young-old" daughter (who can't afford to retire) taking care of an "old-old" parent.

In the future, community health care services will certainly need to be revamped and expanded (Lynn and Adamson 2003). While most elderly enjoy good mental health, only about half of those who acknowledge problems receive *any* treatment at all: Less than 3% receive treatment from *mental health professionals.* As the elderly population grows, we can expect this problem of accessing mental health services to grow as well (Administration on Aging 2001). And as the elderly population ages, the number living alone should also increase. This could very well produce a greater number of poor elderly. (The poverty rate for the "old-old" living alone is about twice the rate for the "young-old" [Administration on Aging 2002a]).

Finally, consider that when the Social Security Act was first passed, approximately 50 workers "supported" each social security recipient. Today, the burden of support falls on fewer than 3 workers for every retiree. What will happen to this ratio in the not too distant future when the aging baby boomers hit retirement age? In the next 30 years, the number of retired workers is expected to double (Social Security Online 2003). (See Figure 6.4.) But with as dynamic a process as aging, any and all projections might very well be shaky. The most recent survey by the AARP, for instance, finds that our jittery economy is prompting big changes in Americans' retirement plans. Indeed, 70% of us now plan on working past 65, and nearly half of us plan on working into our 70s and 80s (AARP 2003c)!

To be sure, the "aging" story is one that will continue to evolve; it is a story that will continue to demand our attention. Thus, old age in America is an area to which all of us must apply careful "second thoughts."

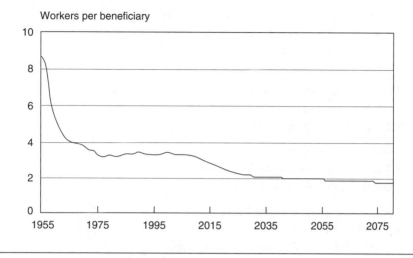

Figure 6.4   Number of Workers Supporting Each Retiree: Ratio of Covered Workers to Social Security Beneficiaries

SOURCE: Social Security Online (2003).

Learning More About It

To learn more about the concept of master status, consult Everett C. Hughes's "Dilemmas and Contradictions of Status," *American Journal of Sociology* 50(5): 353–359, 1945; Howard Becker's *The Outsiders* (Glencoe, IL: Free Press, 1963); or J.L. Simmons's "Public Stereotypes of Deviants," *Social Problems* 13: 223–232, 1966.

To probe more deeply into the process of anticipatory socialization, check Robert K. Merton's *Social Theory and Social Structure* (Glencoe, IL: Free Press, 1957) or "Adult Socialization," an article by Jeylan T. Mortimer and Roberta G. Simmons appearing in the 1978 *Annual Review of Sociology* 4: 421–454.

David Hackett Fischer offers an interesting history of aging in America in *Growing Old in America* (New York: Oxford University Press, 1977).

Todd Nelson's (Editor) book *Ageism: Stereotyping and Prejudice Against Older Persons* (Cambridge, MA: MIT Press, 2002) examines the origins and consequences of negative stereotyping of the elderly.

For an informative and "in their own words" account of making one's home in assisted living facilities, see Jacquelyn Frank's *The Paradox of Aging in Place in Assisted Living* (Westport, CT: Bergin and Garvey, 2002).

To see the latest research on emotions and the aging process, visit Laura Carstensen's "Life Span Development Lab" at Stanford University: <http://www-psych.stanford.edu/~lifespan/>

"Aging in the 21st Century" (in Stanford University's *Difficult Dialogues* series) offers a review of some of the policy implications of our increasing life span and elderly population: <http://www.difficultdialogues.com/DD!/consensus_report/cr_intro.htm>

The following organizations can help you to learn more about aging:

The National Aging Information Center, Administration on Aging
330 Independence Ave., SW, Room 4656, Washington, DC 20201
(202) 619–7501; Web site: <http://www.aoa.dhhs.gov/naic/>

The National Institute on Aging
P.O. Box 8057, Gaithersburg, MD 20898–8057
(800) 222–2225; Web site: <http://www.nia.nih.gov/>

American Association of Retired Persons
601 E Street NW, Washington, DC 20049
(800) 424–3410; Web site: <http://www.aarp.org/>

Exercises

1. Try a little fact-finding yourself. Ask some friends and family members what they believe to be true about the financial and social situations of those 65 and over. For instance, what social characteristics do your subjects associate with the elderly? What percentage of the elderly do your "subjects" believe are still employed? Are the elderly financially secure? Are the elderly happy after retirement? After you've solicited several opinions, compare your results with your library's holdings on the latest census figures or with the results of a recent survey executed by the AARP. How do the social locations of your respondents influence their knowledge of the elderly?

2. It is not always possible to know in advance which status will emerge as one's master status. Consider the following individuals and try to identify the master status for each: Hillary Clinton, Rudy Guiliani, Al Sharpton, Sammy Sosa, Ronald Reagan, Oprah Winfrey, Mother Theresa, Martha Stewart, and yourself. Be prepared to discuss your selections.

3. We've offered the concepts of master status and anticipatory socialization as useful devices for understanding conventional wisdoms regarding old age. Consider some of the other sociological ideas introduced in previous essays. Select and discuss two of them that you feel also offer insight into the misconceptions of old age. (Hint: Do the dynamics of a "self-fulfilling prophecy" feed a negative view of old age?)

Culture Meets Social Structure

Essay 7

Conventional Wisdom Tells Us ... Americans Are Becoming More and More Individualistic

This essay examines social relations in the United States, exploring in particular the characterization of contemporary Americans as increasingly isolated, disconnected, and dangerously individualistic. Here, we argue that social relations in the United States are more multifaceted than conventional wisdom suggests, a result of the complex interplay of social structure and culture.

Community is dead! That is the cry of many a social commentator. Indeed, since the 1970s, a bevy of intellectuals have warned of a growing individualism in America. **Individualism** refers to relational form that prioritizes the individual over any group, community, or institution.

Consider this timeline of claims. In 1976, author Tom Wolfe (1976:143) anointed the "Me Generation," a cohort of "zealous individualists" devoted only to the project of themselves. Three years later, Christopher Lasch (1979) proclaimed that a "culture of narcissism," had "carried the logic of individualism to the extreme of a war of all against all, the pursuit of happiness to the dead end of a narcissistic preoccupation with the self" (p. xv). Through the 1980s and 1990s, scholars wrote of rising selfishness, declining civility, of suburban isolation, and the loss of community. By the millennium's end, many saw Americans as hopelessly disengaged—from everything but themselves. Indeed, political scientist Robert Putnam (1998, 2000) declared the "death of Civic America," while sociologist Amitai Etzioni (1996) described the United States as a nation "heavily burdened with the antisocial consequences of excessive individual liberty" (pp. xvii, xv).

Are these analysts and intellectuals correct in their depictions of the American society? In reviewing social life in the United States during the past four decades, do we indeed find that social relations have slowly moved from something approximating civic community to an anomic world of self-centered strangers? And if so, is such "me-centered" individualism a terminal condition or simply pro tem?

In exploring this issue, sociologist Karen A. Cerulo examined data on American attitudes and behaviors for the past four decades (1960–2000), including figures generated by the Gallup poll, the General Social Survey, and the U.S. Census. (For a full accounting of the study's data sources, see Cerulo 2002.) Cerulo contends that these data fail to confirm an unequivocal shift toward individualism. Rather, data on American attitudes and behaviors provide a very complex and multifaceted picture of U.S. social relations. **Social relations** refer to the types of connections and the patterns of interaction that structure the broader society. Thus, in response to those who depict social actors of the future as isolated, disconnected beings, Cerulo suggests a much more optimistic picture.

To be sure, there are several areas in which national level data support increased individualism. For example, many point to the changing configuration of American families and households as a cue of this phenomenon. And indeed during the past four decades, national data reveal an increase in the percentage of single people, divorced people, and one-person households in the U.S. population. Each of these trends suggests a greater propensity on the part of Americans to "go it alone." Several other indicators confirm the increased "me-centeredness" of this period. For example, when it comes to sociability, Americans generally decreased the time they spent socializing with their immediate neighbors. In turn, Americans increased the time they devoted toward the very individualistic project of personal grooming. The data also show increases in certain attitudes that champion personal freedom. For example, public approval for suicide increased during this period.

But while the indicators just reviewed suggest a definitive shift toward individualism, it is important to note that other national level data question that trend. Indeed, many attitudes and behaviors of the period suggest only a "temporary flirtation" with individualism. Consider abortion, an act often cited as a hallmark of individual freedom. Both abortion rates and Americans' approval ratings for abortion increased from 1970 to 1980. But in 1981, abortion rates began to steadily decrease; post-1980, Americans' approval ratings for abortion proved rather erratic as well. Violent crime rates, murder rates in particular, are often cited as a cue of excessive personal liberty. However, the murder rates recorded for the period in question fail to display the linear increase that would confirm a growing individualism. While U.S. murder rates increased from 1965 to 1975, rates leveled off between 1976 and 1980. From 1981 to 2000, murder rates generally decreased. Finally, consider the popularity of various college majors during the period in question. Business, a field many feel is a trademark of the "me generation," increased in popularity from 1970 to 1985; however, the major saw a precipitous decrease in its popularity after 1985. Art, perhaps the extreme expression of individualism, actually declined during the 1970s and early 1980s, rebounding only slightly after 1985. Now consider majors in education and social science, prototypically non-individualistic in thrust. While the number of such majors temporarily declined in the 1970s, that trend generally reversed after 1981. Taken together, these indicators suggest that the growth of individualistic attitudes and behaviors is not linear and absolute. Often, the growth of individualism is a short-lived, reversible phenomenon.

While some attitudes and behaviors suggest only a temporary shift toward individualism, note that others suggest no movement toward individualism at all. For example, in an increasingly individualistic society, we might expect community-oriented activities such as church membership and church attendance to decrease. Yet these behaviors remained relatively stable over the past four decades. In a period of individualism, we also might expect more and more people to seek the independence of self-employment. Yet here, too, such rates remained relatively stable. In an era of growing individualism, we might expect to find cues of decreased interaction with family and friends. (After all, we found that socializing with neighbors declined.) Yet indicators of parent-child contact or social contacts between adults and their parents, siblings, and friends displayed little change. In a period of individualism, we might expect to see increases in prototypically individualistic acts such as suicide. Yet suicide rates remained stable as well. Note, too, that in an era of growing individualism, we might expect to see changes in Americans' reported levels of satisfaction with their communities. Similarly, we might expect people to lose faith in the communal spirit. Yet Americans' attitudes on these matters remained relatively stable. In total, these data fail to support a growing individualism in America. Rather, the data suggest little change in many relevant attitudes and behaviors.

In reviewing American attitudes and behaviors during the past four decades, one final trend deserves noting. Several indicators clearly challenge any growth in individualism. Rather, much data suggest the sustenance or growth of communally oriented sentiments. For example, if individualism were truly surging, we might expect to see an increase in self-gratifying behaviors such as smoking or alcohol and drug use. Yet such behaviors generally decreased during the past four decades. During an era of individualism, we might expect to see individuals withdrawing their support from community-oriented causes such as higher education, fraternal clubs, and organizations. Yet figures show that voluntary contributions to such causes increased steadily during the period in question. In concert with voluntary spending, government expenditures on social welfare programs, social security, Medicare, and veterans benefits consistently increased during this period as well. So, too, did public support for such spending (albeit in a jagged fashion). Taken together, these data indicate that many of Americans' attitudes and behaviors circa 1960 to 2000 were actually more "other-oriented" than they were "me-oriented."

To be sure, the indicators summarized here constitute only a portion of the many measures that tap social relations in America. We could, of course, increase the number of indicators we examine, but research suggests it would lead us to a similar end. For example, in a recent *New York Times* poll, researchers asked Americans how much importance they attached to 15 specific values. Some seemingly individualistic dimensions such as "being responsible for your own actions" and "being able to stand up for yourself" ranked among the most important values for those sampled. However, very close behind were more communally oriented sentiments such as "being able to communicate your feelings (to others)," "having faith in God," and "having children." In support of increased individualism, Americans ranked "having enough time for one's self" as more important than "being involved in the community." Yet in support of community, Americans ranked "being a good neighbor" as more important than "being financially secure" or "being physically attractive" (Cherlin 1999). Thus, it seems clear that Americans live a multifaceted existence. While Americans have indeed grown more individualistic in some regards, they have grown more community oriented in others, or simply exhibited no change in either direction. Indeed, a careful study of American attitudes and practices firmly suggests that American social relations are a highly complex phenomenon.

Cerulo (2002) suggests that rather than labeling the United States as dangerously individualistic, we should think of American society as an entity that resides in a state of relational polyphony. **Relational polyphony** means that different relational forms—not just individualism—simultaneously constitute American society. Cerulo's work shows that one can enter American society at any point from 1850 to the present and find that four different relational forms coexist: individualism, pluralism, bilateralism, and communalism.

Recall that earlier, we defined individualism as a relational form that prioritizes the individual over any group, community, or institution. Here, we define the remaining three relational forms. **Pluralism** emerges when social interactions are directed toward the peaceful coexistence of multiple groups. Various sectors of a society work to maintain mutual understanding; they work toward a system by which resources can be shared. Under pluralistic conditions, compromise and collaboration represent the dominant modes of social interaction. **Bilateral relations** suggest a condition in which a "them-versus-us" mentality guides social interaction. Dominance over or competition with the "other" represents social interaction's central goal. When bilateralism is in force, conflict and organized competition present the most frequent modes of interaction. Strong bonds are built with in-group members, while connections to out-group members are discouraged. In **communalism**, social actors become connected, albeit temporarily, via a specific task, event, or characteristic. During such periods, a sense of familiarity, "like-mindedness," or "we-ness" emerges. Similarities are stressed over differences; common knowledge is stressed over specialized knowledge. The good of the community takes precedence over any subgroup or individual.

How can these relational forms coexist? We need only look at the present historical moment to understand the phenomenon. In today's society, for example, new communication technologies do greatly facilitate individualism. One can customize and insulate rather than commune, creating a "world of one." Via the Internet, one can create Web sites that celebrate the self. One can downscale the scope of interaction, performing all one's routine tasks—banking, shopping, medical counseling, even romance—all without entering the physical community. In this way, contemporary American society can be reduced to its most basic element, the individual, with each individual remaining only loosely or instrumentally connected—and sometimes, disconnected.

At the same time, contemporary America is mapped according to pluralistic relations. Present-day society exists as a set of overlapping, interlocking "circles" (i.e., "baby boomers," Catholics, gun-control supporters, New Democrats, etc.), and often social action is directed by the ways in which these circles configure and coalesce. Such pluralistic relations became quite visible, for example, in the 2000 presidential election. Candidates could no longer rely on person-to-person connections or blind party loyalty. Rather, constituencies represented a coalition of compatible interest groups.

Of course, contemporary American society does periodically divide according to dualistic conflict. Certain events and issues pit White against Black, male against female, pro-life against pro-choice, big business against government, and so on. Such controversies force "either/or" choices and forge relations on the basis of social actors' bilateral affiliations. In the case of race, we saw this occur with the Rodney King trial, the O.J. Simpson case, or the Amadou Diallo proceedings. Similarly, the Microsoft antitrust case underscored the divide between government and big business. During such periods, social relations often develop in opposition rather than in conjunction with the "other."

And yet it is also true that faced with certain social events, Americans will temporarily ignore social partitions and emphasize collective concerns. Actors ban together (albeit for short, finite spans of time) in a single, targeted point of attention. Such like-mindedness enables actors to form communalistic relations, express shared perspectives, and support a common agenda. We witnessed such relations in widespread efforts aimed at solving national problems, for example, the recovery from the September 11, 2001, terrorist attacks in America or the power blackout that paralyzed the U.S. Northeast and Midwest in 2003. Similarly, we witness communalistic relations in the face of American human interest stories. Recall the intense collective focus that surrounded the deaths of Princess Diana or John F. Kennedy Jr., the Oklahoma City bombing or the execution of Timothy McVeigh. (Gallup polls showed that over 80% of respondents reported paying very close attention to these stories; Gallup 1974–2003.) And finally, we witness such relations in what sociologist Nina Eliasoph (1998) calls the "community of talk." **Communities of talk** revolve around topics about which the large majority of social members can fluently and affably converse: the retirement of pitching great Roger Clemens, basketball star Kobe Bryant's sexual assault case, the latest winner of television's *Survivor,* or the arrest of the "King of Pop," Michael Jackson. Far from the isolated existence attributed to contemporary Americans, communalistic relations infuse society with a sense of group-mindedness.

The aforementioned examples suggest that different relational forms—individualism, pluralism, bilateralism, communalism—are all integral parts of American society. To be sure, the relative concentration of these forms shifts through time, just as the primary melody of a polyphonic composition shifts from voice to voice as the piece progresses. But it is the coexistence of these four relational forms that constitutes social relations in America.

If relational polyphony is the typical state of the American society, why have so many social commentators argued that one relational form, individualism, has come to dominate the United States? Cerulo (2002) argues that two factors help perpetuate claims of a growing individualism. The first involves a predisposition in sociological analysis toward linear models of social relations. **Linear models** invoke a set of bipolar categories (such as communalism versus individualism) to capture changing social relations. Such models describe movement from one relational pole to the other as a unidirectional process, a transition typically triggered by the modernization of society. When we look at some of the linear models so central to sociological analysis (e.g., Tonnies's Geimenschaft versus Gessellschaft, Durkheim's mechanical and organic solidarity, Simmel's small-town relations versus the metropolis, Habermas's or Gidden's distinctions between the public and private sphere), one argument forms a common thread: Modernization drives societies down a one-way path of development; it triggers a steady progression from a "we-centered" to a "me-centered" experience. When so many central models promote a similar point of view, analysts can become blinded to empirical data that contradict that view.

We must also consider the role of culture in perpetuating claims of a growing individualism. **Culture** refers to the values, beliefs, symbols, objects, customs, and conventions that characterize a group or society's way of life. Cerulo (2002) shows that in certain historical eras, one finds what we might call "cultural surges of individualism," eras in which individualistic images overpower the projection of other cultural themes. In the United States, one such surge occurred from 1970 to 1984. During this period, a wide variety of cultural sectors, such as music, best-sellers, film, theater, television, sports, education, law, and science, were saturated with images and messages of growing individualism. Yet it is important to note that the culture of the period did not reflect Americans' *actual* behaviors and attitudes. As we pointed out earlier in this essay, Americans of the era did *not* display a dramatic increase in individualistic practices. Rather, behavioral and attitudinal moves toward individualism were temporary or limited in scope. Thus, the sense of this period as an "era of individualism" must be viewed, in part, as a cultural construction. A **cultural construction** is an image of reality that may not necessarily reflect actual behaviors and attitudes.

Cultural constructions of individualism do not emerge without reason. Such surges appear to be a reaction to a social condition called diffuse instability. **Diffuse instability** refers to a widespread period of flux in which change and uncertainty are distributed *across* the social system. In reviewing decades of U.S. history and cultural production, one finds that cultural constructions of individualism are almost always associated with diffuse instability. In contrast, periods of stability rarely emphasize individualistic themes (Cerulo 2002). Why? It may be that during periods of social confusion and uncertainty, a culture of individualism provides a message of personal control—a message of survival. Cultural constructions of individualism suggest to social actors that in the face of adversity, the individual can fight back and prevail. When social life appears to be slowly eroding, individual initiative can turn the tide. As such, cultural constructions of individualism offer a coping mechanism of sorts, a prescription for personal action at a time when instability derails predictability and threatens established social patterns.

The research discussed in this chapter reminds us that the cultural and the social are not bound by a simple causal relationship. Culture does not simply reflect the social, or vice versa. Rather, each sphere develops in response to the progression of the other, suggesting both the unique integrity of culture and society, as well as the powerful symbiosis between the two. The study of individualism represents one avenue by which to study this symbiotic relationship. But only patient and extensive empirical inquiry will provide us with the full scope of this intricate interaction.

Learning More About It

For the definitive work on the decline of civic America, see Robert D. Putnam's *Bowling Alone: The Collapse and Revival of American Community* (New York: Simon and Schuster, 2000).

Karen A. Cerulo offers an opposing view in "Individualism . . . Pro Tem: Reconsidering U.S. Social Relations," in K.A. Cerulo (Ed.), *Culture in Mind: Toward a Sociology of Culture and Cognition* (pp. 135–171; New York: Routledge, 2002).

For some interesting ideas on community building, see Amitai Etzioni's *Monochrome Society* (New York: New Forum Books, 2003) or Robert Putnam's *Better Together: Restoring American Community* (New York: Simon & Schuster, 2003).

The U.S. Census Bureau offers a wide variety of indicators by which to "track" social relations in America. For trends in marriage, divorce, college majors, suicide, visiting neighbors, church attendance, violent crime, and many, many more, consult the *Statistical Abstracts of the United States,* a book published annually by the U.S. Census Bureau since 1880 (Washington, D.C.).

Exercises

1. In this essay, we mention a number of indicators used as cues of individualism. Check a recent volume of the *Statistical Abstracts of the United States.* Can you locate five additional indicators that could be added to the measures mentioned here? Defend your selection.

2. Relational polyphony can readily be seen in various TV programs. Select five different sitcoms and view two episodes of each show. Which form of social relations appears most often? Offer some interpretation of any patterns you observe.

Socialization and Identity

Essay 8

Conventional Wisdom Tells Us … What's in a Name? That Which We Call a Rose by Any Other Name Would Smell As Sweet

This essay explores the power of names, highlighting the central role of symbols and labels in the construction of identity.

Shakespeare's verse argues for substance over labels. It is a sentiment common to much of the conventional wisdom on names. Adages such as "Sticks and stones may break my bones, but names will never hurt me" or "The names may change, but the story remains the same" and quips like "Call me anything, but don't call me late for dinner," all such truisms consistently downplay the importance of names. Are the labels we give to people and things as inconsequential as conventional wisdom suggests? Do names really lack the power to influence or the force to injure? Would a rose really command such deep respect and awe if it were known as a petunia or a pansy?

A large body of social science literature suggests that conventional wisdom has vastly underestimated the significance of names. Indeed, names in our society function as powerful symbols. **Symbols** are arbitrary signs that come to be endowed with special meaning and, ultimately, gain the ability to influence behaviors, attitudes, and emotions.

The symbolic nature of names makes them much more than a string of alphabetics. Rather, names function as calling cards or personal logos. They signify important aspects of one's history and heritage; they pinpoint an individual's social location and group affiliations. Based on our names, others make important decisions regarding our nature and temperament. In this way, names serve as important symbols of identity. **Identity** refers to those essential characteristics that both link us and distinguish us from other social players and thus establish who we are.

The link between names and identity helps to explain why forgetting someone's name often is viewed as a social *faux pas*. Similarly, we view situations that preclude the linking of name to identity with great pathos. Consider the sadness that surrounds every tomb of an unknown or unnamed soldier. In settings where one's name remains unknown, it is not unusual for an individual to feel alienated or disconnected. Think of those large lecture courses in which neither the professor nor other students know your name.

Names contribute to the construction of identity in a variety of ways. A family surname, for example, provides instant knowledge of an individual's history. Surnames serve as road maps to the past; they guide us through an individual's lineage and archive one's traditional group affiliations and cultural ties. Thus, historically, children who were denied their father's surnames were denied legitimate social locations. Without this signifier to chronicle their paternal pasts, such children were considered faceless and anonymous, with no rightful place in their social environments (Brunet and Bideau 2000; Isaacs 1975; Nagata 1999; Sanabria 2001; Sapkidis 1998). Surnames also tend to be indicators of one's ethnic background. Thus, in the modern world, many states manipulate surnames in ways that forward their current national agendas. A governing body may, for example, create official policy that uses surnames to include or exclude particular communities in the national identity. Consider the case of Japan. After annexing Korea in the 1900s, the Japanese government forced the first wave of Korean immigrants to adopt Japanese surnames. In this way, the government subsumed Koreans under both physical and symbolic control. In the White (British) controlled Jamaica of the 18th century, immigrants were an issue as well. But here, the immigrants were African slaves. Rather than assimilating the group, the government wished to mark that population's separation from Whites. Hence, upon their arrival in Jamaica, slaves were stripped of ancestral forenames and surnames. Furthermore, they were renamed using common English forenames. These truncated labels marked slaves as a distinctive group. Their "missing" surnames also made it clear that slaves lacked the lineage of Whites (Burnard 2001; Fukuoka 1998; Prabhakaran 1999; Scassa 1996; Wang 2002).

A name's ability to pinpoint personal histories leads some individuals to abandon their family surnames and adopt new ones. A well-chosen replacement name can bring one closer to groups or social histories that seem more in vogue, more powerful, or more in-tune with one's future aspirations and endeavors. The entertainment industry is rife with examples of the practice. Many performers readily acknowledge the necessity of name changes in building a successful career. Consequently, Marshall Bruce Mathers's fans now know him as rapper "Eminem." Brian Werner decided "Marilyn Manson" was better suited to a life of shock rock. And credit singer "Queen Latifah" for understanding that names such as Dana

Owens are not the stuff of which pop idols are made. In particular, personalities with ethnic surnames often feel the need for more mainstream, English-sounding names. Thus, fans know Winona Horowitz as "Winona Ryder," Jennifer Anistopoulou as "Jennifer Aniston," and Carlos Irwin Estevez as "Charlie Sheen" (*World Almanac and Book of Facts*, 1998:352–53; www.famousnamechanges.com). Of course, name changing is not restricted to the famous. Often, newly naturalized citizens choose to change their names, selecting something familiar within their adopted nation. And name changing can be political in nature. For example, after the September 11, 2001, terrorist attacks on the United States, some Muslims began legally changing their names to avoid bias and discrimination (Donohue 2002).

In each of these cases, a name change became a tool for impression management. **Impression management** is a process by which individuals manipulate or maneuver their public images so as to elicit certain desired reactions. In the process of impression management, new surnames become the foundation upon which broadly targeted identities are constructed.

First or common names function as powerful symbols as well. Consider the care and consideration frequently given by parents as they set about naming a newborn. Many parents start the process months before the child is born. Such care may represent a worthy investment, for research suggests that the selection of a personal name can have long-term consequences for a child. Several studies show that individuals assess others' potential for success, morality, good health, and warmth on the basis of names. Thus, when asked to rate other people on the basis of first names alone, subjects perceived "James" as highly moral, healthy, warm, and likely to succeed. In contrast, "Melvin" was viewed as a potential failure, lacking good character, good health, or human caring. Similarly, individuals with names that correspond to contemporary norms of popularity—currently these include Jacob, Michael, and Joshua for boys and Emily, Madison, and Hannah for girls—are judged to be more intelligent and better liked than individuals with old-fashioned names such as Arnold, Earl, Fred, Betty, Judy, and Phyllis (Christopher 1998; Etaugh et al. 1999; Joubert 1999; Karylowski et al. 2001; Liddell and Lycett 1998; Mehrabian 2001; Mirsky 2000; Twenge and Manis 1998).

Personal names can influence more than just the perception of performance and ability. Some studies show a significant association between uncommon, peculiar, undesirable, or unique names and actual outcomes such as low academic performance, low professional achievement, and psychological maladjustment (Bruning et al. 2000; De Schipper, Hirschberg, and Sinha 2002; Insaf 2002; Luscri and Mohr 1998; Marlar and Joubert 2002; Twenge and Manis 1998; Willis, Willis, and Grier 1982). Indeed, so strong is the influence of personal names that some nations actually regulate the process of naming. French law, for example, allows officials to reject any name deemed at odds with a child's well-being (Besnard and Desplanques 1993). The Canadian government has set similar standards, refusing to register unusual names for babies. After trying to register the name "Ivory" for their daughter, two Quebec parents were told, "No! Ivory is only a brand of soap." (McLean 1998). While we don't fully regulate naming in the United States, there are limits, especially in the world of business. Nearly 100 years ago, the U.S. Supreme Court ruled that newcomers to the market could not use their personal names if those titles duplicated active names with high market recognition (Quigley 2003). So, if your name is Martha Stewart, Tommy Hilfigger, or Sarah Lee—sorry, you'll have to make a change before you enter the marketplace! Aside from laws, there are strong social norms that govern the practice of naming. **Norms** are social rules or guidelines that direct behavior; they are the "shoulds" and "should nots" of social action, feelings, and thought. In the United States, norms tell us that naming is a very personal affair. That may explain why Jason Black and Frances Schroeder drew the wrath of the public when they tried to "cash in" on the naming of their son. In 2001, the couple announced they were willing to sell a corporate buyer the right to name their child. People were aghast when they posted the "naming rights" on E-Bay and started the bidding at $500,000 (Goldiner 2001)!

In charting the role of personal names, it is interesting to note that child name selection follows some predictable patterns. For example, naming patterns initiate and reinforce certain gender scripts. Parents quite frequently select trendy or decorative names for their daughters, for example, Chloe, Destiny, Lily, or Jade. In contrast, parents prefer traditional or biblical names for their sons—such as David, Ethan, Jacob, or Michael. (Think about it. Have you ever met a man named after a flower, a season, or a concept?) Furthermore, although little boys frequently are given the names of their fathers or grandfathers, little girls rarely share a name with any family member (Lieberson 2000; Satran and Rosenkrantz 2003).

In addition to establishing identity, names often demarcate shifts in identity or changes in social status. In this way, names facilitate a process sociologists refer to as boundary construction. **Boundary construction** is the social partitioning of life experience or centers of interaction. When we cross the boundary from childhood to adulthood, for example, we often drop childlike nicknames—Mikey, Junior, or Princess—in favor of our full birth names. Similarly, when acquaintances become close friends, the shift is often signaled by a name change. Mr. or Ms. becomes "Bob" or "Susan"; William becomes "Bill," or Alison becomes "Ali."

A shift from singlehood to marriage, an occupation change, and a religious conversion are marked by name changes. Thus, in the occupational arena, "Ike," "The Gipper," and "W" all became "Mr. President" when they moved into their new status. In the religious realm, Siddhartha's conversion was signaled by his new name, "Buddha." With a similar experience, Saul became "Paul." In the modern day, a change in religion transformed Cassius Clay into "Mohammed Ali."

Name changes accompany the shifting identities of places as well. With the reemergence of Russia's nationhood, for example, Leningrad reverted to "St. Petersburg." Similarly, with political reorganization, the plot of land once known as Czechoslovakia was renamed as the "Czech Republic" and "Slovenia." And the place once known as Yugoslavia is now called "Bosnia," "Croatia," and "Serbia." Although the physical terrain of these areas remains the same, new names serve to reconfigure each location's political identity.

Changing place names often does more than mark an identity shift. Such changes can also function as tools of social control. Gonzalez Faraco and Murphy (1997) illustrate this condition as they trace the rise and fall of three socially transformative regimes in 20th-century Spain. The authors note that extensive changes to the street names of a town called "Almonte" served as a strategy by which each ruling body announced its relationship to the ruled. Indeed, the street names chosen by each regime proclaimed each government's intentions, methods, philosophy, and ethos. Thus, the Second Republic (1931–1936) chose street names that promoted the regime's educational agenda. In contrast, Franco's oppressive dictatorship (1936–1975) employed intimidating street names. And the Socialist Democracy that followed the Franco regime adopted a clever set of symbolic compromises designed to heal the rifts between the nation's opposing "camps." Azaryahu and Kook (2002) tell a similar story in their study of street names in pre-1948 Haifa and post-1948 Umm el Fahm. The researchers show that the naming of streets in these locations represent variations on the theme of Arab-Palestinian identity. For example, street names in pre-1948 Haifa define Arab identity in the broadest meaning of the term, celebrating culture and politics, Catholics and Muslims, heroes and occasions that traverse locality and time. In contrast, street names in Umm el Fahm project a much narrower version of Arab-Palestinian identity. The overwhelming majority of these names highlight persons and events critical to early Islamic history. The differences one finds in Haifa and Umm el Fahm street names are important, for they reveal the interests and attitudes of local political elites. In studying them, one can concretize a political shift and track a period of changing ideologies. Finally, consider this example from the American South. In 1993, the New Orleans school board launched an effort to lead the population toward greater racial tolerance. The school board mandated that slave owners' names be removed from all city schools. Schools that bore the names of slave owners were renamed after racially tolerant individuals. The seriousness of the school board's intentions was dramatically illustrated in 1997 when President George Washington's (a slave owner) name was removed from one of New Orlean's schools. School board officials renamed the institution after Charles Drew, a pioneering black doctor. Spain, Palestine, the United States: These examples illustrate one common point. By reading the symbolic tapestry created by place names, we learn something about official identity formation in a region. We learn something as well about the ideological premises upon which such identities are built.

Beyond person and place, names can illustrate changing collective identities. In this regard, consider the experience of African Americans in the United States. Note that when the name "Negro" appeared in the United States, it was synonymous with the status of slave. To distance themselves from slavery, free African Americans of that period elected to call themselves "African" rather than "Negro." However, when a movement developed in the 1830s encouraging slaves and their descendants to return to Africa, free African Americans renamed themselves "Colored" or "People of Color." The color term was adopted to underscore disapproval of the "return to Africa" movement. Interestingly, "Black" was repeatedly rejected as a name for this collective and appeared on the scene only with the social and legal changes of the 1960s and 1970s (Isaacs 1975). Currently, the name "African American" is favored, with many arguing that this change will emphasize African Americans' cultural heritage and help to address problems such as racial disparity and poverty (Philogene 1999; Sangmpam 1999).

Postmodern theorists suggest that collective identities generated by shared group names can sometimes prove more harmful than helpful. **Postmodern theory** represents an approach that destabilizes or deconstructs fixed social assumptions and meanings. Collective names imply a unity of identity—a sameness—among all members of a group. In this way, collective names can mask the diversity that exists within groups. Collective names can lead us to conclude that all "Hispanics," "women," or "senior citizens" think or act in identical ways by virtue of their shared classifications. Postmodernists also warn that collective names can give a false sense of distinctiveness to groups. Labeling collectives suggests that "Whites" are profoundly different from "Blacks," "men" irreconcilably different from "women," and "nations" unique unto themselves (Collins 1990; Foucault 1971; Hacking 1995, 1999; Riley 1988; Smith 1991; Wong 2002).

Just as name changes symbolize shifts and movement, they can also function to immortalize certain identities. The name often becomes the tool of choice in poignant and permanent commemorations of extraordinary human efforts. Consider The American Immigrant Wall of Honor located at Ellis Island or the AIDS Memorial Quilt. Special individuals often are honored by attaching their names to buildings or streets. War memorials elicit heightened emotions by listing the names of those they honor. Witness the deeply moving response elicited by the Vietnam War Memorial in Washington, D.C., or the ceremonies for the September 11, 2001, terrorist attacks that have involved reading the victims' names.

Extraordinary athletes have their "numerical names," or numbers, retired, indicating that there will never be another Yankee "Number 7" (Mickey Mantle) or another Jets "Number 12" (Joe Namath). The retirement and return of the Chicago Bull's Michael Jordan is an interesting example. Recall that upon Jordan's 1993 exodus from basketball, "Number 23" was ceremoniously retired by his team. When he returned to the Bulls in 1994, his new beginning was signaled by the assignment of a new "name": "Number 45." These numerical names served to distinguish the old, proven Jordan from the new, mysterious Jordan. Indeed, the National Basketball Association viewed the boundary protected by these symbols to be so sacred that they fined Jordan heavily the first few times he tried to wear his old number during one of his "second-life" games.

Names can be used to indicate possession or ownership. It is not unusual for valuable belongings such as homesteads, boats, aircraft, cars, or pets to be named by their owners. In the same way, conquerors reserved the right to name the continents they discovered or acquired, as well as the indigenous people living there. Columbus, for example, named the indigenous people he met "Indians," a term that came to be used generically for all native peoples. Similarly, colonial populations were frequently renamed by those controlling them so as to reflect the cultural standards of the ruling power. In one case, a mid-19th-century

Spanish governor replaced the Philippine surnames of his charges with Spanish surnames taken from a Madrid directory, as a method of simplifying the job of Spanish tax collectors (Isaacs 1975). Scientists, too, use names to mark their discoveries. Most of us are familiar with "Lucy," the name given to some of the oldest human remains known to contemporary scientists. Indeed, the naming of scientific discoveries is so important that scientists fight hard for the right to name. Witness the multiyear controversy that surrounded heavy elements 104 (discovered in the 1960s), 105 (discovered in the 1970s), and 107 through 109 (discovered in the early 1980s). These elements went nameless, in some cases for decades, because researchers in the field disagreed as to the parties responsible for their discovery. Similar controversies now surround the human genome project as companies and universities fight for the right to patent and trademark thousands of genes and gene fragments. (Browne 1997; *Information Please Almanac* 1997:545; Pollack 2000).

Family names function as a sign of ownership as well. In bestowing their surnames on children, parents identify the children as "theirs." And historically, wives were expected to take the names of their husbands to indicate to whom the women "belonged" (Arichi 1999; Johnson and Scheuble 2002; Suarez 1997). These examples highlight a normative expectation: That which we name belongs to us. This expectation may help to explain why adopted children are more likely to be named after a parent or relative than are biological children. In the absence of shared genes, names become a mode of establishing familial connection. And, indeed, research shows that namesaking generally strengthens the bond between father and child. This link between males, surnames, and possession has been a difficult one to challenge. Interestingly, in places and times in which women have won the right to keep their surnames upon marriage, the large majority choose to name their children in accord with the surnames of their husbands (Auerbach 2003; Furstenburg and Talvitie 1980; Johnson, McAndrew, and Harris 1991; Stodder 1998).

Perhaps the importance of the power of naming is best revealed in research on labeling. **Labeling theory** is built around a basic premise known to sociologists as Thomas's theorem: If we define situations as real, they are real in their consequences. In other words, the names or labels we apply to people, places, or circumstances influence and direct our interactions and thus the emerging reality of the situation.

Thomas's theorem was well documented in a now-famous study of labeling practices in the classroom. After administering intelligence tests to students at the beginning of the academic year, researchers identified to teachers a group of academic "spurters"—that is, children who would show great progress over the course of the approaching school year. In fact, no such group really existed. Rather, researchers randomly assigned students to the spurter category. Yet curiously enough, when intelligence tests were readministered at the end of the academic year, the spurters showed increases in their IQ scores over and above the "nonspurters." Furthermore, the subjective assessments of the teachers indicated that the spurters surpassed nonspurters on a number of socioeducational fronts. The researchers credited these changes to the power of labels: When teachers came to define students as "spurters," they began to interact with them in ways that guaranteed their success (Rosenthal and Jacobson 1968; Schulman 2004).

A famous study in the area of mental health also demonstrates the enormous power of labels. David Rosenhan engaged colleagues to admit themselves to several psychiatric hospitals and to report symptoms of schizophrenia to the admitting psychologists. (Specifically, Rosenhan's colleagues were told to report "hearing voices.") Once admitted to the hospital, however, these pseudopatients displayed no signs of mental disorder. Rather, they engaged in completely normal behavioral routines. Despite the fact that the pseudopatients' psychosis was contrived, Rosenhan notes, the label "schizophrenia" proved more influential in the construction of reality than did the pseudopatients' actual behaviors. Hospital personnel "saw" symptomatic behaviors in their falsely labeled charges. The power of the label schizophrenia caused some normal individuals to remain hospitalized for as long as 52 days (Rosenhan 1973; Schulman 2004).

The labeling phenomenon is not confined to what others "see" in us. Labels also hold the power to influence what we see in ourselves. Recent emphasis on politically correct (PC) speech is founded on this premise. The PC movement suggests that by selecting our labels wisely, we may lead people to more positive self-perceptions. There is, after all, a difference between calling someone "handicapped" and calling that person "physically challenged." The former term implies a fundamental flaw, whereas the latter suggests a surmountable condition. Many believe that applying such simple considerations to the use of positive, versus negative, labels can indeed make a critical difference in self-esteem levels.

Similar logic can be found within the literature on social deviants. Some contend that repeated application of a deviant label—class clown, druggie, slut, troublemaker, and so on—may lead to a self-transformation of the label's "target." Sociologists refer to this phenomenon as secondary deviance. **Secondary deviance** occurs when labeled individuals comes to view themselves according to what they are called. In other words, the labeled individual incorporates the impressions of others into his or her self-identity. Thus, just as positive labels such as "spurter" can benefit an individual, negative or deviant labels can help to ensure that an individual "lives down" to others' expectations (Lemert 1951; Schulman 2004).

The power of names and labels may be best demonstrated by considering the distrust and terror typically associated with "the unnamed." Namelessness is often synonymous with invisibility and exclusion. One can note several examples of this phenomenon. Historically, the Christian child was considered a nonperson until "it" received a name. Indeed, Christian children were not granted full rights to heaven until they were baptized and "marked" by a Christian name. The soul of a child who died before such membership cues could be bestowed was believed to be barred from heaven and condemned to perpetuity "in limbo." Indeed, the body of such a child could not be buried in sacred ground (Aries 1962).

Things that are unnamed can strike terror in social members because, in a very real sense, such things remain beyond our control. The most feared diseases, for example, are those that are so new and different they have not yet been named. The lack of a name implies unknown origins, and thus little hope for a cure. In contrast, the mere presence of a diagnosis, even one that connotes a serious condition, often is viewed as a blessing by patients. Think of the number of times you've heard a relieved patient or family member say, "At least now I know what the problem is."

Alzheimer's disease also illustrates the terror that accompanies namelessness. For many people, the most frightening aspect of Alzheimer's disease is its ability to steal from us the names of formerly familiar people and objects. Generally, our life experiences are rendered understandable via insightful naming and labeling.

In another realm, note that anonymous callers and figures can strike dread in their targets. The namelessness of these intruders renders them beyond our control. Wanted "John Does" are frequently perceived as greater threats than known criminals because of their no-name status. Recall the intensive search efforts for the suspect "John Doe II" following the Oklahoma City bombing. Similarly, note the frantic aura that surrounded the hunt for the unknown "Unabomber." And no time was wasted in putting names to faces after the September 11, 2001, attacks. Fears of namelessness plague us in cyberspace as well. Anonymous communication forums or situations in which people use "fake" names and identities make Internet users uncomfortable and unsure of "who they're dealing with." In these settings, namelessness can threaten the development of trust (Marx 1999).

When we experience disruptive behaviors that appear new or unusual, our first step toward control involves naming. We coined the label "rumble," for example, to characterize the violent and frightening gang fights that began to erupt on urban streets in the 1950s. We applied the label "wilding" to the new and shocking acts of violence by packs of juveniles that emerged as a phenomenon of the 1980s. And we use the term "hacking" to describe those who harm Web sites and machinery by releasing unwanted computer viruses and worms. In essence, naming such phenomena provide us with a sense of control. In addition to control, naming people, places, objects, and events seems to make them more appealing. Thus, marketers work long and hard to get the right "brand name," one that will "hook" potential consumers. Nothing can hurt the image of a product more than locating it in the generic or no-name arena (Grassl 1999).

What's in a name? Obviously more than conventional wisdom implies. Names and labels can effectively reshape an individual's past, present circumstance, or future path. Indeed, research seems to leave little doubt: A rose by any other name . . . would somehow be different.

Learning More About It

For a fascinating examination of the social patterns of naming, see Stanley Lieberson's award winning book *A Matter of Taste* (New Haven, CT: Yale University Press, 2000). For a light-hearted discussion of future trends, consult Pamela Redmond Satran and Linda Rosenkrantz's *Cool Names for Babies* (New York: St. Martin's Griffin, 2003).

Want to trace the popularity of a name or discover the most popular names of the day? Visit the Social Security Web site on names at <http://www.ssa.gov/OACT/babynames/index.html>

Harold Isaacs offers some interesting reflections on collective naming in his now classic treatise, *Idols of the Tribe* (Cambridge: Harvard University Press, 1975). For an interesting discussion of postmodern perspectives on collective naming and identity, see James Wong's article, "What's in a Name: An Examination of Social identities," *Journal for the Theory of Social Behavior* 32(4): 451–464.

For more on the links between symbols and identity, see Karen A. Cerulo's *Identity Designs: The Sights and Sounds of a Nation* (New Brunswick: Rutgers University Press, ASA Rose Book Series, 1995).

For the classic work on impression management, see Erving Goffman's *The Presentation of Self in Everyday Life* (New York: Anchor, 1959). Howard Becker provides a highly readable discussion of labeling in *The Outsiders* (Glencoe, IL: Free Press, 1963). An informative discussion of labeling as it pertains to women comes from Edwin Schur in *Labeling Women Deviant* (Philadelphia: Temple University Press, 1984).

The following organizations and Web sites will help you learn more about names:

American Name Society (Sponsors research on names)
c/o Professor Wayne H. Finke, Dept. of Modern Languages
Baruch College 17 Lexington Ave.
New York, NY 10010–5526
Web site: <http://www.wtns.binghamton.edu/ANS/>

Ancestry.com (Web site facilitating genealogical research)
Web site: <http://www.ancestry.com>

Behind the Name (Web site devoted to information on the history of names)
Web site: <http:// www.www.behindthename.com>

Exercises

1. Choose one or two good friends and intentionally call them by the wrong name several times over the course of a day. Record your friends' reactions. What do these data tell you about the power of personal symbols?

2. Research the names of various buildings on your campus, especially those named for an individual. Taken as a whole, what identity do these names confer on your institution? What lessons of naming can you deduce from the list? Are the norms of naming time-bound? Class-bound? Gender-bound?

Essay 9

Conventional Wisdom Tells Us ... Beauty Is Only Skin Deep

This essay documents the social advantages enjoyed by physically attractive individuals—tall, slim, and beautiful or handsome women and men. We also discuss the powerful role physical attractiveness can play in the construction of self-identity.

"Beauty is only skin deep," goes the old adage. It's a lesson we learn early in life. From youth to old age, we are promised that, ultimately, we will be judged on the basis of our inner qualities and not simply by our appearance.

The conventional wisdom on beauty is echoed on many fronts. Religious doctrines teach us to avoid the vanity of physical beauty and search for the beauty within. Popular Broadway shows such as *Phantom of the Opera* or *Beauty and the Beast,* fairy tales like "The Ugly Duckling," or songs such as "I Love You Just the Way You Are" promote the notion that appearances are too superficial to seriously influence our fate. All in all, our culture warns us not to "judge a book by its cover," for "all that glitters is not gold."

The conventional wisdom on beauty is reassuring, but is it accurate? Do social actors really look beyond appearance when interacting with and evaluating one another?

One finds considerable **cultural inconsistency** surrounding the topic of beauty. Cultural inconsistency refers to a situation in which actual behaviors contradict cultural goals. Cultural inconsistency depicts an imbalance between ideal and real cultures. Although we say that appearances don't matter, our actions indicate something quite to the contrary. Indeed, a large body of research suggests that an individual's level of attractiveness dramatically influences others' assessments, evaluations, and reactions.

Several studies show that attractive individuals—tall, slim, and beautiful or handsome women and men—are better liked and more valued by others than individuals considered to be unattractive (Buss et al. 2001; Kowner and Ogawa 1995; Langlois et al. 2000; Livingston 2001; Zuckerman, Miyake, and Elkin 1995). These preferences are amazingly widespread. In seeking friends, individuals prefer the companionship of attractive versus unattractive people (Marks, Miller, and Maruyama 1981; Reis, Nezlek, and Wheeler 1980; Sprecher and Regan 2002). In the workplace, attractive people are more likely to be hired than their unattractive competitors, even when an experienced personnel officer is responsible for the hiring (Cash and Janda 1984; Marlowe, Schneider, and Nelson 1996; Watkins and Johnston 2000). In courts of law, physically attractive defendants receive more lenient sentences than unattractive defendants (Abwender and Hough 2001; DeSantis and Kayson 1997; Erian et al. 1998; Vrij and Firmin 2002). And within the political arena, attractive candidates regularly garner more votes than unattractive candidates (Ottati and Deiger 2002; Sigelman, Sigelman, and Fowler 1987). Only in the search for a lifetime mate does the influence of physical attractiveness wane. Studies show that people tend to choose long-term partners whom they judge to be of comparable attractiveness (Kalick and Hamilton 1986; Kalmijn 1998; Keller and Young 1996; Murstein 1999; Wong et al. 1991).

The link between physical attractiveness and being liked and rewarded exists at all stages of the life cycle, including infancy and childhood. Studies show, for example, that attractive babies are held, cuddled, kissed, and talked to more frequently than unattractive babies. This pattern holds true even when one restricts the focus to mother-child interactions (Badr and Abdallah 2001; Berscheid 1982; Leinbach and Fagot 1991; Weiss 1998). It is worth noting that babies apparently feel the same way about attractiveness. Studies show that newborns and young infants spend more time looking at pictures of attractive faces than they do pictures of unattractive faces (Rhodes et al. 2002; Rubenstein, Kalakanis, and Langlois 1999; Slater et al. 2000). When attractive children make their way to school, they tend to be more frequently praised and rewarded by teachers than their less attractive counterparts (Clifford and Walster 1973; Kenealy, Frude, and Shaw 1988; Pace et al. 1999; Wapnick, Mazza, and Darrow 2000). Furthermore, studies show that children themselves come to equate attractiveness with high moral character (K.K. Dion 1979; Dion and Berscheid 1974; Langlois and Stephan 1981; Ramsey and Langlois 2002). The typical children's fairy tale is one source of this lesson. Remember Cinderella and her evil stepsisters? Or Snow White and her wicked stepmother, who is disguised as an ugly witch? And how about Oz's beautiful, "good" witch of the North versus the ugly and "wicked" witch of the West? The stories of our youth regularly couple beauty with goodness, while ugliness is usually indicative of wickedness (Ramsey and Langlois 2002).

In addition to issues of liking, reward, and moral character, physically attractive individuals are perceived as having a host of other positive and highly desirable characteristics. Research shows that "beautiful people" are assumed to possess pleasing personalities, personal happiness, great intelligence, mental and physical competence, high status, trustworthiness, and high success in marriage. Furthermore, these perceptions persist even when the facts contradict our assumptions (Andreoletti et al. 2001; Breland 1998; Chia and Alfred 1998; Dion 2001; Dion, Berscheid, and Walster 1972; Feeley 2002; Feingold 1992; Grant et al. 2002; Jackson, Hunter, and Hodge 1995; Jones, Hansson, and Phillips 1978; Perlini et al. 2001; Wilson and Nias 1999; Zaidel, Bava, and Reis 2003; Zebrowitz et al. 2002).

Some researchers feel that our perceptions of attractive people and their lifestyles may create a **self-fulfilling prophecy** (Leonard 1996; Snyder 2001; Zebrowitz, Collins, and Dutta 1998). A self-fulfilling prophecy is a phenomenon whereby that which we believe to be true, in some sense, becomes true for us. Thus, when we expect that handsome men or beautiful women are happy, intelligent, or well placed, we pave the way for expectation to become reality. This may explain why attractive individuals tend to have higher self-esteem and are less prone to psychological disturbances than are unattractive individuals (Jackson 1992; Rudd and Lennon 1999; Taleporos and McCabe 2002).

By contributing to a self-fulfilling prophecy, social reactions to physical appearance may endow handsome men and beautiful women with valuable cultural capital. **Cultural capital** refers to attributes, knowledge, or ways of thinking that can be converted or used for economic advantage. Cultural capital is a concept that was originally introduced by contemporary theorist Pierre Bourdieu. According to Bourdieu (1984), one accumulates cultural capital in conjunction with one's social status. **Social status** refers to the position or location of an individual with reference to characteristics such as age, education, gender, income, race, religion, and so on. The more privileged one's status, the better one's endowment of cultural capital.

Bourdieu argues that an individual's cultural capital works like a good investment. The capital itself—typically defined as family background, education, communication skills, and so on—has inherent value and gains for the individual's entry into "the market." "Working" one's cultural capital enables its "owner" to "buy" or accumulate additional social advantages.

The many studies reviewed in this essay suggest that physical attractiveness also forms another type of cultural capital that operates according to the same dynamic as the one described by Bourdieu. Physical attractiveness provides individuals with an extra resource in meeting life's demands. Beauty places individuals in a preferred, or more powerful, position (Boyatzis and Baloff 1998; Espino and Franz 2002; Finkelstein 1991; Greenhouse 2003; Hunter 2002; Koernig and Page 2001; Lynn and Simons 2000; Mehrabian 2000; Mulford et al. 1998; Saporta and Halpern 2002). As such, appearances are frequently converted to economic gain.

Thinking of beauty as cultural capital helps to explain Americans' propensity for physical alterations. In the United States, we are "lifted," "tucked," "Botoxed," and liposuctioned more than any other country in the world. Over 1.6 million cosmetic surgeries and 5.2 million nonsurgical procedures occur each year, all of them performed for aesthetic reasons rather than reasons of necessity. The under-35 crowd (including teenagers) accounts for 28% of this business, indicating that our concerns with beauty start early (American Society for

Aesthetic Plastic Surgery 2002). National figures also indicate that more than $89.1 billion is spent in the United States each year on cosmetics, perfumes, hair care, and health clubs. This figure has nearly doubled in the past 10 years. Interestingly enough, the figure surpasses the dollar amounts Americans devote each year to higher-education expenses ($87.6 billion), health insurance ($75 million), financial investment counseling ($74.2 million), legal services ($70.4 billion), books ($35.1 billion), and computers, peripherals, and software ($32.9 million) (Bureau of Economic Analysis 2002; *World Almanac* 2003: 109). And it is worth noting that some impose their obsession with beauty on their pets! In 2003, controversy swirled through the prestigious Crufts Dog Show in England. It seems that Danny, a Pekingese who won the show, underwent facial surgery to improve his prospects of victory (Trebay 2003)!

"Buying" beauty is not strictly an American phenomenon. In many Asian and African cultures, for example, a growing value on American facial and skin features has resulted in a dramatic upsurge in eyelid, nose, and facial reconstruction surgery as well as skin-lightening procedures. Reports also show massive increases in cosmetic sales throughout rural China and other Asian nations, and long lines in Moscow as Muscovites fight to purchase Estée Lauder and Christian Dior cosmetics (Branigan 2001; Doggett and Haddad 2000; Kovaleski 1999; Mok 1998; Parker-Pope 1997; Poblete 2000, 2001; Shaffer, Crepaz, and Sun 2000). All in all, human behavior may confirm Aristotle's ancient claim: Beauty may be better than all the letters of recommendation in the world.

The effects of physical attractiveness go beyond our interactions with others. An individual's "attractiveness quotient" also proves one of the most powerful elements in the construction of one's self-identity. **Identity** refers to those essential characteristics that both link us and distinguish us from other social players and thus establish who we are.

Research suggests that physical attractiveness is critical to positive self-assessment. Physical attractiveness greatly boosts one's level of self-esteem and strengthens one's confidence. Unattractiveness, in contrast, appears to sow self-doubt and impede social interaction skills (Cash and Pruzinsky 1990; Figueroa 2003; Garcia 1998; Gergen et al. 2003; Griffiths et al. 2000; Phillips and Hill 1998; Sanderson, Darley, and Messinger 2002; Sharma 2002; Wood, Solomon, and Englis 2003). Some studies suggest, however, that this connection may be race specific. African Americans, for example, are far less likely than Whites to link their appearance to feelings of self-worth (Hebl and Heatherton 1998; Lovejoy 2001; Milkie 1999).

When considering attractiveness and its impact on identity, body weight proves a particularly crucial factor. Each year, Americans spend more than $33 billion on weight loss programs, diet aids, and low-calorie foods in an effort to shed those extra pounds (American Obesity Association 2002; Larkin 1996). We trim down, pump up, tan, tattoo, and even surgically reshape our bodies, all in the hopes that a "new" and more beautiful body will boost our sense of self.

In theory, connections between body weight and identity should be quite straightforward. Throughout the socialization experience, we are exposed to what sociologists call appearance norms. **Socialization** refers to the process by which we learn the norms, values, and beliefs of a social group, as well as our place within that social group. **Appearance norms** refer to a society's generally accepted standards of appropriate body height, body weight, distribution or shape, bone structure, skin color, and so on.

When individuals conform to appearance norms, they enjoy positive feedback from intimates, peers, and social members at large. These reactions enable one to develop a "normal" body image and a heightened sense of self. In contrast, individuals who deviate from appearance norms are likely to be negatively sanctioned. As such, those who stray from average body weight or ableness may develop deviant or negative self-identities (Goffman 1963; Millman 1980; Schur 1984. For recent experimental work, see Abell and Richards 1996; Gergen et al. 2003; Gimlin 2000, 2002; Hurd 2000; Kent 2000; Kostanski and Gullone 1998; Neumark-Sztainer et al. 2002; Pierce and Wardle 1997).

The process sounds straightforward. Yet in the everyday world of experience, body weight and its connection to identity can be quite complex. For example, several studies, as well as testimony found on countless weight loss Web sites, show that when certain individuals move from thin to fat (in American society, a shift from a normal to a deviant body), such individuals nevertheless maintain a slim, and hence "normal," body image. This sense of normalcy often persists even in the face of objective evidence to the contrary, such as scale readings or clothing size (Berscheid 1981; Degher and Hughes 1992; *Do It Yourself Weight Loss* 2001; Gettleman and Thompson 1993; Jenny Craig 2003; Millman 1980). Similarly, some individuals who achieve "normal" bodies via diet, eating habits, illness, or surgery continue to identify themselves as overweight, disproportioned, or disfigured (Altheimer 1994; Rubin, Shmilovitz, and Weiss 1993; Waskul and van der Reit 2002; Williamson et al. 2001).

What explains the failure to incorporate a "new" body into one's identity? Some believe the phenomenon may be a function of one's childhood years—in particular, the "first impressions" such individuals formed of their bodies during their primary socialization. Sociologists define **primary socialization** as the earliest phase of social "training," a period in which we learn basic social skills and form the core of our identities.

Children who develop "slim and trim" images of their bodies often succeed at maintaining that image as they build their adult identities. In essence, that skinny kid of an individual's past can cover her or his adult eyes and obscure the portly grown-up in the mirror (Laslett and Warren 1975; Millman 1980). In contrast, children who are labeled as "fat" or ridiculed during their early years seem never to fully embrace the notion of a normal or thin body, even when they achieve body weight within or below national weight guidelines (Altheimer 1994; Pierce and Wardle 1997; Rubin et al. 1993; Sands and Wardle 2003; Thompson and Stice 2001).

Can those affected by first impressions of their bodies ever synchronize their identities with their current physical condition? Research shows that certain rituals prove helpful in this regard. Sociologists define **rituals** as a set of actions that take on symbolic significance. When body transitions are marked by some sort of "rite of passage," individuals are more likely to adjust their identities to reflect their new weight. So, for instance, patients opting for surgical weight loss may request a "last meal," write a will, or burn old clothing and photographs. Such rituals prove quite powerful in signaling the death of one's "old" body. Similarly, dieters often engage in rituals such as clothing shopping sprees or body-boasting beach vacations to mark the achievement of a target weight. Dieter's report the power of these rituals in signifying a physical "rebirth" (McCabe and Ricciardelli 2003; Rubin et al. 1993, 1994).

Intense social feedback also appears critical to synchronizing identity with body weight. Repeated reaction to one's actual weight can eventually alter faulty self-perceptions. Thus, although the overweight individual may be able to neutralize the numbers that appear during his or her morning weigh-in, that same individual proves unable to ignore repeated stares or blatant comments on weight gain by family, friends, or strangers. Similarly, the newly thin often report the wide-eyed gasps, exclamations, and smiles of those viewing their new bodies for the first time as the factors most significant to their adoption of a true sense of body size (Altheimer 1994; McCabe and Ricciardelli 2003; Rubin et al. 1993, 1994).

Note, however, that some sources of social feedback can hinder the synchronization process. For example, when individuals use TV images to measure their own appearance, they tend to overestimate their body weight. Such overestimations, in turn, negatively impact self-identity. Women appear particularly susceptible to such media influence. Although the media present the "acceptable" male in a variety of shapes and sizes, "acceptable" females rarely deviate from the thin standard (Biocca 1992; Hargreaves and Tiggermann 2002; Harrison 2000; Harrison and Cantor 1997; Myers and Biocca 1992; Myers et al. 1999; Van den Buick 2000; Vartanian, Giant, and Passino 2001).

Work by communication researchers Philip Myers and Frank Biocca (1992; Myers et al. 1999) demonstrates that daily exposure to as little as 30 minutes of TV programming may contribute to the self-overestimation of body size typical among women. Furthermore, these same short periods of TV viewing may indirectly increase the incidence of anorexia nervosa and bulimia among women. (Also see Groesz, Levine, and Murnen 2002; Stice, Spangler, and Agras 2001; and Thomsen et al. 2002.)

Before leaving this discussion of the ideal body, it is important to note that definitions of that ideal can change dramatically as one moves through history or across different racial and ethnic groups. As recently as the 1950s, for example, a Marilyn Monroe-ish figure—5'5" and 135 pounds—was forwarded as the American ideal. But in the past four decades, the ideal body has slimmed down considerably. Images of the 1990s depict that same 5'5" female at under 100 pounds (Wolf 1991)! The movement toward thinness is also illustrated in longitudinal studies of beauty icons such as Miss America winners and *Playboy* centerfolds. Current figures suggest that these icons are approximately 20% thinner than a woman of average size. Indeed, an increasing number of these icons fall within the medically defined range of "undernourished" (Rubenstein and Caballero 2000; Wiseman et al. 1992). But note that such research projects illustrate race-specific standards of attractiveness. For example, African Americans—both men and women—associate fewer negative characteristics with overweight bodies than do Anglo-Americans. Furthermore, in cross-sex relationships, African American males are nearly twice as likely as Anglo-American males to express a preference for heavier females (Hebl and Heatherton 1998; Jackson and McGill 1996; Lovejoy 2001; Milkie 1999; Thompson, Sargent, and Kemper 1996).

Social feedback on weight and the use of such feedback in identity construction illustrates the utility of Charles Horton Cooley's concept, the looking-glass self. **The looking-glass self** refers to a process by which individuals use the reactions of other social members as mirrors by which to view themselves and develop an image of who they are. From Cooley's perspective, individuals who seem unable to "see" their current bodies may be using reactions of the past as their mirrors on the present. Similarly, the use of TV "mirrors" in the definition of self may lead to "fun house" type distortions. The key to accepting one's current body type is collecting appropriate contemporary mirrors and elevating them over those of the past.

Thus far, we have discussed the various effects exerted by an individual's physical appearances. But it is interesting to note that the influence of physical appearance goes beyond the realm of the person. Appearances influence our evaluation of objects as well. Often, we judge the value or goodness of things in accordance with the way they look. Some researchers have discovered, for example, that the architectural style of a home can affect the way in which others describe the atmosphere within the structure. Farmhouses, for instance, are generally identified with trustworthy atmospheres. Colonial-style homes are perceived to be the domains of "go-getters." And Tudor-style homes are associated with leadership (Freudenheim 1988). And, of course, the great chefs have taught us a similar lesson: Looks equal taste. Thus, great chefs underscore the beauty of food. For the connoisseur, the presentation of the food—the way it looks on the plate—is as important as the flavor.

Such links between an object's appearance and notions of quality or identity are at the heart of the marketing industry. Indeed, in the world of advertising and public relations, "packaging" a product so as to convey the right image is truly the name of the game. A product must be more than good. Its appearance and "story" must lure the consumer. The importance of packaging holds true even when the object is a living thing! Indeed, research shows that "good marketing" can change our perception of an animal's attractiveness, and thus its desirability. In one set of studies, labeling an animal as an endangered species increased subjects' perceptions of the animal's attractiveness. Once subjects learned that an animal was endangered, animals routinely thought to be ugly were reassessed as cute, majestic, or lovable. This shift in perception is important, because the same study showed that people are more sympathetic to campaigns designed to save physically attractive animals. Like people, being attractive affords an animal with more cultural capital (Gunnthorsdottir 2001).

Is beauty only skin deep? After reviewing research findings on physical attractiveness, we cannot help but view this conventional wisdom with some skepticism. When it comes to evaluating and reacting to others, ourselves, and even inanimate objects, beauty matters. The more attractive the proverbial "cover of the book," the more likely we are to value its story.

Learning More About It

For a collection of "state of the art" summary essays on physical appearance research, see *Body Image: A Handbook of Theory, Research, and Clinical Practice* edited by Thomas F. Cash and Thomas Pruzinsky (New York/London: Guilford Press, 2002). Jeffrey Sobal and Donna Maurer provide a compelling collection of articles that draws on the symbolic interactionist perspective to examine the ways in which people deal with body image and, in particular, construct, define, and sanction fatness and thinness. See *Interpreting Weight: The Social Management of Fatness and Thinness* (New York: Aldine de Gruyter, 1999).

Kathy Peiss offers a fascinating look at America's beauty culture and the history of the cosmetics industry in *Hope in a Jar: The Making of America's Beauty Culture* (New York: Owl Books, 1999). A similarly engaging history of aesthetic plastic surgery can be found in Sander Gilman's *Making the Body Beautiful: A Cultural History of Aesthetic Surgery* (Princeton, NJ: Princeton University Press, 1999).

In *The Body Project* (New York: Random House, 1997), Joan Jacobs Brumberg draws on 150 years of girls' diaries, providing a fascinating historical account of changing American ideas on the ideal female body. Mimi Nichter offers another personal glimpse of attitudes on body image in *Fat Talk: What Girls and Their Parents Say About Dieting* (Cambridge, MA/London: Harvard University Press, 2000).

Want to see a visual timeline recounting changing images of the ideal female body? Visit the *Discovery Health Channel* at <http://health.discovery.com/centers/weightloss/overyears/weightlosstimeline.html>

The Renfrew Center provides information and educational resources on body image, self-esteem, and weight control. Visit their Web site at <http://www.renfrew.org/info.htm>

Exercises

1. Choose approximately 10 bridal pictures from your local paper. Using conventional cultural standards, choose brides of varying attractiveness. Remove any identifying names and show the pictures you've selected to five "judges." Supply the judges with a 5-point scale, where 5 equals "just right" and 1 equals "inadequate," and have the judges rate the brides on the following standards:

attractive	*sensual*
good-humored	*sophisticated*
happy	*successful*
intelligent	*trustworthy*
pretty	*wealthy*

Check the judges' ratings: Is there any relationship between the answers addressing physical attractiveness and those pertaining to personality characteristics? Now, repeat

Exercise 1 using pictures of men from your local newspaper. In choosing your pictures, be sure to select men who are similarly dressed and of similar ages.

2. For this exercise, you will need to gather 20 to 30 ads that feature both products and people. In making your selections, choose ads for "glamorous" products (perfume, clothing, vacations, and the like), as well as ads for nonglamorous products (antacids, cleansers, insecticides). Analyze the patterns you find (if any) between the type of product being marketed and the attractiveness of the people used in the product's ad.

3. Review the personal ads in three newspapers: the *Village Voice,* your local town newspaper, and your college newspaper. Content-analyze three-days' worth of ads that feature people. Record all the information about their physical appearance—weight, height, facial characteristics, and so on. What do your data tell you about current appearance norms? Using your data, discuss the similarities and differences in the appearance norms that govern each of these three contexts.

Stratification

Essay 10

Conventional Wisdom Tells Us ...
The More We Pay, the More It's Worth

If so, our garbage collectors are worth more than our teachers, and baseball players are worth more than those searching for a cure to AIDS. This essay addresses the inconsistencies often found between what we pay for work and the value we place on it.

Price tags mean a lot to consumers. With time and experience, most consumers come to embrace the notion that "you get what you pay for." To be sure, many shoppers are frequently driven to find a good bargain. But on the whole, Americans seem to equate high price with quality.

Hal Arkes, an Ohio State psychologist, has demonstrated this in an experimental setting. Arkes told experimental subjects to pretend that, by mistake, they had made reservations for a $50 and $100 ski trip, both on the same weekend. Consequently, one reservation would have to be cancelled. Before making a cancellation, subjects were told that travelers overwhelmingly report having more fun on the cheaper $50 trip. Nevertheless, more than half of Arkes subjects chose to cancel the $50 trip, reporting their belief that the more expensive trip just had to be more enjoyable (as reported in Gourville and Soman 2002).

In the "real world," Americans' willingness to equate high prices with quality has led to some ingenious marketing strategies. The founders of Häagen-Dazs ice cream, for example, readily admit to conscious price inflation in introducing their product on the market. Given consumer tendencies to gauge product value and attractiveness by price, the owners of Häagen-Dazs correctly perceived a high price tag as the best path to high sales (Cowe 1990).

Thus business economists Michael J. Silverstein and Neil Fiske (2003) ask: Does that high-priced Starbucks coffee really taste that much better than its Dunkin' Donuts counterpart, or does Starbucks' "double-the-price" cost influence our taste buds?

The more we pay, the more it's worth. The art world has certainly embraced the conventional wisdom. Indeed, the willingness of retired Japanese industrialist Ryoei Saito to pay $85.2 million for Van Gogh's "Portrait of Dr. Gachet" drastically changed the value, not only of that single painting, but of Van Gogh's entire body of work. Similarly, when Bill Gates, the chairman of Microsoft Corporation, paid a record $30 million for a Winslow Homer painting, he set new standards of value for works produced by American artists (Famous Art Reproductions 2003; Vogel 1998).

Conventional wisdom seems "on the money" with regard to patterns of product consumption. However, it is important to note that the adage falls short when we apply it to other economic arenas. For example, in the area of human efforts or work, what we pay is not always a signal of the worth of one's work. Determining the social worth of work requires that we look far beyond an individual's paycheck.

We might begin our inquiry by asking: What do we pay for work? What occupations draw the biggest paychecks in the United States?

Chief executive officers (CEOs) of large corporations earn the highest yearly wages in the United States. For example, the CEOs of the 365 largest corporations in the nation average a yearly salary of $7.4 million. (When one considers stock options and other forms of financial compensation, this salary average increases to $21.8 million per year!) What do these figures mean in relative terms? Currently, the CEOs of America's major corporations earn almost 41 times the salary of the Chief Justice of the Supreme Court, 172 times the average salary of a U.S. schoolteacher, and 274 times the average factory workers' wage (*BusinessWeek Online* 2002; Dent 2003; U.S. Bureau of Labor Statistics 2002; *World Almanac and Book of Facts* 2003).

Close on the heels of the CEOs are major league baseball players. Along with long winter vacations and high adulation, the "boys of summer" enjoy an average yearly wage of $2.5 million (Blum 2003).

Not surprisingly, physicians also fall near the top of the nation's pay scale. But note that within the profession, the distribution of salaries is somewhat varied. A specialized internist (average yearly salary: $126,930) or a psychiatrist (average yearly salary: $113,570), for example, earn significantly less than an anesthesiologist (average yearly salary: $220,000) or a radiologist (average yearly salary: $260,000)! And a general practitioner (average yearly salary: $110,020) may make about the same as the local dentist (average yearly salary: $110,790) (Netreach.com 2003; U.S. Bureau of Labor Statistics 2002).

American lawyers also earn a hefty paycheck. But like physicians, attorneys' financial rewards vary across employment settings. Lawyers employed by manufacturing firms (mean yearly salary: $171,901) earn nearly twice as much as those employed by state and local governments (mean yearly salary: $92,860). And attorneys specializing in administration and management (mean yearly salary: $230,429) earn more than three times the amount of those involved in nonprofit organizations (mean yearly salary: $71,206) (Abbott, Langer, and Associates 2002; U.S. Bureau of Labor Statistics 2002).

We have reviewed some of the highest-paid occupations in America. What occupations generate the smallest paychecks in the United States? The average yearly salaries of apparel sales clerks ($18,200), fast-food cooks ($17,316), cashiers ($16,172), food counter workers ($13,520), and child care workers ($13,052) make these some of the lowest-paid occupations in the United States. And it is worth noting that those who care for our children earn significantly less than those who care for our pets; animal caretakers average $18,270 per year— an average wage that is 40% higher than that of a child care worker (U.S. Bureau of Labor Statistics 2002)!

Are members of highly paid occupations worth the paychecks they collect? Is income the true measure of worth in the United States? **Income** refers to the amount of money earned via an occupation or investments during a specific period of time. One theoretical position in sociology, the Davis-Moore thesis, supports the connection between income and worth. The **Davis-Moore thesis** asserts that social inequality is beneficial to the overall functioning of society. According to Davis and Moore, the high salaries and social rewards attached to certain occupations reflect the importance of these occupations to society. Furthermore, high salaries and social rewards ensure that talented and qualified individuals are well motivated to pursue a society's vital jobs. Inequality, then, is an important source of occupational motivation; income variation ultimately works to the benefit of society as a whole (Davis and Moore 1945; Jeffries and Ransford 1980).

The Davis-Moore thesis represents a functional analysis of society. A **functional analysis** focuses on the interrelationships between the various parts of a society. The approach is ultimately concerned with the ways in which such interrelationships contribute to social order. But not all sociologists share this functionalist view.

Proponents of conflict theory question the social benefits of salary discrepancies. **Conflict theorists** analyze social organization and social interactions by attending to the differential resources controlled by different sectors of a society. Conflict theorists note that certain occupational salaries far outweigh the occupation's contribution to society. Furthermore, negative attitudes and bias can prevent some people from occupying jobs for which they nonetheless are qualified. Thus, conflict theorists suggest that salary variations reflect discrepancies in wealth and power, discrepancies that allow a select group of individuals to determine the financial rewards of various occupations (Tumin 1967). **Wealth** refers to the totality of money and resources controlled by an individual (or a family). **Power** is the ability of groups and/or individuals to get what they want even in the face of resistance. Consider, for example, that in 2002, the average CEO salary increased by 6%, one of the smallest increases on record. Still, CEOs of the biggest U.S. companies managed to award themselves these extra dollars while holding their workers to a modest 2% increase (*Business Week Online* 2002; U.S. Department of Labor 2002). The conflict perspective suggests that these salary increases are not reflective of the CEOs' social contributions. Rather, the increases occurred because the CEOs had the capacity, or the power, to command them.

Similar reasoning is used to explain the multimillion dollar salaries of some baseball stars. From the conflict perspective, these megasalaries do not reflect the contributions of these athletes. Rather, wealthy team owners pay the salaries because they are convinced that they will reap the financial benefits of such investments. Baseball stars can generate huge baseball revenues for club owners by attracting paying customers to the stadium gates and to home TV screens.

Note that income, wealth, and power do not tell the whole story when it comes to defining the social worth of one's work. Worth is also a function of occupational prestige. **Occupational prestige** refers to the respect or recognition one's occupational position commands. Occupational prestige is determined by a variety of job-related factors: the nature of the job, the educational requirements for the job, honors or titles associated with the job, the job's use of "brainpower" versus "brute strength," and the stature of the organizations and groups affiliated with the job.

Periodically, Americans give insight into the prestige factor by rating hundreds of U.S. occupations. Researchers then use such ratings to form an occupational prestige scale. The **occupational prestige scale** provides relative ratings of select occupations as collected from a representative national sample of Americans. In reviewing these ratings, we can quickly see that prestige complicates the road to worth. High income, power, and prestige do not always travel together (Gilbert 2003).

CEOs, for example, enjoy great wealth and can wield immense power. Yet the prestige associated with this occupation is comparatively weak. CEOs score only 72 when rated on the 100-point prestige scale. Doctors and dentists earn similar average salaries, yet doctors enjoy significantly more prestige for their work, earning a rating of 86 versus a 72 rating for dentists.

Bank tellers and secretaries find themselves near the bottom of the income scale. Yet their prestige ratings are more moderate in magnitude; these occupations receive rankings of 43 and 46, respectively. And a rating of 65 suggests that if prestige were currency or power, U.S. teachers would take home much larger paychecks.

Occupational prestige ratings also can take us beyond the workplace and into the realm of general American values. Often, such insight presents a disturbing commentary. Consider that the lifesaving acts of a firefighter (rated 53) are given no more social recognition than the cosmetic acts of a dental hygienist (rated 52). Similarly, police officers, our legally sanctioned agents of power (rated 59), appear only slightly more valued than the actors who entertain us (rated 58). The "information highway" seemingly has bulldozed the heartland, for the farmers who grow our food appear equal in prestige to the telephone operator who answers our information questions (both rated 40). Trades that played a central role in building the nation—carpenters, masons, and miners—no longer command our favor when it comes to prestige (their ratings are 39, 36, and 26, respectively). And, interestingly, the midwife who delivers a baby (rated 23) fares slightly worse than the waitress who delivers food (rated 28), the bellhop who delivers bags (rated 27), and the bartender who delivers drinks (rated 25) (General Social Survey 1999).

When we note that income, power, and prestige are not always a "package deal," we come to realize the complexity of the U.S. stratification system. The **stratification system** ranks individuals hierarchically with regard to their control of a society's resources, privileges, and rewards.

Those on the highest rungs of the stratification ladder enjoy a critical combination of wealth, power, and prestige. Knowing this helps to explain why electricians or plumbers are rarely considered members of the "upper crust." Their incomes may be high, but their prestige levels are relatively low because of a lack of higher education, title, and the use of manual labor in their jobs. Similarly, major league baseball players rarely are classified among the elite. Although their incomes are high, their level of prestige is moderate (rated 65). Furthermore, the historic baseball strike of 1995 suggests that the high income associated with this occupation does not always translate into power.

Individuals who enjoy high income and prestige but are barred from the inner circles of power will never gain full entry to the American upper class. Indeed, many argue that it is this very condition that impedes the progress of political minorities—African Americans, Hispanics, women, youth, and so on—in our nation. Our public rhetoric suggests open access to advanced education, good jobs, and thus high incomes, but our behaviors often block members of minorities from entering the professional and social networks through which power is "brokered."

The more we pay, the more it's worth. Conventional wisdom needs some qualification here. When it comes to the value of certain objects, conventional wisdom may be accurate, but with regard to other aspects of the economy—such as human effort or work—research suggests that the more we pay simply means the more we pay.

Learning More About It

For a good review of occupations in the United States, see Irene Padavic and Barbara Reskin's *Women, Men and Work,* 2nd edition. (Thousand Oaks, CA: Pine Forge Press, 2002).

The definitive work on the three dimensions of stratification—wealth, prestige, and power—can be found in Max Weber's classic work *Economy and Society* (New York: Bedminster 1968; original work published 1922).

For a classic review of the functionalist versus conflict perspectives on stratification, see Arthur Stinchcombe's article, "Some Empirical Consequences of the Davis-Moore Theory of Stratification," *American Sociological Review* 28(5) 1963.

The U.S. Bureau of Labor Statistics maintains a Web site through which you can access the *Occupational Outlook Handbook.* There, one can learn about the nature of hundreds of occupations along with information on training, earnings, working conditions, and job outlooks. Visit the site at <http://stats.bls.gov/oco/>

How many years would it take you to earn the same amount of money that either Coca-Cola's, Exxon's, or Walt Disney's CEO earns in a year? How much would you be earning if your salary increased at the rate of CEOs? *Executive Paywatch* allows you to compare your salary with that of over 200 U.S. CEOs. Access this Web site at <http://www.aflcio.org/corporateamerica/paywatch/ceou/>

Exercises

1. Make a list of all the occupations mentioned in this essay. Classify each occupation with regard to the gender, race, and ethnicity of those typically associated with the occupation. What patterns can you determine with reference to income and prestige as the occupations vary by gender, race, and ethnicity?

2. Ask 10 of your relatives and/or friends to list their occupations. Then ask them to rate the prestige of the occupation on a 100-point scale. Compare the occupation ratings given by your "subjects" with the national ratings found in your library's copy of the General Social Survey. Did your subjects underestimate, overestimate, or pinpoint their prestige levels? If errors were made, were there any patterns to these errors that might be related to the age, ethnicity, gender, or race of your subjects?

Essay 11

Conventional Wisdom Tells Us . . . Money Is the Root of All Evil

This essay documents the impact of income on issues of mortality and life chances. Money, with all its alleged downfalls, can still mean the difference between life and death.

When it comes to issues of wealth and poverty, conventional wisdom spins a compelling tale. On the one hand, we are warned of money's ills. Money is touted as the "root of all evil," an intoxicating drug with the power to enslave us. (Charles Dickens's "Scrooge" could tell us something about that!) Biblical scripture contains similar cautions, noting that one "cannot serve God and money." And adages of popular culture warn that "money can't buy happiness or love."

In conjunction with admonitions regarding the perils of wealth, conventional wisdom often paints a rather comforting picture of poverty. From Shakespeare, one hears that "poor and content is rich, and rich enough." In the modern era, Gershwin promoted a similar sentiment, writing that "plenty o' nuttin" is plenty enough. These messages reflect a more general belief that poverty brings serenity and simplicity to one's life. The poor are lauded as free of the possessions that can cloud the mind and tempt the spirit. Indeed, the conventional wisdom on poverty suggests that it can breed great character. Such beliefs may explain why politicians—Abraham Lincoln, Richard Nixon, and Bill Clinton among them—love to remind us of their humble beginnings.

Is money the root of all evil, and poverty a blessing in disguise? The everyday world of wealth and poverty contradicts such conventional wisdom. Indeed, when we review the connections between one's wallet and one's well-being, it becomes quite clear that the difference between wealth and poverty can literally have life-and-death consequences.

Consider, for example, the issue of mortality. **Mortality rates** document the number of deaths per each 1,000 (or 10,000 or 100,000) members of the population. Such rates suggest that the length of one's life is greatly influenced by one's socioeconomic status. **Socioeconomic status** refers to a particular social location defined with reference to education, occupation, and financial resources.

Those in America who have the highest socioeconomic status live significantly longer than those who have the lowest status. In fact, some sources suggest that a privileged person's life span can exceed that of a disadvantaged person by as much as three to seven years. Patterns of infant mortality paint a similar picture. **Infant mortality rates** gauge the number of deaths per 1,000 live births for children under one year of age. Rates of infant mortality are twice as high among the economically disadvantaged as they are among the privileged (Cockerham 2004; Mirowsky, Ross, and Reynolds 2000; National Center for Health Statistics 2001; Robert and House 2000).

The link between poverty and mortality stems, in part, from issues of health care. The economically disadvantaged have less access to health care than do members of any other socioeconomic status. Furthermore, the quality of care received by the disadvantaged is significantly worse than that enjoyed by those with higher incomes. Thus, people at the bottom of the U.S. economic hierarchy face the greatest risk of contracting illness and disease. When the disadvantaged get sick, they are more likely to die from their ailments than those who are more economically privileged (Cockerham 2004; National Center for Health Statistics 2001).

Poor individuals, for example, are much more likely to suffer fatal heart attacks or fatal strokes or to die from cancer than members of any other socioeconomic status. Interestingly, these economic patterns of health hold true even for diseases nearly eradicated by modern medicine. Disadvantaged patients are several times more likely to die of tuberculosis, for example, than their more privileged counterparts. Similarly, the poor are more likely than are members of any other socioeconomic strata to die from generally nonfatal illnesses, such as influenza, stomach ulcers, and syphilis. These trends led former U.S. Surgeon General C. Everett Koop to remark, "When I look back on my years in office, the things I banged my head against were all poverty" (Cockerham 2004; Mirowsky et al. 2000; National Center for Health Statistics 2001; Robert and House 2000).

Poverty's relationship to life and death, to health and well-being, is a worldwide phenomenon. According to the World Health Organization, 1.3 billion people around the world—just over 20% of the world population—suffer from serious illnesses attributable to poverty (World Health Organization 1999, 2000). Poor sanitation, unvaried diet, and malnutrition all set the stage for this condition. The lack of medical care also greatly contributes to the high rates of death and disease among the poor. Note that in the world's most disadvantaged nations, such as Angola, Chad, or Malawi, there are fewer than 5 doctors for every 100,000 of the country's inhabitants! Nations with slightly more resources do not fare much better.

Throughout Indonesia and approximately two-thirds of the African nations, there are fewer than 40 doctors for every 100,000 people (World Health Organization 1998).

The effects of world poverty seem especially harsh when one considers the plight of children. Despite the technological advancements of the 20th century, 10 million children worldwide will never see their fifth birthdays. In the poorest nations of the world, such as Afghanistan, Guinea Bissau, or Sierra Leone, approximately 1 in 5 children face this sad plight. And it is important to note that 60% of those children who die before the age of five will not succumb to incurable diseases or tragic accidents. Rather, their deaths will be linked to malnutrition, a clearly solvable problem (World Health Organization 2003).

Poverty also helps to explain the short life expectancies of those living in the poor nations of the world. **Life expectancy** refers to the average number of years that a specified population can expect to live. For example, although a U.S. citizen can expect to live approximately 77 years, individuals in most African nations can expect to live for roughly 50 years. For some nations, life expectancy is significantly lower. In Afghanistan, the average citizen lives for 46 years. In Angola, the average life span is 40 years. And in Mozambique, average life expectancy is only 34 years! (Population Reference Bureau 2003). Clearly, for many parts of our world community, poverty can be viewed as the leading cause of death.

Poverty's link to mortality goes beyond issues of health and hygiene. Simple membership in a society's lower economic status, regardless of one's health, increases the risk of premature death. The sinking of the *Titanic* in 1912 offers a stark illustration of this phenomenon. Among passengers on that ill-fated ship, socioeconomic status was a major determinant of survival or death. When disaster strikes on the high seas, norms dictate that women and children should be the first evacuated. On the *Titanic,* however, that norm apparently applied only to wealthier passengers. Forty-five percent of the women in third class met their deaths in contrast to the 16% death rate of women in second class and the 3% death rate of women in first class. What explains the discrepancy? Historians tell us that first-class passengers (both male and female) were given the first opportunity to abandon ship, while those in third class were ordered—sometimes forced at gunpoint—to stay in their rooms. It was only when the wealthy had been safely evacuated from the ship that third-class passengers were permitted to leave. Thus, for many aboard the *Titanic,* mere membership in the ranks of the poor proved to be a fatal affiliation (Hall 1986; Lord 1981; Zeitlin, Lutterman, and Russell 1977).

The link between poverty and mortality, so dramatically witnessed on the decks of the *Titanic,* haunts every corner of American life. In the United States, poverty doubles one's chances of being murdered, raped, or assaulted. Similarly, members of the lower economic strata are more likely than others to die as a result of occupational hazards—that is, from diseases such as black lung, from machinery injuries, and the like. Among children, those of the lower class are more likely to drown, to die in fires, to be murdered, or to be killed in auto accidents than their more affluent counterparts. And during wars, the sons of the poor are most likely to serve in the military and therefore most likely to be casualties (Cockerham

2004; Dunne 1986; Kids Count 2003; National Center for Health Statistics 1998; Reiman 2004).

Physical health, life, and death—poverty influences all of these. But the negative effects of low socioeconomic status extend beyond physical well-being. Many studies document that poverty can also negatively influence mental and emotional states. For example, more than one-third of the poor report worrying all or most of the time that their household incomes will be insufficient to meet their basic family expenses. Similarly, the poor are less likely to report feelings of happiness, hope, or satisfaction than their more wealthy counterparts. As a result, the poor are more likely to greet the day with trepidation, despair, and depression than with enthusiasm, drive, and stamina (Cockerham 2003, 2004; McEwen and Seeman 1999; McLeod and Nonnemaker 2000).

Negative life events also befall the disadvantaged more frequently than those of any other socioeconomic status. **Negative life events** refer to major and undesirable changes in one's day-to-day existence, such as the loss of a spouse, divorce, or unemployment. For example, divorce occurs most frequently among the poor, with rates steadily decreasing as one moves up the socioeconomic hierarchy. Similarly, job loss and unemployment are most common among those of the lower socioeconomic strata. The frequency with which the poor experience such events affects their mental and emotional well-being as well. Negative life events have been linked to increases in depression, low self-esteem, and increased use of drugs and alcohol (Cockerham 2003, 2004; McEwen and Seeman 1999; McLeod and Nonnemaker 2000; U.S. Census Bureau 2002, Table 598).

One's socioeconomic status can also influence an individual's ability to effectively cope with life's struggles; the poor again appear at a disadvantage in this regard. Consider that family members typically constitute the support networks of the poor. This stands in contrast to the networks of the privileged, which typically consist of friends, neighbors, and colleagues. The restricted outlets of the poor are not without cost. Research indicates that the poor experience less security in social exchanges with nonfamily members and greater distrust and fear of the "outside world" than those in more privileged segments of the population (Cockerham 2003, 2004).

Poverty's links to premature death, physical disease, and poor mental and emotional health suggest that membership in the lowest socioeconomic strata can severely limit an individual's life chances. **Life chances** are the odds of one's obtaining desirable resources, positive experiences, and opportunities for a long and successful life.

Poverty damages the general quality of life. The condition also limits one's ability to improve or change one's circumstances. In the face of disease, depression, unrest, or danger, it becomes hard to summon the motivation necessary for upward mobility.

Given the debilitating consequences of poverty, why have societies been so ineffective at combating it? Sociologist Herbert Gans (1971) suggests that poverty may serve some positive social functions for society. In this regard, he offers a functional analysis of poverty. A **functional analysis** focuses on the interrelationships between the various parts of a society. The approach is ultimately concerned with the ways in which such interrelationships contribute to social order.

Consider the economic benefits afforded by the existence of poverty. The poor constitute an accessible pool of cheap labor. They fill jobs that are highly undesirable yet completely necessary to a functioning society: garbage collector, janitor, poultry processor, and so on. The existence of poverty also generates jobs for those in other socioeconomic strata. Social workers, welfare agents, and public defenders, for example, occupy positions created either to service the poor or to isolate them from the rest of society. A society's poor also provide a ready market for imperfect or damaged goods. By consuming products that others would not consider, the poor help many manufacturers avoid financial loss.

At a social level, the poor provide a measuring rod against which those of other socio-economic statuses gauge their performance. In this way, the continued existence of a poor class reassures the more privileged of their status and worth. Finally, the poor often function as social scapegoats, symbols by which the larger society reaffirms its laws and values. The poor are more likely to be arrested and convicted of crimes than are members of any other socioeconomic strata (Reiman 2004). By focusing the social audience on the "sins" of the poor, societies can effectively convey the message that crime doesn't pay.

Reviewing the realities of money and poverty and their place in a society casts serious doubt on conventional wisdom. Money may not guarantee happiness; it may not buy love. Money may trigger greed and, ultimately, personal pain. Yet the disadvantages of money wane in comparison to the absence of money and its effects. Poverty has clear, negative consequences for social actors. In fact, it can be argued that poverty has been a more destructive force in this nation than any medical disease or any international threat. Yet poverty also has clear, positive social functions for society as a whole. Perhaps this point best explains a harsh fact of our times: Despite society's "war on poverty," poverty has proven a tenacious opponent. The battle wages on, with casualties growing in number. Yet victory over poverty may come at a cost too high for the nonpoor to embrace.

Learning More About It

Two poignant accounts of the lives and conflicts faced by those near the bottom of the economic scale are offered in Richard Sennett's and Jonathan Cobb's *The Hidden Injuries of Class* (New York: Vintage, 1972) and Barbara Ehrenreich's *Nickel and Dimed: On (Not) Getting By In America* (New York: Henry Holt and Co., 2001).

Paul Krugman provides a very engaging look at the growing economic divide in America. See "For Richer," *New York Times* Magazine Section, October 20, 2002, pp. 62–67. A more in-depth treatment of the topic can be found in Dennis Gilbert's *The American Class Structure in an Age of Growing Inequality* (Belmont, CA: Wadsworth/Thomson Learning, 2003).

Jeffrey Reiman offers a highly readable look at the ways in which poverty influences justice in *The Rich Get Richer and the Poor Get Prison* (Boston: Allyn & Bacon, 2004).

The World Health Organization provides a wealth of information on global health patterns. Their Web site provides a variety of reports and surveys that fully document the effects of poverty on health and life chances. Visit them at <http://www.who.int>

The following organizations can help you learn more about poverty:

Center for Community Change
1000 Wisconsin Avenue, NW, Washington DC 20007
(202) 342–0519 Web site: <http:www.communitychange.org/default.asp>

National Center for Children in Poverty
215 W. 125th Street, 3rd Floor, New York, NY 10027
(646) 284–9600 Web site: <http://www.nccp.org/>

National Coalition for the Homeless
1012 Fourteenth St., NW, #600, Washington DC 20005–3471
(202) 737–6444 Web site: <http://www.nationalhomeless.org/>

Exercises

1. Essay 6, on aging, introduced the concept of master status. Consider the ways in which an individual's financial position can function as a master status in our society. What auxiliary traits or characteristics are presumed to accompany the status of rich? Of poor? Under what conditions does one's financial status fail to operate as a master status?

2. Consider the ways in which money affects the life chances of a college student. Being as systematic as possible, identify academic and nonacademic activities that increase one's chances of successfully negotiating a college career. How does the ready availability of cash facilitate or impede these various activities? What are the implications of your findings?

Essay 12

Conventional Wisdom Tells Us . . . You've Come a Long Way, Baby

In the past 30 years, women have made great strides toward equality with men, but have they journeyed far enough? Here, we focus on gender relations in the home, the schools, and in the workplace, illustrating the gains and losses faced by women and men in the current era.

D rop in on any historical period, and chances are great that you will find evidence of a past filled with gender inequality.

- *Dateline, preindustrial Europe:* Artisan guilds limit apprenticeships to men, thereby ensuring the exclusion of women from their ranks and consequently from the master crafts (Howell 1986).

- *The shores of colonial America:* The Doctrine of Coverture, which subsumes a woman's legal identity and rights to those of her husband, is adopted from British common law (Blackstone [1765–1769] 1979).

- *United States, circa 1870:* The "conservation of energy" theme is used to support the argument that education is dangerous for women. The development of the mind is thought to occur at the expense of the reproductive organs (Clarke 1873).

- *The State of Virginia, 1894:* The U.S. Supreme Court rules that the word "person" in a Virginia regulation was properly equated with "male," not "female," and thereby upholds the state's decision to deny a law license to a "nonperson" female (Renzetti and Curran 1989).

- *Turn-of-the-century America:* Twenty-six U.S. states embrace the doctrine of "separate spheres" and pass laws prohibiting the employment of married women. The doctrine asserts that a woman's place is in the home, while a man's is in the public work sphere (Padavic and Reskin 2002; Skolnick 1991).

- *Sharpsburg, Maryland 1989:* A female participant in a historical re-creation of the Civil War battle of Antietam is forced to leave the event. She was evicted by a park ranger who told her that women were not allowed to portray Civil War soldiers at reenactments. (In fact, more than 250 women fought on both sides of the Civil War; 5 women died at the battle of Antietam) (Marcus 2002).

"You've come a long way, baby." No doubt, you have heard this phrase used to acknowledge the dramatic change in women's social roles and achievements. Today, much has improved for women. Thousands of women have moved into traditionally male jobs. Marital status is no longer a legal barrier to the employment of women. Court rulings have struck down gender-based job restrictions. Women participate in higher education at rates equal to or greater than men, and the law has made concerted efforts to advance and protect the legal rights of women. Even the historical record is slowly but surely being corrected. Yet despite the long way that "baby" has traveled, a careful assessment of gender relations in the United States indicates that "baby" has a long haul ahead.

Obstacles to gender equality begin with gender socialization. **Gender socialization** refers to the process by which individuals learn the culturally approved expectations and behaviors for males and females. Even in a child's earliest moments of life, gender typing, with all its implications, proves a routine practice. **Gender typing** refers to gender-based expectations and behaviors. Several early studies documented parents' differential treatment of male and female infants. An observational study by Goldberg and Lewis (1969), for example, revealed mothers unconsciously rewarding and reinforcing passivity and dependency in girls while rewarding action and independence in boys. In another early study by Lake (1975), researchers asked 30 first-time parents to describe their newborn infants. The exercise revealed that parents' responses were heavily influenced by prominent gender stereotypes. **Stereotypes** are generalizations applied to all members of a group. Thus, daughters were most often described using adjectives such as "tiny," "soft," and "delicate." In contrast, boys were most frequently described with adjectives such as "strong," "alert," and "coordinated" (also see Rubin, Provenzano, and Luria 1974; Sweeney and Bradbard 1988; and more recently Karraker, Vogel, and Lake 1995). Other studies on gender typing in infancy uncovered similar patterns. For example, when the infants were dressed in blue clothing and identified as boys, women participating in the study described the infant in masculine terms and engaged in more aggressive (bouncing and lifting) play. When the *very same* infants were dressed in pink and identified as girls, women participating in the study described the infants in feminine terms, handled them more tenderly, and offered the "girls" a doll (Bonner

1984; Will, Self, and Dalton 1976). Similarly, when asked to assess the crawling ability of their babies, mothers overestimated the ability of their sons and underestimated the ability of their daughters. In actual performance, infant boys and girls displayed identical levels of crawling ability (Mondschein, Adolph, and Tamis-LeMonda 2000). Gender typing in infancy is a widespread phenomenon. Even in a society that actively promotes gender equality, Sweden, there is nonetheless evidence of differential treatment of male and female infants by mothers (Heimann 2002).

Often, the gender typing of infants occurs in subtle ways. Several studies, for example, have focused on gender differences in vocalizations of both infants and parents. In one study, both mothers and fathers perceived their crying infant girls more negatively as the crying increased. Increased crying by sons, on the other hand, led their mothers to rate them as "more powerful" (Teichner, Ames, and Kerig 1997). Another study found that babies who "sounded" like boys (i.e., babies with less nasal vocalizations) received higher favorability ratings by adults (Bloom, Moore-Schoenmakers, and Masataka 1999)! And research has also documented that fathers sing more playfully and expressively to sons, while mothers do the same with daughters (Trehub, Hill, and Kamenetsky 1997).

Gender typing continues during the toddler years. Observation studies of toddlers reveal that parents are rougher and more active with sons than they are with daughters. Studies also show that parents teach their toddlers different lessons on independence. For example, fathers teach boys to "fend for themselves," while encouraging daughters to "ask for help." These distinctions occur even among parents who claim identical child-rearing techniques with reference to their male versus female children (Basow 1992; Lindsey and Mize 2001; Lips, 1993; Lytton and Romny 1991; Richardson 1988; Ross and Taylor 1989; Witkin-Lanoil 1984). Parents also engage in more implicit gender scripting. In storytelling about their own pasts, for example, fathers tell stories with stronger autonomy themes than do mothers, and sons hear these stories more than daughters (Fiese and Skillman 2000). Similarly, parents' playground interactions encourage risk-taking behaviors in sons and perceived injury vulnerability in girls (Morrongiello and Dawber 1999). Daughters also seem to model fear and avoidance reactions of mothers to a greater degree than sons (Gerull and Rapee 2002). Finally, consider a behavior pattern known as the "stroller effect." Research shows that fathers are more likely to push strollers when the child is in it; mothers are more likely to push empty strollers. Such behavior delivers strong nonverbal messages concerning the gender scripting of power and responsibility (Mitchell et al. 1992).

Overall, studies of parental gender typing show that parents' ideas and beliefs about gender influence the child's socialization to gender roles (Witt 1997). However, parents are not the only family members to contribute to the process. Siblings are also involved in gender typing. Studies show, for example, that boys with older brothers and girls with older sisters engage in more sex-typed behaviors than children with other-sex siblings (Rust et al. 2000). Indeed, well before their third birthdays, children display knowledge of gender stereotyping of familiar family activities (Pouline-Dubois et al. 2002). Preschool children also prove to be quite aware of gender-typed competencies and occupations (Levy, Sadovsky, and Troseth 2000).

The gender typing of infants and toddlers is not confined to the home. From child care settings (Chick, Heilman-Houser, and Hunter 2002) to tee-ball fields (Landers and Fine 2001), observation data document the prevalence of gender stereotyping. In peer play activities, girls are more likely to engage in pretend play, while boys are more likely to engage in physical play (Lindsey and Mize 2001). Young boys also seem particularly concerned about proper gender-typed behavior: They are more likely than girls to present themselves as engaging in gender-appropriate play and having gender-appropriate toy preferences when in front of same-sex peers (Banerjee and Lintern 2000). Gender typing can also result in a strikingly different educational experience for boys and for girls. For example, research documents that elementary and junior high school teachers give more attention and praise to male students. Furthermore, boys tend to dominate classroom communication and receive more support than girls do when working through intellectual problems (Chira 1992; Sadker and Sadker 1985, 1998; Thorne 1995). Overall, younger generations seem to be learning the same lessons taught to older generations. And middle school students appear no more flexible than college students with regard to gender roles for women (Mills and Mills 1996).

Social scientists contend that such differential treatment can have long-term consequences. Teacher response patterns send an implicit message that male efforts are more valuable than female efforts. Teachers' gender-driven responses also appear to perpetuate stereotypes of learning. For example, gender stereotypes suggest that boys are more skilled at math and science than girls. Yet more than 100 studies document that during the elementary and middle school years, girls actually perform equal to or better than boys in math and science. Some suggest that the decline in girls' math skills and interest during the high school years occurs because teachers begin tracking boys and girls in drastically different directions. Teachers urge boys to value math and science skills, while girls are taught to devalue them (Feingold 1988; Hyde, Fennema, and Lamon 1990). Female high school seniors are more likely than males to be advised against taking additional math courses (U.S. Department of Education 1997). Parents contribute to the mix by perceiving sons as more competent in the sciences and by expecting more from them (Andre et al. 1999; Brownlow, Jacobi, and Rogers 2000; Dai 2002). Students' own gender biases about their competencies also influence different education and career plans for male and female students (Brownlow et al. 2000; Correll 2001; Guimond and Roussel 2001; Keller 2002).

Teachers', parents', and students' perceptions and actions are not without consequences. Longitudinal data (data collected at multiple points in time) show that 7th- and 10th-grade boys and girls have a similar liking for both math and science. By the 12th grade, however, boys are more likely than girls to report enjoying math and science (U.S. Department of Education 1997). Gender differences in actual performance also increase over time. A study of high-scoring male and female math students found that despite a similar starting point in elementary school, the male students' math performance accelerated faster as years in school progressed (Leahey and Guo 2001). And to come full circle, such performance differences have been attributed to pedagogical approaches that are male- rather than female-friendly (Strand and Mayfield 2000). Given these dynamics, perhaps it is to be anticipated that junior high school students today express career interests that fall along traditional gender paths (Lupart and Cannon 2002). Furthermore, lack of training in math and science also serves to keep females out of lucrative career paths in engineering and the sciences (Mitra 2002).

Perhaps the most telling "lesson" regarding the relationship between gender and education, however, is that schooling leads to greater financial benefits for males than it does for females. For every level of educational attainment, median earnings for women are lower than those for men. At the start of the new millennium, a female high school graduate's earnings were on par with those of a male high school dropout (U.S. Department of Education 2002). Indeed, it takes a college degree for a female worker to exceed the average earnings of a male with a high school diploma (*World Almanac* 2003). In the last decade, full-time male workers with college degrees had median annual incomes that were approximately $15,000 higher than their female counterparts. (National Center for Education Statistics 2003). In 2000, a male with a bachelor's degree or higher earned 31% more than a female with the same level of education (U.S. Department of Education 2002). The gender gap in earnings grows still larger for those with graduate training. In 2000, American males with master's degrees had a median annual income of nearly $60,000 per year, whereas females with the same amount of graduate training averaged just over $40,000 per year. Males with professional degrees earned over $81,000, while their female counterparts earned under $46,000 (U.S. Census Bureau 2002, Table 664). The lower financial returns of education for women is made more exasperating when one realizes that women are increasingly participating in advanced education. By the end of the 1990s, 58% of those enrolled in graduate school were women (U.S. Department of Education 2002).

In addition to parents and the schools, the mass media contribute to gender inequality by prioritizing the male experience in explicit ways. While their numbers have grown over the years, women are still underrepresented in prime-time television programming as well as in leading roles in film (Eschholz, Bufkin, and Long 2002; Signorielli and Bacue 1999). Furthermore, in comparing the presentation of male versus female characters, one finds that males are more likely to be portrayed as aggressive, powerful, and accomplished, while females are more likely to be playing minor roles and frequently depicted as either attractive sexual objects obsessed with appearance and dating or as troublesome, bothersome shrews (Elasmar, Hasegawa, and Brain 1999; Kalisch and Kalisch 1984; Lauzen and Dozier 2002; Sidel 1991; Vande Berg and Streckfuss 1992).

Television commercials present more of the same—males exercise power and authority, while women are shown in family settings or as sex objects (Coltrane and Messineo 2000). Even in commercials using *animated* spokescharacters (e.g., the Energizer Bunny, Tony the Tiger, or Ronald McDonald), females are underrepresented—most such characters are male (Peirce and McBride 1999)! These trends can be observed in other media messages as well.

Exposure to images of women in magazine ads, for instance, can reinforce stereotypes about gender roles (Curry, Arriagada, and Cornwell 2002; Lafky et al. 1996). Similarly, music videos also deliver clear gender scripts: Males should be aggressive and dominant, while females should be lovable and dependent or relegated to the background (if seen at all) (Alexander 1999; Seidman 1992).

The media prioritize males in subtle ways as well. One study challenged viewers to turn on their TV sets, close their eyes, flip through the channels, and note the gender of the first voice they heard on each station. With few exceptions, the voice turned out to be male, a trend suggesting that men are the appropriate gatekeepers of the airways (Atkin 1982; Courtney and Whipple 1983). A more recent study on commercial voice-over work suggests that this "flip and listen" challenge would yield similar results today. Although there has been an increase in female voice-overs in recent years, over 70% are still male (Bartsch et al. 2000).

It is important to note that gender bias seeps beyond prime-time programming and other adult-geared media. Children's programming also retains a clear male bias. Television programming for children, such as Teletubbies and Barney, although depicting some change in gender messages nonetheless primarily reinforces gender stereotypes for girls (Powell and Abels 2002). Cartoons, likewise, reinforce traditional gender scripts. They overrepresent males and portray female characters in stereotypical ways, such as in family roles and acting fearful, romantic, polite, emotional or supportive (Klein, Shiffman, and Welka 2000; Leaper et al. 2002). A recent study focusing on educational science programs found that male characters outnumbered female characters by two to one. When females did appear on the shows, they were seldom seen in the role of expert scientist. Most frequently, females were seen in supportive roles such as apprentices, assistants, or pupils (Steinke and Long 1996).

Network officials defend this imbalance in children's programming as a valid, indeed sensible, marketing call—nothing more. Marketing research shows that although girls will watch male-dominated shows, boys will not "cross over" to female-dominated programs. And because boys watch more TV than girls, networks bow to the preference of their male audience members (Carter 1991). Perhaps marketing considerations help explain the imbalance found in video games as well. Recent studies of Nintendo, Sony PlayStation, and Sega Genesis games found that female characters are missing from most of these video games. When females are present in games, they are often portrayed in ways that reinforce the idea of women as sex objects or as victims of violence (Beasley and Standley 2002; Dietz 1998).

When boys and girls become men and women, they carry learned gender differences into the domestic sphere. Thus, despite current rhetoric to the contrary, the division of labor on the domestic front is anything but equal. A recent study by the Center for the Ethnography of Everyday Life reports that American men average 16 hours of housework a week compared with 27 hours for women (University of Michigan 2002). The amount of housework done by men stays the same regardless of whether their wives are full-time homemakers or work outside the home (Bird 1999). When it comes to household chores, marriage (as well as cohabitation) reduces the workload for men and increases it for women (Gupta 1999; South and

Spitze 1994). The actual chores done by men and women also follow gender scripts: Women cook and clean and do laundry, while men do yard work and home repairs (Robinson and Godbey 1997). While the amount of household labor done by men did increase from 1965 to 1985, their domestic contributions have essentially stalled in recent years (University of Michigan 2002). And the overall narrowing of the gap between women's and men's contributions to housework can be attributed to the fact that women have been systematically cutting back on the number of hours they spend on housework (Bianchi et al. 2000). Interestingly enough, even "academic" households can't escape the gender scripts of housework: Female college professors do considerably more household work than their male colleagues, especially when they are married and have children (Suitor, Mecom, and Feld 2001). Finally, in addition to doing about 70% of the household chores (Bianchi et al. 2000), women also bear the primary responsibility for managing family organization and schedules (Daly 2001; Zimmerman et al. 2001).

Most sociologists agree that the greatest strides toward gender equality have been made within the workplace. Despite such strides, however, the old industrial practice of separating work along gender lines continues. Sex segregation is common practice in many workplaces and within many occupations. **Sex segregation** in the work sphere refers to the separation of male and female workers by job tasks or occupational categories. When it comes to women and work, it is very clear that sex segregation still thrives. Approximately 30% of all working women are found in just 10 occupations. Only 2 of the occupations, managers/administrators and supervisors/proprietors in sales, show up on the top-10 list of men's occupations. One out of every four women workers can be found in "administrative support occupations" (Padavic and Reskin 2002). Ninety-three percent of registered nurses, 97% of receptionists, 97% of child care workers, 98% of secretaries, and 98% of dental hygienists are female (U.S. Census Bureau 2002, Table 588). The histories of these occupations point to an economic motive for such segregation. Within these areas, employers used female workers to reduce their wage costs. Employers were able to pay female workers lower wages than males. Employers also thought that women were less likely to be susceptible to the organization efforts of unions. Furthermore, by confining their hiring to young, single women, employers ensured a high worker turnover in their businesses (young, single women left their jobs to marry), as well as a continuous supply of inexperienced, low-wage workers (Padavic and Reskin 2002).

We may be tempted to think that sex segregation can lead to certain positive outcomes. For example, an abundance of women within certain occupations suggests arenas of power born from numbers. However, it is important to note that there is a negative relationship between the percentage of female workers within an occupation and that occupation's earnings. Occupations dominated by women enjoy less pay, less prestige, and less power than occupations dominated by males. Female-dominated industries also fare less well on health insurance coverage than do male-dominated industries (Dewar 2000). Furthermore, once an occupation becomes female dominated, it is effectively abandoned by men. The opposite trend—male displacement of female workers—is unusual (Padavic and Reskin 2002). Indeed, it is a trend typically limited to instances where immigrant men replaced native-born women, as they did in American textile mills or in the cigar-making industry (Hartman 1976; Kessler-Harris 2003). Men moving into female work has also occurred when there has been a compelling financial incentive. With Title IX of the 1972 Higher Education Act, for instance, salaries for college coaches of female teams had to be brought in-line with those for male teams. With this change, there was a marked increase in the number of men taking positions as coaches for women's collegiate programs (Padavic and Reskin 2002). In general, however, men have little motivation to enter lower-paying, lower-status, female-dominated occupations. Those who do are apt to encounter challenges to their masculinity and witness eventual wage erosion in the occupation (Catanzarite 2003; Cross and Bagilhole 2002).

In general, male workers dominate in relatively high-paying precision production, craft, repair and protective service occupations (U.S. Department of Labor 2002). In addition, the most prestigious professions are primarily the domains of men. Only 10% of engineers, 20% of dentists, 23% of architects, 29% of lawyers, and 29% of physicians are female. Less than 5% of top management positions are held by women (Sharpe 1994; U.S. Census Bureau 2002, Table 588).

Women who do enter nontraditional occupations are likely to face gender segregation within the occupation. For example, females in medicine are most likely to specialize in pediatrics and gynecology, while neurosurgery and radiology remain the preserve of male physicians (Epstein 1988; *World Almanac* 2003). Female physicians are also underrepresented in leadership positions (Zimmerman 2000). Similar patterns are found in the legal profession. Women are underrepresented in prestigious and lucrative settings; they are also less likely to "make partner" than their male counterparts (Hull and Nelson 2000; Kay and Hagan 1999, 1998). In professional specialty occupations, men are much more likely than women to be in the highest-paying professions (e.g., engineers and mathematical and computer scientists). Women are more likely to work in lower-paying occupations, such as teaching (U.S. Department of Labor 2002). The picture fails to brighten in service-oriented work. In the realm of real estate, for example, women sell homes, while men sell commercial properties (Thomas and Reskin 1990). (Guess which is the more lucrative branch of the field?) In the world of waiting tables, gender segregation persists. Expensive restaurants tend to hire waiters; inexpensive eateries and diners hire waitresses (Padavic and Reskin 2002). Even in the "work of God," sex segregation exists. Women clergy are overrepresented in low-status, subordinate congregational positions (Sullins 2000).

The gender segregation of jobs and occupations takes a financial toll on women. For example, in 2001, the median weekly earnings for full-time male workers were $672, and for female workers, weekly earnings averaged $511 (U.S. Department of Labor 2002). This disparity means that women must work about 16 months to earn the 12-month wage of men. Such pay discrepancies are reflected in a statistic known as the **pay gap**. The pay gap refers to a ratio calculated when women's earnings are divided by men's earnings. Historically, a pay gap favoring men over women is a well-established tradition. Currently, the pay gap is approximately 76%—that is, for every $10,000 paid the average male worker, the average female worker is paid around $7,600. While the gap did narrow through the 1980s, it has maintained itself over the last decade (U.S. Department of Labor 2002). Not surprisingly, the wage discrepancies can be found even among professionals working in the very lucrative world of Wall Street. Compensation of women in the securities industry during the longest bull market on record was less than their male counterparts (Roth 1999).

The pay gap can vary according to the age, race, and educational level of workers. For example, the gap increases when we compare the salaries of older female and male workers with those just entering the workforce. Similarly, the gap increases when we compare the salaries of African American or Hispanic female workers with those of their male counterparts. Female college graduates face a larger pay gap vis-à-vis their male counterparts (72%) than is found between female and male high school dropouts (76%) (U.S. Department of Labor 2002).

Ironically, one area in which women do appear to be achieving equity is in the realms of disease and mortality. Traditionally, women have enjoyed a health advantage over men. Females display lower rates of infant mortality than males. Females enjoy longer life spans than males. Male death rates generally are higher than female death rates within all age categories. But as women embrace more of the behaviors traditionally associated with the male role (such as alcohol consumption, smoking, and so on), and as they make inroads into male occupations, their health advantage may be waning.

For instance, the U.S. Surgeon General links the increased incidence of smoking among women with increased rates of lung cancer. (Today, levels of smoking in men and women are almost identical.) The Surgeon General reports that since 1950, there has been a 600% jump in women's death rates from lung cancer (Pampel 2002; U.S. Surgeon General 2001). Today, lung cancer is the leading cause of cancer deaths for both men and women. Indeed, since 1987, more women have died of lung cancer each year than have died from breast cancer (American Cancer Society 2003). Similarly, women's increased representation in the workforce has been linked to increases in female heart disease. Heart disease is now the leading cause of death for women. Through the 1990s, cardiovascular disease mortality trends for women actually increased, while trends for men decreased. In 2000, 505,661 women died from cardiovascular disease compared with 440,175 men (American Heart Association 2002a).

Despite women's greater representation in cancer and heart disease rates, however, several studies show that the female experience receives only secondary consideration by medical researchers. There is still a common perception that heart disease is not a significant problem for women. Chest pain in women is often attributed to noncardiac causes. Note, too, that women report more problems in accessing health care than men do. The majority of cardiovascular procedures are conducted on men; most randomized studies on treatment focus only on males (American Heart Association 2002b; Commonwealth Fund 1994, 2000). As a result, heart disease in women tends to be less effectively detected and treated than it is in men. Thirty-eight percent of female heart attack victims will die within one year of their attacks; 25% of male victims will suffer the same fate (American Heart Association 2003).

Indeed, cardiovascular disease kills approximately 65,000 more women than men each year (American Heart Association 2002a).

In general, women's health care reflects many of the gender stereotypes and discrepancies documented throughout this essay. To make this point painfully clear, consider that gender differences exist with regard to the experience of pain. Again, gender scripts help explain the difference. The nurturing and empathic roles for women make them more likely to see pain in others and to experience more pain themselves. Gender scripts are also evident in the medical field's reactions: Women's pain has been taken less seriously and too often discounted (Wartik 2002). Clearly, the social and economic contexts of women's lives are not unrelated to women's health and health care issues. During the 1990s, activists aggressively lobbied Congress to obtain a more equitable share of funding for women's health issues. A recent Institute of Medicine (IOM) report stressed the need for research on the biological and physiological differences between men and women with regard to disease and medical practice and therapies (IOM 2001). There is increasing recognition that gender equity is an essential part of health care policy reform (Moss 2002; Strobino, Grason, and Mikovitz 2002).

The longest journey begins with the first step. Women have taken that step, but their journey is far from complete. Perhaps the greatest evidence of the distance yet to be covered is found in the area of politics. Governorships, senate seats, and house seats are noteworthy for their near absence of women. Only six (although this is an all-time high) women currently serve as governors; only 73 of 535 seats in the 108th Congress are held by women—14 in the Senate and 59 in the House of Representatives (Center for American Woman and Politics 2003). Social psychologist Sandra Lipsitz Bem (1993) contends that the male dominance of political power has created a male-centered culture and social structure. Such an environment works to the clear advantage of men. A male-centered perspective on the world dictates a set of social arrangements that systematically meets the needs of men, while leaving women's needs unmet or handled as "special cases."

Witness, for instance, the influence of the male perspective within the legal arena, specifically no-fault divorce laws. Such laws treat parties to a divorce as equal players despite their unequal work and occupational histories. Present social arrangements are such that a husband's earning power is enhanced over the course of a marriage. Consequently, in the wake of no-fault divorce laws, ex-wives typically experience a decrease in their standard of living, while ex-husbands typically enjoy an increase (Peterson 1996). Or consider a criticism of the Unemployment Insurance (UI) system. Many states exclude part-time workers from eligibility. Since women account for 70% of all part-time workers, such policies are particularly harsh on females (Institute for Women's Policy Research 2001). The Temporary Assistance to Needy Families (TANF) program has been criticized for forcing mothers to prioritize wage work (in low-paying female jobs) over child care responsibilities (Oliker 2000). Indeed, family support and occupational segregation issues have been systematically neglected as critical elements to any welfare or workforce reform efforts (Jones-DeWeever, Peterson, and Song 2003).

Male-centered social arrangements also permeate current disability policies. Such policies recognize nearly all "male" illnesses and medical procedures (circumcision, prostate surgery, and so on) as potentially eligible for compensation. In contrast, the female condition of pregnancy is defined as a "special condition" unique to women and therefore ineligible for coverage. In essence, models or standards of normalcy and behavior are male oriented, a situation that automatically puts women at a disadvantage (Bem 1993; Crocker 1985).

By increasing their numbers and voice in the political arena, women may achieve an effective "check" on social inequality. It is worth noting that in recent years, women have made important strides in the area of voter turnout: In every presidential election since 1980, the percentage of female voters exceeded the percentage of male voters (U.S. Census Bureau 2002, Table 393). Without these kinds of developments, it will remain far too easy to sustain policies and practices that work to the disadvantage of women. Gender inequality will continue to be business as usual.

Learning More About It

An interesting and provocative discussion of gender inequality is offered by social psychologist Sandra Lipsitz Bem in *The Lenses of Gender: Transforming the Debate on Sexual Inequality* (New Haven: Yale University Press, 1993).

For a concise and very accessible introduction to a sociological analysis of our gendered lives, see Laura Kramer's *The Sociology of Gender: A Brief Introduction* (Los Angeles: Roxbury, 2001).

For a rather extensive collection of articles on gender (as well as race and class) in the media see Gail Dines and Jean Humez's (Eds.) book: *Gender, Race and Class in Media: A Text-Reader* (Thousand Oaks: Sage Publications, 2003).

A very readable and interesting discussion of the working woman's disproportional domestic duties is offered by Arlie Russell Hochschild (with Anne Machung) in *The Second Shift: Working Parents and the Revolution at Home* (New York: Penguin, 2003).

In *Mismatch: The Growing Gulf Between Women and Men* (New York: Scribner, 2003b), Andrew Hacker examines the widening divide between men and women as evidenced in marriage patterns, divorce trends, career paths, politics, and so on.

Irene Padavic and Barbara Reskin have constructed a very readable review of gender and its relationship to work. Readers can consult *Women and Men at Work,* 2nd edition (Thousand Oaks, CA: Pine Forge Press, 2002).

Three recent *Annual Review of Sociology* articles should help the reader become well-grounded in individual and organizational level approaches to understanding sex inequality in the workplace: Barbara Reskin, Debra McBrier, and Julie Kmec's "The Determinants and Consequences of Workplace Sex and Race Composition," *Annual Review of Sociology* 25: 335–361, 1999; Barbara Reskin's "Getting It Right: Sex and Race Inequality in Work Organizations," *Annual Review of Sociology* 26: 707–709, 2000; and Tanja van der Lippe and Liset van Dijk's "Comparative Research on Women's Employment," *Annual Review of Sociology* 28: 221–241, 2002.

The following organizations can also help you learn more about gender relations in society:

Center for American Women and Politics
Eagleton Institute of Politics, Rutgers University
New Brunswick, NJ 08901
(732) 932–9384; Web site: <http://www.rci.rutgers.edu/~cawp/>

Society for the Advancement of Women's Health Research
1828 L Street, NW, Suite 625, Washington, DC 200036
(202) 223–8224; Web site: <http://www.womens-health.org/>

Institute for Women's Policy Research
1400 20th Street, NW, Suite 104, Washington, DC 20036
(202) 785–5100; Web site: <http://www.iwpr.org> (Once on the page, click the link for "The Status of Women in the States" to see how each of the 50 states ranks on indicators such as political participation, earnings, health and well-being, social autonomy, etc. FYI: Three states tie for being the "best" for women—Massachusetts, Minnesota, and Vermont. The single worst state for women is Mississippi.)

Exercises

1. Using your own experiences and the experiences of friends and classmates, construct a list of paying jobs typically performed by adolescent boys and girls. Be sure to note the activities, duration, and rate of pay that normally characterize these jobs. Discuss the anticipatory socialization (see Essay 6) implications of your findings.

2. Using your college catalog, examine the gender distribution across the various academic departments and administrative levels. Note the total number and percentage of female faculty and administrators. Are women equally likely to appear in all fields and levels of work? Within specific fields and departments, is there any evidence of job-level segregation? (For example, are women more likely to occupy adjunct or assistant professor positions?) Review some recent course registration materials and see whether there is any pattern to the courses assigned to female faculty. Are your findings consistent with the image projected by your institution in its promotional materials?

3. Observe parents with small children in some public setting. Identify 5 to 10 gender lessons being provided by the nonverbal exchanges you observe.

4. Visit the *Institute for Women's Policy Research* Web site and review the information found via the "Status of Women in the States" link. Do you think that the indicators for assessing the status of women are reasonable ones? Are there areas or issues of life that are overlooked or slighted? Would the same indicators work for assessing the status of men?

Essay 13

Conventional Wisdom Tells Us ... America Is the Land of Equal Opportunity

Is the United States a level playing field for all Americans despite race? In this essay, we review the many arenas of continued segregation and racism in the United States. Furthermore, we explore the basis for determining one's race, noting that with all of the implications the classification holds, categorizing race is, at best, a tenuous process.

Several years ago, an editorial in the *Wall Street Journal* (1993) urged civil rights leaders to tone down the rhetoric on racism. The authors argued that although pockets of racism may still exist, equality is winning the day in the United States. Ten years later, the majority of White Americans think that Blacks in their communities have an equal chance of getting jobs for which they are qualified (80%) or getting affordable housing (81%). Ninety-two percent believe that Black children have as good a chance as White children to go to a good public school (ABC News 2003). Most recently, a vocal group of Americans (including the Bush Whitehouse) urged the Supreme Court to reject racial preferences in college admissions. These reports highlight a rather popular sentiment held by many Americans today: If African Americans, Hispanic Americans, or Native Americans fail to succeed, the fault must lie with members of these groups and not with the system at large.

Respondents in one national survey were asked why African Americans have worse jobs, income, and housing than White Americans. Forty-seven percent of White respondents agreed with a statement that offered "a lack of motivation and willpower among Blacks" as an explanation for the phenomenon. Only 31% of Whites (as opposed to 60% of Blacks) feel that Blacks' disadvantaged positions with regard to jobs, income, and housing are mainly due to discrimination (*Public Perspective* 2001). In a National Opinion Research Center (NORC) questionnaire designed to tap *true* rather than *socially appropriate* responses regarding racial/ethnic stereotypes, 62% of respondents rated African Americans as "lazier" than Whites (*Diversity Digest* 1998). Seventy-one percent of Americans think that Blacks, like other past minority groups, should overcome prejudice and work their way up in society without any special favors (General Social Survey 1998). A 2003 Roper poll found that 49% of Americans think that affirmative action programs unfairly discriminate against Whites (Roper Center 2003).

Current conventional wisdom suggests that racial inequality and discrimination are things of the past. Progress has been made, and the nation is now a "level playing field." Are such claims accurate? Has racial equality been achieved in the United States? Furthermore, when inequalities do arise, are they rightfully attributable to race or racism?

Before answering these questions, it is important to define the terms we will be using in this essay. **Race** is typically defined as a group of individuals who share a common genetic heritage or obvious physical characteristics that are deemed socially significant. **Racism** refers to prejudice and discrimination based on the belief that one race is superior to another. **Prejudice** refers to an unfavorable prejudgment of an individual based on the individual's group membership. **Discrimination** refers to unfavorable treatment of individuals on the basis of their group membership.

Public opinion polls do suggest that race relations have improved in the past few years. In 1997, only 31% of Americans thought race relations in the United States were good or excellent. Today, 52% of Americans hold this view. Still, racial divisions in America persist. For example, while a majority of White Americans (54%) have a positive view on race relations in the United States, only 44% of Blacks see it this way. Sixty-six percent of Whites but only 28% of Blacks believe that Blacks receive equal treatment from the police (ABC News/ *Washington Post* 2003). Fifty-five percent of Whites but 83% of Blacks say that racial or ethnic profiling is widespread (Jefferson and Hughes 2003). Nearly one-quarter of Black men report experiencing discrimination in their public lives on a *daily* basis (Gallup Poll 2003). And while nearly half of White Americans oppose affirmative action programs, 70% of Blacks and 63% of Hispanics favor affirmative action (Gallup Poll 2003).

Housing patterns in the United States further underscore America's racial divide. Only 46% of Blacks believe that they have as good a chance as Whites to get affordable housing— 81% of Whites believe this to be true (ABC News/*Washington Post* 2003). In home-buying decisions, Black neighborhood composition matters to White buyers (Emerson, Yancey, and Chai 2001). Other studies find that Blacks are more willing than Whites to live in integrated neighborhoods. While Blacks are comfortable with a 50/50 racial divide, Whites are reluctant to move into areas where more than one-fifth of residents are Black (Krysan 2002; Krysan and Farley 2002).

Attitudes on neighborhood living arrangements reflect actual residential patterns in the United States. Despite the civil rights movement, affirmative action programs, and other equality initiatives, housing segregation is still a fact of American life: A third of Blacks and more than half of Whites live on blocks that are racially homogeneous (*Economist* 2003). In a phenomenon referred to as "tipping," figures show that White residents begin to relocate from neighborhoods when the African American population exceeds the 8% threshold. With African Americans constituting approximately 12% of the U.S. population, the tipping phenomenon makes full integration virtually impossible (Chideya 1995). Research also finds that Blacks, regardless of income, are less successful than Whites in escaping poor neighborhoods (Crowder 2001). Interestingly enough, even when minorities are successful in moving to the suburbs, segregation levels remain stable (Stuart 2003). The practice of "exclusionary zoning" (setting housing construction standards at levels to exclude low and moderate housing developments) also works to keep residential segregation alive (Institute on Race & Poverty 1998). Indeed, housing segregation practices have contributed to the creation of **concentrated-poverty neighborhoods**. This term refers to neighborhoods in which 40% or more of the population is at or below the poverty level. Poverty became more and more concentrated through the 1980s, before the trend was reversed during the 1990s. Still, the share of all high-poverty neighborhoods that are predominantly Black remains high: 39% (Kingsley and Pettit 2003).

Segregated living imposes other financial burdens on racial and ethnic minorities. Minorities living in central cities encounter a shrinking job market: Between 1993 and 1998, more than 14 million jobs were created in the United States, but only 13% of them were located in central cities. The picture becomes even more bleak when we consider "entry-level" jobs. While the entry-level labor *pool* resides in urban areas, the majority of entry-level *jobs* (70%) are located in White suburbs (Institute on Race & Poverty 2002). Ironically, those minorities who try to rectify this mismatch by buying cars for commuting to the suburbs may well find themselves the victims of racial bias in dealer-arranged car loans (Henriques 2000; *New York Times* 2003a).

Furthermore, studies show that home loan applications for Blacks and Hispanics are rejected at a higher rate than those for Whites, regardless of applicants' income levels (Brenner and Spayd 1993; Conner and Smith 1991; Dedman 1989; Institute on Race & Poverty 1998; *Progressive* 2000). And when loans are approved, they are often at less generous amounts and terms and at higher lending rates (*Progressive* 2000). It is not surprising then that Blacks and Hispanics are less likely to own homes and average lower equity in their homes than do Whites (Flippen 2001; Institute on Race & Poverty 2002). When one considers the centrality of home ownership in determining an individual's overall wealth, it becomes clear that the implications of discriminatory practices in the home loan business and the minimal appreciation of homes in minority neighborhoods are profound and long-lasting.

Some sociologists contend that race segregation ultimately translates into knowledge segregation. Despite record national funding in 2001 to bridge the digital divide, the divide remains wide (Dickard 2002). Sixty-one percent of White households have computers versus only 37% of Black and 40% of Hispanic households (U.S. Census Bureau 2002, Table 1135). And Internet access is higher for White households (60%) than for Black (40%) or Hispanic (32%) households (Dickard 2002). Proposed cuts in federal funding will only further disadvantage minorities.

Race bears direct links to inequality in American schools as well. In 1954, the U.S. Supreme Court's *Brown v. Board of Education* decision ordered American schools to desegregate with all deliberate speed. Yet, after 50 years, full integration still eludes schools. In many cases, White communities effectively circumvented the desegregation ruling by relocating their children to private schools. In Mississippi, for instance, court-ordered desegregation was met with a dramatic increase in private segregationist academies (Andrews 2002). In the 1990s, Supreme Court rulings put an end to many desegregation plans in school districts across the nation (Orfield and Eaton 2003). Today, our nation's courts, once champions of desegregation efforts, are declaring more and more school districts "unitary" and therefore released from desegregation plans (Baldas 2003). Public schools are becoming increasingly non-White, with minority enrollments approaching 40%, almost double minority enrollments of the 1960s (Frankenberg, Lee, and Orfield 2003a). From 1972 to 2000, the percentage of White students in public schools dropped from 78% to 61% (U.S. Department of Education 2002). In public schools, nearly half of White students attend schools that are 90% to 100% White (Reardon and Yun 2002). These developments mean that lower levels of interracial exposure—or what some are calling a "resegregation trend"—are occurring in numerous school districts across the nation (Frankenberg and Lee 2002). A resegregation trend has also emerged in private schools. In 1997 to 1998, the average Black private school student was enrolled in a school that was only 34% White—in reality, Black and White private school students are attending separate schools (Reardon and Yun 2002). Residential patterns help explain this development, since over 40% of private schools are located in central cities (Alt and Peter 2002). Even charter schools, touted as solutions to failing public education, are as or more segregated than public schools (Frankenberg et al. 2003b).

When we realize the very strong tie between intensely segregated schools and concentrated poverty, we are that much closer to understanding the inherent inequality of school segregation. Research clearly demonstrates that economically disadvantaged students and schools underperform their more affluent counterparts (Frankenberg and Lee 2002; Orfield et al. 1996; Taubman Center 1999; U.S. Department of Education 2002). The least-advantaged students begin their formal schooling in lower-quality schools. The formal schooling experiences of poor and minority children reinforce and magnify the inequalities between disadvantaged and advantaged students (Lee and Burkam 2002). Not surprisingly, then, academic performance gaps between minority and White students are growing (Gewertz 2003).

Parents who can afford to send their children to private schools reap rewards for their financial investments. Private schools offer advantages over public schools in terms of student/teacher ratios and educational outcomes. Teacher satisfaction across a variety of measures (class size, availability of educational materials, colleagues, parental support, and teaching) is higher in private schools (Alt and Peter 2002). In general, however, private schools have a lower proportion of minority students than do public schools. Within the public school sector, significant contrasts exist between public schools located in predominantly White versus predominantly non-White neighborhoods. Because most public school budgets are tied to local economic resources, schools in wealthy, White neighborhoods fare better than schools in poor, non-White neighborhoods (Cummings 2003). Consider, for instance, that despite the fact that almost all public schools now have access to the Internet, there are still noteworthy differences between White and minority public schools. For example, there is a 20 percentage-point gap between predominantly White schools with instructional Internet classrooms (85%) and predominantly minority schools with such classrooms (64%). In predominantly White public schools, there are six students per instructional computer, while in public schools with high minority enrollments, there are eight students per computer. Continuous Internet connection is available in 80% of White public schools and in 74% of school with high minority enrollments (Cattagni and Farris 2001).

Sociologist Jonathan Kozol (1991, 1995, 2001) dramatically documented the vast resource differences that characterize White versus non-White schools. For example, Kozol found that the poor resources of one predominantly African American Chicago Southside school forced chemistry teachers to use popcorn poppers as Bunsen burners. In contrast, students in a nearby predominantly White suburban school were enjoying a facility that housed seven gyms, an Olympic-sized pool, and separate studios for fencing, dance instruction, and wrestling. Similarly, Kozol found that PS 261 in the South Bronx housed 400 more students than permitted by local fire codes. Just a few bus stops away in the wealthy Riverdale section of the Bronx, PS 24 touted class sizes well below the city average.

In addition to the unequal distribution of resources, researchers note that the lessons taught in predominantly White versus predominantly non-White schools can differ dramatically. Students in predominantly White schools learn to be self-directed, inquisitive, and ambitious. In contrast, students in predominantly non-White schools are taught to obey rules and maintain the status quo (Bowles and Gintis 1976, 2002; Kozol 1991; Miron 1997; Polakow 1993).

After graduation, former students find that racial boundaries are maintained within the workplace as well. In 2002, race discrimination charges were the largest category of filings with the Equal Employment Opportunity Commission (close to 30,000 out of a total of 84,500 filings) (EEOC 2003). Controlled "**paired testing**" hiring experiments (where two equally qualified candidates of different races each apply for the same job) reveal that hiring discrimination is pervasive, affecting approximately 20% of African American job applicants (Bendick, Jackson, and Reinoso 1999; Urban Institute 1999). Other research indicates that employers' perceptions of job candidates' merits are often biased by racial stereotypes (Moss and Tilly 2001). Such findings have prompted a call for a "national report card" on discrimination as well as an expanded "paired testing" program in order to promote public understanding of the prevalence of racial discrimination (Urban Institute 1999).

Once on the job, discrimination continues as minorities on average earn less than Whites. In 2001, the median household income for non-Hispanic Whites, Blacks, and Hispanics was $46,305, $29,470 and $33,565, respectively (DeNavas-Walt and Cleveland 2002). Black men with college degrees earn only 78% of what their White counterparts earn, and Hispanic men with college degrees earn 81%. These gaps grow still larger when minority women enter the equation. Black women working full-time earn only 64% and Hispanic women working full-time earn only 52% of their White male counterparts' wages (National Committee on Pay Equity 2002). Blacks and Hispanics have poverty rates that are nearly three times as high as the rates for Whites (U.S. Census Bureau 2002b)

Evidence of the racial divide makes its way into the entertainment sphere as well. Perhaps one of the most telling signs of racial inequality is found in children's books—a source regarded by some to be important primers for a society's culture. A recent content analysis of children's books found a dearth of Black characters. In addition, depictions of egalitarian interracial interactions were rare (Pescosolido, Grauerholz, and Milkie 1997). Put down the books and pick up the TV remote, and the racial divide reappears. Blacks and Whites in the United States form two distinct TV viewing audiences. Indeed, with the exception of NFL Monday Night Football, there is virtually no overlap between Black and White viewers in the Nielson ratings for the highest-rated top-10 primetime television programs (Ebenkamp 2003; Nielsen Media Research 2003). And while multiethnic TV series have increased in recent years, shows that could be characterized as Black-character-dominant have declined (Freeman 2002).

Clearly, many inequalities still exist in the various sectors of U.S. society. Yet many contend that such inequalities are not the product of racism. Many continue to believe that race, as a biological attribute, indicates some inherent differences in individuals' ability to achieve.

At first glance, this argument may appear valid. Biology would appear to be the unequivocal determinant of racial group distinctions. Thus, different biologies could conceivably lead to different levels of ability. Yet a biological definition of race does not produce a simple or clear racial classification scheme. In fact, identifying groups who share obvious physical characteristics proves a less-than-obvious task.

Using a biological definition of race, biologists and physical anthropologists can "find" as few as 3 or as many as 200+ different races. These classifications are muddied further when we note that generations of intergroup marriage and breeding ensure that no "pure" races exist. Indeed, a remarkable similarity exists across the genes of all humans: Of the DNA molecules that account for racial categories, 95% to 99% are common across all humans (Shipman 1994). Thus, if the human essence is "all in the genes," then racial similarities, not distinctions, are most noteworthy. The genome project has offered consistent evidence that there is only one race: the human race (Angier 2000).

From a biological perspective, "racial differences" are best understood as beneficial, adaptive changes for our human species (Molnar 1991). For instance, the dark skin of peoples living near the equator serves as vital protection against dangerous sun rays. Similarly, the longer, narrow noses found among those living in colder northern climates help to warm the air before it reaches the temperature-sensitive lungs. If the earth were to shift on its axis so that the Northern Hemisphere moved into direct line with the sun, we would expect an adaptive change in the skin color and nose configurations of the northern population (Rensberger 1981). Geography, then, is central to the variations we so readily attribute to race (Lehrman 2003; "Race: The Power of an Illusion" 2003).

A biological approach to the race issue is really insufficient for understanding the dynamics of racial categories. Noted biological anthropologist Alan Goodman has observed that race is not about biology, but rather about an *idea* we *ascribe* to biology ("Race: The Power of an Illusion" 2003). The respected *New England Journal of Medicine* has asserted that "race is biologically meaningless" (Kristof 2003). Indeed, the task of identifying discrete racial categories has largely been abandoned by many physical anthropologists. Sociologists suggest that race is more properly understood as a *social* rather than a biological phenomenon: Race is socially constructed. The **social construction of reality** occurs when individuals create images, ideas, and beliefs about society based on their social interactions.

The social constructionist approach suggests that racial categories emerge from social interaction, social perception, and social opinion. Historians, for instance, observe that the idea of biologically based races was advanced as a way to defend slavery in North America— that is, as a way to justify the unequal treatment of slaves in a land promoting equality (Lee 2003; "Race: The Power of an Illusion" 2003). Social encounters repeatedly expose individuals to specific definitions of race. If these definitions suggest clear and natural boundaries and rankings between various groups of people, the definitions can institutionalize racism as part of a society's stock of knowledge. Such definitions come to reify, or substantiate, racial distinctions that may not be supported in fact. **Reification** refers to the process by which the subjective or abstract erroneously comes to be treated as objective fact or reality. From such a perspective, we must view race as a characteristic that resides in the "eye of the beholder." Change the group doing the perceiving and defining—that is, change the eye of the beholder—and you will change the racial distinctions being made.

For example, it is estimated that more than 70% of Black Americans have some White ancestors (Kilker 1993; Roberts 1975). Yet this biological lineage does not alter public perception. Despite evidence of White ancestry, such individuals are still classified as Black. U.S. classification patterns resulted from a long-standing legal practice that mandated percentage or "one drop of blood" standards for determining racial classifications. Until 1983, for instance, the law of Louisiana dictated that individuals with one-thirty-second of "Negro blood" were properly classified as belonging to the Black race. In the 2000 census, respondents were able to identify themselves as bi- or multiracial by checking more than one race category. Interestingly, however, the "one drop of blood" rule seems to be making a comeback. The U.S. Office of Management and Budget guidelines dictated that anyone marking "White" and any other non-White category be counted as non-White (Goldstein and Morning 2002). Were we to change the standards used for racial classification, however, very different designations of race would emerge. In Brazil, for example, any individual who has "some" White ancestry is classified as belonging to the White race. Consequently, by Brazilian standards, most Black Americans would be classified as White (Denton and Massey 1989).

At first glance, perceptual differences of race may not seem very significant. Such differences merely underscore a major premise of the sociological perspective: Social context is an important factor in understanding, explaining, or predicting human attitudes and behaviors (see the introductory essay). **Social context** refers to the broad social and historical circumstances surrounding an act or an event. But the intriguing nature of race as a social creation becomes clearer when we view it as a significant social status. **Social status** refers to the position or location of an individual with reference to characteristics such as age, education, gender, income, race, religion, and so on.

All of us have many different relationships; social actors all possess a status set. A **status set** refers to the collection of statuses that a social actor occupies. Some of the statuses we occupy are the result of our own personal efforts; these are achieved statuses. An **achieved status** is one earned or gained through personal effort. One's statuses as Red Cross volunteer, parent, or worker are all achieved statuses. In contrast, some of our statuses are "assigned" to us, independent of our personal efforts, desires, or preferences; these are ascribed statuses. An **ascribed status** is one assigned or given without regard to a person's efforts or desires. Age, gender, and racial status are all ascribed statuses.

The average reader of this book will occupy many of the following statuses (try classifying each as "achieved" or "ascribed"): son or daughter, student, friend, spouse, sibling, male or female, citizen, voter, consumer, employee. Often, however, one of our many statuses will dominate the rest. This dominant status forms a master status (see Essay 6). A **master status** is a single social status that overpowers all other social positions occupied by an individual. A master status directs the way in which others see, define, and relate to an individual.

If we consider race in light of these status distinctions, we begin to more fully appreciate the implications of race as a social creation. For although race is a social creation, it is also an ascribed status. As such, race is imposed on the individual; one's race is beyond one's control. Race also frequently serves as a master status. As a master status, race has the ability to influence the social identity and life chances of an individual. **Identity** refers to those essential characteristics that both link us and distinguish us from other social players and thus establish who we are. **Life chances** refer to one's odds of obtaining desirable resources, positive experiences, and opportunities for a long and successful life. For races classified as social minorities, this influence is often negative. A **social minority** is a group regarded as subordinate or inferior to a majority or dominant group. Social minorities are excluded from full participation in society; they experience inferior positions of prestige, wealth, and power.

Note the irony here. Ascribed master statuses are beyond the individual's control. They are assigned, yet they have a remarkable capacity to control the individual. Indeed, certain ascribed master statuses can prove more important to one's identity than personal efforts. The irony intensifies when we acknowledge that race, an assigned status, is nonetheless a social creation. Racial designations can change as audience perceptions change.

The significance of these last few points becomes more apparent when we reconsider the real-life consequences of racial designations:

- In 2001, the poverty rate was 7.8% for Whites, 22.7% for Blacks, and 21.4% for Hispanics (Proctor and Dalaker 2002).
- In 2000, 93% of White children but only 87% of Black children and 75% of Hispanic children were covered by health insurance (U.S. Department of Health and Human Services 2002).
- Approximately 26% of the White population earns at least a college degree compared with only 16.5% of the African American population and approximately 11% of Hispanic Americans (U.S. Census Bureau 2002, Table 208).
- The high school dropout rates for 16- to 24 year-olds reach 7.3% for Whites, 10.9% for Blacks, and 27% for Hispanics (U.S. Department of Education 2003).
- As of 2000, the average life expectancy for Whites was just over 77 years. Life expectancy for African Americans was almost 6 years shorter, at 71.7 years (U.S. Census Bureau 2002, Table 91).
- The infant mortality rate for White babies is under 6 deaths per 1,000 live births. The rate for African American babies is almost 15 deaths (Children's Defense Fund 2002).

Indeed, take any set of statistics regarding life chances—health and illness rates, divorce rates, crime victimization rates, death rates, and so on—and you will undoubtedly come to the conclusion that race matters.

This essay suggests that racial distinctions cannot be equated with biological or genetic differences. Race is not a simple matter of physiology. Rather, racial distinctions are more properly understood as social creations. Skin color proves the primary marker of racial distinctions in U.S. society; other cultures have focused on such characteristics as height or hair and eye color. No matter what a society's marker, once certain characteristics are deemed worthier than others—that is, once racial categories are created—powerful social processes such as prejudice and discrimination are set into motion.

Still, race has proven itself a highly dynamic process; the human species has shown a remarkable capacity to adapt to environmental demands. The pressing question for today and the near future is whether our social definition of race will prove equally adaptive to changes in our social and cultural environments. It is presently projected that by the year 2050, the United States will be a land where Whites will be a numerical minority. Given these projected demographic changes, rethinking the race issue may well be a social and cultural necessity. Perhaps by stressing the *social* nature and origins of racial distinctions, we will find that such distinctions are more amenable to change than conventional wisdom currently allows.

Learning More About It

To learn more about the continued presence of racial inequality in the United States, see the most recent edition of Andrew Hacker's *Two Nations: Black and White, Separate, Hostile, Unequal* (New York: Simon and Schuster, 2003b). Statistical tables and analyses are included.

W.E.B. Du Bois offers a classic treatise on the dynamics of U.S. race relations in *The Souls of Black Folks* (New York: Penguin, 1982; original work published 1903). Cornel West thoughtfully grapples with issues of race in a more contemporary book entitled *Race Matters* (New York: Random House, 1994). Similarly engaging is F. James Davis's very readable book *Who Is Black: One Nation's Definition* (University Park, PA: Penn State University Press, 1991). The work offers a history of the "one drop rule. An excerpt from the book can be found in the PBS *Frontline* show, "Jefferson's Blood: Mixed Race America: Who is Black? One Nation's Definition." See: <http://www.pbs.org/wgbh/pages/frontline/shows/jefferson/mixed/onedrop.html>

In *The Declining Significance of Race: Blacks and Changing American Institutions,* 2nd edition (Chicago: University of Chicago Press, 1980), William Julius Wilson posits the controversial thesis that social class is more significant than race in defining opportunities for African Americans. In a later work, Wilson gives special attention to the plight of Blacks caught in the grip of the inner-city underclass. See *The Truly Disadvantaged: The Inner City, The Underclass, and Public Policy* (Chicago: University of Chicago Press, Reprint Edition, 1990).

New York Times correspondents offer a series of essays that capture how race is experienced in our day-to-day lives and relationships in *How Race Is Lived in America* (New York: Times Books, 2001).

You can also consult the following organizations/sites to learn more about race and ethnic relations in America and abroad:

Equal Employment Opportunity Commission
1801 L Street NW
Washington, DC 20507
1(800) 669–4000
Web site: <http://www/eeoc.gov.>

Institute on Race and Poverty
415 Law Center
229 19th Ave. South
Minneapolis, MN 55455
    E-mail: *irp@tc.umn.edu*; Web site: <*http: //www1.umn.edu/irp/.*>

AntiRacismNet (an international online network for those interested in supporting the fight against racism)
<*http://www.antiracismnet.org/main.html*>
E-mail: antiracism@antiracismnet.org

National Urban League
120 Wall Street
New York, NY 10005

1 (201) 558–5300
E-mail: info@nul.org
<Web site: http://www.nul.org>

On the PBS Web site, you can "re-view" the station's recent series on race: *Race: The Power of an Illusion.*" In addition to accessing each program segment, you can also pose questions to some of the most eminent scientists in the field: <http://www.pbs.org/race/000_General/ 000_00-Home.htm>

Exercises

1. Imagine that height is a critical marker for social ranking in the United States: shortness valued, tallness devalued. Speculate on the ways in which the social structure of your hometown might change if residential, educational, and occupational patterns influenced by prejudice and discrimination were based on human height.

2. Racial categories are social creations that emerge from social interaction. Gather a sample of ads from two magazines that target different classes of readers. For instance, one magazine might be targeting an elite readership (for example, *Martha Stewart Living* or *Gourmet*), whereas the second might target a more general, less affluent readership (for example, *Family Circle* or *Good Housekeeping*). Are racial lessons delivered through these ads? Do the ads indicate any differences in life aspirations by race or ethnic group? Consider the data on life chances as presented in this essay. How does reality compare to the lifestyles projected in your sample ads?

Deviance, Crime, and Social Control

Essay 14

Conventional Wisdom Tells Us ... Violence Is on the Rise in the United States—No One Is Safe

In recent decades, Americans have wrestled with a growing fear of violence. Is that fear justified? Here we review the state of violence in America, and we explore those instances in which the public's fears of violence are justified and those in which they are exaggerated. As such, the essay explores the many problems surrounding the detection and perception of danger and crime.

James Martin, 55, was a programs analyst at the National Oceanic Atmospheric Administration. He was a Civil War enthusiast and the father of an 11-year-old son. Conrad Johnson, 35, was a Maryland bus driver for 10+ years. He had two children and a wife, all of whom he loved. Linda Franklin, 47, was an analyst with the FBI's cyber division. A wife and mother, she boasted one other major accomplishment: She was a proud breast cancer survivor. Three lives, three separate paths. Yet one critical element drew these 3 together and tragically connected them to 10 other horribly unlucky people. Martin, Franklin, and Johnson belonged to the group of 13 who were killed or injured by the "D.C. Snipers" in the fall of 2002.

It was a fall like no other in the Washington, D.C., area. Public space became dangerous turf, with routine trips to the post office, the local food store, or hardware shop becoming potentially life-threatening events. In the space of a few short weeks, people were changing their way of "being." Trips to the store were made only out of absolute necessity. Area middle schools and high schools were relocating their outdoor sporting events. People were simply "looking over their shoulders" . . . until October 24, 2002. On that day, snipers John Allen Muhammad and John Lee Malvo were finally captured.

The D.C. Sniper story is not the most famous of the decade; it is not the most unusual or the most brutal narrative of our time. Rather, this entire incident represents just one of many violent events—events that, some argue, have become a routine feature of modern life.

When Americans are asked to name the country's most troubling problems, they rank violent crime very high on the list (Gallup 1976–2003). Drive-by shootings, gang warfare, metal detectors at the doors of our schools, yellow and orange terror alerts: In the "new" millennium, these images have become all too common, and they are images that can provoke a sense of fear and panic. Americans are acting on their fears. Recent polls show that Americans are increasing the number of protective measures they take against murderers and other violent criminals. Record numbers are installing special locks or alarms in their homes, buying dogs or guns for protection, changing their nighttime walking patterns, and minimizing contact with strangers (Wirthlin Report 2001).

Is the rising fear of violence justified? Is conventional wisdom correct in suggesting that our streets have become more dangerous than ever before? Just how likely is it that any one of us will become the victim of a violent crime?

Americans do indeed face a greater risk of violence than the inhabitants of many other nations in the world. Murder, for example, as well as violent crimes such as assault, rape, and robbery occur three to eight times more frequently in the United States than in the developed nations of Europe. The United States also has higher rates of violent crime than nations suffering from intense poverty or political turmoil—places such as Costa Rica, Croatia, Greece, India, Indonesia, Yemen, and so on (Interpol 2003; Nationmaster 2003).

Rates of violence in the United States relative to rates found in other world nations suggest that violence is a serious problem for Americans. At first glance, such rates seem to support the conventional wisdom that violence is on the rise. However, recent international statistics tell us that things in the United States may be changing. The tide of violence may be turning in Americans' favor.

Each year, the FBI provides statistics on crime in the *Uniform Crime Reports Index for Serious Crime* (hereafter referred to as the *UCRs*). According to the *UCRs,* violent crime in the United States reached an all-time high in 1992; the nation had over 1.92 million incidents of murder, rape, robbery, and aggravated assault. But recent statistics show that the number of violent crimes has dropped significantly. In 2002, the nation had approximately 1.44 million acts of violence. That number represents nearly a 25% decrease in the violent crime rate. Many are hopeful that this trend will continue into the new century (U.S. Department of Justice 2002).

To be sure, many will argue that official statistics such as the *UCRs* grossly underestimate violence in America. **Victimization studies,** that is, statistics based on victims' self-reports and not the reports of police, present a picture of violent crime that differs significantly from the one painted by the FBI. For example, statistics from the National Crime Victimization

Survey estimate that just over 7 million Americans fell victim to violent crime in 2001 (U.S. Department of Justice 2001b). Similarly, the Family Violence Prevention Fund (2003) argues that as many as 3 million women experience domestic abuse each year (also see Tjaden and Thoennes 2000). And both the Administration of Children and Families (2001) and the Children's Defense Fund (2000) contend that between 1 and 3 million cases of child abuse occur in the United States each year.

Just as some researchers criticize the *UCRs* for underestimating violent crime, other researchers criticize victimization studies for overestimating the problem. Which statistics are correct? Experts in the field disagree, but the key point to remember is this: *All* statistics on violent crime—*UCRs* and victimization surveys alike—show a similar decrease in the violent crime rate from 1992 to the present.

If, as statistics suggest, violent crime is waning, then what explains Americans' persistent—even increasing—fear of violence? Even with decreasing rates, does violent crime occur with staggering frequency?

Violent crime cannot be described as a frequent event. Indeed, within the world of crime, violence is quite rare. FBI statistics show that, overall, property crimes (e.g., arson, auto theft, burglary, and larceny) occur 7.3 times more often than violent crimes. (Victimization surveys suggest a similar relationship, with property crime rates 6.75 times higher than violent crime rates.) More specifically, the FBI notes that the typical American is 132 times more likely to be burglarized than murdered and 77 times more likely to be a victim of theft than of rape. Indeed, when it comes to fatal victimization, statistics show that Americans are more likely to take their own lives than to be killed by violent criminals (U.S. Census Bureau 2002, Table 100; U.S. Department of Justice 2001b, 2002).

Given the relative rarity of violent crime, what other factors might explain Americans' growing fear of violence? Some suggest this fear may be linked to the perceived randomness of such crimes. Americans tend to view violence as an event that can strike anyone at any time. As conventional wisdom states, "No one is safe." Crime statistics, however, do not substantiate this image (Macmillan 2001). Consider the act of murder. Most Americans picture murder as an unpredictable attack that is likely to be perpetrated by a stranger. Yet "friendly murders"—that is, murders committed by relatives, friends, or acquaintances of the victim—are over three times more common than murders perpetrated by strangers. Furthermore, far from being random, murder exhibits several striking social patterns. For example, murder is a crime of the young. An individual's risk of being murdered peaks at age 25, regardless of race or gender. (Recall from Essay 6 that senior citizens are most fearful of violent crime, yet crime statistics show that seniors are least likely to become murder victims.) Murder also is a "male" crime; more than 85% of all perpetrators and 70% of all victims are male. Note, too, that murder systematically varies by race; it is an overwhelmingly intraracial crime. Whites tend to murder other Whites, Blacks tend to murder other Blacks, and so on. The crime of murder also occurs disproportionately among the poor. In addition, socioeconomic status appears related to when and how a murder occurs. Members of the

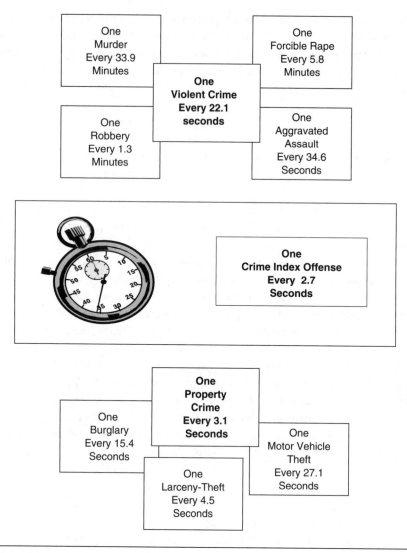

Figure 14.1   FBI Time Clock, 2000
SOURCE: U. S. Department of Justice (2001a).

lower socioeconomic strata, for instance, are most likely to be murdered on a Saturday night, and the grizzly event is likely to involve alcohol and emotions. In contrast, members of the upper strata are murdered with equal frequency during all days and times of the week. In addition, murders among the "privileged" typically result from premeditation rather than passion (U.S. Department of Justice 2002).

Statistics on other violent crimes dispel the myth of random violence as well. Rape, for example, is rarely the product of a surprise attack. Indeed, rapes by strangers account for only about a third of such crimes. Similarly, simple assault usually takes place between intimates, the result of a building animosity between two individuals. Intimacy is especially character- istic of assaults involving female victims. Women are several times more likely to be attacked by an intimate or an acquaintance than they are to be attacked by a stranger (U.S. Census Bureau 2002, Table 296; U.S. Department of Justice 2001b, 2002).

Our visions of violence seem not to match the realities of the world around us (Altheide 2002; Glassner 1999). Contrary to perceptions of violence on the rise, high frequency of occurrence, and randomness of violent events, violent crimes are relatively rare, highly patterned, and decreasing in recent years. Given these facts, what else might explain Americans' persistent fears and misperceptions?

One might be tempted to explain these fears by referring to the high personal cost of violence—namely, serious injury or death. However, if the risk of injury or death alone stimulated such fears, we would find similar trepidation surrounding other high-injury and high-mortality settings. Consider the area of occupational-related injuries and deaths. Although fewer than 20,000 Americans are murdered each year, some studies estimate that over 60,000 U.S. workers die annually due to occupational disease or unsafe working condi- tions. Similarly, while the FBI estimates that approximately 1.7 million Americans become victims of violent crime, some estimates suggest that nearly 4 million suffer physical harm on the job. Despite the staggering figures on occupational disease and death, Americans' fear of the work setting is negligible relative to their fear of violent crime (Leigh et al. 1997; Reiman 2004; U.S. Census Bureau 2002, Table 621). Now consider life on American roads. Americans are more than twice as likely to die in automobile accidents as they are to be mur- dered, and nearly twice as likely to be injured in an automobile accident as they are to be injured by a violent criminal. However, few would cite a level of fear that precludes one's "taking to the roads" (*World Almanac* 2003).

Considerations regarding the reality and cost of violent crime contribute little to our understanding of Americans' intense fear of violence. Violence in the United States is clearly a problem, but violence does not appear to warrant the level of fear expressed by the American public. As a result, some sociologists contend that Americans' fear of violence may in part be socially constructed. The **social construction of reality** occurs when indi- viduals create images, ideas, and beliefs about society based on their social interactions. The social constructionist approach suggests that certain social encounters expose individ- uals repeatedly to information on violence—information that suggests that violent crime is on the rise and that it occurs frequently, randomly, or at the hands of strangers. As a result, these data—even though they represent misinformation—come to form the public's "reality" of violence.

The mass media, especially television, are the greatest source of misinformation on violence. The National Television Violence Study (1996–1998) as well as longitudinal research conducted by scholars at the Annenberg School of Communication (Diefenbach and West 2001; Gerbner et al. 2002) provide a wealth of evidence on this point. Researchers involved in these projects have meticulously analyzed the content found in sample weeks of prime-time and daytime television. Their findings show that the rates of violent crime in "TV land" are disproportionately high compared with real-world figures.

Sixty one percent of television programs contain some type of violence. During any week-night, viewers see an average of 3 violent acts per hour. On Saturday mornings, a time period dominated by child viewers, the rate of violence increases to 18 violent acts per hour. Furthermore, some studies estimate that by the time most children leave high school, they have viewed approximately 13,000 murders on TV! The figures on TV violence are signifi-cant, for they suggest a world quite different from everyday reality. In the real world, less than 1% of all Americans become involved in violence. In TV land, 64% of all characters are involved in violence. Therefore, those who rely on television as their window on reality may come to view the world as a perilously dangerous place (Diefenbach and West 2001; Gerbner et al 2002; National Television Violence Study 1996–1998).

To substantiate this claim, the Annenberg research group regularly compares both heavy and light television viewers with regard to their perceptions of violence. Respondents partic-ipating in these studies are asked a series of questions requiring them to estimate rates of murder, rape, and assault. Respondents are generally presented with two choices in making these estimates. One choice typically reflects real rates of violence in the United States, whereas the other choice better reflects rates of violence in TV land.

In each of the Annenberg studies, results consistently show that heavy television viewers are much more likely to overestimate rates of violence than those who watch little or no tele-vision. Heavy television viewers routinely favor TV-land estimates of violence over real-world estimates. Furthermore, heavy television viewers perceive the world to be a more dangerous place than those who watch little or no TV. Thus, heavy viewers are more likely than light viewers to take the protective measures mentioned earlier: installing special locks or alarms in their homes, buying dogs or guns for protection, or changing their nighttime walking patterns (Diefenbach and West 2001; Gerbner et al. 2002; Signorielli, Gerbner, and Morgan 1995; Signorielli and Morgan 1988).

Complementing the social constructionist view, some suggest that Americans' dispropor-tionate fear of violent crime emerges from a long-standing cultural value that supports a fear of strangers. A **cultural value** is a general sentiment that people share regarding what is good or bad, right or wrong, desirable or undesirable. A **fear of strangers** refers to a dread or suspicion of those who look, behave, or speak differently from oneself. Such fears can ultimately make the world seem unfamiliar and dangerous.

In the United States, cultural values instill a sense of mistrust and foreboding toward those we do not know. Couple this phenomenon with the fact that most Americans view violent crime as "stranger crime," and the misinformation that links violence to an already feared social category—strangers—serves to exacerbate and perpetuate public fears of such crimes (McDonald 2003; President's Commission on Law Enforcement and Administration of Justice 1968).

The public's misplaced fears and misperceptions of violence are not without serious consequences. Such misconceptions sometimes result in the ineffective control of the crime. For example, high-profile murder cases such as the Rabbi Fred Neulandert case in New Jersey, the Toni Riggs case in Detroit, or the Susan Smith case in South Carolina illustrate the danger of equating murder with strangers. In these cases, the murder victims were killed by immediate family members: Neulandert and Riggs murdered their spouses; Smith murdered her children. Yet in all cases, resistance to the notion of "friendly" murder initially led to the detention of innocent people. (The false leads in the Riggs and Smith cases also involved Black males; indeed, 35 Black males were questioned in the Smith case.) Such "mistakes" substantiate the power of socially constructed scripts—scripts that depict the "typical" nature of murder and the "probable" perpetrator of the crime (Brown 1994; McDonald 2003).

Misplaced fears and misperceptions of violence also can detract attention from the critical sites of violence in the United States. To be sure, Americans display greater concern for violent crimes on our nation's streets than they do for violence in the home. Yet sociologist Richard Gelles notes that aside from the police and the military, the family is the single most violent institution in our society (Gelles and Loseke 1993; Gelles and Straus 1988; Mignon, Larson, and Holmes 2002; Ruane 1993; Straus 2001; Straus and Gelles 1990; Straus, Gelles, and Steinmetz 1980).

Finally, some worry that the constant bombardment of violent media programming, as well as the ways in which violent stories are told—for example, the vantage point of the viewer, the context of violence, the response of other characters to the perpetrator—will eventually desensitize readers and viewers to real-world violence. Constant media exposure may make readers and viewers more tolerant of violent acts in the real world (Cerulo 1998; Gerbner et al. 2002; National Television Violence Study 1996–1998).

If Americans' fear of violence is socially constructed and our perceptions of violent crime are inaccurate, should society shift its attention from the issue of violence? We suggest nothing of the kind. To be sure, any instance of violence represents one death or one injury too many. In this sense, violence may indeed be all too common in the United States. As a nation, we appear to be making strides in reducing the incidence of violence. Can levels of violence in the United States be further reduced? It is difficult to say, but any solutions to the violence problem require us to adopt a more accurate picture of the scope and patterns that characterize violent crime in America.

Learning More About It

To keep track of yearly increases and decreases in violent crime, visit the FBI's Web site and read the FBI's *Uniform Crime Reports.* The address is <http://www.fbi.gov/ ucr/01cius.htm>

One can also follow results from the National Crime Victimization Survey at the Justice Department's Web site: <http://www.ojp.usdoj.gov/bjs/glance/tables/viotrdtab.htm>

Mary R. Jackman provides a wonderful summary of current research on violence in her article "Violence in Social Life," *Annual Review of Sociology* 28: 387–415, 2002.

The *National Crime Prevention Council* provides information on building safer, stronger communities. Visit their Web site at <http://www.ncpc.org/>

Barry Glassner offers an engaging look at the culture of fear in America. See T*he Culture of Fear: Why Americans Are Afraid of the Wrong Things* (New York: Basic Books, 1999). David Altheide offers a very readable excursion on the media's role in creating a culture of fear. See *Creating Fear: News and the Construction of Crisis* (New York: Aldine de Gruyter, 2002).

The *National Television Violence Study (1996–1998)* provides a comprehensive look at the amount of violence on TV, its nature, and the contexts in which it is presented (Thousand Oaks, CA: Sage). Jonathan L. Freeman provides a meta-analysis of research on violence, attempting to determine what we know to date on the effects of media violence; see *Media Violence and Its Effects on Aggression: Assessing the Scientific Evidence* (Toronto: University of Toronto Press, 2002). And Jennings Bryant and Dolf Zillmann have assembled an informative collection of articles on cultivation analysis and other media theories. See *Media Effects: Advances in Theory and Research,* 2nd edition (Mahwah, NJ: Lawrence Erlbaum, 2002).

Karen A. Cerulo explores ways in which the media may be increasing public tolerance of violence. Consult *Deciphering Violence: The Cognitive Structure of Right and Wrong* (New York: Routledge, 1998).

A classic essay by Georg Simmel, "The Stranger," offers an insightful exploration into our cultural beliefs about those we do not know; see *The Sociology of Georg Simmel,* edited by K. Wolff (pp. 402–408, New York: Free Press, 1950b).

Silvia Mignon, Calvin Larson, and William Holmes offer an exhaustive review of family violence in *Family Abuse: Consequences, Theories, and Responses* (Boston: Allyn & Bacon, 2002).

Exercises

1. Interview from 10 to 15 people about their working "models" of crime. Be sure to obtain information on such things as the appearance of the typical criminal, the location of the typical crime, the typical criminal offense, and so on. Determine whether a general model emerges, and discuss how this model allows certain acts to escape the label "criminal."

2. This essay provides a detailed profile of the social patterns of murder: age, gender, site, and social class. Go to your local or university library and collect similar statistics for the crimes of burglary, larceny, and auto theft. Based on your data, speculate on the ways in which the "face" of murder differs from the "face" of property crimes.

3. Visit the FBI's Web page (<http://www.fbi.gov>) and secure the most recent rates for murder, rape, assault, and robbery. Then create a "multiple-choice" test designed to tap

individuals' perceptions of violent crime rates. Your survey might include questions such as the following:

In the United States, _____ murders occur each year:

(a) 5,000   (b) 20,000   (c) 50,000   (d) 100,000

Administer your survey to 10 to 15 people you know to be avid TV watchers and 10 to 15 people you know to be only occasional TV watchers. Compare the answers of heavy and light TV viewers. Which group better estimated the actual violent crime rate?

Essay 15

Conventional Wisdom
Tells Us . . . There Ought to Be a Law

There's no social ill that the law can't fix . . . or at least that is what many Americans believe. In this essay, we review various social functions of the law. We also consider whether or not we are overly dependent on this tool of formal social control.

"There ought to be a law" . . . it's a phrase that expresses Americans' penchant for the law. In the United States, no social realm is exempt from the rule of law. Indeed, law is a pervasive feature of American society. Family, civic duties, education, business and commerce, religion, government, even birth and death are regulated by law. Leave this world without your legal pass (i.e., a will or a trust) and your "life" (as it were) will become the domain of probate courts and lawyers.

Americans pride themselves on being a land of laws. The U.S. Constitution, our most cherished legal document, is invoked by liberal and conservative, law-abiding and law-violating individuals alike. Americans trust in the law and symbolically display it as "blind" to status differences. The law, it is argued, renders all parties equal before the scales of justice. No one in the United States, not even the president, is considered above the law. (A few years back, Kenneth Starr rather dramatically reminded Bill Clinton of this fact.) Americans expect great things of the law and are quick to express their displeasure and disappointment when the law behaves badly. (A decision by a Michigan judge to settle a holiday visitation conflict by flipping a coin received national coverage in February 2002. One party to the conflict felt the judge's behavior made a mockery of the judicial process; the judge's superiors agreed that the incident hurt the judicial process [Ashenfelter 2002]).

Many sociologists contend that social control represents the dominant function of the law. **Social control** refers to the process of enforcing social norms. **Norms** are social rules or guidelines that direct behavior. Social control can be informal or formal. **Informal social control** can be initiated by any party; no special status or training is required. It includes such mechanisms as socialization, gossip, ridicule, shaming, praise, or rewards. **Formal social control** is state centered. The law as a tool of formal social control is legitimated and enforced by the power of the state.

In recognizing the law's social control function, we acknowledge it as a vehicle for achieving and maintaining social order and stability. The law steps in when informal social control tactics fail to get the job done. For the most part, people readily appreciate the social control function of the law. Most would agree that certain behaviors—murder, robbery, assault, burglary, arson—are clearly social wrongs deserving the law's attention. Few would question the need to regulate such norm violations. Indeed, most would rail at the dangers posed by the absence of law in response to these behaviors.

The law, however, serves other social functions—functions about which one finds less public consensus. In addition to operating as a tool of social control, the law can function as a tool of **social engineering**. In this capacity, the law is constructed to satisfy social wants and to bring about desired social change.

Law for the sake of social engineering poses dilemmas for societies. Whose wants and desires should such law promote? Whose ideas of right and wrong should the law encode? Can we rightfully enact law that pushes forward a specific moral agenda?

Despite the dilemmas posed by socially engineered law, there is no shortage of statutes and regulations that fit into this category. Indeed, the United States boasts a substantial historical record in which certain groups have legislated right and wrong—even amid the outcries of others. The "roaring 20s" provide perhaps the most notorious example of this process. In 1919, the National Prohibition Act (a.k.a. the Volstead Act) made the sale, manufacture, and transportation of liquor, beer, and wine illegal in the United States. In part, the Volstead Act resulted from efforts of middle-class groups to counteract the vices of newly arrived immigrants (Gusfield 1963). As is the case for many instances of social engineering law, however, not everyone agreed with the act's definition of right and wrong. As a result, the passage of the Volstead Act spurred several unintended consequences. For example, outlawed "saloons" were quickly replaced by newly devised "speakeasies." Hardware stores began to stock and sell portable stills. Libraries supplied instructional books and pamphlets needed for distilling homemade "hootch." California vintners (who actually expanded their acreage during Prohibition) introduced "Vine-glo," a grape juice that with proper care and time (60 days) could be turned into wine. Brewers followed suit, manufacturing and selling "wort," a half-brewed liquid that could be turned into beer with the simple addition of yeast. And since the Volstead Act allowed the sale of alcohol for medicinal purposes, doctors began writing alcohol prescriptions, and pharmacists began filling them in unprecedented numbers (Time-Life Books 1988). In short, Americans responded to the social-engineering nature of the Volstead Act by designing creative ways in which to avoid, evade, and ignore the law.

Americans' rebellious response to the Volstead Act was not an isolated incident. Many argue that certain drug laws have encouraged similar activities (Campos 1998). Here again, the actions of moral entrepreneurs have had unintended consequences. **Moral entrepreneurs** are individuals who seek to legally regulate behaviors that they consider morally reprehensible. Like Prohibition, efforts to criminalize certain drugs have created an extremely lucrative black market in illicit drugs. Drugs that have a negligible pharmaceutical value now command hundreds of dollars on the streets. Furthermore, the financial incentive associated with drug trafficking has provided an irresistible career option for certain individuals. Some would also argue that the legal prohibition of particular drugs assures that increasingly potent and harmful forms of illicit drugs will continue to enter the illegal drug market. Former Baltimore Mayor Schmoke maintains that this scenario accurately describes the emergence of crack cocaine (Mills 1992).

The examples just cited illustrate the dangers posed when we use law as a tool of social engineering. Equating the law with general public sentiment is a tricky business. In modern, complex societies where there are multiple "publics," there is no simple relationship between public opinion and the law. Thus, the ability to translate social wants and desires into law involves social power more than social consensus. Why have antismoking campaigns and legislation been so successful? Some would argue that it's all about power and status politics—smoking is inversely related to social class and status (Tuggle and Holmes 1997).

When special interests successfully mobilize resources on behalf of their own causes, the "law" can come to contradict the general public will. In such cases, Americans cling to a belief in equality before the law, but they also understand that lawmakers consider some people more equal than others. Consider these words about U.S. lawmakers penned by noted legal scholar Lawrence Friedman (1975):

> They know that 100 wealthy, powerful constituents passionately opposed to socialized medicine, outweigh thousands of poor, weak constituents, mildly in favor of it. Most people . . . remain quiet and obscure . . . This is the "silent majority" . . . (P. 164).

While these words were written more than a quarter of a century ago, they prove timely. Recent failed efforts to achieve health care reform by the U.S. Congress offer compelling evidence in this regard: A single, silent majority still encounters great difficulty when attempting to make its voice heard over that of a smaller but more powerful special interest group.

Is it socially harmful when law becomes disconnected from general public opinion? Some maintain that laws that contradict public sentiment breed contempt and, more important, disregard. Consider the following examples. Unrealistic speed limits have invited many drivers to disregard traffic laws. Sunday "blue laws" or laws prohibiting the sales of cigarettes and alcohol to minors have placed many merchants on the wrong side of the law. Many middle- and upper-class families procure child care providers and housekeepers as a means of making their busy lives easier, but some individuals do so at the cost of violating tax and immigration laws.

Social control or social engineering: Regardless of its social function, law is a dominant force in American society. One legal scholar observes that our devotion to reason leads us to legally regulate more and more of our social interactions. We use the law to satisfy our metaphysical anxieties (Campos 1998). As these formal rules come to dominate our lives, the potential for legal work grows and grows. Since the 1960s, the law represents the fastest-growing profession in the United States (Vago 2003). Our nation averages more lawyers per person than any other modern industrial society. And despite the high population density of lawyers, the law is still a popular career option for college graduates. During the 1990s, approximately 40,000 law degrees were conferred annually (U.S. Census Bureau 2002, Table 281).

Against this backdrop of a legally saturated society, the United States has also acquired a reputation as a rather litigious society. Many argue that lawsuits have become Americans' favorite pastime. Have you ever sustained a burn from an overly hot cup of coffee? Sue! (In 1992, a New Mexico woman sued McDonald's for compensatory and punitive damages after sustaining third-degree burns when a cup of McDonald's coffee spilled into her lap.) Has your favorite sports team been hurt by unpopular trades? Sue! (In 1997, fans of the Florida Marlins turned into plaintiffs when they filed a lawsuit over the breakup of the 1997 World Series title team.) Are you unhappy with the job your parents are doing? Sue! (In the early 1990s, a child sought and obtained a "divorce" from his biological parents (Tippet 1993). Not pleased with the census-driven reapportionment of congressional seats? Sue! (In 2001, Utah sued the Census Bureau in an effort to secure a House seat lost to North Carolina). Are you an overweight fan of fast foods? Sue! (In 2002, several Americans filed lawsuits against McDonald's, Burger King, etc., arguing that the chains had not provided adequate warning about the dangers of overeating fast foods.) Not pleased that your high school wants you to share the valedictorian title with another student? Sue! (In spring of 2003, a New Jersey high school student sued her Moorestown school district and won the right to be the solo class valedictorian.) Indeed each year, Americans address the wrongs they experience in life by filing civil lawsuits. **Civil lawsuits** are generally private legal proceedings for the enforcement of a right or the redressing of a wrong.

High-profile cases such as those just mentioned receive much popular press and prompt many to conclude that Americans are an excessively litigious group. Indeed, President Bush (as well as many others) believes that frivolous lawsuits are the cause of an emerging health care crisis that sees physicians abandoning their medical practices because of high malpractice insurance premiums. The issue strikes President Bush as important enough to be part of his domestic agenda and reelection campaign efforts (Stolberg 2003a). Some social observers expect the malpractice lawsuit reform effort to be a particularly interesting exchange since it pits two high-power interest groups against each other: doctors and lawyers (Stolberg 2003b). The charge of excessive litigation is also made with regard to **class action suits**, or litigation where one or more persons bring a civil lawsuit on behalf of other similarly situated individuals. To be sure, some regard malpractice suits and class action suits as threats to health care and to big business, and as negative manifestations of greedy plaintiffs and still greedier lawyers. Others, however, are less inclined to cast litigation in such a negative light. Ever-increasing malpractice insurance premiums may be attributed to the pecuniary interests of insurance companies who want to recover stiff Wall Street losses of the past few years. A recent report by the Missouri Department of Insurance maintains that the number of malpractice claims is actually trending down, not up (Stearns 2003). Others argue that lawsuits are essential tools for achieving social justice and reform. What can't be achieved via legislation or regulation might nonetheless be accomplished via litigation (Hensler 2001). John Banzhaf, a key legal player in the current efforts to sue the junk-food industry, believes that such action may help America come to grips with its increasing obesity problems and thereby serve the public interest (Gumbel 2002).

While Americans may seem enamored with legal remedies, it is important to note that the law is not our most-utilized social control tool. More than one-third of Americans will experience legal problems each year, but only about 10% of us will take the matter to an attorney (Vago 1997). Even after legal proceedings are initiated, it is unlikely that the matter will progress to trial: Either parties settle cases or judges decide them on legal motions. Consequently, there are those who argue that that charges of a litigation explosion in the United States are unfounded (Glaberson 1999; Moller 1996). For some, the most notable change in legal work has been the increase in work for corporations and the government, while work for individual clients has remained relatively stable (Heinz, Nelson, and Laumann 2001). Similarly, while there is growing concern about the use of class action suits, in fact such suits constitute a very small percentage of the total civil caseload (Hensler 2001). Instead, much litigation is essentially a business matter, that is, businesses suing other businesses (Heinz et al. 2001). Furthermore, in recent years, more and more alternative dispute resolution (ADR) processes such as mediation and arbitration are being considered as reasonable alternatives to adjudication.

Contrary to the notion of a litigation explosion, some statistics suggest that America is a nation of legal restraint. For example, California's State Judicial Council reports a significant decline in personal injury and motor vehicle lawsuit filings in that state since the late 1980s: 39% and 46%, respectively (Consumer Attorneys of California 1995). Similarly, a recent study of Wisconsin lawyers reveals that the typical lawyer will turn down more cases than he accepts (Kritzer 1997).

What explains this legal restraint? One contributing factor is cost. The practice of law is expensive. Many Americans with legal problems cannot afford to resolve them via the law. (Indeed, the high cost of legal action is one reason that some persons resort to a class action suit—it can make the cost of litigation more affordable for persons suffering moderate financial loses.) This is true despite the fact that lawyers frequently accept cases on a contingency fee basis. In contingency fee cases, attorneys receive compensation only if they prevail in collecting damages for their clients. While this arrangement can motivate attorneys to seek high damages, it also assures that attorneys will refrain from taking meritless or weak cases. Pursuing no-win cases is a losing proposition. Thus, despite the rather common belief that contingency fee arrangements encourage litigation, the evidence does not support this view. A recent study by the U.S. Department of Justice reveals that punitive damages were awarded in only 3% of jury verdicts reached in the 75 largest counties of the country (U.S. Department of Justice 1995). Punitive damages in product liability cases are even rarer (Moller 1996). Taken together, expense and smaller financial payoffs keep many wronged individuals out of court. In its *2002 Annual Report,* the Judicial Council of California credits declines in personal injury filings to increased costs of litigation as well as to shrinking damage awards (Judicial Council of California 2002).

The high cost of the law assures that most of those facing social wrongs will react by adopting some informal, extralegal response. Some will avoid contact or refuse to cooperate with those who do them wrong. Others may resort to gossip or direct scorn against wrong-doers. Certain individuals elect to settle scores by seeking revenge. Indeed, many incidents of personal violence, as well as property crimes, can be attributed to such revenge seeking, or "self-help" behaviors (Black 1998). Most of us, however, are likely to respond to wrongs against us by "lumping" them; we will, in effect, turn the other cheek. Indeed, tolerance is "the most common response of aggrieved people everywhere" (Black 1998). **Tolerance** refers to inaction in the face of some offense.

The juxtaposition of tolerance vis-à-vis the law is a compelling reminder of the need to develop our sociological vision. The law is a social phenomenon, and as such it varies greatly within its social environment. Understanding its availability, distribution, usage, nonusage, and even its suspension requires us to analyze the law in light of social context. A timely illustration of this point is found in the legal actions of the Bush administration and of Attorney General John Ashcroft in their efforts to combat terrorism. Immediately after the September 11, 2001, terrorist attacks on America, in October 2001, the president signed the USA Patriot Act. This act strengthens all federal investigations by broadening the information-gathering, surveillance, and detention powers of the Justice Department and by limiting judicial oversight of these activities. Attorney General John Ashcroft defends the act as an essential tool for fighting terrorism. Critics of the act see it as a serious threat to fundamental constitutional rights. (In July 2003, the American Civil Liberties Union filed a federal lawsuit on the grounds that a major section of the Patriot Act violates the privacy, due process, and free speech rights of citizens.) Exactly how the courts will respond to this expansion of power and charges of constitutional violations remains to be seen, although early federal appellate rulings indicate that the courts will follow the historical trend and support the claims of security threats over claims of constitutional affronts (Lewis 2003). And to add yet another layer to the social context of this latest legal controversy, a random survey of Americans in June 2003 found the majority (61%) did *not* think that average Americans should have to give up their own rights and freedoms in order to combat terrorism, while 10% were undecided, and 29% would support such developments (Flashpoints 2003).

Despite its cultural importance, the law does not represent the whole story of social control in our society. Instead, we must view the law as one form of control among many. Pursuing such second thoughts about the law will help us see how it is that our very demand for the law and social control can contribute to much of the extralegal activity in our society.

Learning More About It

Paul Campos offers a compelling analysis of our addiction to the law in his book *Jurismania: The Madness of American Law* (New York: Oxford, 1998).

A thorough review of the theory and techniques of conflict management can be found in Donald Black's *The Social Structure of Right and Wrong* (San Diego: Academic Press, 1998).

For an analysis of how the law can be used as a tool of moral entrepreneurs, see Joseph Gusfield's classic work on prohibition, *Symbolic Crusade: Status Politics and the American Temperance Movement* (Urbana, IL: University of Illinois Press, 1963).

An interesting review of American's appetite for fast food, social change, and litigation is found in Andrew Gumbel's "Fast Food Nation: An Appetite for Litigation." In the *Independent. co.uk:* <http://news.independent.co.uk/world/americas/story. jsp?story=302005>

The following organizations can help you learn more about law in American society:

Rand Institute for Civil Justice
Web site: <http://www.rand.org/icj/>

Consumer Attorneys of California
Web site: *http://www.caoc.com/*

National Lawyers Guild
126 University Place, 5th Floor, New York, NY 10003
(212) 627–2656; Web site: <http://www.nlg.org/>

Trial Lawyers for Public Justice
Web site: <http://www.tlpj.org/>

More information about the Patriot Act can be found at the following Web sites:

Center for Public Integrity
Web site: <http://www.publicintegrity.org/>

American Civil Liberties Union
Web site: <http://www.aclu.org/>

Exercises

1. Donald Black's (1976) theory of law asserts that social intimates (such as family members) are less likely to use the law against each other than are nonintimates. Identify and speculate as to alternate means of social control that might prove to be particularly effective in family settings.

2. Consider the legal and extralegal ramifications of formally regulating our social relations in cyberspace. How have we tried to regulate cyberspace relations via the law? What do you see as some of the most likely extralegal responses to these legal rules?

Essay 16

Conventional Wisdom Tells Us . . . Honesty Is the Best Policy

. . . except, of course, when reporting your income, revealing your age, sparing the feelings of another—the list can go on and on. In this essay, we explore the conditions under which lying is viewed as normal. In so doing, we use lying as a case study that aptly demonstrates both the pervasiveness and the relative nature of deviance.

"Honesty is the best policy," wrote Ben Franklin. From an early age, parents and teachers urge us to embrace this sentiment. We learn cultural fables and tales that verify the value of truthfulness—remember Pinocchio or George Washington and the cherry tree? Similarly, religious doctrines turn honesty into law with lessons such as "Thou shalt not lie." In civics class, individuals learn that perjury—lying while under oath—is an illegal act.

Prohibitions against lying are among the earliest norms to which individuals are socialized. **Norms** are social rules or guidelines that direct behavior. They are the "shoulds" and "should nots" of social action, feelings, and thought. These lessons continue throughout life. As we grow older, we witness firsthand the ways in which dishonesty can lead to the downfall of individuals, families, careers, communities—even presidencies. Indeed, many social commentators identify the Watergate incident, and the high-level lying that accompanied it, as the basis for today's widespread public distrust of the U.S. government. The Iran Contra scandal and the Clinton-Lewinsky affair added fuel to the fire—so much so that recent polls suggest less than 70% of Americans trust the federal government (Ekman 2001; Leone 1994; National Public Radio 1999).

But if honesty is the best policy, how do we understand the findings of a recent survey that documents widespread dishonesty in our high schools and colleges? Eighty percent of high school students at the top of their classes have admitted to cheating on their way to the top (ECI 2002). A study conducted across 23 college campuses found that 38% of undergraduates admitted to plagiarizing Internet materials and passing them off as their own work. Many students claim their cheating is "no big deal," while others assert it is essential for besting the competition and landing the top jobs after college (ECI 2002; Rimer 2003).

If honesty is the best policy, how do we understand the deceit that is rampant in corporate America? Many Enron employees as well as countless investors had their financial futures destroyed because they believed the fraudulent bookkeeping by J.P. Morgan Chase and Citigroup and the lies by Enron's CEO, Ken Lay (Eichenwald and Atlas 2003). Andersen Worldwide, the once highly respected auditing firm, stands accused of destroying evidence relevant to the Enron investigation. MCI (formerly WorldCom Inc) is working its way out of a bankruptcy brought on by massive accounting fraud (Lavelle 2003; Rosenbush and Haddad 2003). In recent years, one major corporation after another—IBM, Microsoft, Xerox—has had to issue restatements of their financials in order to "get the numbers right." Corporate boards of directors are supposed to keep a watchful eye on CEOs, but in too many cases (like WorldCom and Tyco), the boards fail to keep anyone in check (Byrne et al. 2002; Eichenwald 2003).

And if honesty is the best policy, how do we understand the scandal that has rocked the Roman Catholic Church for the last few years? Hundreds of priests stand accused of sexually molesting young charges and parishioners. The scope of the scandal escalated as we slowly discovered the reactions of the church hierarchy. In the summer of 2003, the public learned of a 40-year-old Vatican document that instructed bishops to cover up sex crimes. The document was described by one defense attorney as a "blueprint for deception" (CBS News 2003). Bishops across the United States kept the illicit behaviors of clergy under wraps by reassigning errant priests and/or buying the silence of victims.

Even now, as we struggle to makes sense of our transformed "post–9/11" society, we repeatedly must come to terms with the honesty issue. Dishonest claims and fraudulent documents paved the way for the terrorists' sinister activities in the months and days before the deadly attacks. Since September 11, 2001, there has been increasing interest in and demand for research and technology that will improve our ability to uncover lies and deceptive behaviors (Glovin 2003). And perhaps in coming full circle, Americans are learning more about the possibly deceitful practices of our own government in its efforts to manipulate public reaction and combat terrorism. An internal Environmental Protection Agency (EPA) report has acknowledged that the agency, under prompting by the White House, misled the public by declaring the "ground zero" vicinity, around the World Trade Center in New York City after 9/11, to be safe *before* any air testing results were obtained. The White House has also been accused of politically manhandling the EPA by insisting that all EPA press releases regarding air quality at ground zero be cleared by the National Security Agency (Fitzpatrick 2003; Kay 2003). Months after President Bush declared "major fighting" in the Iraq war to be over,

Americans were trying to discern the truth about the start of the war. Did the president deliberately lie to Congress and the people about weapons of mass destruction and Iraq's ties to al-Qaeda as a way to secure support for launching the war in March of 2003? A June 2003 University of Maryland poll found that more than half of the respondents believed that President Bush "stretched the truth" when making the case for war (Yahoo News 2003). In the fall of 2003, after weeks of discussing the claims and counterclaims regarding Saddam Hussein's connection to 9/11, social commentators warned that President Bush was teetering on the edge of being a "serial exaggerator" and reminded him that "stark honesty" is the best weapon for maintaining public confidence in his leadership (*New York Times* 2003b; Simendinger 2003).

Clearly, we would be lying to say that our culture firmly endorses honesty as the best policy. The conventional wisdom regarding the virtue of honesty is strong, yet we must also note that almost as early as we learn prohibitions against lying, we also learn how to rationalize the telling of lies. We learn that "little white lies" are not as serious as "real lies." We learn that context matters: Lying to strangers is not as serious as lying to friends; lying to peers is more excusable than lying to parents or authorities. We learn that lies don't count if we cross our fingers or wink while telling them. And we learn that lies told under duress are not as awful as premeditated or "barefaced lies" (Bussey 1999; Ekman 2001; Lawson 2000; Williams 2001).

Thus, despite conventional wisdom to the contrary, lying stands as a ubiquitous social practice. Children lie to parents, and parents lie to grandparents. Employees lie to employers, and employers lie to regulators. Confessors lie to clergy, and clergy lie to congregations. Presidents lie to Congress and the public, and governments lie to the people. Indeed, there may be no social sphere to which lying is a stranger (DePaulo, Kashy, and Kirkendol 1996; Ekman 2001).

What explains the prevalence of lies when conventional wisdom so strongly supports honesty? What accounts for the discrepancies between what we say about lies and what we do? Is lying wrong? Is it deviant or not?

To start, we must first appreciate the role of values in our often contradictory stance on honesty. A **value** refers to a general sentiment regarding what is good or bad, right or wrong, desirable or undesirable. Values can be powerful motivators that "drive" our behaviors. In reviewing the previous list of dishonest activities of students, corporate executives, clergy, and political leaders, it is easy to identify some overriding or motivating values. Some students, for instance, cheat in the name of getting good grades or good jobs. Some CEOs engage in creative bookkeeping in order to achieve personal success and wealth. The church hierarchy is interested in preserving the integrity of that institution, and some bishops were willing to mislead parishioners about the conduct of priests in the hope of maintaining that integrity. And some of our political leaders might well be willing to engage in hyperbole and thus stretch the truth in the name of fighting terrorism. In short, for some, the pursuit of high and noble values can invite expedient behavior—we do whatever we must to achieve what we think is worthy or desirable. Unfortunately, however, expedient behavior often takes us into the realm of deviance (Merton 1938).

Deviance is typically defined as any act that violates a norm. Definitions of deviance are rarely "black and white." Rather, determining what is deviant is a relative process, because norms can vary with time, setting, or public consciousness. Thus, today's deviant behaviors may be tomorrow's convention. (Think of some "deviant behaviors" that subsequently entered the realm of conformity: long hair on men, jeans on students, living together before marriage, smoking among women.) *Ideally,* norms reflect or are consistent with our values. A culture that promotes the value of family should direct people to marry and have children. A culture that promotes democracy should direct people to vote and participate in community affairs. Values and norms *should* coincide, but that doesn't always happen. They can get out of balance with each other. Frequently, values dominate; we are willing to do anything to accomplish our values or goals. When values dominate, expedient behavior rules, and the normative order can be compromised. If expedient behaviors violate social norms, we enter the realm of deviance. While honesty may be the best policy, dishonesty is often the most expedient way to achieve, succeed, manage, and win. Thus, if I am truly convinced that the grade is everything, I may find it easy to lie and claim the work of others as my own. Similarly, if financial success means everything to me, I might find it easy to lie about company profits if it will help boost stock prices. If protecting the church from scandal is my highest priority, I might find it easy to lie about the reason for reassigning priests. And if fighting terrorism is my goal, I might find it very easy to say what I must to get the job done.

Because lying, like all deviant acts, is variable, sociologists distinguish between two types of lies: deviant lies and normal lies. **Deviant lies** are falsehoods always judged to be wrong by a society; they represent a socially unacceptable practice, one that can devastate the trust that enables interaction within a complex society of strangers. **Normal lies** are a socially acceptable practice linked to productive social outcomes. Individuals rationalize and legitimate normal lies as the means to a noble end: the good of one's family, colleagues, or country. A lie's relative deviancy or normalcy depends on who tells it; when, where, and why it is told; to whom it is told; and the outcome of its telling (Barnes 1994; Burke 1995; Hope 1995; Manning 1974, 1984; Ruane et al. 1994; Ryan 1996; Seiter, Bruschke, and Bai 2002; Zagorin 1996).

For example, withholding your AIDS diagnosis from your elderly mother may be viewed as an act of mercy. In contrast, withholding the diagnosis from a sex partner would probably be viewed as immoral or potentially criminal. Similarly, lying about one's age to engage a new romantic interest is likely to be defined as significantly less offensive than lying about one's age to secure Social Security benefits. As with all forms of deviance, lie classification is based on context. We cannot classify a lie as deviant or normal on the basis of objectively stated criteria. In being slow to judge President Bush's stated reasons for going to war, Americans are trying to carefully assess the context of any alleged misstatements.

Although deviant lies can destroy social relations, normal lies can function as a strategic tool in the maintenance of social order. Normal lies become a "lubricant" of social life; they allow both the user and receiver of lies to edit social reality. Normal lies can facilitate ongoing interaction (Goffman 1974; Goleman 1985; Sacks 1975).

If our boss misses a lunch date with us, we tell her or him it was "no big deal," even if the missed appointment led to considerable inconvenience in our day. Similarly, we tell a soldier's parents that their son or daughter died a painless death even if circumstances suggest otherwise. In both of these cases, the normal lie represents a crucial mechanism for preserving necessary social routines (Burke 1995; Hope 1995).

In the same way, normal lies also are important in maintaining civil social environments. Thus, when a truthful child announces someone's obesity, foul smell, or physical disability while on a shopping trip at the mall, parents are quick to instruct him or her in the polite albeit deceptive practices of less-than-honest tact. Similarly, the daily contact between neighbors inherent in most city and suburban layouts leads us to tell a rather bothersome neighbor that she or he is "really no trouble at all." In both of these cases, honesty would surely prove a socially destructive policy—the normal lie allows individuals to preserve the interaction environment.

What processes allow us to normalize an otherwise deviant behavior such as lying? In a classic article, sociologists Gresham Sykes and David Matza (1957) identify five specific techniques of neutralization that prove useful in this regard. **Techniques of neutralization** are methods of rationalizing deviant behavior. In essence, these techniques allow actors to suspend the control typically exerted by social norms. Freed from norms in this way, social actors can engage in deviance. Using the techniques of neutralization—denial of responsibility, denial of injury, denial of victim, condemning the condemner, and appealing to higher loyalties—individuals effectively explain away the deviant aspects of a behavior such as lying. Individuals convince themselves that their actions, even if norm violating, were justified given the circumstance. Once an individual has learned to use these techniques, she or he can apply them to any deviant arena, thereby facilitating an array of deviant behaviors: stealing, fraud, vandalism, personal violence, and so on.

Employing Sykes and Matza's techniques, then, one might *deny responsibility* for a lie, attributing the action to something beyond one's control: "My boss forced me to say he wasn't in." One might *deny injury* of the lie, arguing that the behavior caused no real harm: "Yes, I lied about my age. What's the harm?" One might *deny the victim* of the lie by arguing that the person harmed by the lie deserves such a fate: "I told her that her presentation was perfect. I can't wait for it to bomb; she deserves it." *Condemning one's condemner* allows an individual to neutralize a lie by shifting the focus to how often one's accuser lies: "Yes, I lied about where I was tonight, but how often have you lied to me about that very thing?" Finally, *appealing to higher loyalties* neutralizes lying by connecting it to some greater good: "I didn't tell my wife I was unfaithful because I didn't want to jeopardize our family."

Just as individuals learn to neutralize certain lies, they also learn appropriate reactions to normal lies. With time and experience, individuals learn that challenging normal lies can be counterproductive. Such challenges can disrupt the social scripts that make collective existence possible. **Social scripts** document the shared expectations that govern those interacting within a particular setting or context.

If the social audience wishes to maintain smooth social exchange, then each member must learn to tolerate certain lies. By doing so, individuals downplay deviations from the social script. Like actors on a stage, individuals ignore momentary lapses and faux pas so that the "performance" can continue (Goffman 1959, 1974).

The U.S. military policy of "Don't ask, don't tell," for example, is built on such logic. Military officials look the other way to avoid the potential disruption embodied in a truthful response to the question of homosexuality. Similarly, the spouse who fails to question a partner's change in routine or habit may do so in an effort to shield the marriage from the threat posed by potential truths.

A variety of social settings require that we take someone at their word or accept things at face value. We learn to listen with half an ear, to take things "with a grain of salt," or to recognize that people don't always "say what they mean or mean what they say." Paul Ekman, an eminent researcher on deceit, maintains that successful liars most often depend on willfully innocent dupes (Ekman 2001). In the end, these strategies or roles offer support and tolerance for the normal lie.

This discussion of lying raises important points about deviance in general. Despite norms forbidding it, deviance happens. Studies show that nearly every member of the U.S. population engages in some deviant behaviors during their lifetime (Adler and Lamber 1993; Goode 1997:36–37). Indeed, Emile Durkheim ([1938] 1966), a central figure in sociology, suggested that deviance would occur even in a society of saints.

Theorist Edwin Lemert contended that certain types of deviance are universal. Everyone, at one time or another, engages in such acts. Lemert referred to these universal occurrences of deviance as primary deviance. **Primary deviance** refers to isolated violations of norms. Such acts are not viewed as deviant by those committing them and often result in no social sanctions. Deviance remains primary in nature as long as such acts "are rationalized or otherwise dealt with as functions of a socially acceptable role" (Lemert 1951:75–76). (Note that normal lying fits easily within this category.)

Herein lies the importance of techniques of neutralization and social scripts of tolerance. The techniques and scripts can keep us and our behaviors within the confines of primary deviance. They can keep us from moving to a more significant type of deviance, which Lemert refers to as secondary deviance. **Secondary deviance** occurs when a labeled individual comes to view herself or himself according to that which she or he is called.

Although all of us engage in primary deviance, relatively few of us become ensnared by secondary deviance. The techniques of neutralization allow the social actor to rationalize periodic infractions of the rules. Social scripts of tolerance allow the social audience to accept such infractions as well. As such, social audiences refrain from publicly labeling the "neutralized" actor as deviant. By anchoring an individual in primary deviance, the techniques of neutralization ease the return to a conforming status. Understand, then, that when CEOs defend creative bookkeeping as a required part of their job or when bishops act in ways to "spare" the faithful unnecessary details about the reassignment of clergy, they are in effect working to maintain the primary status of their deviance.

When it comes to norms on lying, or any other social behavior, conformity may be, as conventional wisdom suggests, the best policy. However, when we understand the complexity involved in the workings of norm violations, we cannot help but note that deviating from the "best policy" may not be all that deviant after all.

Learning More About It

"The Lie," by Georg Simmel, is a classic sociological essay on the topic. See *The Sociology of Georg Simmel,* edited by K. Wolff (New York: Free Press, 1950a, pp. 312–316). Paul Ekman's *Telling Lies* (New York: W.W. Norton, 2001) is a highly readable and comprehensive examination of experimental research on lying. For a comprehensive sociological review of lying, see J. Barnes's *A Pack of Lies: Toward a Sociology of Lying* (New York: Cambridge University Press, 1994). *Social Research,* a sociological journal, sponsored a special issue on truth telling, lying, and self-deception; see *Social Research* 63 (Fall) 1996. And finally, lying is just one of the many annoying interactions examined by Robin Kowalski in *Complaining, Teasing, and Other Annoying Behaviors* (New Haven, CT: Yale University Press, 2003).

Carl Hausman examines lies in advertising, retail, politics, and the media and offers tips on how we might better equip ourselves for spotting and stopping falsehoods in his book *Lies We Live By: Defeating Double-Talk and Deception in Advertising, Politics and the Media* (New York: Routledge, 2000). Jeremy Campbell considers the benefits of falsehood and suggests that lying may be natural, if not instinctual, in his book The *Liar's Tale: A History of Falsehood* (New York: Norton, 2001).

For a detailed consideration of normal lying in an occupational setting, consult Janet Ruane, Karen Cerulo, and Judith Gerson's 1994 article, "Professional Deceit: Normal Lying in an Occupational Setting," *Sociological Focus* 27 (2): 91–109. In their 2002 article, "The Effects of Salesperson Compensation on Perceptions of Salesperson Honesty," *Journal of Applied Social Psychology* 42(4): 719–731, Robert Straughan and Michael Lynn examine how the perception of honesty is affected by whether one works for commissions or salary. For an engaging review of how a variation on the normal lie operates in the world of students, see Stan Bernstein's 1972 article, "Getting It Done: Notes on Student Fritters," *Urban Life and Culture* 1 (October): 2.

For an explicit discussion on how corporate culture influences deceit in business practices see Nikos Passas's "Anomie and Corporate Deviance," *Contemporary Crises* 14: 157–178, 1990.

Michiel de Vries examines the honesty of 10,000 politicians in 17 countries in "Can You Afford Honesty? A Comparative Analysis of Ethos and Ethics in Local Government," *Administration & Society* 34(3): 309–334, 2002. While honesty is found to be a universal value, it is also the case that organizational contingencies greatly influence the practice of honesty.

Gresham Sykes and David Matza's 1957 article, "Techniques of Neutralization: A Theory of Delinquency," *American Sociological Review* 22: 664–670, offers readers some insight into the dynamics that feed the legitimation process.

Exercises

1. Consider the normal lie as it exists in the world of advertising. Collect a sample of ads targeting different audiences: adults versus children, men versus women, yuppies versus the elderly. Is there any pattern in the ads' reliance on normal lying as a marketing technique? What would be the ramifications of unmasking the normal lie in advertising?

2. Consider the function of normal lying in the successful completion of the student role. Are there ways in which dishonesty has been institutionalized in the student role? What do your own experiences and the experiences of your friends suggest are the important sources of such deception?

3. Select and carefully follow the media coverage of a current "scandal." Discuss the relevance of the concepts of primary and secondary deviance. Identify and document the techniques of neutralization that are being used to control or limit the public's perception of deviance.

Social Institutions

MARRIAGE AND FAMILY

Essay 17

Conventional Wisdom Tells Us ... The Nuclear Family Is the Backbone of American Society

Mom, dad, and the kids—is this the unit on which American social life is built? This essay documents the history of family in America, showing that the nuclear family is a relatively recent phenomenon and one that soon may be replaced by other forms of family. In addition, the stability of the nuclear family is explored in light of idyllic stereotypes.

A tour of Broadway, listening to a top-40 radio station, or hearing a speech by a major political figure—all show us to be a nation hooked on nostalgia. We yearn for the "good old days," a time when life was simpler, the nation was prosperous, and nuclear families prayed and stayed together.

A return to the family—this plea rests at the heart of current rhetoric. Today's popular culture touts the world of the Andersons (*Father Knows Best*), the Cleavers (*Leave It to Beaver*), the Cunninghams (*Happy Days*) and most recently the Barones (*Everybody Loves Raymond*) as an American ideal. One social observer has speculated that the popularity of the television series *The Sopranos* may be due to protagonist Tony's traditional "yearning for yesterday" views (Teachout 2002). Working dads, stay-at-home moms, and carefree yet respectful kids: Conventional wisdom promotes such units as the cornerstone of this nation.

Many believe that only a return to our nuclear "roots" can provide a cure for our ills. Only the rebirth of nuclear family dominance can restore the backbone of our floundering society. The **nuclear family** refers to a self-contained, self-satisfying unit composed of father,

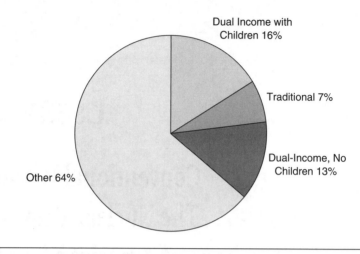

Figure 17.1   Major Types of U.S. Households, 2002

Traditional Households consist of married couples with children where *only the husband* is in the labor force.
SOURCE: Population Reference Bureau.

mother, and children. Are conventional sentiments correct? Will a return to this nation's nuclear roots bring stability to American society?

At present, only 7% of American households contain what some would say is the *most traditional* nuclear family (i.e., a working dad, a stay-at-home mom and kids) (see Figure 17.1) (Population Reference Bureau 2003a). Even if we restrict our focus to *married couples* (as opposed to households), still only 13% fit this particular nuclear model (see Figure 17.1.) (AmeriStat 2003d). From the children's point of view, there is little that resembles the Cleavers or the Andersons. In 2002, 62% of children lived in families that had *both* parents in the labor force. Close to 30% of children lived in single-parent families: 23% (or 16.5 million) lived in mother-only families, 5% (3.3 million) lived in father-only families, and 4% lived in households with neither parent present (Fields 2003). Perhaps equally telling is the number of households without kids: 52% of family households have no children under 18 (U.S. Census Bureau 2002)! With such a departure from the traditional nuclear family, are we charting new terrain? History suggests not.

A macro-level analysis of family in America suggests that nonnuclear family forms are common in America's past. A **macro-level analysis** focuses on broad, large-scale social patterns as they exist across contexts or through time. The shape and form of the "typical" American family has changed quite frequently throughout our nation's history. Indeed, historically speaking, the nuclear family is a fairly recent as well as a relatively rare phenomenon. Knowing this, it is difficult to identify the nuclear family as either *the* traditional family format or the rock upon which our nation was built. Furthermore, social history reveals that the nuclear family's effects on American society have often proved less positive than nostalgic images suggest.

Historically, American families have displayed a variety of forms. In preindustrial times, the word *family* conjured up an image quite different from the nuclear ideal. Preindustrial families were truly interdependent economic units. All members of the household—parents, children, and quite often boarders or lodgers—made some contribution to the family's economic livelihood. Work tasks overlapped gender and age groups. However, frequently parental contributions were ended by early mortality. In the preindustrial era, average life expectancy was only 45 years (Rubin 1996). One-third to one-half of colonial children had lost at least one parent by the time they reached 21 years of age (Greven 1970).

During the early stages of industrialization, the face of the family changed. Many families of the era began to approximate the "dad-mom-and-the-kids" model. Yet early industrialization also was a time when the number of extended families in the United States reached its historical high. An **extended family** is a unit containing parent(s), children, and other blood relatives such as grandparents or aunts and uncles. Although the extended family has never been a dominant form in U.S. society, 20% of this period's families contained grandparents, aunts, uncles, or cousins (Hareven 1978).

The stay-at-home mom, a mom who focused exclusively on social activities and household management, first appeared in America's middle-class Victorian families. This new role for Victorian women, however, came on the backs of working-class mothers and children. Many women and children of the working class were hired as domestics for middle-class families. In the early days of industrialization, such women and children were also frequently employed as factory workers. Only as industrialization advanced were working-class women relegated to the home sphere (Padavic and Reskin 2002). By the late 1800s, a typical family included a mother who worked exclusively at home.

Children, however, continued to work outside the home for wages. Indeed, in New England, an 1866 Massachusetts legislative report hailed child labor as a boon to society (TenBensel, Rheinberger, and Radbill 1997). Throughout the Northeast, children were regularly employed in industry or the mines (Bodnar 1987; Schneiderman 1967). In the South, children comprised nearly one-fourth of all textile workers employed at the turn of the century (Wertheimer 1977). Across the nation, approximately 20% of American children were relegated to orphanages because parents could not afford to raise them (Katz 1986).

The modern nuclear family that Americans so admire did not fully come into its own until the 1950s. A careful review of families emerging from this period suggests a unit that both confirms and contradicts conventional wisdom's idyllic models.

Historian Stephanie Coontz (2000) notes that the nuclear unit of the 1950s emerged as a product of the times. The family model of the era developed in response to a distinct set of socioeconomic factors. The post–World War II decade saw great industrial expansion in the United States. The nation enjoyed a tremendous increase in real wages. Furthermore, Americans experienced an all-time high in their personal savings, a condition that resulted largely from U.S. war efforts. The nuclear family became a salient symbol of our country's newfound prosperity.

Consumerism was a significant hallmark of 1950s nuclear families. Spending devoted to products that enhanced family life brought significant increases in our nation's GNP (gross national product). Indeed, the buying power of the 1950s family was phenomenal. During the postwar era, for example, home ownership increased dramatically. There were 6.5 million more homeowners in 1955 than in 1948 (Layman 1995). Federal subsidies enabled families to buy homes with minimal down payments and low-interest (2%–3%) guaranteed 30-year mortgages. It is estimated that half the suburban homes of the 1950s were financed in this way (Coontz 2000).

Consumerism added a new dimension to the American family. By 1950, 60% of all U.S. households owned a car (Layman 1995). Cars, cheap gas, and new highways made mobility a part of family life. The purchase of television sets converted the home into both an entertainment and consumer center. In 1950, there were 1.5 million TV sets in the United States. A year later, there were 15 million (Knauer 1998)! Indeed, 86% of the U.S. population owned TVs by the decade's end, bringing about a 50% decrease in movie theater attendance (Jones 1980). In 1954, Swanson Foods introduced a new food product to complement our fondness for the tube: the frozen TV dinner (Layman 1995). Advertisers took advantage of the new medium to sell their products to the American public like never before. By the end of the 50s, 2 out of every 10 minutes of TV programming were devoted to advertising (Layman 1995).

Other new and improved tools and appliances (power mowers, electric floor polishers) made the home an efficient and comfortable place to live. Shopping malls appeared on the suburban landscape for ease of access by the growing suburban population (Layman 1995). The growth of the credit card industry strengthened the nuclear family's consumer patterns and encouraged a "buy now, pay later" mentality (Dizard and Gadlin 1990; Ritzer 1995). And pay later we did. Some would argue that the debt-laden 1990s are the legacy of the spend-and-grow mentality established in the 1950s.

The buying power of the 1950s nuclear family suggested a unit with the potential to fulfill all needs. At first glance, this development may seem to be a positive aspect of the era, but some argue that it marked the beginning of a harmful trend in our society—the decline of community commitment. Such critics contend that by emphasizing the "private" values of the individual and the family, the nuclear unit intensified individualism and weakened civic altruism (Bellah et al. 1985; Collier 1991; Sennett 1977). Thus, the seeds of our later decades of self-indulgence and excess may well have been planted in the nuclear family era of the 1950s. As historian Coontz (2000) observes, "The private family . . . was a halfway house on the road to modern 'me-first' individualism" (p. 98).

Consumerism, however, is only a part of the nuclear family's legacy. There were profound changes in domestic behavior patterns as well. In contrast to the ideal lives enjoyed by the Andersons, the Cleavers, or the Cunninghams, home life of the 1950s showed some problematic developments.

For example, couples married at younger ages than earlier generations had. The formation of a nuclear family was an integral part of "making it" in the United States. As a result, many people moved rapidly toward that goal. But the trend toward early marriage was not without cost. National polls showed that 20% of the period's married couples rated their marriages as unhappy—interestingly enough, this figure is higher than any displayed in recent General Social Surveys. In the heyday of the nuclear family, millions of couples resolved their marital differences by living apart (Komarovsky 1962; May 1988; Mintz and Kellogg 1988).

The 1950s also saw couples starting families at younger ages than their predecessors. In addition, families were larger and grew more quickly than families of previous decades. More than ever before or since, married couples faced enormous pressure to have children. Indeed, *Life* magazine declared children to be a built-in recession cure (Jones 1980). But the emphasis on childbearing had some unintended consequences. The period saw a substantial increase in fertility rates, largely due to teenage pregnancies. (Kids were having kids—sound familiar?) Half of all 1950s brides were teenagers who had children within 15 months of getting married (Ahlburg and DeVita 1992). The number of out-of-wedlock babies placed for adoption increased by 80% between 1944 and 1955, and the proportion of pregnant brides doubled during this era (Coontz 2000).

City living was largely abandoned by families in the 1950s. The new young families of the era put down roots in the suburbs, which seemed ideal for breaking with old traditions. The suburbs were well suited to the newly emerging idea of the family as a self-contained unit, a unit that would supplant the community as the center of emotional investment and satisfaction. Fully 83% of the population growth in the 1950s occurred in the suburbs. Indeed, *Fortune* magazine noted that more people arrived in the suburbs each year than had ever arrived at Ellis Island (Jones 1980).

Changing family lifestyles brought changes to the workplace as well. By 1952, 2 million more women were in the workforce than had been there during World War II. This time, however, female entry into the workplace was not fueled by patriotic duty. Rather, many women were entering the workforce to cover the rising costs and debts associated with the nuclear family's consumer mentality (Rubin 1996). Others went to work to help young husbands complete educational and career goals.

The working women of the 1950s faced a workplace less receptive to them than it had been to the "Rosie the Riveters" of the World-War-II era. The industries that had welcomed women during the war years now preferred to keep American women at home or in dead-end jobs. Popular magazines of the day ran articles examining the social menace and private dysfunction of working women.

The pressures and rejections faced by women in the workplace had important links to the amazing increase in production and use of newly developed tranquilizers: 462,000 pounds of tranquilizers were consumed in 1958, and 1.15 million pounds of tranquilizers were consumed in 1959! Consumers were overwhelmingly female (Coontz 2000).

In considering the realities of the nuclear family, it becomes clear that neither it nor any other family form can be a remedy for social ills. Debates on the virtue of the "good old days" or attempts to identify the "perfect family" form thus seem an exercise in futility. Each historical period, with its own combination of economic, political, and social forces, redefines perfection.

These thoughts may help us to better appreciate the risk entailed in trying to build current social policy around institutions whose times may have come and gone. Perhaps the best course of action today is to resist nostalgic "retrofitting" and instead assist the family in making adaptive changes to our current social circumstances. Such changes may well be the new "traditions" that future generations will yearn to restore.

Learning More About It

Stephanie Coontz offers a detailed historical review of the American family from colonial times to the present in *The Way We Never Were: American Families and the Nostalgia Trap* (New York: Basic, 2000). In particular, the author systematically debunks many of our most cherished family myths.

For a detailed and thoroughly entertaining account of the 1950s generation and beyond, readers should consult Landon Jones's *Great Expectations* (New York: Ballantine Books, 1980).

For reflections on the current state of the American family, see Stephanie Coontz's *The Way We Really Are: Coming to Terms with America's Changing Families* (New York: Basic, 1998).

Expressing America: A Critique of the Global Credit Card Society, by George Ritzer (Thousand Oaks, CA: Pine Forge, 1995), presents a sociologically informed analysis of the growth of consumerism and the credit industry. *Explorations in the Sociology of Consumption: Fast Food, Credit Cards, and Casinos,* by George Ritzer (Thousand Oaks, CA: Sage, 2001), examines the irrational consequences of consumption.

For some of the latest research and key issues facing family policymakers today, see "The Changing Structure of the Family 2002" at Stanford's *Difficult Dialogues* series: <http://www.difficultdialogues.com/DD2/index.html>

The following organizations and sites can also help you learn more about family life:

Children's Rights Council
6200 Editors Park Drive, Suite 103
Hyattsville, MD 20782
(301) 559–3120; Web site: <http://www.gocrc.com/>

Research and Training Center on Family Support and Children's Mental Health
Web site: <http://www.rtc.pdx.edu/>

Exercises

1. Use your sociological imagination to identify some key factors that prompt our present nostalgia for the past. For example, think in terms of historical and social developments that may help to explain why the past looks so good to us now.

2. We noted in this essay that nuclear families were a product of specific historic and socioeconomic conditions. Consider a family type common to the 1990s, the "blended family." Blended families are units that consist of previously married spouses and their children from former marriages. What are the current historic and socioeconomic conditions that explain the blended-family phenomenon? What social policy changes might enhance the success of this family form?

Essay 18

Conventional Wisdom Tells Us ...
Marriage Is a Failing Institution

High divorce rates, couples living together, the need for "space," fear of commit-ment—have such trends doomed the institution of marriage? Here, we discuss research suggesting that the practice of marriage is alive and well despite con-ventional wisdom to the contrary. We also note the historical "popularity" of divorce in America and speculate on why such a trend marks our culture.

Politicians say it and social commentators lament it: Many of our current social and economic problems stem from deteriorating family values. The conventional wisdom on the matter suggests that high divorce rates are jeopardizing the future of marriage and the family. Many fear that "till death us do part" has become a promise of the past. Are such fears well-grounded? Is marriage really a failing institution?

Most research on the matter suggests little cause for such alarm. Indeed, a variety of indi-cators document that marriage remains one of society's most viable social institutions. **Marriage** refers to a socially approved economic and sexual union. A **social institution** consists of behavior patterns, social roles, and norms, all of which combine to form a system that ultimately fulfills an important need or function for a society.

The United States has the highest marriage rate of any modern industrial society (United Nations 2002). Most young adults plan to marry at some point in time, although the age of first marriage is increasing. Higher ages for first marriage is itself a good sign for the insti-tution, since they are associated with increased marital stability (Bramlett and Mosher 2002). The overwhelming majority of women (76%) are married by age 30 (Bramlett and Mosher 2002; National Center for Health Statistics 2002b). Past the age of 30, the percentage of married women is at least four times higher than the percentage of those who never married (Bramlett and Mosher 2002). Even "Generation X-ERs," children who were born at the same time our divorce rate was doubling, are still supporting marriage. Indeed, of all age groups, members of Generation X are least likely to identify divorce as the best option for troubled marriages (Hamilton and Wingert 1998). They are also likely to emphasize marriage as the foundation for future happiness (Arnett 2000).

In the United States, the marriage institution enjoys much "positive press." For Americans, marriage appears to be a key to happiness. The majority of married adults in the United States (64%) indicate that they are *very* happy with their marriages (General Social Survey 1998). Other polls find even higher percentages reporting great satisfaction with their marriages (Bowman 1999). To be sure, the link between marriage and happiness is not unique to the United States. Recent studies involving as many as 64 countries also document that married individuals reported higher levels of happiness (Doyle 2002; Stack and Eshleman 1998). Furthermore, marital bliss appears to have a halo effect. Surveys show that married couples are twice as likely as the never-married or the divorced to report feeling very happy about life in general (Bowman 1999; Smith 1997).

In addition to raising individuals' happiness quotient, marriage also makes us healthy and wealthy (if not wise). In addition to boosting financial well-being, marriage is also associated with emotional and health benefits and the reduction of risky behaviors (AmeriStat 2003c; Bramlett and Mosher 2002; National Center for Health Statistics 2001; Pienta, Hayward, and Jenkins 2000; Simon 2002; Waite 2000). Perhaps the biggest benefit of pledging "till death us do part" is reducing our chances of death. There is evidence that marriage helps keep us alive: Both married men and women show significantly lower risks of dying than the unmarried, and the effect is not simply due to married individuals selecting healthy partners. The lower mortality benefit remains even after health status is controlled (Bramlett and Mosher 2002; Lillard and Waite 1995).

Marriage in the United States occurs with great frequency and generates high overall satisfaction for those who enter the union. What, then, explains the alarm sounded by many regarding the institution's failure? Recent changes in the American household are a concern to some. The 2000 census found that 52% of households were maintained by married couples—this figure is down from 55% in the 1990 census and from 71% in the 1970 census. The second most common household (at 26%) consists of people living alone—a figure that has steadily increased from 17% in 1970. (Fields and Casper 2001; Simmons and O'Neill 2001). In the past 40 years, we've also seen a 1,000% increase in the number of unmarried, cohabiting couples. It is estimated that today over half of all first marriages are preceded by living together—a practice that was virtually nonexistent in earlier eras (National Marriage Project 2003). Typically, though, divorce is cited as the primary threat to the health of the marriage institution. While the divorce rate has recently declined in the United States (the 2001 rate of 4.0 per 1,000 population is the lowest in the last quarter century), our nation still displays the highest divorce rate in the world (Blankenhorn 2003; United Nations 2000; *World*

Almanac 2003). Yet note that our propensity toward divorce is not a recent or modern phenomenon.

Divorce is a rather old practice in America. The United States has ranked Number 1 on the divorce scale since the late 1800s. The first American divorce was recorded in 1639 and occurred in Puritan Massachusetts (Riley [1991] 1997). The Puritans viewed unsuccessful marriages as obstacles to the harmony deemed important to their society. Consequently, divorce was regarded as a necessary tool for the *safeguard* of marriage, family, and community (Riley [1991] 1997; Salmon 1986; Weisberg 1975).

By the Revolutionary War, divorce was a firmly established practice in the colonies, one defended via the revolutionary values and rhetoric of our newly formed nation. Thomas Jefferson, for example, in preparing notes for a divorce case in Virginia, defended the right to a divorce, using the principles of "independence" and "happiness" (Riley [1991] 1997). In 1832, divorce entered the White House. Andrew Jackson was elected to the presidency despite a much publicized marriage to a divorced woman (Owsley 1977).

By the mid-1800s, divorce was characterized as a right of those whose freedom was compromised by an unsuccessful marriage. In the years following the Civil War, the U.S. divorce rate increased faster than the rates of both general population growth and married population growth (Riley [1991] 1997). By World War I, this nation witnessed one divorce for every nine marriages (Glick and Sung-Ling 1986). For a short time after World War II, there was one divorce for every three marriages of women over 30! In 1960, the U.S. divorce rate began to increase annually, until the rate doubled and peaked in 1982. Today, it's thought that nearly half of recent first marriages may end in divorce (Kreider and Fields 2002). When viewed within its historical context, it is clear that divorce is an American tradition.

In considering high divorce rates in the United States, we must take care not to interpret these figures as an indictment of the marriage institution. Despite lack of success in first-time marriages, most divorced individuals do remarry, and half do so within about 3 years (Kreider and Fields 2002). Fifty-four percent of divorced women remarry within 5 years, and 75% remarry within 10 years (Bramlett and Mosher 2002). High remarriage rates indicate that divorce is clearly a rejection of a specific partner and not a rejection of marriage itself. Indeed, these remarriage patterns have prompted some observers of the family to recognize a new variation on our standard practice of monogamy: namely, serial monogamy. **Monogamy** refers to an exclusive union: for example, one man married to one woman at one time. **Serial monogamy** refers to the practice of successive, multiple marriages—that is, over the course of a lifetime, a person enters into successive monogamous unions.

The prevalence of serial monogamy in the United States suggests that the old adage "Once burned, twice shy" does not seem to apply to people who have been divorced. Indeed, the inclination to remarry—even after one has been "burned"—may provide the greatest testimony to the importance of marriage as a social institution.

Is there a positive side to divorce? Some research suggests that divorce does provide a latent function in U.S. society. A **latent function** is an unintended benefit or consequence of a social practice or pattern. Studies show that as divorce rates in the United States increase, so do rates of marital satisfaction. Considering high divorce rates in conjunction with increasing marital satisfaction suggests that in the long run, divorce may make marriage a healthier institution (Veroff, Douvan, and Kulka 1981). By dissolving unhappy unions, divorce frees individuals to create new and happy unions. Within happy marriages, fear of divorce also may encourage continued dedication to maintaining a successful union. Since most divorces are followed by remarriages, divorce can also be seen as giving people opportunities for growth and second chances in life (Hetherington and Kelly 2002; Visher, Visher, and Pasley 2003).

Any latent functions aside, divorce certainly carries several manifest dysfunctions as well. A **manifest dysfunction** refers to an obvious negative consequence of a social practice or pattern. For example, divorce has highly negative effects on the emotional well-being of ex-spouses. Research documents that ex-spouses face an increased incidence of psychological distress, depression, loneliness, and alcohol use (Hope, Rodgers, and Power, 1999; Johnson and Wu 2002; National Center for Health Statistics 2001). Financial hardship also plagues victims of divorce. Such hardship targets divorced women in particular, as studies show significant decreases in the standard of living for divorced women and their children (Bartfeld 2000; Peterson 1996; Sorenson 1990; Whitehead 1993). Among economically disadvantaged women, poverty rates for divorced women exceed those of never-married women (Lichter, Graefe, and Brown 2003).

Each year, about 1 million children must deal with the aftermath of parental divorce (National Marriage Project 2003). The children of a divorce often pay an undeniably high price for this breakup. Such children display greater emotional conflict than children from intact families, conflicts that can persist into adulthood (Amato 2000; Amato and Sobolewskei 2001; Lauer and Lauer 1991; Orbuch, Thornton, and Cancio 2000; Wallerstein and Blakeslee 1990). Children of divorce also suffer in terms of their academic achievement, self-concepts and social relations (Amato 2001a; Reifman et al. 2001). The effects of divorce can follow children into their adult relationships: Young adults from divorced families report less trust in or commitment to their own romantic relationships (Jacquet and Surra 2001). Experiencing a parental divorce at an early age also is associated with poor mental health in early and young adulthood (Chase-Lansdale, Cherlin, and Kiernan 1995; Cherlin, Chase-Lansdale, and McRae 1998).

Divorce can erode bonds between parents and children, especially those between fathers and their children (Amato and Sobolewski 2001; Scott and Church 2001). Furthermore, the children of divorce are likely to "lose" one of their parents. Despite a growing trend toward joint parental custody of children, the number of fathers living apart from their children continues to grow (Leite and McKenry 2002). In 2002, of the nearly 20 million children living with just one parent, 16.5 million lived with their mothers, and only 3.3 million lived with their fathers (Fields 2003). While one-quarter of noncustodial fathers see their children at least once a week, approximately one-third have no contact at all over the course of the year (Nord and Zill 1996). In general, there is a gradual withdrawal of fathers from their children's lives. And as visits with noncustodial parents decrease, so does the receipt of child support payments (Doherty, Kouneski, and Erikson 1996). The most recent census data indicates that only 36% of parents without joint custody or visitation arrangement receive any child support payments (U.S. Census Bureau 2000f). Lack of child support is not the only risk of "out of touch" fathers. Absent fathers can impact negatively on a son's self-esteem and his ability to form intimate relationships (Balcom 2002). Having an absent father also may increase the risk of early sexual activity among daughters (Ellis et al. 2003; McLanahan 2002).

Although divorce clearly poses serious problems for a society, the practice appears firmly rooted in the United States. Ironically, some suggest that the prevalence of divorce in our nation may stem from the heightened health and longevity of Americans. Historian Lawrence Stone (1989) argues that divorce is the functional substitute for death. In earlier periods of our history, marriages—good and bad alike—were typically terminated by death. The high mortality rates that characterized colonial America, for example, guaranteed that most marriages lasted less than 12 years (Fox and Quit 1980). But as life spans grew longer and longer, marriages faced new tests. In the current day, promises of "till death us do part" now constitute oaths that can traverse decades. Surely, such a profound demographic shift has had an effect on our divorce rates (Wells 1982).

In addition to increased life expectancy, some contend that the ready availability of divorce in the United States helps to explain the prevalence of the practice. By 1970, every state in the union permitted divorce. In that same year, no-fault divorce was introduced in California, and many states quickly followed suit.

Yet although easy access may contribute to the high rate of divorce in the United States, history reveals that the "absence" of a divorce option does little to save bad marriages. For example, in states that were slow to recognize divorce as a legal option (typically, the southern states), marriages were far from indissoluble. In lieu of legal divorce, other adaptations were readily devised: annulments, desertion, migratory divorces (divorces sought after relocations to other states), premarital contracts, and separation agreements. Indeed, South Carolina's refusal to recognize divorce resulted in a curious development in the state's inheritance laws: Mistresses (another popular adaptation to troubled marriages) were legally precluded from inheriting *any more than 25%* of a husband's estate (Riley [1991] 1997).

But longer life spans or ease of access do not tell the whole story regarding divorce in America. Our high divorce rates must be examined in light of some core American values. Consider, for example, American values relating to romantic love. Americans have long identified romantic love as the most important dimension of marriage. Indeed, it is the power and passion of love that convinces us to separate from our **families of orientation** (the families into which we are born) and form new unions with others.

The principle of a love-based marriage guarantees excitement and euphoria for the individuals involved. But linking marriage to romantic love simultaneously introduces a high risk to the institution as a whole. Consider, for instance, that research suggests that the rating of love as an important basis for marriage is more likely in societies that allow premarital and extramarital sexual relations (deMunck and Korotayev 1999). Furthermore, love is a fickle enterprise. When the sparks of passion die, love can be fleeting. Love's fickle nature is exacerbated by the fact that people frequently fall in love with possibilities rather than realities— that is, they fall for what they *want* their future spouses to be rather than what they are (Berscheid and Hatfield 1983). Assumed similarity is common for married couples, but it is greatest for people who are dating (Schul and Vinokur 2000; Watson, Hubbard, and Wiese 2000). We also find ourselves juggling competing notions of love as we move through our lives. These competing views can make love an ambiguous basis for marriage and guarantee that individuals will have to work hard and compromise and change in order to keep love and marriages going (Swidler 2001).

In short, love, especially passionate love, can and often does fade. And faded love can leave a marriage with no raison d'être, making it a union ripe for divorce. Indeed, some of the earliest U.S. divorce petitions—filed in the 1600s and 1700s—referenced lost affections and love as a justification for divorce (Riley [1991] 1997). Knowing this, love may not be the strongest foundation for the marriage institution. Indeed, many other cultures of the world do not base marriages on love; some regard a loved-based marriage as a foolish endeavor (Jankowiak and Fischer 1992) (see Box 18.1). Instead, marriages are arranged for practical, social, or economic reasons. There is some indication that these alternate factors result in more stable unions with higher survival rates than those motivated by love (Dion and Dion 1996; Levine 1993).

Box 18.1   Love as a Questionable Basis for Marriage

Longing to Belong
Saira Shah

At 17, I was so homesick for a country I'd never known that I let my Afghan relatives begin to arrange my marriage.

My brother and sister Tahir and Safia, and my elderly aunt Amina and I were all attending the wedding of my uncle's son. Although my uncle's home was closer than I'd ever been, I was not yet inside Afghanistan. This branch of my family lived in Peshawar, Pakistan. On seeing two unmarried daughters in the company of a female chaperone, my uncle obviously concluded that we had been sent to be married. I was taken aback by the visceral longing I felt to be part of this world.... If I allowed my uncle to arrange a marriage for me, I would belong. Over the next few days, the man my family wished me to marry was introduced into the inner sanctum.... My putative fiancé ... sent a constant flow of lavish gifts. I was busy examining my hoard when my uncle's wife announced that he was on the phone. My intended was a favorite of hers; she had taken it upon herself to promote the match. As she handed me the receiver, he delivered a line culled straight from a Hindi movie: "We shall have a love-match, *ach-cha?*" Enough was enough. I slammed down the phone and went to find Aunt Amina. When she had heard me out, she said: "I'm glad that finally you've stopped this silly wild goose chase for your roots. I'll have to extricate you from this mess. . . . "My uncle's wife was sitting on her prayer platform in the drawing room. Amina stormed in, scattering servants before her like chaff. "Your relative . . ." was Amina's opening salvo, ". . . has been making obscene remarks to my niece . . . Over the *telephone!*" "How dare you!" her rival began . . . It gave Amina exactly the opportunity she needed to move in for the kill. "What? Do you support this lewd conduct? Are we living in an American movie? Since when have young people of mixed sexes been permitted to speak to each other on the telephone? Let alone to talk—as I regret to inform you your nephew did—of love! Since when has love had anything to do with marriage? What a dangerous and absurd concept!"

Excerpt from "Longing to Belong," *The New York Times Magazine*, September 21, 2003.

Romantic love is only one American value that may be linked to the nation's high divorce rates. The pursuit of personal freedom, self-actualization, and self-gratification—all values on which the establishment and expansion of our country were based—are also quite compatible with our well-exercised "right" to divorce. Consider that the westward expansion of this country was fueled, in part, by settlers who carried the spirit of rugged individualism. Many who migrated to the West did so without the support or company of recalcitrant spouses. Under such conditions, liberal divorce laws in Western states and territories proved to be a valuable mechanism for resolving such migratory conflicts.

Liberal divorce policies also proved a boon to self-actualizing business entrepreneurs. For example, when social pressure from antidivorce factions saw Nevada increase its divorce residency requirement from six months to a year, Nevada businesspeople vigorously protested the change. Such a change posed a threat to the valuable revenues typically generated by the "divorce trade." Thus, in the interest of capturing more and more of the dollars spent in pursuing a divorce, Nevada eventually dropped its residency requirement to six weeks (Riley [1991] 1997).

If core American values contribute to high divorce rates, then a reversal of divorce trends in the United States may demand major cultural changes—changes that would be difficult to execute. For example, increasing marital stability may require that love give way to less romantic criteria in making marriage decisions. Yet that such a shift would be made seems highly unlikely. A cursory review of television programming, movie plots, literature, or music clearly demonstrates that Americans are "in love" with the notion of love. Viewers of romantic programming tend to have higher idealistic expectations of love (Segrin and Nabi 2002). Furthermore, surveys from the 1960s through the 1980s document an increase in Americans' commitment to love as the basis for marriage (Simpson, Campbell, and Berscheid 1986). More recently, an overwhelming majority of American college students indicated that they would not be willing to enter into a loveless marriage. Decidedly larger numbers of non-American students, however, were willing to entertain this possibility (Levine 1993).

Similarly, individualism's dire effects on many a happy marriage suggest that decreasing divorce rates may require an exchange of individualism for concerns of community. Again, however, such a change is unlikely. Individualism is arguably the "defining" American value. (Consider again, for instance, that single-person households are the second most common living arrangements in the United States today). Proposed solutions to other social problems, such as welfare, poverty, and homelessness, recommend a recommitment to individual accomplishment and responsibility. The "me-generation" of the 1980s, the decline in social connections, and the economic threats of the 1990s have put concerns for "Number 1" at the forefront of American attentions (Collier 1991; Etzioni 1994, 1996; Putnam 2000).

In contrast, many feel that concerns for community have gradually come to occupy the "back burner" of the American agenda. In recent years, national leaders such as former Speaker of the House Newt Gingrich have been known to fight community-minded programs (i.e., the National Youth Corp), arguing that volunteerism should be a "personal decision" rather than an institutionalized practice. Some social scientists contend that the average U.S. citizen may now share the Gingrich mentality. Robert Putnam, a political scientist who examines trends in community participation, notes a marked decline in civic involvement. He argues that few U.S. citizens are actively engaged in solving problems such as crime, drug abuse, homelessness, and unemployment—all threats to community stability (Putnam 1995, 1996, 2000).

As community loses its place on the American agenda, some speculate that family has come to fill the void. In many ways, family has become the substitute for community. In contrast to the America of the 1930s and 1940s, where "God, Home, and Country" were the rule, the America of recent decades finds religion and civic concerns overpowered by issues of family. According to a recent Gallup poll, staying home with family (25%) is second only to watching television (26%) as American's favorite way of spending an evening (Gallup Poll 2001). A growing percentage of American youth report that having a good marriage and family life is extremely important to them (National Marriage Project 2003). As we move into young adulthood, our sense of family obligation increases (Fuligni and Pedersen 2002). As we age, the emotional support we receive from our families is an important resource, one that increases our life expectancies (Ross and Mirowsky 2002). And the family is the backbone of supportive services for the aged and the disabled (AARP 2003b).

Ironically, Americans' heavy investments in family may make this unit increasingly vulnerable to the practice of divorce. When family experiences fail to yield the expected emotional benefits, American cultural traditions and laws make it possible to "cut our losses" and invest anew. Oddly enough, our restricted family focus may render the family more, rather than less, vulnerable to disruption (Giddens 1992).

In considering the reasons for high divorce rates in the United States, one additional factor requires attention. Certain social structural changes also mitigate the likelihood of waning divorce rates. For example, increased labor force participation of both married and unmarried women and high geographic mobility both create social contexts that increase the risk of marital dissolution (South 2001; South and Lloyd 1995). The practice of cohabiting before marriage is growing—about half of all first marriages are preceded by cohabitation. Yet the evidence suggests that marriages preceded by cohabitation tend to have higher divorce rates (National Marriage Project 2003). Furthermore, it is estimated that 40% of children spend time in a cohabiting family (Bumpass and Lu 2000). Such arrangements as well as the reality of having divorced parents may offer children counterproductive lessons about commitment (Amato 2001b). The rise in single-person households over the last few decades may make it easier for some individuals to contemplate the prospect of "going it alone" after a divorce. Last, decreasing marital fertility may mean that some unhappy spouses will perceive fewer obstacles to divorce.

Is marriage a failing institution? Hardly. But along with the health of marriage in America comes the health of divorce. Arguably, divorce is itself an established institution, one which facilitates the pursuit of some core American values. Without some changes to these values, we can well expect both high marriage rates and high divorce rates to be a rather permanent feature of our society.

Learning More About It

Much of the historical data on divorce in this essay were obtained from Glenda Riley's book, *Divorce: An American Tradition* (New York: Oxford University Press, 1991; University of Nebraska Press, Reprint, 1997).

Ann Swidler's *Talk of Love: How Culture Matters* (Chicago: University of Chicago Press, 2001) explores the different meanings and myths of love in American culture.

The Ties that Bind: Perspectives on Marriage and Cohabitation (New York: Aldine de Gruyter, 2000) is an edited volume (by Linda Waite, Christine Bachrach, Michelle Hindin, Elizabeth Thomson and Arland Thorton) that explores a range of topics relevant to our marriage practices—marital commitment, ethnicity and beliefs about marriage, marital values in context, the transformation of the meaning of marriage, and so on.

The late 1990s saw the emergence of a new "marriage movement" that is embraced by the Bush Whitehouse and informs various government policies (i.e., welfare reform). The PBS documentary *Let's Get Married* (November 2002) provided a brief introduction to the marriage movement and its reception by citizens and politicians alike: <http://www.pbs.org/wgbh/pages/frontline/shows/marriage/etc/script.htm>

A very readable review of how children fare without fathers is offered by Sara McLanahan in "Life Without Father: What Happens to the Children?" *Contexts* 1 (Spring): 35–44.

You can visit *Public Agenda Online* and click on the *Issue Guides* link to find an overview of major family issues and competing perspectives on future policy, and to review public opinion on an assortment of family topics: <*http://www.publicagend.org*>

James Lincoln Collier offers a rather thorough and highly readable review of the moral transformation of American society in his book *The Rise of Selfishness in America* (New York: Oxford University Press, 1991). In *The Spirit of Community: The Reinvention of American Society* (Touchstone Books, 1994), Amitai Etzioni explores the connection between individual rights, responsibilities, community, and the role of family in this mix. Robert Putnam's *Bowling Alone: The Collapse and Revival of American Community* (New York: Simon and Schuster, 2000) offers evidence that he claims documents the decline of social capital in American society in recent decades. Robert Wuthnow offers an interesting rebuttal to the "lost community" argument in *Loose Connections: Civic Involvement in America's Fragmented Communities* (Cambridge, MA: Harvard University Press, 1998).

Exercises

1. Trying to understand divorce in America provides a good opportunity for exercising our sociological imagination. Divorce, as it currently stands in our society, is not just a "private trouble"—a personal failing of the individual. Rather, it is a "public issue"—a phenomenon tied to myriad broader social, cultural, and historical events. Confusing public issues with private troubles results in misinformed social policy. Public issues cannot be remedied with individual-oriented solutions appropriate to private troubles. Instead, public issues require that we pay attention to changes in social forces that are larger than and transcend individuals. Recognizing divorce as a public issue, identify three appropriate targets for our reform efforts.

2. Go to your local or university library and collect recent statistics on national divorce rates, broken down by the following groups: African Americans, Asian Americans, Hispanics, and Whites of Western European origin. Attempt to explain any differences you find using information on the cultural values held within each group.

3. Love is the basis on which current American marriages are built. Think of at least two other possible foundations for the institution of marriage. In each case, what are the likely ramifications of changing the "rules" of choosing a mate?

Social Institutions

THE ECONOMY

Essay 19

Conventional Wisdom Tells Us ...
Welfare Is Ruining This Country

A frequently expressed opinion when talk turns to welfare reform is that too many people are on the dole and too many recipients have other options. In this essay, we review some of the least understood dimensions of welfare and explore exactly where welfare moneys are going.

Charges against the United States welfare system abound in conventional wisdom. Welfare recipients are thought to be lazy people. They are accused of lacking the motivation to earn an honest living, preferring instead to take handouts from the government. Furthermore, many believe that the welfare rolls are continuously growing and riddled with fraud. It is often discussed as a program plagued by able-bodied con artists—people with no financial need—who nonetheless manage to collect welfare checks.

Conventional wisdom also tells us that welfare fails to help those on the dole. Rather, it creates further dependency among its recipients. As such, many argue that welfare expenditures are ruining this nation. Welfare represents too great a burden for a government facing unsettled financial times.

Is the conventional wisdom regarding welfare accurate? Is welfare simply a tax on the economy, one destroying American initiative? A fair assessment of the system requires us to evaluate the many charges against it.

Many of the common and persistent beliefs about welfare are largely a product of the AFDC (Aid to Families with Dependent Children) era of public assistance. Concerns about AFDC helped fuel the clamor for welfare reform. Reform materialized in 1996 with the passage of the Personal Responsibility and Work Opportunity Reconciliation Act (PRWORA), which abolished the AFDC program and replaced it with a new, time-limited Temporary Assistance to Needy Families (TANF). TANF is a "welfare-to-work" program. It gives states much flexibility in structuring their welfare programs, but it imposes a restriction on federal funding: Families are subject to a lifetime limit of five years of support. TANF was implemented in all 50 states within 18 months of its 1996 passage (California was the last state to put TANF into effect). In this essay, we will look back at the AFDC era as well as the current TANF program to see whether there is any basis for common views about welfare.

Are welfare rolls spinning out of control? Data suggest that the answer to the question is no. In 1993 (the AFDC period), just over 5% of the total population were on AFDC welfare rolls. In 1997, during the AFDC to TANF transition, the figure had dropped to less than 4%. Today it's estimated that only about 2% of the population are TANF recipients (U.S. Department of Health and Human Services 2002b; Waldfogel 2003). Thus, no matter the era we examine, the welfare ranks are small.

Do welfare recipients live "high on the hog" and have more and more kids to keep the benefits flowing? In the pre-welfare reform period, the average monthly cash benefits to an AFDC family amounted to under $500, an amount that was insufficient for lifting families out of poverty. Under the TANF program, cash benefits are even less. A recent congressional report shows that $349 is the average monthly cash payment for a program family. Also note that in both eras, AFDC and TANF, the typical welfare family is small. A typical AFDC family consisted of a mother and one or two children; in the TANF program, two in five families have only one child. (Administration for Children and Families 2002).

Are welfare recipients simply lazy? No doubt some are. After all, laziness is a trait found in all social groups. However, it would be wrong to assume that the *typical* welfare recipient is a social loafer. In both the AFDC and the TANF eras, a mother with dependent children represents the average welfare recipient. And today, despite the challenges posed by child care, more than a quarter of TANF adult recipients are employed (Administration for Children and Families 2002; U.S. Department of Labor 1998).

To be sure, the perceived positive value of work is the cornerstone of TANF: To receive temporary assistance, recipients *must* get job training or find work. At first glance, this would seem like a step in the right direction. TANF should provide some strong incentives that will move individuals from welfare to work. What could be wrong with this reasoning and policy? If you listen to the critics, there's plenty wrong.

Consider again the typical welfare recipient: Ninety percent of all adult welfare recipients are women, and most are single parents (Administration for Children and Families 2002). Critics of the "welfare to work" reform raise two key objections. First, TANF forces poor mothers to choose work *over* caring for their children. Eligibility requirements make full-time mothering, a choice for the economically advantaged, a nonoption for the poor (Boushey 2002; Jones-DeWeever, Peterson, and Song 2003; Oliker 2000). Second, critics charge that TANF work requirements do little to combat the root cause of welfare: poverty. The disturbing truth is that many of the jobs currently available in our country—especially service sector jobs earmarked for women—simply pay too little to keep a family from the grips of poverty (Edin and Lein 1997a; Padavic and Reskin 2002; Rangarajan 1998). The **poverty threshold** is the federal government's designation of the total annual income a family requires to meet its basic needs. Currently, the poverty threshold for a family of three (e.g,. a mother and two children) is $14,494—that is, a family (as well as every person in it) whose income is below this amount is designated as "poor." (This figure is adjusted annually for inflation.) In 2002, 34.6 million people were below the poverty threshold (Proctor and Dalaker 2002). Poverty thresholds can be contrasted with **poverty guidelines**—that is, amounts used for *administrative* purposes to determine eligibility for certain federal programs. The 2003 poverty guideline for a family of three was $15,260 (U.S. Census Bureau 2003; U.S. Department of Health and Human Services 2003a).

Full-time workers at minimum-wage jobs (a condition for 2% of women over 16 years of age) earn approximately $10,000 a year. This amount would fail to put *any* working parent above the poverty threshold (U.S. Census Bureau 2003; *World Almanac* 2003). Indeed, an analysis of Los Angeles County's welfare-to-work program finds that 78% of current and former welfare recipients who entered the labor force since 1998 were nonetheless earning incomes below the poverty threshold (Rivera 2003). Even for those families who leave TANF, the average monthly income is close to the poverty threshold (Acts, Loprest, and Roberts 2001).

As counterintuitive as it may seem, accepting a minimum- or low-wage job can actually prove a "costly" proposition for the poor. Employment can deprive former welfare recipients of other essential benefits, such as food stamps, housing assistance, and health care (Edin and Lein 1997a; Rangarajan 1998). Follow-up studies find that many former TANF recipients are unaware that they may still be eligible for food stamps and Medicaid benefits after they leave the welfare rolls (Quint, Widom, and Moore 2001). Census data indicate that working actually hurts the chances of health care coverage for the poor: 54.5% of the working poor have health insurance, while 63.4% of nonworking poor are covered (Mills 2001). Other follow-up research on newly employed welfare recipients indicates a similar outcome—new workers experience a decline in access to employment based health insurance post-TANF reforms (Jones-DeWeever et al. 2003). For some, "work first" employment has come at the cost of pursuing postsecondary education (Jones-DeWeever et al. 2003; Mazzeo, Rab, and Eachus 2003). Welfare-to-work programs also appear to have an adverse effect on partici- pants' adolescent children who are experiencing increases in below-average performances, repeating grades, and in receiving special education services (MDRC 2003).

Low-paying jobs also fail to provide a solution to a major obstacle facing poor female heads of households: child care (Hartmann and Yi 2001; Rangarajan 1998). In the major urban areas of 49 out of 50 states, it is more costly to provide a four-year-old with child care for a year than to pay a year's tuition for an older child at a public college (Schulman 2000). On average, working families devote 9% of their yearly earnings to child care. Child care, then, can easily be the second-largest expense (behind rent or mortgages) in a family budget

(Giannerelli, Adelman, and Schmidt 2003). As family income *decreases*, the proportion spent on child care *increases*. A family in poverty must be prepared to devote over a third of its income to child care costs (Smith 2000). A recent report by the Children's Defense Fund charges that every state's child care subsidy system comes up short on quality and availability. Some states have unreasonably low income cutoffs (e.g., $25,000 for a family of three), others have excessively high copayments, and still others are strapped for the resources to fund programs and as a result have long waiting lists (Children's Defense Fund 2001). At present, even when all federal funding is combined, only one in four eligible children are assisted with child care subsidies (National Council of Churches 2003). Without much-needed increases in TANF reauthorization funding, it is estimated that hundreds of thousands of children in working families will lose access to child care assistance in the near future (Fremstad 2003; Parrott and Mezey 2003).

The harsh truth is that hard work does not necessarily save one from the need for government assistance. In 2001, nearly 5% of those in the labor force were classified as "working poor"—that is, these individuals are employed but not making enough to get above the poverty threshold (U.S. Department of Labor 2003). Furthermore, the majority of the working poor (60%) are poor *despite holding full-time jobs* (U.S. Department of Labor 2002b). Homelessness—perhaps the most visible marker of poverty—offers additional evidence that work and poverty are not mutually exclusive. The U.S. Conference of Mayors' 2002 survey found that 22% of the urban homeless are employed. Their earnings, however, are not enough to pay for a place to live (U.S. Conference of Mayors 2002).

The plight of the working poor is especially stark when we the consider the effects on the family. For example, a family of four, with both parents working full-time at minimum wage jobs, will just barely keep their collective heads above the poverty line (using either the current poverty threshold or poverty guideline figures). Change the picture to a single-parent family—where only one parent's salary pays the bills—and the family will almost certainly fall into the clutches of poverty. The poverty rate for a working mother with children under 18 years of age at home is 21%; when the children at home are under 6 years of age, the rate climbs to 30% (U.S. Census Bureau 2002c). The financial state of children in single-parent homes is quite precarious: Such children are *four and one-half times more likely* to be poor as their counterparts in a two-parent family (Administration for Children and Families 2002). With the development of unforeseen hardships such as illness, layoffs, home or car repairs, and so on, a hardworking, lower-income family could be plunged into official poverty. A hardworking family could all too easily find itself in need of welfare.

Do those who enter the welfare system become hopelessly dependent on it? The recent overhaul of the U.S. welfare program was tied to this assumption. Yet a large body of research proves that the assumption is false. Those who turn to the government for financial help tend not to seek that assistance for very long. Despite the rather prevalent belief that welfare is a chronic dependency condition (that is, a long-lasting condition assumed to destroy one's will to work), most people receive assistance for relatively short periods of time. One-third of those receiving food stamps leave the program within four months. Similarly, between 1993 and 1995, 31% of AFDC recipients spent only four months or less in the program, and over one-half were off the program in a year or less (U.S. Department of Health and Human Services 2002b).

The welfare changes introduced by TANF mandate relatively short assistance periods. In general, an adult-headed family is limited to 60 months of TANF-funded assistance *over its lifetime.* States are free to set shorter time limits if they so desire. Twenty states have done so (Schott 2000). Given the mandated time limits, many TANF recipients are motivated to leave welfare as soon as they begin working in order to "stop the clock" on their lifetime eligibility. In North Carolina, for instance, the average length of stay on the state's "Work First" TANF program is 6 to 8 months (Spivey 2002). Recent analysis of individuals who have left welfare during the "welfare-to-work" reform period indicates that about a quarter of leavers do return to welfare within 12 months of their exit. But these returners don't stay for long: More than two-thirds leave welfare rolls again within the year (Bavier 2001). The short-term nature of individuals' tenure with welfare is really a long-term trend. Such findings would seem to confirm that welfare is not an enticing lifelong choice.

It is also important to note that most welfare stays are not the result of being born to poverty. Rather, ordinary life events such as unemployment, illness, or divorce can easily push one into poverty. Consider for instance, that in 2001, nearly 15% of Americans were without health care insurance (Cooper 2002). Only about half of those in the workforce participate in medical health care programs (U.S. Census Bureau 2002, Table 139). Imagine, then, the potentially devastating financial consequences for those families facing a medical emergency. Given the relative ease with which one can slip into poverty, it is actually quite remarkable that only a very small percentage of American families remain permanently poor and therefore permanently tied to welfare programs.

Suppose we were all to agree that most welfare recipients are hardworking, honest individuals who simply need some temporary help. Isn't it still the case that the welfare system represents too great a financial burden for our country? To answer this question accurately, we must carefully distinguish among the terms *poverty, public assistance programs* (a.k.a. welfare programs), and *social insurance programs* of the welfare state.

Poverty refers to an economic state where one's annual income is below the threshold judged necessary to support a predetermined minimal standard of living. For the first time since the early 1990s, the national poverty rate is increasing, hovering at just over 12% of the population in 2002 (Proctor and Dalaker 2003). In the United States, we have experienced double-digit poverty rates for the last quarter of a century. Yet it is important to note that the percentage of families receiving AFDC/TANF over this same time period has never climbed out of the single digits. Recall that a few years prior to TANF reforms (in 1993), just over 5% of the population was on welfare. In 1997, under 4% of the total population was on welfare. Welfare reform of the last few years is credited with cutting welfare caseloads in half (Miller 2002; Waldfogel 2003). Estimates today put the percentage of recipients at just over 2% of the population (U.S. Department of Health and Human Services 2002b; Waldfogel 2003). Similarly, since TANF reform the number of children receiving benefits has been cut in half and is presently at an all-time low rate of less than 6%. Only a small percentage of the total population receive food stamps: 6% in 2000. For the past quarter century, the percentage of all Americans who receive SSI (Supplemental Security Income for elderly, blind, or disabled individuals meeting income eligibility) has held fairly constant at just over 2% (U.S. Department of Health and Human Services 2002b). Clearly, only a small percentage of Americans participate in "traditional" welfare programs. More surprising, however, is the fact that only a portion of those *living in poverty* enter the welfare system; these individuals enter the system via public assistance programs.

Public assistance programs are those directed exclusively at the eligible poor—that is, recipients must meet income and, most recently, behavioral requirements. One might think that once determined to be eligible, families would rush to receive their due. This is hardly the case. Just over half of families eligible for TANF enroll and receive benefits. Similarly, only half of those eligible for food stamps participate in that program (U.S. Department of Health and Human Services 2002b). Only 44% of households below the poverty threshold receive Medicaid benefits (U.S. Census Bureau 2002, Table 514). Less than 3% of the population is considered "dependent" on welfare—that is, receiving more than 50% of its total yearly income from TANF, food stamps, and/or SSI. (And the government agency issuing this figure admits it is an overestimate given the way that "dependency" is actually calculated.) These figures would suggest that public assistance is a safety net that many Americans would rather live without (U.S. Department of Health and Human Services 2002b).

As recently as the late 1980s, less than 1% of the annual federal budget was devoted to the now defunct mainstay of our welfare system, the AFDC (Rubin 1996). Federal spending for AFDC's replacement, TANF, was capped at $16.4 billion a year through 2002. The administration has since frozen TANF funding at 16.5 billion a year through 2007 (Children's Monitor 2003; Parrott 2002). By way of comparison, our current defense spending was close to $350 billion in 2002 (U.S. Census Bureau 2002, Table 485). This amount, of course, significantly increased with the 2003 war in Iraq.

As these figures show, America's financial burdens lie not with antipoverty public assistance programs like AFDC and TANF, but elsewhere. More specifically, America's financial woes are located in social insurance programs like Social Security and Medicare. **Social insurance programs** are those that require payroll contributions from future beneficiaries. Neither eligibility for nor benefits from these programs are linked to financial need.

The 2002 federal expenditures (estimated) for Social Security and Medicare reached over $459 and $226 billion, respectively (U.S. Census Bureau 2002, Table 450). Thus, in reality, social insurance programs—not antipoverty public assistance programs—are our largest "welfare" expenditures. Indeed, these social insurance programs constitute the largest part of what we have come to define as America's "welfare state"—a state that transcends poverty per se and instead offers protection based on our more general rights of citizenship (Bowles and Gintis 1982). For the 2004 Health and Human Services Budget, 3.5% of the funds are directed at TANF, while 47.6% are earmarked for Medicare (U.S. Department of Health and Human Services 2003b).

When we turn to facts and figures, we can quickly discredit the conventional wisdom on welfare. Yet we must also concede that year after year, conventional wisdom on this subject overpowers facts and figures. Why?

Some of our misconceptions regarding welfare no doubt are fueled by the profound changes occurring in the economic and occupational structure of our society. Americans today face a growing gap between the rich and poor—a gap that is setting all-time "highs" and "lows." Simply put, the rich are getting richer, and the poor are getting poorer (Center on Budget and Policy Priorities 2002). This long-standing trend makes the United States the most unequal democracy in the world (Boshara 2003). From 1977 to 1989, the incomes of the wealthiest 1% of Americans nearly doubled, whereas the remainder of the population saw either no improvement or a decline in their incomes (Mandel 1992). A Congressional Budget Office study found that from 1979 to 1997, the top 1% of families saw their after-tax incomes rise 157%; middle-income families experienced a 10% gain (Krugman 2002). The most recent census data show that the average income of the top 5% of the population was $260,464 in 2001. For this same time period, the average yearly income *for every other income category* fell (Center on Budget and Policy Priorities 2002). The wealthiest fifth of American households received over 50% of the total national income. The bottom fifth of American households received less than 5% of the total national income (see Table 19.1) (Greenstein and Shapiro 2003). Another telling way to understand the concentration of wealth in the hands of the few is by looking at the increases in millionaires and "deca-millionaires" (individuals worth $10 million or more). In the past 20 years, the number of millionaires in the United States has doubled (so that we have almost 5 million today), while the number of "deca-millionaires" has tripled, reaching almost 240,000 today (Boshara 2003).

Table 19.1   Income Distribution: Percentage of National Income and Average Incomes for Selection Portions of American Households (After Taxes), 2000

	Percentage of National Income	Average Income
Top 1%	15.5%	$862,700
Top One-fifth	51.3%	$141,400
Next One-fifth	20.2%	$59,200
Next One-fifth	14.6%	$41,900
Next One-fifth	9.7%	$29,000
Bottom One-fifth	4.9%	$13,700

SOURCE: Center on Budget and Policy Priorities (2003).

In the face of present economic circumstances, intergenerational upward mobility is no longer a birthright for most Americans. **Intergenerational upward mobility** refers to social status gains by children vis-à-vis their parents. In the 1950s, the average male worker could expect a 50% increase in income over the course of his working lifetime. This expectation is no longer a safe bet for the average worker. Rather, present-day workers find themselves competing in a global economy. As a result of this turn of events, many American jobs have been lost to other countries, and wages for low-skill jobs have suffered a marked decline. Furthermore, present-day workers find themselves in an occupational landscape that is increasingly dominated by computer-related and service industry jobs (Berman 2001; Hecker 2001; Padavic and Reskin 2002). Yet for one-third of these fast-growing occupations, workers can anticipate low to very low annual earnings (i.e., a max of $25,760 a year) (U.S. Census Bureau 2002, Table 589). Again looking ahead, most new jobs will be concentrated in occupations that require work-related training. Indeed, jobs requiring only the shortest of training periods (one month or less) are expected to grow the fastest. Unfortunately, jobs requiring little on-the-job training have low wages—only 60% of the mean for all wage and salary workers (Hecker 2001). Consequently, many of those entering the labor force in the next few years will be faced with modest- or lower-paying jobs.

Shifts in the occupational and economic structure of our society have shaken the very core of American values. Americans invest heavily in the idea that they can and will work their way up the socioeconomic ladder; the economic shifts described here threaten that belief. The growing inability to achieve the "American Dream" has left many people frustrated and searching for someone to blame. In this regard, the poor—and welfare recipients in particular—are easy scapegoats. The logic of the welfare system is completely inconsistent with fundamental American values: individual effort, equal opportunity, success, and upward mobility. Rather than promoting hard work and achievement, welfare programs are thought to institutionalize qualities that are directly opposite. In this way, welfare recipients come to constitute an out-group in our society (Feagin 1975; Lewis 1978). **Out-groups** are considered undesirable and are thought to hold values and beliefs foreign to one's own. An out-group is identified as such by an **in-group**, which holds itself in high esteem and demands loyalty from its members.

Individuals who can avoid public assistance, regardless of their exact income, can count themselves as members of the hardworking in-group. Indeed, it is the negative image of the welfare out-group that keeps many poor and near-poor from accessing various forms of public assistance: "I may be poor, but I'm not on welfare."

The power of American values explains why we cling to conventional wisdom regarding welfare. This power also can help us better understand why relatively few Americans denigrate society's wealthy sector, even when that wealth is gained at the expense of the working and middle class. The General Social Survey (GSS) has found that fully 57% of respondents agreed that "people should be allowed to accumulate as much wealth as they can even if some make millions while others live in poverty." Less than 30% of respondents disagreed with this sentiment (GSS 2000). After all, a rising tide lifts all boats. To be sure, those on the upper rungs of the U.S. stratification ladder are indeed accumulating wealth. Over the past 30 years, we have witnessed a 2,500% rise in CEO incomes (Krugman 2002). At present, the average salary of top corporate executives is 411 times higher than that of the average hourly worker! In 2001, the CEO of Home Depot received a total compensation package of $41,105,409— enough to support 1,611 average workers and 3,837 minimum-wage workers (AFL-CIO 2003). When we value individual effort and opportunity, tolerance of wealth must be expected. We embrace the old adage that "what's good for GM (or more recently GE) is good for America." (In his last full year running GE, CEO Jack Welch was paid $123 million; his retirement package included perks worth at least $2 million a year [Krugman 2002]). The wealthiest have already arrived where many of us would like to go. They are proof to us that individual efforts can pay off; they are proof that the American Dream, to which we are so committed, lives on.

To sustain the power of American values, we must lay the blame for poverty on the poor themselves. There is, of course, a certain irony and destructiveness to this process. Personalizing poverty deflects our attention from the social causes of poverty, such as changing occupational structure and lack of education. Such a stance lessens the likelihood that we will successfully reduce poverty. Indeed, without major social changes, social reproduction theory suggests that the American Dream will continue to elude the poor. **Social reproduction theory** maintains that existing social, cultural, and economic arrangements work to "reproduce" in future generations the social class divisions of the present generation. Princeton economist Paul Krugman identifies corporate culture and boardroom handshakes as the invisible force behind the recent explosion in CEO pay (Krugman 2002).

One proponent of social reproduction theory, Pierre Bourdieu (1977a, 1977b), maintains that the aspirations of lower-class children are adversely affected by their class position. The lower-class child is immersed in a social world hostile to the American Dream. The objective realities of the lower-class environment deflate hopes of success; the restricted opportunity structure inherent in a lower-class location leads to reduced life aspirations.

Social reproduction is not the only obstacle to poverty reduction. Structural functionalists remind us that the elimination of poverty is highly unlikely as long as the poor among us serve valuable social functions. **Structural functionalism** is a theoretical approach that stresses social order. Proponents contend that society is a collection of interdependent parts that function together to produce consensus and stability. **Social functions** refer to the intended and unintended social consequences of various behaviors and practices.

Personalizing poverty sustains a lower class. The lower class, in turn, fulfills many needs for those in other social locations. For example, the poor provide society with a cheap labor pool. They also create countless job opportunities for others: for those wishing to help them—social workers, policymakers, and so on—as well as for those wishing to control them—police and corrections officers. The poor even provide financial opportunities for those wishing to take advantage of them—loan sharks, for example, and corporations seeking tax breaks via the food discard market (Funiciello 1990; Gans 1971; Jacobs 1988). And sustaining the poverty out-group enables the social mainstream to better define and reaffirm some of its most fundamental values and beliefs.

In light of these functions, we must reexamine the notion that welfare is ruining this country. Welfare may breed dependency, but dependency for whom? Given the social functions of the poor, welfare may breed a social dependency of the masses on the few, as the poor ultimately serve as vehicles by which mainstream values are assured.

Learning More About It

If you want to learn more about the reality and challenges of working for poverty-level wages see Barbara Ehrenreich's best-selling *Nickle and Dimed: On (Not) Getting By in America* (New York: Owl Books, 2001).

To read more about the gender and racial base of poverty, see Diana M. Pearce's 1983 article, "The Feminization of Ghetto Poverty," *Society* 21(1): 70–74. See also J. Devine and J.D. Wright's *The Greatest of Evils* (New York: Aldine de Gruyter, 1993) or Kathryn Edin's and Laura Lein's *Making Ends Meet: How Single Mothers Survive Welfare and Low-Wage Work* (New York: Russell Sage, 1997b).

To learn more about the poor as social scapegoats, see Jeffrey Reiman's book, *The Rich Get Richer and The Poor Get Prison,* 7th edition (Boston: Allyn & Bacon, 2004).

The classic work on the functions of poverty is Herbert Gans's "The Uses of Poverty: The Poor Pay for All," *Social Policy* (summer): 20–24, 1971.

To learn more about the growing inequality of wealth in America, you can access the study, "Pulling Apart A State-by-State Analysis of Income Trends" at the Economic Policy Institute's Web page: <http://www.epinet.org/content.cfm/studies_pullingapart>

The following organization and sites can also help you learn more about welfare:

Administration for Children and Families
U.S. Department of Health and Human Services
Web site: <http://www.dhhs.gov/>

U.S. Department of Labor's Welfare-to-Work Highlights
Web site: <http://wtw.doleta.gov/>

Welfare Information Network (WIN)
Web site: <http://www.financeprojectinfo.org/win/>

National Coalition for the Homeless
Web site: <http://www.nationalhomeless.org>

Exercises

1. American values are one explanation for the triumph of conventional wisdom over facts. Choose another concept from the material covered thus far in your course and provide an alternate explanation of why welfare gets such a "bum rap."

2. The cutoff level for official poverty is arbitrary. Identify five different consequences of setting the cutoff point higher; identify five consequences of setting the cutoff point lower. Are the consequences you identify primarily functional or dysfunctional for mainstream Americans?

Essay 20

Conventional Wisdom Tells Us . . . Immigrants Are Ruining This Nation

"Why don't you go back where you came from?" This angry cry seems to be getting more and more familiar as the United States faces the highest levels of immigration in its history. Is immigration ruining this nation? This essay reviews the historical impact and future trends of immigration in the United States.

"Why don't you go back where you came from?" This is a familiar taunt that most of us have heard. Here in the United States, it is a question often born of ethnic and racial prejudice. And, increasingly, feelings of prejudice target members of immigrant groups. **Prejudice** refers to the prejudgment of individuals on the basis of their group membership. **Immigrant groups** contain individuals who have left their homelands in pursuit of new lives in new countries.

Immigration has always been a fact of American life. The earliest European settlers were immigrants to the 3 to 8 million Native Americans who already occupied the continent. In the first census, in 1790, approximately one in five Americans was an "immigrant" slave brought from Africa (U.S. Census Bureau 1993). Since the early 1800s, over 68 million immigrants have arrived in the United States (U.S. Immigration and Naturalization Service 2002). Undeniably, most Americans are truly indebted to their immigrant ancestors—all but 0.8% of us are descendants of immigrants (Schuman and Olufs 1995).

Between 1970 and 2000, the immigrant population of the United States nearly tripled (Schmidley 2001). Since 1990, an average of one million *documented* immigrants have entered the United States each year. Immigrants accounted for one-third of U.S. population growth in the 1990s and for 40% of growth between 2000 and 2001 (Kent and Mather 2002). The *number* of foreign-born residents today is about twice the number during the great immigration period of the early 20th century (Martin and Midgley 1999). At present, 11.5% of the U.S. population was born abroad (Schmidley 2003). Indeed, the Census Bureau expects that immigration and higher fertility rates among foreign-born women will continue to fuel population growth for decades to come (Kent and Mather 2002). In light of such developments, the conventional wisdom on immigration suggests that the phenomenon has gotten out of hand. More and more, public sentiments urge severe limitations on the acceptance of new immigrants to our shores (Church 1993).

Given America's immigration history, the current conventional wisdom on the subject is ironic. We find ourselves casting doubt on the value of immigrants in a nation long considered the "land of immigrants."

Table 20.1 reveals that our immigrant roots are well established. As evidenced by annual parades and festivals, a great many "hyphenated-Americans" take pride in their diverse ancestral roots. At the same time, our daily newspapers and television newscasts document anti-immigration sentiments that currently run high and are frequently violent. Commentaries filled with fear, distrust, and hate are becoming a staple of talk-radio broadcasts. The Federation for American Immigration Reform (FAIR) has called for severe reductions in U.S. immigrations in order to combat excessive population growth, environmental degradation, and job loss (Martin and Midgley 1999). And the tragic events of the September 11, 2001, terrorist attacks have prompted many Americans to rethink the wisdom of freely embracing foreigners.

Table 20.1   Total and Percentage Foreign-Born for U.S. Population: 1900–2000 (Numbers in Thousands)

	Foreign-Born	
	Total	Percentage
1900	10,341	13.6
1910	13,516	14.7
1920	13,921	13.2
1930	14,204	11.6
1940	11,595	8.8
1950	10,347	6.9
1960	9,738	5.4
1970	9,619	4.7
1980	14,080	6.2
1990	19,767	7.9
2000	31,108	11.1

SOURCE: U.S. Census Bureau (2000c).

Is the current conventional wisdom on immigration justified? Do these sentiments reflect a new anti-immigration trend? Or are these anti-immigration sentiments more common and long-standing than we realize?

The immigration history of the United States is nothing if not complex. Despite the message delivered by the "Lady in the Harbor," the United States has seldom greeted immigrants with totally open arms. Descendants of the first immigrant settlers, White Anglo-Saxon Protestants from England, were slow to welcome other newcomers. Rather, they expressed concern about "new" and undesirable immigrants and organized against those arriving from Germany, Ireland, Poland, Italy, and other White ethnic countries (Fallows 1983). The 1850s saw the rise of a political party—the Know-Nothings—whose unifying theme was decidedly anti-immigration. In the 1860s, James Blaine of Maine sought to curb Catholic immigration by seeking an amendment to the U.S. Constitution banning states from providing aid to schools controlled by religious groups. His efforts established the groundwork for restrictions on government aid to religious schools and the current school voucher debate (Cohen and Gray 2003). In the same decade that the Statue of Liberty first beckoned immigrants to our shores, a group of U.S. residents founded the first all-WASP (White Anglo-Saxon Protestant) country club; these residents also established the Social Register, a list identifying the exclusive "founding" families of the United States (Baltzell 1987). In the 1920s, President Hoover freely expressed clear anti-immigration sentiments when he encouraged New York City's mayor, Fiorello La Guardia, the son of immigrants, to go back where he belonged. The mass migration period of 1880 to 1924 saw nativists and politicians working hard to restrict immigration. Campaigns to impose literacy tests in order to hold the tide on immigration were repeatedly mounted in the late 1800s and early 1900s. And from 1921 to the mid-60s, the government used a quota system to regulate and limit immigration. In 1965, Congress passed a new law that replaced quotas with a complex system that grants priorities to three categories: foreigners with relatives living in the United States, people needed to fill vacant jobs, and refugees. These changes produced a major shift in immigration patterns (more and more immigrants originating in Latin America and Asia) and renewed calls for immigration reform (Martin and Midgley 1999). These examples suggest that although the United States proudly touts its immigration history, immigration in the United States has always been characterized by a love–hate relationship.

Americans' love–hate stance toward immigration may be the product of certain core cultural values. A **cultural value** is a general sentiment that people share regarding what is good or bad, right or wrong, desirable or undesirable.

We are a nation strongly committed to economic opportunity and advancement. At various times and to various parties, the labor of immigrants has provided one sure route to economic betterment. For example, estimates suggest that nearly half of colonial-era European immigrants came to America as indentured servants who were willing to work off their debts for a chance at a better life in the new land. Similarly, the forced immigration of African slaves provided cheap labor for the South's labor-intensive agricultural development

Table 20.2   Hourly Compensation Costs for Production Workers in Select Countries/Areas, 2001 (in U.S. Dollars)

Sri Lanka	.48
Mexico	2.34
Taiwan	5.70
Hong Kong	5.96
Korea	8.09
United States	20.32

SOURCE: U.S. Bureau of Labor Statistics (2003).

(Daniels 1990). The construction of the transcontinental railroad and the economic development of the West depended on the willing and able labor of Chinese immigrants, and Japanese immigrants were welcomed as cheap, reliable labor for Hawaiian sugar plantations. By 1910, immigrants constituted 14% of our national population, yet they made up more than one-half of the industrial labor force (National Park Service 1998). In short, immigration has benefited many U.S. enterprises, industries, and corporations.

The ties that link immigrants to traditional American cultural values have not only benefited big business but also advanced the lives of countless immigrants as well. Indeed, the crush of immigrants in the mid-19th century was prompted by the immigrants' hopes that they could escape their own poverty via the economic expansion that was taking place in the United States. Such promises of economic betterment continue to attract immigrants to our shores, even amidst current trends toward economic globalization. The promise proves a potent one. Throughout the early 1990s, even the lowest-paying jobs in the United States were an improvement over those most new immigrants left behind. Wages for unskilled labor in the United States, for example, were 7 times higher than wages in South Korea, 10 to 15 times higher than wages in Central America, and 35 times higher than wages in China (Baker et al. 1993; Bonacich et al. 1994; Braun 1991; Peterson 1992). Today, American workers continue to fare better than many other workers of the world. Witness the compensation figures for production workers listed in Table 20.2.

The cultural emphasis on economic advancement and opportunity helps to explain the affinity between the United States and immigrants, but such emphasis also helps to explain our long history of resisting immigrants. American tolerance for immigrants decreases whenever immigrants prove a threat to the economic well-being of "traditional" American workers. Indeed, the strongest support for immigration restrictions has often come from organized labor (Schuman and Olufs 1995).

Recall that Chinese immigrants played a critical role in the construction of the transcontinental railroad. However, the Chinese Exclusion Act of 1882 was passed when Chinese immigrants began to be viewed as a threat to the White labor force. Similarly, Mexicans were welcome immigrants to the United States during the labor shortages imposed by World War II and again during the farm labor shortages of the 1950s. However, in the 1960s and the

1980s, when traditionally White labor jobs were in jeopardy, attempts were made to stem the flow of Mexican immigrants (Schuman and Olufs 1995).

In the 1990s, economic changes created a double bind for the traditional American workforce. Specifically, many low-wage jobs left the United States for more profitable locations abroad. (Again, see Table 20.2 to understand the financial incentives that tempted employers to move their jobs out of the United States.) At the same time, more and more foreign workers entered America and offered direct competition for the low-wage jobs that remained. These economic realities played a role in fueling current anti-immigration sentiments.

Americans' avoidance attitude toward immigration is further explained by referring to the basic processes of group dynamics. We refer specifically to conventional patterns by which in-groups and out-groups develop. The people who constitute the group to which one belongs form an in-group. An **in-group** holds itself in high esteem and demands loyalty from its members. In-groups then define others as members of an out-group. **Out-groups** are considered undesirable and are thought to hold values and beliefs foreign to one's own. American society consists of a variety of ethnic groups. These groups are frequently ranked relative to their tenure in the country, but each wave of immigration to a country establishes new population configurations. In general, the most established immigrant groups cast themselves in the role of the in-group. Such groups define themselves as the "senior" and thus most valid representatives of a nation. These in-groups cast those that follow them in the role of out-groups. Recent arrivals are stigmatized as foreign elements to an established mold (Spain 1999).

Research demonstrates that members of an in-group carry unrealistically positive views of their group. At the same time, in-group members share unrealistically negative views of the out-group (Hewstone, Rubin, and Willis 2002; Tajfel 1982). As groups improve their status, they are more likely to display in-group bias (Guimond, Dif, and Aupy 2002). Threats to in-groups can increase the derogation of lower-status out-groups (Cadinu and Reggiori 2002; Hopkins and Rae 2001). Low-status minorities are the most susceptible to in-group devaluation (Rudman, Feinberg, and Fairchild 2002). Exposure to prejudice about out-groups can increase the negative evaluations of those groups and hinder social ties with them and thus reinforce destructive social dynamics (Levin, VanLaar, and Sidanius 2003; Tropp 2003). Because newcomers are viewed relative to those with earlier claims, the very process of immigration perpetuates social conflict. Indeed, the mechanics of immigration seem to guarantee a hostile boundary between the old and the new, between established ethnic groups versus recent arrivals.

In light of Americans' historical relationship with immigrants, should we simply dismiss current anti-immigration sentiments as "business as usual"? Perhaps not.

Figure 20.1 reveals the European background of earlier generations of immigrants to the United States. Indeed, these European origins are frequently credited with facilitating past immigrants' transition to U.S. culture. The many shared customs and characteristics and the spatial dispersion of various European ethnic groups facilitated the assimilation of each new European immigrant wave. **Assimilation** is the process by which immigrant groups come to adopt the dominant culture of their new homeland as their own.

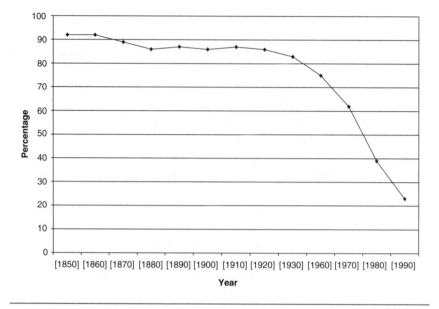

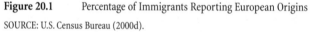

Figure 20.1   Percentage of Immigrants Reporting European Origins

SOURCE: U.S. Census Bureau (2000d).

Today, the vast majority of immigrants are from Asian or Latin American nations (see Figure 20.2). Table 20.3 lists the top 15 sources of immigrants in 2002. By the year 2050, most immigrants will hail from Latin America, Asia, Africa, the Middle East, or the Pacific Islands (Schmidley 2003). On one hand, these shifts in immigration patterns should hardly be cause for concern. The immigration history of these new groups, like the history of previous immigrant groups, has been relatively successful. Asian households, for example, have the highest median income of *all* (native and foreign-born) households (Schmidley 2001). The Asian-born also have the lowest unemployment and the lowest poverty rates of any minority group in the United States today (Proctor and Dalaker 2002; U.S. Census Bureau 2000b). Asians have the highest high school and college graduation rates and are more likely than any other group to obtain graduate degrees (U.S. Census Bureau 2002, Table 36).

Hispanic immigrants to the United States can point to similar triumphs. Although it is true that the economic conditions of Hispanic Americans tend to lag behind national averages, the median income of households increased from 1995 to 2000 and reached an average of $33,455 in 2000. The percentage of Hispanic households with incomes over $100,000 has doubled in the last 20 years (U.S. Census Bureau 2002, Table 652). The educational profile of Hispanics has improved greatly over the last several years. Over the past two decades, the percentage of Hispanics obtaining every level of educational degrees from associate's to

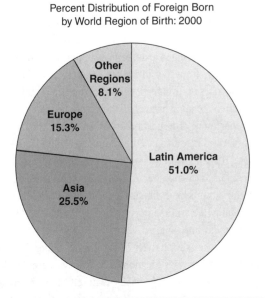

Percent Distribution of Foreign Born
by World Region of Birth: 2000

Figure 20.2   Foreign-Born Regional Background: U.S. 2000

SOURCE: U.S. Census Bureau (2000e).

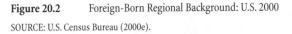

Table 20.3   Top 15 Countries of Origin for U.S. Immigrants, 2002

1. Mexico
2. India
3. China
4. Philippines
5. Vietnam
6. El Salvador
7. Cuba
8. Bosnia-Herzegovina
9. Dominican Republic
10. Ukraine
11. Korea
12. Russia
13. Haiti
14. Canada
15. Colombia

SOURCE: United States Immigration and Naturalization Service (2002).

first-professional has increased by two times or more (U.S. Census Bureau 2002, Table 277). And during this same time period, Hispanics (along with Asians) have experienced the fastest growth in graduate and professional school enrollments (U.S. Department of Education 2003). Hispanic households also reaffirm important core American values. The family, for instance, is greatly respected in Hispanic culture, a sentiment reflected in high rates of marriage and low rates of divorce for Hispanic Americans (U.S. Census Bureau 2002, Table 46). Hispanic children are more likely than their Black counterparts to be living in two-parent homes (U.S. Department of Education 2003). Hispanic American youth also report the strongest sense of family duty during young adulthood (Fuligni and Pedersen 2002). And in terms of politics, the Hispanic vote will surely receive more and more attention in local, state, and national elections as the number of Hispanic voters continues to grow.

While the faces of immigrants have changed in the past 50 years, intergenerational assimilation and upward mobility are still the norm (Card, DiNardo, and Estes 1998; Myers and Cranford 1998). Of the foreign-born who arrived in the United States before 1970, 80.5% have obtained citizenship. Of those who arrived in the United States during the 1970s, 67% obtained citizenship. Citizenship rates for more recent arrivals are decidedly lower (under 50%), but it is expected these rates will increase with efforts to promote citizenship and accelerate the naturalization process. Mexico's recent approval of dual citizenship is also expected to increase the number of naturalized citizens among this very large group of foreign-born residents (Martin and Midgley 1999; Schmidley 2003). There also is a very clear association between length of time in the United States and both income and home owner-ship rates. And the eventual mastery of the English language is another key to immigrants' economic success. Historically, the shift from speaking another language to speaking English has occurred over three generations. Among recent immigrants, however, the shift seems to be occurring within two generations (Martin and Midgley 1999; Portes 2002).

In light of the general success rates posted by recent immigrants in general and by many Asian and Hispanic Americans, we must consider that current anti-immigration sentiments may be based on issues of race. Visible physical differences, as well as a lack of familiar cultural practices, make the assimilation of "new" immigrant groups more difficult than it was for earlier immigrants. New, non-European immigrants may lack the physical and cultural similarities necessary for eventual acceptance as part of society's in-group.

If immigration and population trends develop as predicted, anti-immigration sentiments fueled by issues of race may get worse before they get better. Demographers tell us that the dominant White population of U.S. society will be very close to becoming a numerical minority by the year 2050. By 2050, African Americans, Hispanics, Asian Americans, and Native Americans are expected to account for almost half the U.S. population (U.S. Census Bureau 2002, Table 16). If these projections are accurate, future immigration, in a very profound sense, will change the status quo. The practice of assimilation may necessarily give way to multiculturalism. **Multiculturalism** accentuates rather than dilutes ethnic and racial differences. Such an environment might strip in-groups of dominance and power. In contrast to the adversarial stance of the in-group/out-group design, a multicultural structure demands that all groups be viewed as equally valued contributors to the mainstream culture.

Immigration projections suggest that the United States is moving closer to being a microcosm of the world. Our nation will experience an increase in the diversity that already characterizes the younger generations of Americans. Such changes could bring us closer to fully realizing the motto that appears on all U.S. currency: *E Pluribus Unum,* one formed from many. Thus, current and future attitudes toward immigrants in America will hinge on our readiness to deal with fundamental population changes.

Certainly, some Americans will resist this development, arguing that it threatens our national identity and changes our national "face." Contemporary movements against bilingual education are evidence of such resistance. Nevertheless, others will view our changing population as a positive economic opportunity. Consider the fact that economists forecast a very different world for coming generations of Americans. More and more of us will be earning our livings in the service sector of an increasingly global, postindustrial economy. Postindustrial economies place a high premium on knowledge and information (Drucker 1993). Future job markets will demand and reward better-educated and more literate workers (Hecker 2001; Sum, Kirsch, and Taggart 2002). Immigration bodes well for educational advancement. Immigrant parents and children have higher education aspirations than native-born individuals. Immigrant students equal or exceed the educational attainment of their native-born counterparts (Vernez and Abrahamse 1996). Some studies also indicate that bilingualism is positively associated with educational aspirations and achievements as well as self-esteem (Feliciano 2001; St-Hilaire 2002; Portes 2002). Multilingual workers will clearly occupy a position of advantage in an increasingly global economy and workplace (Portes 2002).

Framed in this way, new immigration patterns may help supply us with a new source of cultural capital (Archdeacon 1992). **Cultural capital** refers to attributes, knowledge, or ways of thinking that can be converted or used for economic advantage. Interestingly enough, as we witness various indicators attesting to the force of globalization, we also see more and more ethnic groups asserting their identities and pushing for political recognition and autonomy (Guillen 2001). By their familiarity with cultures now central to the world market, immigrants to the United States may well give our nation a competitive edge in a global playing field. Once again, immigrants to the United States may be the national resource that makes the United States a significant player in a new world economy.

Learning More About It

In *Legacies: The Story of the Immigrant Second Generation,* Alejandro Portes and Ruben G. Rumbaut present findings from a longitudinal study investigating how children of foreign parents adapt in terms of family, school, identity, self-esteem, ambition, and so on. (Berkeley, CA: University of California Press, 2001).

Richard Alba and Victor Nee offer an insightful review of assimilation of current immigrants in *Remaking the American Mainstream: Assimilation and Contemporary Immigration* (Cambridge, MA: Harvard University Press, 2003).

George Borgas offers a thorough discussion of the economic impact of immigrants in his book, *Heaven's Door: Immigration Policy and the American Economy* (Princeton: Princeton University Press, 2001).

Those interested in an in-depth consideration of diversity issues facing today's college students should consult David Schuman and Dick Olufs's *Diversity on Campus* (Boston: Allyn & Bacon, 1995).

For an interesting and now classic discussion of the underside of American values, see Philip Slater's *The Pursuit of Loneliness: American Culture at the Breaking Point* (Boston: Beacon Press, 1970).

The U.S. Immigration and Naturalization Service offers a wealth of information on immigration. Visit their Web site at: <http://www.immigration.gov/>

You can test your immigration knowledge by taking an interactive pop quiz at the U.S. Census Bureau's foreign-born population page: <http://www.census.gov/population/www/socdemo/>

Exercises

1. Visit a library that has back copies of local telephone directories. Examine the entries in the yellow pages for a variety of categories—beauty salons, physicians, restaurants, and so on. What insights about immigration patterns can be gleaned from your data as you move from year to year?

2. Prepare several in-depth interviews with first-generation Americans—that is, people who were born in other countries and immigrated to the United States. Find out about the conditions of their immigration, the reception they received in their new communities, and, if appropriate, the reception they received at their new workplaces or their new schools. Try to vary the immigration background of your interview subjects; that is, choose individuals who came from different foreign countries. Consider whether one's status as an immigrant functions as a master status (see Essay 6 or 12).

3. Use your own college community to locate children of recent immigrants. Prepare an interview guide that will allow you to explore whether these individuals exist in two social worlds or cultures. (For example, how do language, food, fashion patterns, and so on vary from school to home?)

Social Institutions

MEDIA AND TECHNOLOGY

Essay 21

Conventional Wisdom Tells Us . . .
Technology Is Taking Over Our Lives

This essay examines new communication technologies and explores their role in contemporary social life. We begin by considering the ways in which technology has changed the development of community and intimacy. We explore as well the impact of new technologies on our definitions of social relations, social actors, and the public and private spheres.

L ook around. No matter where you are, you will see the signs. Technology rules the day. On the road? Electronic message boards and Amber Alert systems are sending immediate updates on road conditions, emergencies, or criminal matters. Now look at the drivers around you. Drive time has become talk time as more and more of us keep in touch with family and work via our cell phones. Check the scene at work or school. Everyone seems to have cell phones in their pockets and laptops on their shoulders. See something extraordinary in your travels? Grab the cell and send a picture! Hear a funny joke or a juicy piece of gossip? Share the wealth—e-mail it to your best friend!

These days, it is easy to stay connected to family and friends. But the information boom is about much more than our social lives. Increasingly, governments, corporations, and law enforcement agencies are privy to our comings and goings. Surveillance cameras or electronic toll devices can record our physical whereabouts. "Cookies" can track our travels and tastes as we browse through cyberspace. Crime-fighting computers and medical data banks can verify our identities; they know us, right down to the chromosomes in our DNA. Even the mundane trip to the grocery store carries a technological flair. Computerized registers are able to "scan" our items and immediately deliver customized coupons that fit our tastes.

The **new communication technologies**—developments such as fiber optics, the Internet, rapid satellite transmissions, and virtual reality imaging—can take us to places that we've never been before. While sitting in front of our computer screens or Web TVs, we might participate in a virtual march on Washington; we might support our favorite cause via online volunteer work; we might tour an art gallery, a historic site, or a home we are thinking about purchasing. Movies can be delivered on demand to our computers; the biggest concert tour of the year may be simulcast on the Internet. Opportunity is knocking . . . although for some it may not always be an easy door to open. Computer users really must become computer "techies" who can troubleshoot their way through various hardware and software problems. Luckily, this knowledge will serve the techie well in the future. Appliances, cars, and homes of tomorrow will all be "smart" and require consumers to be programming savvy. Down time may be gone time. The Internet is never closed; technology whirls on, 24/7.

Conventional wisdom suggests that technological advancements are taking over our lives. Critics charge that we are slaves to our hi-tech toys, drowning in a sea of points, clicks, and wireless connections. Indeed, many believe we spend so much time with the new products of technology that we have forgotten or withdrawn from the "real" world. Is conventional wisdom correct in its anti-technology stance? Have we lost control of our lives . . . or merely learned a different way to live them? A number of sociologists are examining these issues in detail. Their research suggests that new communication technologies may be less "dangerous" than critics suggest.

What is it that people fear about the new communication technologies? One common concern involves the issue of inequality. Some researchers argue that new communication technologies are creating a digital divide. A **digital divide** refers to the formation of an information underclass–a portion of the population that cannot afford to access and capitalize on the things that new technologies have to offer. To be sure, *all* technological innovations result in a digital divide. Radios and televisions, telephones and automobiles–all seemed to be a luxury of the wealthy when first introduced. But as these technologies were diffused within the society at large, some of the access inequalities tended to disappear. New communication technologies are following this developmental pattern. For example, the racial and gender divides that once characterized computer access and usage have largely disappeared. Income and educational differences in access and usage have also diminished somewhat. Yet in the areas of income and education, much work remains. It is still the case that the wealthier and more educated an individual, the more technologically proficient they tend to be (Katz and Rice 2002:34).

Conventional wisdom also argues that new communication technologies are destroying people's involvement in civic and community life. Critics fear that individuals are substituting online activity for more traditional offline affiliations–an experience that critics contend is inferior to traditional modes of civic activity. Some fear that Internet users may be overwhelmed with available information. As a result, users may participate in selected interest groups that do little more than reinforce their existing beliefs. Others fear that users may encounter online activists who are much more extreme than their offline counterparts. Such encounters could be intimidating, resulting in users' complete withdrawal from the civic arena. Still others contend that users may decide navigating the dense terrain of the Internet simply is not worth their effort (Calhoun 1998; Katz and Rice 2002:132). While such fears abound, recent studies on the Internet and community fail to lend them much credence. Current research suggests that online interactions tend to supplement, not replace, offline community involvements. In addition, heavy Internet use is actually associated with high levels of participation in offline voluntary organizations and politics. Thus, far from being overwhelmed or exceptionally selective, Internet users tend to be highly interested in a wide array of current events and highly involved in civic and political activities (Katz and Rice 2002; Kraut et al. 2002; Wellman et al. 2001).

Note too that during the past few years there has been a remarkable growth in **e-philanthropy**, that is, online or "cyber giving." For example, Networkforgood.org (formerly Helping.org), AOL's charity-oriented Web site, has posted steady traffic and growth since its inception in the late 1990s. In the 1999 holiday giving season, the site received over $600,000 in online donations. For the 2001 holiday season, donations totaled $2.7 million (*USA Today* 2002). E-philanthropy has also seen success in the area of online volunteering. The largest Web site for online volunteering is VolunteerMatch.org. This site connects potential volunteers with nonprofit groups. An individual simply submits a list of volunteering contingencies (i.e., the distance one is willing to travel, the time frame for one's volunteer work, and the type of cause or issue with which one wants to be associated). The site then searches for an organization that matches an individual's criteria. Since its launch in 1998, VolunteerMatch has generated over 1,000,000 volunteer referrals (VolunteerMatch *Annual Report* 2002).

E-philanthropy received a significant boost in the days following the September 11, 2001, terrorist attacks on America. On Sept 10th, there were but a few dozen donations to AOL's Networkforgood.org. On Sept 14th, there were 12,000 donations totaling more than $1.26 million. Indeed, in the first six months following 9/11, it is estimated that 10% of relief donations (or $150 million) came via the Internet. The Red Cross alone raised over $63 million online after 9/11 (Larose and Wallace 2003). September 11 also had a clear impact on online volunteering. The number of matches made between nonprofits and volunteers doubled from pre- to post-9/11. Prior to 9/11, approximately 20,000 matches a month were made. Thirty days after 9/11, the number of matches was running close to 40,000 (Miller 2002). On 9/11 alone, Volunteermatch.com made 4,500 volunteer referrals (VolunteerMatch 2002).

Early studies of Internet users also give cause for optimism about the prospects of e-philanthropy. A 1999 study of "socially engaged" Internet users found that a core group of 7.5 million Americans had already begun to embrace online philanthropy and another 7.3 million were characterized as being on the verge of joining the wave (Craver et al. 1999). In 2002, a study by *The Chronicle of Philanthropy* found that the nation's largest charities raised $124.5 million online (Larose and Wallace 2003). The increasing popularity of e-philanthropy may be due to its complementary tie to our daily work patterns: 71% of all online donations are made at work. Since many of us are online during a normal working day, e-giving has become a quick and satisfying way to support our charitable causes (*Business Wire* 2002). Another study by the Independent Sector found that 10% of Internet users went online to search for volunteer opportunities (Independent Sector 2001). Perhaps most encouraging with regard to online volunteering is the finding that one-fifth of VolunteerMatch.com participants report that they are newcomers to volunteering, indicating that e-philanthropy is mobilizing a previously disengaged population (VolunteerMatch 2002).

Beyond civic activity, critics of new communication technologies voice other concerns. Fears regarding the Internet and the destruction of community are matched by concerns for technology's effect on intimacy. In many ways, the intimacy debate centers on the difference between direct and mediated communication. According to conventional wisdom, intimacy demands **direct communication**, face-to-face or physically copresent exchange. For intimacy to grow, we must "be" with others, see, hear, and touch them. Only then is a relationship "real." But online communication is **mediated communication**—an indirect connection funneled through a mechanical medium. Many feel that mediation makes communication impersonal, fleeting, and ingenuous. As such, it is an inappropriate means by which to establish deep and lasting connections.

The bias against mediated communication as a vehicle of intimacy is well established. Indeed, many would argue that those who build "technological ties" are really isolates and loners living fantasy lives and creating anonymous, meaningless worlds. To be sure, there are some well-executed studies that support these concerns. Certain works suggest that some Internet users become unduly drawn into cyberspace and thus neglect their offline relationships (see e.g., Nie and Erbring 2000; Schroeder and Ledger 1998; Shapiro and Leone 1999). Other studies contend that the anonymity of Internet communication creates identity conflict and confusion (Turkle 1996, 1997). But in the final analysis, a greater number of studies forward a positive picture of technology's role in intimate relationships. Research shows that the Internet complements and enhances preexisting relationships. The Internet also facilitates new friendships and bonds that might not otherwise have been possible. Researchers at UCLA, for example, have shown that, increasingly, the Internet is becoming people's media of choice for connecting with significant others. Consider that more than 100 million Americans used the Internet to make emotional connections with friends and loved ones in response to the 9/11 attacks (UCLA Internet Report 2002). Note that these individuals consciously chose e-mail over telephone or letter writing as a method of linking to others. The Pew Foundation's (2000) "Internet and American Life Project" forwards similar conclusions. According to Pew, Internet users report that online communication improves relationships with family members and friends. Furthermore, users report that online communication allowed them to establish new friendships with people beyond their geographical sphere of action. Thus, as Katz and Rice conclude, "the Internet is quite a social environment, inhabited by quite social folks (Katz and Rice 2002:264).

Sociologists Karen A. Cerulo and Janet M. Ruane suggest that an accurate assessment of new communication technologies will require a more flexible way of conceptualizing social relations. **Social relations** refer to the types of connections and the patterns of interaction that structure the broader society. Traditionally, sociologists have argued that physical copresence is integral to important relationships—relationships that enable communities, friendships, and intimacy. Thus, physical copresence has become the standard by which to judge the quality and importance of interaction. Cerulo and Ruane suggest that "bodies" may not be the most important part of the intimacy equation. Rather, the cognitive context in which communication occurs may make certain forms of direct and mediated exchange equally valuable and "real." Frequent and balanced interaction among individuals with overlapping backgrounds, strong and long-term bonds, the development of trust—these are the qualities that make us feel connected to others. When these things are present, in online or offline settings, individuals perceive the interaction to be central to their lives (Cerulo 1997; Cerulo and Ruane 1998; Cerulo, Ruane, and Chayko 1992; Chayko 2002).

The American courts have taken such ideas to heart. Indeed, over the past decade, the courts have substantially broadened their definition of intimacy. A New Jersey court, for example, entertained a divorce and adultery case in which the "third party" and the offending spouse never physically met. The courts considered an online romance, void of any physical contact, as sufficient grounds for divorce by reason of adultery. Similarly, in a Massachusetts custody battle, a probate judge granted a mother custody of her children and permitted her to leave the state and move to New York. The judge granted the children's father two weekend visits per month and two weekly visits–*virtual* visits made possible through Internet conferencing technology. The father's lawyers protested, arguing that "you can't hug a computer." But in the judge's estimation, the children's physical presence was not vital to a meaningful visit.

Embedded in concerns of intimacy is the notion that technology dehumanizes the species. Philosophers such as Adorno, Ellul, Heidegger, and Marcuse, dystopia works such as George Orwell's *1984* or Stanley Kubrick's *2001: A Space Odyssey* all promote a similarly frightening message. Technology has transformed our person-to-person world into a cold, anonymous person-to-machine existence. Technology "does to us" and "takes from us," all in the name of progress. Ultimately, it robs us of initiative, control, and basic human emotions. Supporters of this argument say that the "proof is in the pudding." Technology has made everyday USA into a surreal scene. Sociability is gone. We are lonely beings in a crowd, preferring our cell phones and palm pilots to interactions with those around us.

Sociologists Byron Reeves and Clifford Nass are unconvinced by the dehumanization argument. In its place, Reeves and Nass forward an idea they call "The Media Equation." Don't let the mathematical term put you off. The equation is quite simple. The media equation states that "media equals real life" (Reeves and Nass 1996:5). In forwarding this notion, Reeves and Nass present us with an interesting proposition. They force us to reconsider the very meaning of the term *social actor.*

Who is a social actor? Is the title restricted to another living, breathing human being . . . or can it be a television . . . a computer . . . a Web site? Reeves and Nass demonstrate that social actors respond to all of these entities in the same fundamentally social way.

Rather than technology dehumanizing people, people humanize technology! To prove the point, Reeves and Nass revisited a number of classic social science experiments designed to test person-to-person responses in social interaction. The researchers redid these experiments, making one critical change: Each experiment now tested person-to-computer interaction. In all cases, the results supported the media equation, demonstrating that people interact with media just as they interact with other humans. Indeed, even the most technologically sophisticated people treat boxes of circuitry as if they were other human beings. People are polite to computers; they respond to praise from them and view them as teammates. People like computers with personalities similar to their own. They find masculine-sounding computers extroverted, driven, and intelligent while they judge feminine-sounding computers knowledgeable about love and relationships. They alter their body posture, their moods, according to the size and perspective of the images on the screens before them (Nass and Moon 2000; Nass, Moon, and Carney 1999; Reeves and Nass 1996).

The work of Reeves and Nass suggests that new technologies have blurred the boundaries between people and objects, allowing both to operate as viable actors in the social terrain. We are witnessing similar changes with reference to the boundaries that distinguish people and animals or the living from the dead. Via virtual imaging, new communication technologies create a reality in which seemingly anything can happen—be it talking to your dog and having him or her answer back . . . experiencing a passionate romance with the man or woman of your dreams . . . or engaging in a conversation with a spouse, friend, or parent who is no longer alive. Just make-believe? On the one hand, yes. However, technology's projection of animals, fantasies, and spirits as viable social actors has had tangible consequences. In the past 10 years, we have witnessed increases in behaviors that confirm the reality of such images. Americans are, for example, spending more time with their pets, buying them clothes, furniture, taking them to spas, to psychotherapists and psychics, bringing them to work, and sending them to vacation resorts. Similarly, Americans are spending more time and money on mediums and other activities designed to contact spirits and angels. Mediums such as John Edwards and James Van Praugh have become media stars! (Indeed, the waiting time for a private reading with John Edwards is nearly three years!) Furthermore, Americans are gobbling up technological products that merge sounds and images of past and present. CDs and videos that bring us duets between the living and the dead are now hot properties. And at this writing, Frank Sinatra, deceased for several years, is slated to "appear live" at Radio City Music Hall, where he will be accompanied by a full concert orchestra and the world-famous Rockettes. Even though Sinatra's part in the concert will be nothing more than a digitally remastered video projected on the big screen and digitally synchronized with live action, people are paying as much as $100 for a chance to "see and hear" him one last time. So . . . who is a social actor? Is the title reserved for a living, breathing human being? New technologies make the question a complicated one to answer (Cerulo and Ruane 1997, 2004).

Technology does offer a potentially frightening "Big Brother" scenario when we consider the issue of privacy. The popularity and growth of electronic surveillance has a chilling effect on many social observers. In a world of ever-increasing anonymity, we must rely on alternate ways of facilitating trust and maintaining social order. Surely, this is the very idea behind electronic satellite "boxes" used to keep track of an increasing number of parolees. These devices allow the government to monitor convicted felons as they move about in local communities (Lee 2002). But surveillance has also entered the world of ordinary, law-abiding citizens. The never-blinking security camera has become a mainstay of social control in our stranger-based and now terrorist-threatened society. While an overwhelming majority of the 2-million-plus closed-circuit television systems currently used in the United States are operated by private entities (Murphy 2002), interest in surveillance of public places has increased since 9/11. Indeed, it is estimated that the average New Yorker is captured on video approximately 75 times throughout the day (Murphy 2002).

Surveillance tapes, of course, know no distinction between the private and public realms. Behaviors that social actors may intend as private backstage exchanges (a furtive kiss in a parking deck) may very well play as front-stage performances on security video screens. Surveillance also occurs on less obvious levels. Our movements over the course of a day can be traced via electronic toll and parking passes, phone records, and credit card activity. And as many people have haplessly discovered, our travels on the Internet can be far too public an affair. Computer cookies can reveal our interests and decision making (Rosen 2001).

While opportunities for the misuse of surveillance tools abound, it is nonetheless true that technology clearly enhances our privacy. Our ability to live a totally anonymous or secluded existence is supported by technology that enables us to work, play, and conduct all of our social and business affairs without ever going public (Nock 1993). With this view, electronic surveillance is not an ogre, but rather a response to the social changes of modern, urban living. Clearly, technology offers a solution to the social control dilemma posed by the fact that we desire and lead increasingly private lives.

Since 9/11, Americans appear to be more tolerant of governmental surveillance and seemingly more willing to regard any opposition to the government's watchful eye as unpatriotic (Murphy 2002). Indeed, with the passing of the USA Patriot Act (in October 2001), the government, in the name of fighting terrorism, is able to collect a staggering array of private information about individuals. To date, the response of Americans to this expansion of invasive government power has been remarkably tame, especially when we consider just how opposed we are to any commercial intrusions (Liptak 2002). Consider, for instance, that in the first four days of its availability, more than 10 million Americans registered their phone numbers with the national "Do Not Call" list in order to stop telemarketing calls. The Federal Trade Commission (FTC) expects that 60 million phone numbers will be registered during the first year of the registry (Ho 2003). Similarly, we consider SPAM to be the bane of the Internet—an affront to our online privacy (although experts acknowledge that it is much more than this). On an average day, consumers use the Internet to forward more than 85,000 examples of SPAM to the FTC, all in a concerted effort to help that agency fight these unwanted electronic intrusions (Gleick 2003). Clearly, we value our privacy, but we also, for now, appear willing to draw distinctions between governmental and commercial intrusions and between what we think are invasions of law-abiding versus law-violating individuals

(Liptak 2002). Our discerning response suggests that high tech itself isn't viewed as the culprit. Rather, we are willing to judge technology by the "cause" it serves.

Technology: new-fangled, oppressive devices—or new, essential tools of social life? If history proves informative, we will likely find some truth in both views. We can also be confident about a few other things. Just as we get comfortable with the latest innovations, still more advanced bells and whistles will arrive to push our buttons and sound new alarms. New technologies will prompt new debates about the pros and cons of high tech living. And society will take it all in its technological stride.

Learning More About It

For a very thorough and balanced treatment of new communication technologies, both the pros and cons, see James E. Katz and Ronald E. Rice's *Social Consequences of Internet Use: Access, Involvement and Interaction* (Cambridge, MA: MIT Press, 2002).

For a wonderful collection of articles exploring the role of new communication technologies in community and intimacy formation, see Barry Wellman and Caroline Haythornthwaite's *The Internet in Everyday Life* (Oxford, UK: Blackwell, 2002).

To read Byron Reeves and Clifford Nass's fascinating work on the humanization of technology, see *The Media Equation* (New York: Cambridge University Press, 1996).

Jeffrey Rosen offers a fascinating excursion into privacy and the Internet. See *The Unwanted Gaze: The Destruction of Privacy in America* (New York: Knopf, 2001).

Exercises

1. Visit an online chat group. You can participate or just watch. However,

    -   visit the same group three times, and
    -   spend at least 30 minutes during each visit

How did your chat group visits compare to face-to-face interactions? Is intimacy possible in these forums? Did you feel more vulnerable to other interactants in the online forums . . . less vulnerable? Were you less honest in your online discussions . . . more honest? Is online communication more useful for some tasks than others?

2. Select five charity mailings (from different organizations) that you have received in the recent past. Access each organization's Web site. Do a systematic comparison of the "snail mail" pitch versus online presentations and appeals. What similarities and difference do you find, especially with regard to each organization's ability to personalize its message and requests?

Social Institutions

EDUCATION

Essay 22

Conventional Wisdom Tells Us...
Education Is the Great Equalizer

Conventional wisdom tells us that educating the masses will bring equal opportunities to people of all races, ethnicities, and genders. In this essay, we explore the truth of this claim and review the progress we have made in bringing quality education to all.

The United States has earned a reputation as the land of opportunity, and the opportunity that so many of us desire is the improvement of our socioeconomic lot. Intergenerational upward mobility is a key dimension of the American Dream. **Intergenerational upward mobility** refers to social status gains by children vis-à-vis their parents.

Historically, education has been offered as the route by which such mobility can best be realized. Our free common public school system, established just prior to the Civil War, was founded on the principle that everyone, regardless of social background, should be educated. Lester Ward, a prominent sociologist of the late 1800s, thought that universal education would eliminate the inequalities associated with social class, race, and gender. Similarly, educational reformer Horace Mann promoted an expanded educational system as the antidote to poverty (Katz 1971).

Such sentiments have survived the test of time. We are a nation fueled by the belief that education will lead to equal opportunity for individual achievement and success. Former "education president" George Bush (the elder) aptly captured this cultural value, characterizing education as the "great lifting mechanism of an egalitarian society. It represents our most proven pathway to a better life."

The conventional wisdom on education reflects a structural functionalist view of society. **Structural functionalism** is a theoretical approach that stresses social order. Proponents contend that society is a collection of interdependent parts that function together to produce consensus and stability. This perspective links education to social stability in two ways. First, in taking their place in the education system, students learn the key norms, values, and beliefs of American culture. Second, by affording all students a chance to develop their skills and talents, education can channel the "best and the brightest" to key social positions.

Does the conventional view of education paint an accurate portrait? Is America's education system really the great equalizer?

To be sure, the American education system has grown dramatically over the past century. At the turn of the last century, only 10% of U.S. youth earned high school degrees, and only 2% earned college degrees (Vinorskis 1992). By World War I, primary education became compulsory in every state; by World War II, the same was true for secondary education.

In 2002, just over 84% of Americans 25 and older had earned a high school degree, and about 27% had earned a bachelor's degree or higher (U.S. Census Bureau 2003b). Higher education is also seen as a possibility for more and more Americans. The percentage of high school graduates who immediately enroll in college is taken as an indicator of the *accessibility* of higher education. In 2001, 62% of high school graduates were enrolled in college for the following fall semester; in 1972, only 49% of high school graduates immediately enrolled in college (U.S. Department of Education 2003).

The face of our nation's college population has become more socially diverse as well. At the turn of the 20th century, college students were primarily the sons of White, upper-class professionals. In contrast, today's college population includes the sons and daughters of all social classes and all racial and ethnic groups. Currently, minority students account for approximately 28% of the total enrollment at colleges and universities (National Center for Education Statistics 2003).

In support of conventional wisdom, one must note a strong and positive association between income and education. In 2001, for example, the average yearly earnings for those with advanced degrees crested $72,000; in contrast, those lacking a high school degree saw average yearly earnings of $18,793.00 (U.S. Census Bureau 2003b). As educational levels increase, the poverty rate for the working poor decreases (U.S. Department of Labor 2003b). (See Figure 22.1.) Furthermore, those with higher levels of educational achievement report higher levels of good or excellent health, regardless of actual income. Mortality rates of college-educated adults (aged 24–64) are less than half those of individuals with only a high school degree (AmeriStat 2002). And as educational achievement increases, so does individuals' civic involvement: Both voter registration and turnout increase with education (U.S. Department of Education 2002, 2003). The benefits of education seem to touch even those who detour from life's conventional path: Prisoners' exposure to educational programs while incarcerated is associated with lower rates of recidivism (American Federation of Teachers 2002; Batiuk 1997).

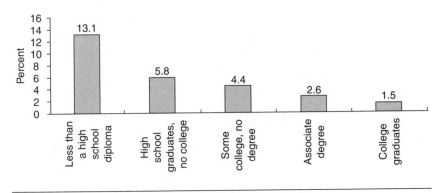

Figure 22.1   Poverty Rates by Education

SOURCE: Monthly Labor Review (2003).

These data were collected in the 2002 Annual Social and Economic Supplement to the *Current Population Survey.* For more information see *A Profile of the Working Poor, 2001* (U.S. Census Bureau).

The statistics just quoted suggest that education's links to "the good life" are right on target. However, on closer examination, one finds several situations that can weaken the strength of that bond. Education's "lifting mechanism" may not be fully functional for all social groups.

Research verifies that the economically disadvantaged fail to reap the benefits of higher education. The pattern is very clear: As income decreases, so does the percentage of students who enroll in college. The pattern is in part explained by the preparation of students. Lower-income high school graduates are less academically qualified for college than are their wealthier counterparts. Yet even when we look only at those students who are qualified for admission to a four-year college, the relationship between income and enrollment stubbornly persists: The higher the income, the higher the enrollment rate. (U.S. Department of Education 2002). (See Figure 22.2.)

Evidence also suggests that a college education is becoming increasingly less affordable to all but the wealthiest of families. In 1980, middle-class families spent 4% of their annual incomes on college education; in 2000, they spent 7%. In 1980, low-income families spent 13% of their annual incomes on college costs; in 2000, they spent 20%. Only families in the top 20% of the income distribution haven't felt this pinch—such families spent but 2% of their annual incomes on college costs in both 1980 and 2000 (Immerwahr 2002). Unfortunately, federal and state financial aid hasn't allowed middle- and lower-income families to keep pace with the increasing costs of higher education. In 1976, the maximum Pell Grant (federal awards for financially needy students) covered 84% of tuition costs at

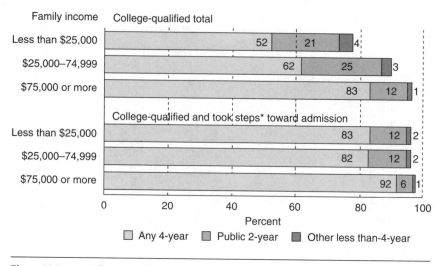

Family income   College-qualified total

Figure 22.2   College Bound by Family Income

Percentage of College-Qualified 1992 High School Graduates Who Enrolled in Postsecondary Education by 1994, by Family Income

*Took a college admissions test (SAT or ACT) and applied for admission to a four-year institution.

SOURCE: U.S. Department of Education (1988/1994).

NOTE: The four-year College Qualification Index is based on high school GPA, senior class rank, NELS 1992 aptitude test, SAT or ACT scores, and curricular rigor.

public four-year colleges. Today, Pell Grants cover only 39% of those tuition expenses (Public Interest Research Group [PIRG] 2002). The future doesn't look any brighter given the expected negative impact of new government formula for awarding Pell Grants (Winter 2003). To be sure, federal grants and loans are a component of most college students' finance strategies—64% of students graduate with student loan debt, with the average debt close to $17,000. Low-income students, however, are more likely to face a debt burden. In 2000, 71% of student borrowers from families earning less than $20,000 a year graduated with debt compared with 44% of students from families with incomes of over $100,000 a year (PIRG 2002).

For some students, the answer to the high cost of a college education is the community college. It's estimated that 42% of college students attend public two-year institutions, and enrollment numbers are expected to grow in the next decade (Immerwahr 2002; U.S. Department of Education 2002). Two-year community colleges have been described as the "safety net" for a state's educational system. They have played a particularly important role for first-generation college students as well as for low-income students (Callan 2003). Indeed, recent increases in college enrollments for low socioeconomic status (SES) students have been largely confined to two-year institutions (U.S. Department of Education 1997). As valuable a role as community colleges play, however, it is important to note the caveats of pursuing a college career via this route. Community colleges simply don't yield the same long-term dividends of four-year institutions. Only half of community college students with the goal of obtaining a bachelor's degree actually transfer to four-year institutions. And transfer students are still less likely than those who started at four-year institutions to actually complete a bachelor's degree: 44% versus 63% (U.S. Department of Education 2003). The implications of terminating college with an associate's versus a bachelor's degree are striking when we focus on the financial payoff of higher education. Annual earnings for an associates versus a bachelor's degree are estimated at $38,000 and $49,000 respectively. Estimates of differences in terms of lifetime earnings are $1,525,000 versus $1,974,000 (Employment Policy Foundation 2001).

The greatest financial return on a college degree is reserved for graduates of elite or selective private colleges (Coleman and Rainwater 1978; Hoxby 2001; Useem and Karabel 1986). Harvard economist Caroline Hoxby has determined that students attending the top-ranked selective colleges earn back their educational investments many times over during their working careers. Indeed, the ultimate value of attending an elite school is reflected in one of her more telling findings: Choosing a "free ride" at a third-tier private college (e.g., Georgetown or University of Virginia) is not as smart as *paying* for an education at a top-tier institution (e.g., Harvard or Johns Hopkins), since the lifetime return on the latter investment is so very lucrative (Hoxby 2001). "Selective" colleges, however, are very selective about their student bodies. Gatekeeping practices, escalating costs (the growth rate of college costs is 3% higher than the overall inflation rate; Chiodo and Owyang 2003), and increasing use of merit- rather than need-based financial aid packages by elite universities ensure that access to such institutions is restricted largely to members of the most privileged social classes. Educational ability proves less important than family background in gaining admission to Ivy League institutions (Karen 1990; Persell and Cookson 1990).

Education's equalizing mechanism often seems to fail ethnic and racial minorities as well. Both high school and college completion rates are lower for African Americans, Hispanic Americans, and Native Americans than they are for Whites (U.S. Census Bureau 2002, Table 208; U.S. Department of Education 2003). Despite recent increases in the percentage of African American and Hispanic American high school graduates who go on to attend college, these figures continue to lag behind the percentage recorded for Whites. In terms of the perceived accessibility of higher education, minority students see a more difficult transition path than do White students: In 2001, 64% of white high school graduates immediately went on to college compared with 55% of African American high school graduates and 52% of Hispanic high school graduates (U.S. Department of Education 2002, 2003). As with low-SES students, some minority high school graduates are more likely to attend two-year rather than four-year colleges or universities than are their White counterparts: 40% of Latino students are enrolled in two-year colleges compared with 25% of White college students (Fry 2002;

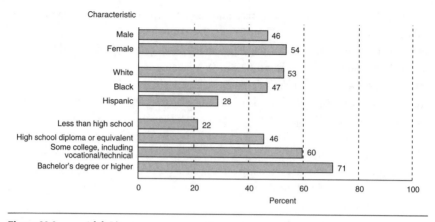

Figure 22.3   Adult Literacy

READING HABITS OF ADULTS: Percentage of adults age 25 and above who reported having read regularly, by selected characteristics: 1999

SOURCE: U.S. Department of Education (2000).

NOTE: The category "having read regularly" consists of people who reported doing all three of the following activities: read a newspaper at least once a week, read one or more magazines regularly, and read a book in the past six months. Adults were asked about their reading habits for literature printed in English.

U.S. Department of Education 2002). Furthermore, minority students are less likely to pursue graduate education (Carter and Wilson 1993; U.S. Department of Education 2003). The financial burden of financing higher education is also particularly harsh on minority students: 55% of African American students and 58% of Hispanic students carry unmanageable debt burdens after college graduation, compared with 40% of all subsidized student loan borrowers (PIRG 2002).

Low educational achievement does more than deprive people of degrees and earnings. Low educational achievement imposes heavy costs on literacy. **Literacy** refers to the ability to use printed and written information to function in society. Literacy levels range from a low of 1 to a high of 5. Level 3 proficiency is regarded as the minimum level needed for success in today's work world. Only about half of those aged 16 to 65 reach this level of literacy (Sum, Kirsch, and Taggart 2002). Simply put, as education levels increase, so does literacy. Reading a newspaper once a week, regularly reading one or more magazines, and reading a book in the past six months are much more likely to be reported by individuals with bachelor degrees or higher than by those with less than a high school degree: 71% versus 22%. (See Figure 22.3.) Similarly, more extensive reading habits (i.e., reading a *daily* paper, regularly reading *five* or more magazines, and so on) are more characteristic of those with college degrees (U.S. Department of Education 2001).

The cycle of low educational achievement is hard to break: Children of high school dropouts are three times more likely to quit high school as are children whose parents have attended college (U.S. Department of Education 1997). Dropout rates of students from the bottom 20% of incomes are six times higher than rates of students from the top 20% of incomes (Kaufman et al. 2001). Students whose parents have only a high school degree are less likely than their peers to enroll in a four-year college, and if they do enroll, they are less likely to graduate (U.S. Department of Education 2002). The lower parents' levels of education, the more time it takes for their children to complete their college degrees (U.S. Department of Education 2003). To be sure, a college education is an expensive investment, one that takes careful planning and financial preparation. Even on this front, however, there are dynamics that hinder equal educational opportunity for all: Families with the lowest incomes and the least-educated parents face the greatest uncertainty and know the least about the costs of attending college (Horn, Chen, and Chapman 2003; U.S. Department of Education 2001).

Perhaps the most dramatic failure of education's equalizing powers is witnessed in the area of gender. The educational history of women in the United States bespeaks little in the way of equal opportunity or achievement. In the 1900s, the doors to high schools and subsequently colleges were opened to women. Indeed, in 1907, there were 110 women's colleges in the United States. However, only 32% of these women's colleges met even the most basic standards of a true higher-education program. Rather, most women's colleges were engaged in the task of preparing women for their "place" in society—that is, as homemakers. Government aid policies of the era reinforced this traditional tracking. Vocational training such as cooking, sewing, and home economics qualified for federal subsidies; commercial training did not (Stock 1978).

Women who wanted a "real" higher education were limited by restrictive college admission policies. Most elite schools of the East simply refused to accept women. Western institutions had more liberal policies, but such policies were generally driven by financial motives. Western colleges admitted women in an effort to ward off financial disaster. The most blatant example of this practice, however, occurred at the University of Chicago. Faced with bankruptcy in 1873, the university decided to admit women. When the financial situation of the university improved, the institution's stance toward female admissions changed dramatically. Women were immediately relegated to a separate junior college (Stock 1978).

The post–World War II era further compromised women's access to education. Prior to World War II, the percentage of women attending college increased steadily. However, postwar college admissions gave absolute priority to war veterans. Such policies forced women back into the home, despite the work they had done during the war to keep America productive (Stock 1978). Furthermore, the postwar policy signaled the beginning of a long-term trend. Even today, women do not enjoy educational returns equal to those of men; the financial benefits of education are significantly less for women than for men at every level of educational achievement (see Essay 12).

Instances of class, racial, ethnic, and gender inequality lead many to doubt the conventional wisdom on education. Indeed, conflict theorists question education's ability to equalize. **Conflict theorists** analyze social organization and social interactions by attending to the differential resources controlled by different sectors of a society. Conflict theorists suggest that the U.S. education system actually transmits inequality from one generation to the next (Bidwell and Friedkin 1988; Bowles and Gintis 1976, 2002; Kozol 1991, 1995; Swartz 2003; Weis 1988).

The conflict view of education parallels structural functionalism in acknowledging the role of education within the socialization process. **Socialization** refers to the process by which we learn the norms, values, and beliefs of a social group, as well as our place within that social group. But in contrast to structural functionalists, conflict theorists argue that the goals of socialization vary according to the social class of students.

In Essay 13, we noted Jonathan Kozol's observations regarding racial inequalities in U.S. schools. Kozol argued that Whites and non-Whites often learn different lessons within American schools. Kozol notes similar inequalities in comparisons of various social classes. (Indeed, Kozol argues that much racial inequality in the United States is fueled by factors that link minority racial status to low economic status.)

Through their elementary and high school education, lower- and working-class students are taught attitudes and skills that best prepare them for supervised or labor-intensive occupations. These include respect for authority, passivity, the willingness to obey orders, and so on (Solomon, Battistich, and Hom 1996). In contrast, middle- and upper-class children are taught skills essential to management-level jobs and professional careers—that is, responsibility and dependability. College and postcollege education offer privileged students continued training in the management and professional skills. The underrepresentation of lower- and working-class students at the college level and beyond excludes such students from similar training and, ostensibly, from upward career mobility (Kozol 1991).

Beyond socialization, the funding and delivery of education can also maintain and reinforce class divisions. Consider, for instance, the fact that local property taxes fund a large portion of public school budgets (Hoxby 1998; U.S. Department of Education 2003). Affluent school districts (less than 5% of students living in poverty) receive local revenues that are three times the amount of those found in impoverished districts (35% of students living in poverty) or approximately $6,000 of local revenues per student versus $2,000 per student (U.S. Department of Education 2003). State governments do try to close this gap by directing more state general revenues to poor school districts, but they do so without total success. In 2000, for instance, school districts with intermediate levels of poverty received up to 18% less in state revenue per student (U.S. Department of Education 2003). While the Bush administration's No Child Left Behind Act of 2001 drew praise for focusing attention on the educational needs of low-income and minority students, it has since been criticized as being largely an unfunded and therefore empty mandate (Rentner et al. 2003).

As critical as it is, the amount of money spent on education doesn't tell the whole story. In the past decade, federal, state, and local governments have invested more than $40 billion to put computers in schools and connect students to the Internet. To be sure, significant improvement has been made on the ed-tech front. The percentage of schools with Internet access in 2001 was 99%, up from just 35% in 1994. Still, a disturbing digital divide remains. Income and minority status impedes some students' travels on the information highway. Just over 80% of children in the lowest-income families use computers in school; 89% of their highest-income peers do so (Dickard, Honey, and Wilhelm 2003). Schools with a 50% or more minority enrollment are less likely to have instructional classrooms with Internet access than are schools with less than 6% minority enrollments: 64% versus 85% (U.S. Census Bureau 2002, Table 236). The gaps become much wider as we follow students home from school. Only 33% of students in the lowest-income households use computers at home compared with 95% of children in the highest-income households! Racial inequalities still exist, though they are much less striking (Katz and Rice 2002). Thirty-two percent of Hispanic students, 40% of African American students, and 60% of White students have Internet access at home. Some have described these developments as tantamount to sending today's poor and minority students home to study without the benefit of any books (Dickard et al. 2003)! Given the increasing importance of technological skills, these discrepancies do not bode well for future employment opportunities and community development (Benton Foundation 2002).

Research also indicates that the size of schools and the number of students in classrooms can also make for very unequal educational experiences. Mid-sized schools offer the most positive environments for learning. Large schools (900+ students), however, dominate central city school districts. As the size of school increases, so does the reporting of serious student problems such as apathy, dropping out, and drug use (U.S. Department of Education 2003). Overcrowding is another problem that diminishes the educational experience for students. Approximately 8% of our public schools are severely overcrowded (i.e., operating at 25% above their student capacity). Severe overcrowding is more likely in schools with more than a 50% minority enrollment (U.S. Department of Education 2001).

Teachers themselves may also play a role in transmitting educational inequality (Brophy 1983). Public schools with high minority enrollments are more likely to employ teachers lacking experience (U.S. Department of Education 2003). Studies also show that the social characteristics of students often affect teacher expectations of student performance. Low expectations are most likely to be found in the most disadvantaged schools—inner-city schools with large enrollments of poor and minority students (Hallinan and Sorensen 1985; Kozol 1991; Lumsden 1997; Solomon et al. 1996).

Teachers' social characteristics can also influence their performance expectations. High-status teachers frequently display rather low expectations for their poor and minority students (Alexander, Entwisle, and Thompson 1987). But in this regard, there is also some encouraging news. Teachers who hold positive performance expectations appear to motivate positive results in their students. Indeed, high expectations and demands for academic excellence appear to offset the otherwise negative effects associated with class, race, and ethnicity (Hoffer, Greeley, and Coleman 1987; Mehan et al. 1994).

Finally, conflict theorists cite tracking as an important source of educational inequality. **Tracking** is a practice by which students are divided into groups or classes based on perceived ability. Although tracking is meant to group students in terms of academic ability, in reality it tends to create economic, racial, and ethnic clusters. Since the 1980s, the *form* of tracking has been modified from total program (e.g., college prep tracks vs. vocational tracks) to course-level distinctions (e.g., honors courses in English, history, math, etc.), yet the inequality of the system remains. Studies that compare the performance of low-, medium-, and high-ability tracks show that tracking benefits only the high-ability groups (French and Rothman 1990; Lucas 1999; Shavit and Featherman 1988). And while theoretically, students should be able to achieve mobility within the system, downward movement is much more likely than upward (Lucas 1999). Thus, critics of tracking argue, the practice does little to equalize opportunity; its most ardent opponents argue that tracking creates de jure segregation in our schools (Nelson 2001). There is evidence that tracking fosters a self-fulfilling prophecy (Eder 1981; Lucas 1999; Nelson 2001). A **self-fulfilling prophecy** is a phenomenon whereby that which we believe to be true, in some sense, becomes true for us. Within the tracking system, students do as well or as poorly as they are expected (or given the opportunity) to do (Alexander and Cook 1982; Goodlad 1984; Hochschild 2001; Nelson 2001; Strum 1993; Vanfossen, Jones, and Spade 1987; Williams 2002).

The inequalities found in the U.S. education system are likely to grow worse in the near future. The current recession is taking a hard toll on education. Across the nation, state budget crises were laid at the feet of students. From 2001/02 to 2002/03, we witnessed four-year college tuitions and fees increase 10% nationally. During this same period, two-year college tuitions and fees increased 8% nationally. State college and university spending, however, grew only 1% nationally. Seventeen states decreased their funding for student financial aid (Trombley 2003). This development is especially worrisome given the short- and long-range forecasts for higher education enrollments. By the end of the decade, we should see the largest high school graduating class in history. Our nation's demographics indicate that low-income and minority students will abound among these graduates (Callan 2003). Blocking their access to higher education would have ramifications for generations to come. American youth must be ready to compete in an increasingly global and information-driven economy. Forecasted changes in the job market indicate an increasing demand for better-educated and more literate workers (Hecker 2001; Sum et al. 2002). The Employment Policy Foundation estimates that American jobs requiring college degrees will increase by 20 million over the next several years. The Foundation also estimates that given our present college graduation rates, there will be a 33% shortfall in the number of educationally qualified workers (Employment Policy Foundation 2002). Clearly, an education system that fails to offer quality public education and restricts access to college and postcollege training guarantees a bleak future for the "undereducated" (Barton 1997; Hochschild 2001). Students who are absent from these settings will also be chronically absent from the jobs of tomorrow and upward mobility.

The inequalities found in the U.S. education system present an unavoidable irony. Education can indeed be a great equalizer, but at present, it is not. This tool of upward mobility is most likely to be placed in the hands of those who are already located in advantaged positions. Thus, rather than creating opportunity, the current educational system more accurately sustains the status quo. Our greatest educational challenge, then, may be to devise an ideology that can resolve such contradictions within the system.

Learning More About It

For an interesting history of the links between education and credentials, see Randall Collins's *The Credential Society: An Historical Sociology of Education* (New York: Academic Press, 1979).

A now-classic critique of the American education system comes from Samuel Bowles and Herbert Gintis in *Schooling in Capitalist America: Educational Reform and the Contradictions of Economic Life* (New York: Basic Books, 1976). A more recent presentation of the argument can be found in Jonathan Kozol's books *Savage Inequalities* (New York: Crown, 1991) or *Amazing Grace: The Lives of Children and the Conscience of a Nation* (New York: Crown, 1995).

William Bowen and Derek Bok offer a comprehensive review of affirmative action in higher education and examine the role of selective and wealthy institutions in the reproduction of social elites in *The Shape of the River: Long-Term Consequences of Considering Race in College and University Admissions* (Princeton: Princeton University Press, 2000).

The following organizations and sites can help you learn more about various issues in education:

The National Center for Public Policy and Higher Education
Web site: <http://www.highereducation.org/>

Once at the site, you might want to look at a report on how the states compare on higher education: "Measuring Up 2000: The State-by-State Report Card for Higher Education."

National Assessment Governing Board (Responsible for issuing the "Nation's Report Card")
800 North Capital St. NW, Suite 825, Washington, DC 20002
(202) 357–6938; Web site: <http://www.nagb.org>

National Institute for Literacy
800 Connecticut Ave., NW, Suite 200, Washington, DC 20006–2712
(202) 632–1500; Web site: <http://www.nifl.gov>

U.S. Department of Education
600 Independence Ave, SW, Washington, DC 20202–0498
1–800–USA–LEARN; Web site: <http://www.ed.gov/>

Peterson's Education Center
202 Carnegie Center, Princeton, NJ 08540
(609) 243–9111; Web site: <http://www.petersons.com/>

Exercises

1. Obtain a college catalogue from each of the following categories: (a) an Ivy League college, (b) a four-year state college, and (c) a local community college. Compare the mission statement contained in each school's catalogue. Also compare each school's programs of study and the types of courses it offers. Use your data to prepare a discussion regarding the equal opportunity philosophy of U.S. colleges and universities.

2. Access the most recent edition of the *World Almanac*. Obtain information on the following four items: high school graduation rate by state, student–teacher ratio per state, per capita personal income per state, and state revenues for the public schools. Identify those states that represent the top five and the bottom five of each data category. Is there any overlap in these top five and bottom five groups? Speculate on your findings.

Conclusion

Why Do Conventional Wisdoms Persist?

L ove knows no reason. . . . Beauty is only skin deep. . . . Honesty is the best policy. . . . Education is the great equalizer. These statements represent just a few of the conventional wisdoms that we so often hear throughout our lives.

In the introduction to this book, we noted that many of these adages contain some elements of truth. Within certain settings or under certain conditions, conventional wisdom can prove accurate. Yet throughout *Second Thoughts,* we have also noted that social reality is generally much more involved and much more complex than conventional wisdom would have us believe. Traditional adages and popular sayings rarely provide us with a complete picture of the broader social world. Knowing this, one might ask why individuals continue to embrace conventional wisdom. Given the limited usefulness of such assertions and tenets, why do such adages persist?

The Positive Functions of Conventional Wisdom

Conventional wisdom represents a people's attempt at "knowing." Such adages promise some insight into what is actually occurring. In this way, a culture's conventional wisdom comes to serve a variety of positive social functions; conventional wisdom can induce many productive outcomes for those who invoke them. Here, we speak specifically to five positive social functions served by conventional wisdom.

First, by providing an explanation for an unexpected or mysterious occurrence, *conventional wisdom helps social members confront the unknown and dispel the fear the unknown can generate.* When conventional wisdom proclaims that "immigrants are ruining this country," it provides members of a society with a tangible explanation for their increasing inability to "make ends meet." Similarly, when conventional wisdom advises us to "fear strangers," it offers up the usual suspects for the perennial and always frightening problems of crime, violence, loneliness, and chaos.

By identifying the causes for looming social problems, conventional wisdom not only dispels fear, it also implies a hopeful resolution. As we noted in Essay 8, naming a problem's cause can increase our sense of control and encourage us to believe that a solution cannot be far away. Furthermore, identifying the cause of frightening social conditions offers a protective shield to the broader population. For example, consider a frequently heard bit of wisdom of the 1980s and 1990s: "Homeless people are mentally ill." Here, conventional wisdom cites a reason for a phenomenon most Americans find foreign and frightening. In addition, identifying mental illness as the instigator of the homeless condition gives most "sane" people a secure guarantee—homelessness could never happen to them. This piece of wisdom, like so many other adages, locates the source of a problem within the individual. Thus, as long as other social members distinguish themselves from the "problemmed" individual, they can protect themselves from the problem itself.

Second, *conventional wisdom also can function to maintain social stability.* Consider the common belief, "Every dog has its day." This adage urges people to be patient, to keep striving, or to leave revenge to fate—all attributes necessary for peaceful coexistence. Similarly, consider the adage, "Education is the great equalizer." This belief provides an incentive for citizen commitment to an institution whose greatest social contribution may be the consignment to the population of national customs, norms, and values. In the same way, conventional wisdom that warns that "united we stand, divided we fall" can effectively squelch protest or disagreement. Such a sentiment can enhance cooperation and dedication to a particular group or goal.

In these examples, and others like them, conventional wisdom "steers" a population toward behaviors that maintain smooth social operations. It keeps societies balanced by making constructive effort a matter of "common knowledge."

Third, under certain conditions, *conventional wisdom can function to legitimate the actions of those who invoke it.* Often, speakers will create or tap popular adages with a specific goal in mind. In such cases, conventional wisdom takes on the guise of political, religious, or social rhetoric. "Wisdom" emerges as strategically selected and stylized speech delivered to influence an individual or group.

As rhetoric, conventional wisdom proves effective in instituting policy or law because it promotes a vision of sound "common sense." For example, we witness politically conservative members of the U.S. Congress forwarding wisdom such as "Welfare is ruining this country" or "Welfare breeds dependency." They do so because such rhetoric projects a prudent justification for shaving federal contributions to this cause. Similarly, politicians often espouse wisdom that claims that "capital punishment deters murderers" or "affirmative action programs favor unqualified minorities." They offer these claims, despite factual evidence to the contrary, because such rhetoric effectively employs popular assumptions in the service of the speaker's special interests.

Fourth, at yet another level, *conventional wisdom can strengthen or solidify a social group's identity.* Conventional wisdom often underscores shared values or attributes. In so doing, such beliefs can enhance collective identity. Adages such as "Great minds think alike" or "Like father like son" and sayings such as "The apple doesn't fall far from the tree" or "Birds of a feather flock together" bond individuals by accentuating their similarities. Such wisdom unites individuals by underscoring the common ground they share.

In some cases, however, note that conventional wisdom supports solidarity by creating a "them-versus-us" milieu. Such approaches may unite the members of one group by accentuating the group's hatred or fear of others. For example, Whites who feel threatened by the influx of non-White immigrants to the United States may readily espouse wisdom that advises individuals to "stick with their own kind." As like-minded individuals rally around such wisdom, White group solidarity can be heightened. Similarly, males who find it difficult to accept growing numbers of females in the workplace may rally around the traditional adage, "A woman's place is in the home." Using conventional wisdom to legitimate their fears, the threatened group can comfortably join in opposition.

Fifth, it is important to note that *conventional wisdom is often created or tapped as a tool for power maintenance.* When certain religious traditions defined "the love of money as the root of all evil," such wisdom effectively maintained the divide between the "haves" and the "have-nots." Dissuading the masses from the struggle for material goods allows those in power to maintain their control over limited resources. (Note that such reasoning led social philosopher Karl Marx to refer to religion as "the opium of the people." Marx argued that religion promoted a passive acceptance among the poor of an unfair economic structure.) Similarly, adages such as "You've come a long way baby" or "Good things come to those who wait" serve to dampen efforts toward gender, racial, or ethnic equality. If common consensus suggests that minority group goals have been satisfactorily achieved or addressed, then the continued struggle toward true equality becomes difficult to sustain.

Conventional Wisdom as Knowledge

Whatever its functions, conventional wisdom appears to offer individuals an intelligence boost—a phenomenon social psychologist David Myers (2002:16) refers to as the "I-knew-it-all-along" effect. No matter what happens, there exists a conventional wisdom to cover or explain social behaviors; there always exists a saying or belief that predicts all outcomes. Herein lies conventional wisdom's most troubling feature: A society's "common knowledge" simultaneously proclaims contradictory "facts." For example, conventional wisdom assures us that "haste makes waste," while at the same time warning us that "he who hesitates is lost." Whereas one adage suggests that "too many cooks spoil the broth," another claims that "many hands make light work."

All in all, conventional wisdoms abound for every possible behavior and outcome. Such claims form a stockpile of knowledge to which socialization affords us access. Once introduced to a culture's conventional wisdom, social actors draw on this stockpile of ancient and contemporary adages to make almost any discovery seem like common sense. Thus, when I discover that separation intensifies my romantic attraction, I confirm the phenomenon by saying, "Absence makes the heart grow fonder." If, instead, separation dampens the fires of my romance, I confirm my experiences noting, "Out of sight is out of mind." Indeed, conventional wisdom allows me to confirm any of my impressions and experiences—whatever they might be—and thereby frames those experiences as if they constitute a general norm or the ultimate truth.

The drawbacks of conventional wisdom are heightened by the fact that once introduced, these wisdoms take on lives of their own. Such adages become a "taken-for-granted" part of our culture; they state what is known, implicitly suggesting that such topics need not be further considered. In this way, conventional wisdom constitutes tenacious knowledge—information that endures even if there's no empirical evidence to support it. The mere passing of time, the longevity of an idea or belief, becomes a sufficient indicator of a tenet's veracity. Facts or observations that contradict the adage lose out to the test of time.

The "staying power" of conventional wisdom may be tied to dimensions of wisdom per se. Indeed, equating conventional adages with wisdom may help to accentuate their appeal. Wisdom is a highly valued commodity in our society. It is born of good judgment and experience. Furthermore, it can offer us a sense of inner peace—an ability to live with what we know. Wisdom cannot be taught; courses in wisdom are not part of the college curriculum. Indeed, our formal education experiences often convince us that wisdom is not to be found in books or in research. Rather, wisdom emerges from the ordinary, the common, the everyday. In the final analysis, the wise person is one who has "lived."

In turning to our experiences for wisdom, however, we return to a problem cited earlier and explored at some length in this book's introduction—namely, the limitations of experientially based knowledge. If we base our wisdom solely on personal experiences, we will probably build dubious knowledge. Although our speculations about various social topics typically start with personal experiences, such experiences may not offer us the best empirical evidence for verification.

Our experiences are subjective and therefore vulnerable to distortion and personal bias. They require a "correction" factor, one that can control for distortions emerging from personal prejudices or sloppy thinking. Social scientific inquiry offers one such correction factor. The sociological approach to knowledge follows a set of standardized rules and procedures that can maximize our chances of obtaining valid and reliable knowledge. Although sociology may start with what we already know, good sociology does not end there. Rather, good sociology explores commonsense notions about the social world by collecting and comparing varied reports and observations in the interest of building an all-encompassing picture of reality.

In Closing

Joseph Story, an early Associate Justice of the U.S. Supreme Court, is quoted as saying: "Human wisdom is the aggregate of all human experience, constantly accumulating, selecting and reorganizing its own materials." Story's statement suggests that true wisdom requires a wealth of experience. It is in that spirit that we prepared *Second Thoughts*. In each essay, we proposed a wisdom that requires us to consider myriad experiences and facts. We advocated an approach to knowledge that remains open-ended, a stance that treats new information as an opportunity to rethink what we know. In this way, we cast all social actors as perpetual students of their environment—students who regularly question assumptions and who seek to see beyond themselves.

Learning More About It

The flaws inherent in relying on conventional wisdom for knowledge are effectively portrayed in a 1949 classic by sociologist Paul Lazarsfeld, entitled "The American Soldier: An Expository Review," *Public Opinion Quarterly* 13(3): 378–380. A similarly striking demonstration comes from social psychologist Karl Halvor Teigen in his 1986 article, "Old Truths or Fresh Insights?: A Study of Students' Evaluations of Proverbs," *Journal of British Social Psychology* 25(1): 43–50. Both provide interesting and very readable excursions on this topic.

In a related vein, anthropologist Claude Levi-Strauss explores the origins of myth in his book *The Raw and the Cooked: Introduction to a Science of Mythology* (New York: Harper & Row, 1964).

Howard Kahane and Nancy Cavender provide a detailed exploration of both the tools and pitfalls of everyday reasoning and problem solving in *Logic and Contemporary Rhetoric: The Use of Reason in Everyday Life,* 9th edition (Belmont, CA: Wadsworth, 2002).

References

Abbott, Langer, and Associates. 2002. "Non-Firm Attorneys Make Up to $600,00+." (http://www. abbott-langer.com/lawsumm.html)

ABC News/*Washington Post.* 2003. "Race Relations." (January 20). (http://abcnews.go.com/sections/us/ DailyNews/poll_race030123.html)

Abell, S. C., and Richards, M. H. 1996. "The Relationship Between Body Shape Satisfaction and Self-Esteem: An Investigation of Gender and Class Differences." *Journal of Youth and Adolescence* 25 (October): 691–703.

Abwender, D. A., and Hough, K. 2001. "Interactive Effects of Characteristics of Defendant and Mock Juror on U.S. Participants' Judgment and Sentencing Recommendations." *Journal of Social Psychology* 141(5): 603–615.

Acts, G., Loprest, P., and Roberts, T. 2001. *Final Synthesis Report of Findings From ASPE Leavers Grants.* Washington, DC: Urban Institute.

Adams, R. G., and Allan, G. (Eds.). 1998. *Placing Friendship in Context.* Cambridge: Cambridge University Press.

Adler, P. A., and Adler, P. 1998. *Peer Power: Preadolescent Culture and Identity.* New Brunswick, NJ: Rutgers University Press.

Adler, S. J., and Lamber, W. 1993. "Common Criminals: Just About Everyone Violates Some Laws, Even Model Citizens." *Wall Street Journal* (March 12): A6.

Administration on Aging. 1996. "Aging into the 21st Century." (http://www.aoa.dhhs.gov/aoa/stats/ statpage.html)

_____. 1997. "A Profile of Older Americans: 1997." (http://www.aoa.dhhs.gov/aoa/stats/profile/)

_____. 2001. "Older Adults and Mental Health: Issues and Opportunities." (http://www.aoa.gov/mh/ report2001)

_____. 2002a. "A Profile of Older Americans: 2002." (http://www.aoa.dhhs.gov/prof/statistics/profile/ profiles2002asp)

_____. 2002b. "Family Caregiver Fact Sheet." (http://wwwaoa.gov/press/fact/alpha/fact_family_ care/)

Administration for Children & Families. 2001. "Child Maltreatment 2001." (www.acf.hhs.gov/programs/ cb/publications/cm01/chapterthree.htm)

_____. 2002. *Temporary Assistance for Needy Families Program (TANF) Fourth Annual Report to Congress.* (http://www.acf.dhhs.gov/programs/opre/ar2001/indexar.htm)

Affleck, G., Tennan, H., and Apter, A. 2000. "Optimism, Pessimism and Daily Life with Chronic Illness." Pp. 580–602 in E. C. Chang (Ed.), *Optimism and Pessimism.* Washington, DC: APA Books.

AFL-CIO. 2003. "2002 Trends in Executive Pay." (http://www.aflcio.org/corporateamerica/paywatch)

Ahlburg, D., and DeVita, C. 1992. "New Realities of the American Family." *Population Bulletin* 47(2): Washington, DC: Population Reference Bureau.

Alba, R., and Nee, V. 2003. *Remaking the American Mainstream: Assimilation and Contemporary Immigration.* Cambridge, MA: Harvard University Press.

Alexander, K., and Cook, M. 1982. "Curricula and Coursework: A Surprise Ending to a Familiar Story." *American Sociological Review* 47: 626–640.

Alexander, K., Entwisle, D., and Thompson, M. 1987. "School Performance, Status Relations, and the Structure of Sentiment: Bringing the Teachers Back In." *American Sociological Review* 52(5): 665–682.

Alexander, S. 1999. "The Gender Role Paradox in Youth Culture: An Analysis of Women in Music Videos." *Michigan Sociological Review* 13 (Fall): 46–64.

Allan, G. 1989. *Friendship: Developing a Sociological Perspective.* Boulder, CO: Westview.

_____. 1998a. "Friendship, Sociology and Social Structure." *Journal of Social and Personal Relationships* 15(5): 685–702.

_____. 1998b. "Reflections on Context." Pp. 183–194 in *Placing Friendship in Context,* R. G. Adams and G. Allan (Eds.). Cambridge: Cambridge University Press.

Alper, S., Tjosvold, D., and Law, K. S. 2000. "Conflict Management, Efficacy, and Performance in Organizational Teams." *Personnel Psychology* 53(3): 625–642.

Alt, M., and Peter, K. 2002. "Private Schools A Brief Portrait" (NCES 2002–013). Washington, DC: U.S. Department of Education.

Altheide, D. 2002. *Creating Fear: News and the Construction of Crisis.* New York: Aldine de Gruyter.

Altheimer, E. 1994. *Weight Loss and the Distortion of Body Image.* Henry Rutgers Scholars Thesis, Rutgers University, New Brunswick, NJ.

Amabile, T. M., and Kabat, L. G. 1982. "When Self-Descriptions Contradict Behavior." *Social Cognition* 1: 311–335.

Amato, P. 2000. "The Consequences of Divorce for Adults and Children." *Journal of Marriage and the Family* 62(4): 1269–1287.

_____. 2001a. "Children of Divorce in the 1990s: An Update of the Amato and Keith (1991) Meta-Analysis." *Journal of Family Psychology* 15(3): 355–370.

_____. 2001b. "What Children Learn from Divorce." *Population Today* (January).

Amato, P., and Sobolewski, J. 2001. "The Effects of Divorce and Marital Discord on Adult Children's Psychological Well-Being." *American Sociological Review* 66(6): 900–921.

Amato, P. R., and Fowler, F. 2002. "Parenting Practices, Child Adjustment and Family Diversity." *Journal of Marriage and the Family* 64(3): 703–716.

American Association of Retired Persons (AARP). 2001. *Having Fun As We Age: A Survey of Adult Funstyles 2001.* (http://research.aarp.org)

_____. 2003a. *These Four Walls . . . Americans 45+ Talk About Home and Community.* (http:// research.aarp.org)

_____. 2003b. *Beyond 50.03: A Report to the Nation on Independent Living and Disability.* (http://research.aarp.org)

_____. 2003c. *Staying Ahead of the Curve 2003: The AARP Working in Retirement Study.* (http://research.aarp.org)

American Cancer Society. 2003. *Cancer Facts & Figures 2003.* Atlanta, GA: American Cancer Society. (www.cancer.org)

American Enterprise. 1992. *Women, Men, Marriages and Ministers* (January/February): 106.

American Federation of Teachers. 2002. "College Classes for Prison Inmates Get Reprieve." *AFT on Campus* (April): 11.

American Heart Association. 2002a. *Heart Disease and Stroke Statistics-2003 Update.* Dallas, TX: American Heart Association.

_____. 2002b. "Is It Gender Difference or Gender Bias?" (http://www.americanheart.org/presenter.jhtml?identifier=2633)

_____. 2003. "Statistical Fact Sheet—Women and Cardiovascular Diseases." (http://www.american heart. org/presenter.jhtml?identifier=3000941)

_____. 2003a. "New Study Says People Take Mental Stress To Heart." (http://www.amhrt.org//presenter.jhtml?identifier=3001555)

American Obesity Association. 2002. "AOA Fact Sheets." (http://www.obesity.org/subs/fastfacts/Obesity_Consumer_Protect.shtml)

American Psychological Association. 1997. "The Different Kinds of Stress." (http://helping.apa.org/work/stress4.html)

American Society for Aesthetic Plastic Surgery. 2002. *Cosmetic Surgery National Data Bank.* New York: ASAPS Communications.

AmeriStat. 2002. "Higher Education Means Lower Mortality Rates." Population Reference Bureau. (http://www.prb.org)

_____. 2003a. "How Many High School Dropouts Are There in the U.S.?" Population Reference Bureau. (http://www.prb.org)

_____. 2003b. "Having Children Later or Not at All." Population Reference Bureau. (http://www.prb. org)

_____. 2003c. "Marriage Boosts Individuals' Earnings." (http://www.ameristat.org/)

Amodeo, N. P. 2001. "Be More Cooperative to Be More Competitive." *Journal of Rural Cooperation* 29(2): 115–124.

Andre, T. Whigham, M., Hendrickson, A., and Chambers, S. 1999. "Competency Beliefs, Positive Affect and Gender Stereotypes of Elemntary Students and Their Parents About Science Versus Other School Subjects." *Journal of Research in Science Teaching* 36(6): 719–747.

Andreoletti, C., Zebrowitz, L. A., Leslie, A., and Lachman, M. E. 2001. "Physical Appearance and Control Beliefs in Young, Middle-Aged, and Older Adults." *Personality and Social Psychology Bulletin* 27(8): 969–981.

Andrews, K. 2002. "Movement-Countermovement Dynamics and the Emergence of New Institutions: The Case of 'White Flight' Schools in Mississippi." *Social Forces* 80(3): 911–936.

Aneshensel, C. 1992. "Social Stress: Theory and Research." *Annual Review of Sociology* 18: 15–38.

Angier, N. 2000. "Do Races Differ? Not Really, Genes Show." *The New York Times.* (http://www.nytimes.com/library/national/science/082200sci-genetics-race.html)

Archdeacon, T. 1992. "Reflections on Immigration to Europe in Light of U.S. Immigration History." *International Migration Review* 26 (Summer): 524–548.

Arichi, M. 1999. "Is It Radical? Women's Right To Keep Their Own Surnames After Marriage." *Women's Studies International Forum* 22(4): 411–415.

Aries, P. 1962. *Centuries of Childhood: A Social History of Family Life.* R. Baldick, Trans. New York: Knopf.

Arnett, J. 2000. "High Hopes in a Grim World: Emerging Adults' View of their Futures and 'Generation X.'" *Youth & Society* 31(3): 267–286.

Aronson, E. 1980. *The Social Animal.* San Francisco: Freeman.

Aronson, E., and Cope, V. 1968. "My Enemy's Enemy Is My Friend." *Journal of Personality and Social Psychology* 8: 8–12.

Aronson, E., and Thibodeau, R. 1992. "The Jigsaw Classroom: A Cooperative Strategy for Reducing Prejudice." In J. Lynch, C. Modgil, and S. Modgil (Eds.), *Cultural Diversity in the Schools*. London: Falmer.

Ashenfelter, D. 2002. "Controversy Follows Coin Flip by Judge." *Detroit Free Press* (Feb 4). (http://www.freep.com/news/locway/toss4_20020204.htm)

Association for Children for Enforcement of Support. 2003. "Child Support Statistics." (http://www.childsupport-aces.org/.)

Atkin, C. 1982. "Changing Male and Female Roles." In M. Schwartz (Ed.), *TV and Teens: Experts Look at the Issues*. Reading, MA: Addison-Wesley.

Auerbach, J. A. 2003. "Passing Father's Surname On To Child Questioned." *Family Law* 228(71): 10.

Axelrod, R. 1984. *The Evolution of Cooperation*. New York: Basic Books.

———. 1997. *The Complexity of Cooperation*. Princeton, NJ: Princeton University Press.

Azaryahu, M., and Kook, R. 2002. "Mapping the Nation: Street Names and Arab-Palestinian Identity: Three Case Studies." *Nations and Nationalism* 8(2): 195–213.

Babbie, E. 1994. *What Is Society: Reflections on Freedom, Order, and Change*. Thousand Oaks, CA: Pine Forge.

———. 1998. *Observing Ourselves: Essays in Social Research*. Prospect Heights, IL: Waveland.

———. 2001 *The Practice of Social Research*. 9th ed. Belmont, CA: Wadsworth.

Bachu, A., and O'Connell, M. 2001. "Fertility of American Women: June 2000." *Current Population Reports* (P20–543RV). Washington, DC: U.S. Census Bureau.

Badr, L. K., and Abdallah, B. 2001. "Physical Attractiveness of Premature Infants Affects Outcome at Discharge from NICU." *Infant Behavior and Development* 24(1): 129–133.

Baker, S., Smith, G., Weiner, E., and Harbrecht, D. 1993. "The Mexican Worker." *Business Week* (April 19): 84–92.

Balcom, D. 2002. "Absent Fathers: Effects on Abandoned Sons." Pp. 100–110 in A. Hunter and C. Forden (Eds.), *Readings in the Psychology of Gender: Exploring Our Differences and Commonalities*. Needham Heights, MA: Allyn & Bacon.

Baldas, T. 2003. "Saying Goodbye to Desegregation Plans." *National Law Journal* 25: 85.

Baltzell, E. D. 1987. *The Protestant Establishment: Aristocracy and Caste in America*. New Haven, CT: Yale University Press.

Banerjee, R., and Lintern, V. 2000. "Boys Will Be Boys: The Effect of Social Evaluation Concerns on Gender-Typing. *Social Development* 9(3): 397–408.

Barnes, J. A. 1994. *A Pack of Lies: Toward a Sociology of Lying*. New York: Cambridge University Press.

Bartfeld, J. 2000. "Child Support and the Postdivorce Economic Well-Being of Mothers, Fathers, and Children." *Demography* 37(2): 203–213.

Barton, P. 1997. *Toward Inequality: Disturbing Trends in Higher Education*. Educational Testing Service. Princeton, NJ: Policy Information Center.

Bartsch, R., Burnett, T., Diller, T., and Rankin-Williams, E. 2000. "Gender Representation in Television Commercials: Updating an Update." *Sex Roles* 43(9–10): 735–743.

Basow, S. 1992. *Gender: Stereotypes and Roles*. 3d ed. Monterey, CA: Brooks/Cole.

Batiuk, M. 1997. "The State of Post-Secondary Correctional Education in Ohio." *Journal of Correctional Education* 48(2): 70–72.

Bavier, R. 2001. "Welfare Reform Data from the Survey of Income and Program Participation." *Monthly Labor Review* (July): 13–24.

Beasley, B., and Standley, T. 2002. "Shirts vs Skins: Clothing as an Indicator of Gender Role Stereotyping in Video Games." *Mass Communication and Society* 5(3): 279–293.

Becker, H. 1963. *The Outsiders.* Glencoe, IL: Free Press.

Bellah, R., Madssen, R., Sullivan, W., Swidler, A., and Tipton, S. 1985. *Habits of the Heart: Individualism and Commitment in American Life.* Berkeley: University of California Press.

Bem, S. L. 1993. *The Lenses of Gender: Transforming the Debate on Sexual Inequality.* New Haven, CT: Yale University Press.

Bendick, M. Jackson, C., and Reinoso, V. 1999. Pp. 140–151 in F. Pincus and H. Ehrlich (Eds.), *Race and Ethnic Conflict: Contending Views on Prejudice, Discrimination, and Ethnoviolence.* 2d ed. Boulder, CO: Westview.

Bendor, J., and Swistak, P. 1997. "The Evolutionary Stability of Cooperation." *American Political Science Review* 91 (June): 290–307.

Bennett, N. G., Bloom, D. E., and Craig, P. H. 1992. "American Marriage Patterns in Transition." In S. J. South and S. E. Tolnay (Eds.), *The Changing American Family: Sociological and Demographic Perspectives.* Boulder, CO: Westview.

Benton Foundation. 2002. "Toward Digital Inclusion for Underserved Youth: A Transatlantic Roundtable." (http://www.benton.org/)

Berger, P. 1963. *Invitation to Sociology.* New York: Anchor Books.

Berman, J. 2001. "Industry Output and Employment Projections to 2010." *Monthly Labor Review* (November): 39–56.

Bernstein, S. 1972. "Getting It Done: Notes on Student Fritters." *Urban Life and Culture* 1 (October): 2.

Berscheid, E. 1981. "An Overview of the Psychological Effects of Physical Attractiveness and Some Comments Upon the Psychological Effects of Knowledge on the Effects of Physical Attractiveness." In W. Lucker, K. Ribbens, and J. A. McNamera (Eds.), *Logical Aspects of Facial Form.* Ann Arbor: University of Michigan Press.

_____. 1982. "America's Obsession With Beautiful People." *U.S. News and World Report* (January 11): 59–61.

Berscheid, E., and Hatfield, E. 1983. *Interpersonal Attraction.* 2d ed. Reading, MA: Addison-Wesley.

Besnard, P., and Desplanques, G. 1993. *La Cote des Prénoms en 1994.* Paris: Balland.

Best, J. 2001. *Damned Lies and Statistics: Untangling Numbers from the Media, Politicians, and Activists.* Berkeley: University of California Press.

Bianchi, S., Milkie, M., Sayer, L., and Robinson, J. 2000. "Is Anyone Doing the Housework? Trends in the Gender Division of Household Labor." *Social Forces* 79(1): 191–229.

Bidwell, C., and Friedkin, N. 1988. "The Sociology of Education." Pp. 449–471 in N. Smelser (Ed.), *Handbook of Sociology.* Newbury Park, CA: Sage.

Bird, C. 1999. "Gender, Household Labor and Psychological Distress: The Impact of the Amount and Division of Housework." *Journal of Health and Social Behavior* 40: 32–44.

Bishop, J. E. 1986. "'All For One . . . One For All?' Don't Bet On It." *Wall Street Journal* (December 4): 31.

Bisin, A., Topa, G., and Verdier, T. 2002. "Religious Intermarriage and Socialization in the U.S." (http://www.econ.nyu.edu/user/topage/papers/jpe1202.pdf.)

Black, D. 1976. *The Behavior of Law.* New York: Academic Press.

_____. 1998. *The Social Structure of Right and Wrong.* San Diego, CA: Academic Press.

Blackstone, W. [1765–1769] 1979. *Commentaries on the Laws of England*. Chicago: University of Chicago Press.

Blake, R. R., and Moulton, J. S. 1979. "Intergroup Problem Solving in Organizations: From Theory to Practice." In W. G. Austin and S. Worschel (Eds.), *The Social Psychology of Intergroup Relations*. Monterey, CA: Brooks/Cole.

Blankenhorn, D. 2003. "The Marriage Problem." *American Experiment Quarterly* 6(1): 61–71.

Bleiszner, R., and Adams, R. C. 1992. *Adult Friendships*. Newbury Park, CA: Sage.

Bloom, K., Moore-Schoenmakers, K., and Masataka, N. 1999. "Nasality of Infant Vocalizations Determines Gender Bias in Adult Favorability Ratings." *Journal of Nonverbal Behavior* 23(3): 219–236.

Blum, R. 2003. "Baseball's Average Salary Tops 2.5 Million U.S.: A-Rod Outearns Devil Rays." (http://ca.sports.yahoo.com/030403/6/sisv.html)

Bodnar, J. 1987. "Socialization and Adaptation: Immigrant Families in Scranton." In H. Graff (Ed.), *Growing Up in America: Historical Experiences*. Detroit, MI: Wayne State University Press.

Bonacich, E., Cheng, L., Chinchilla, N., Hamilton, N., and Ong, P. (Eds.). 1994. *Global Production: The Apparel Industry in the Pacific Rim*. Philadelphia: Temple University Press.

Bonner, J. 1984. *Research Presented in "The Two Brains."* Public Broadcasting System Telecast.

Borgas, G. 1990. *Friends or Strangers: The Impact of Immigrants on the U.S. Economy*. New York: Basic Books.

_____. 2001. *Heaven's Door: Immigration Policy and the American Economy*. Princeton, NJ: Princeton University Press.

Boshara, R. 2003. "The $6,000 Solution." *The Atlantic Monthly* (January/February): 91–95.

Bourdieu, P. 1977a. "Cultural Reproduction and Social Reproduction." In J. Karabel and A. H. Halsey (Eds.), *Power and Ideology in Education*. New York: Oxford University Press.

_____. 1977b. *Outline of a Theory of Practice*. Cambridge: Cambridge University Press.

_____. 1984. *Distinction: A Social Critique of the Judgment of Taste*. Cambridge: Harvard University Press.

Boushey, H. 2002. "'This Country is Not Woman-Friendly or Child-Friendly': Talking about the Challenge of Moving from Welfare-to-Work." *Journal of Poverty* 6(2): 81–115.

Bowen, W., and Bok, D. 2000. *The Shape of the River: Long-Term Consequences of Considering Race in College and University Admissions*. Princeton, NJ: Princeton University Press.

Bowles, S., and Gintis, H. 1976. *Schooling in Capitalist America: Educational Reform and the Contradictions of Economic Life*. New York: Basic Books.

_____. 1982. "The Crisis of Liberal Democratic Capitalism: The Case of the U.S." *Politics and Society* 11: 51–59.

_____. 2002. "Schooling in Capitalist America Revisited." *Sociology of Education* 75(1): 1–18.

Bowman, K. 1999. "Living Happily Ever After: Marriage Under the Microscope." *The Public Perspective* (April/May).

Boyatzis, C. J., and Baloff, P. 1998. "Effects of Perceived Attractiveness and Academic Success on Early Adolescent Peer Popularity." *Journal of Genetic Psychology* 159(3): 337–345.

Bramlett, M., and Mosher, W. 2002. "Cohabitation, Marriage, Divorce, and Remarriage in the United States." National Center for Health Statistics. *Vital Health Stat* 23(22).

Brandenburger, A. M., and Nalebuff, B. J. 1996. *Co-Opetition*. New York: Doubleday.

Branigan, T. 2001. "Women: In The Eye of the Beholder: Black and Asian Women Are Spending Thousands on Plastic Surgery–to Look More Caucasian." *Guardian* 2: 10.

Braun, D. D. 1991. *The Rich Get Richer.* Chicago: Nelson Hall.

Breland, A. M. 1998. "A Model for Differential Perceptions of Competence Based on Skin Tone Among African Americans." *Journal of Multicultural Counseling and Development* 26(4): 294–312.

Brenner, J. G., and Spayd, L. 1993. "A Pattern of Bias in Mortgage Loans." *Washington Post* (July 8).

Brophy, J. 1983. "Research on the Self-Fulfilling Prophecy and Teacher Expectations." *Journal of Educational Psychology* 75: 631–661.

Brown, J. F. 1994. "35 Black Men Quizzed in Union, S.C." *Afro-American* (November 12): A1.

Browne, M. W. 1997. "Naming of 6 Elements to End Long Disputes." *The New York Times* (March 4) C5.

Brownlow, S., Jacobi, T., and Rogers, M. 2000. "Science Anxiety as a Function of Gender and Experience." Sex Roles 42, (1–2): 119–131.

Brumberg, J. J. 1997. *The Body Project: An Intimate History of American Girls.* New York: Random House.

Brunet, G., and Bideau, A. 2000. Surnames: History of the Family and History of Populations." *History of the Family* 5(2): 153–161.

Bruning, J. L., Polinko, N. K., Zerbst, J. I., and Buckingham, J. T. 2000. "The Effect on Expected Job Success of the Connotative Meanings of Names and Nicknames." *Journal of Social Psychology* 140(2): 197–201.

Bryan, J. H., and Walbek, N. H. 1970. "Preaching and Practicing Generosity." *Child Development* 41: 329–353.

Bryan, S. 1996. "Work-Related Stress: An Ethical Perspective." *Business Ethics* 5(2): 103–108.

Bryant, J., and Zillmann, D. 2002. *Media Effects: Advances in Theory and Research.* 2d. ed. Mahwah, NJ: Lawrence Erlbaum.

Bumpass, L., and Lu, H. 2000. "Trends in Cohabitation and Implications for Children's Family Contexts in the United States." *Population Studies* 54(1): 29–41.

Bureau of Economic Analysis. 2002. "National Income and Product Account Tables." (http://www.bea.gov/bea/dn/nipaweb/TableViewFixed.asp)

Burke, F. V., Jr. 1995. "Lying During Crisis Negotiations: A Costly Means to Expedient Resolution." *Criminal Justice Ethics* 14 (Winter/Spring): 49–62.

Burnard, T. 2001. "Slave Naming Patterns: Onomastics and the Taxonomy of Race in Eighteenth-Century Jamaica." *Journal of Interdisciplinary History* 31(3): 325–346.

Burton, R. P. D. 1998. "Global Integrative Meaning as a Mediating Factor in the Relationship Between Social Roles and Psychological Distress." *Journal of Health and Social Behavior* 39: 201–215.

BusinessWeek Online. 2002. "Executive Pay." (http://www.businessweek.com/magazine/content/03_16/b3829002.htm)

Business Wire. 2002. "71% of Online Donors Give Weekdays from 9 a.m. to 6 p.m., Kintera Study Reports; Workplace Giving Important Factor in Rise of e-Philanthropy." *Business Wire* (November 14).

Buss, D. M., Shackelford, T. K., Kirkpatrick, L. A., and Larsen, R. J. 2001. "A Half Century of Mate Preferences: The Cultural Evolution of Values." *Journal of Marriage and the Family* 63(2): 491–503.

Bussey, K. 1999. "Children's Categorization and Evaluation of Different Types of Lies and Truths." *Child Development* 70(6): 1338–1347.

Button, J., and Rosenbaum, W. 1990. "Gray Power, Gray Peril or Gray Myth?: The Political Impact of the Aging in Local Sunbelt Politics." *Social Science Quarterly* 71(1): 25–38.

Byrne, J., Arndt, M., Zellner, W., and McNamee, M. 2002. "Restoring Trust in Corporate America." *Business Week* (June 24): 30–36.

Cadinu, M., and Reggiori, C. 2002. "Discrimination of a Low-Status Outgroup: The Role of Ingroup Threat." *European Journal of Social Psychology* 32(4): 501–515.

Calhoun, C. 1998. "Community Without Propinquity' Revisited: Communications Technology and the Transformation of the Urban Public Sphere." *Sociological Inquiry* 68(3): 373–397.

Calhoun, L. G., and Tedeschi, R. G. 2001. "Posttraumatic Growth: The Positive Lessons of Loss." Pp. 157–172 in R. A. Neimeyer (Ed.), *Meaning, Construction, and the Experience of Loss.* Washington, DC: American Psychological Association.

Callan, P. 2003. "A Different Kind of Recession." *National Crosstalk* (Winter).

Campbell. J. 2001. *The Liar's Tale: A History of Falsehood.* New York: Norton.

Campos, P. 1998. *Jurismania: The Madness of American Law.* New York: Oxford University Press.

Card, D., DiNardo, J., and Estes, E. 1998. "The More Things Change: Immigrants and Children of Immigrants in the 1940's, the 1970's and the 1990's." Joint Center on Poverty Research. (http://www. jcpr.org)

Carley, K. M., and Krackhardt, D. 1996. "Cognitive Inconsistencies and Non-Symmetric Friendship." *Social Networks* 18(1): 1–27.

Carstensen, L. Pasupathi, M., Mayr, U., and J Nesselroade. 2000. "Emotion Experience in the Daily Lives of Older and Younger Adults." *Journal of Personality and Social Psychology* 79: 644–655.

Carter, B. 1991. "Children's T.V., Where Boys Are King." *The New York Times* (May 1): A1.

Carter, D., and Wilson, R. 1993. *Minorities in Higher Education.* Washington, DC: American Council on Education.

Cash, T. F., and Janda, L. H. 1984. "The Eye of the Beholder." *Psychology Today* (December): 46–52.

Cash, T. F., and Pruzinsky, T. 1990. "The Psychology of Physical Appearance: Aesthetics, Attributes, and Images." In T. F. Cash and T. Pruzinsky (Eds.), *Body Images: Development, Deviance, and Change.* New York: Guilford.

———. (Eds.). 2002. *Body Image: A Handbook of Theory, Research, and Clinical Practice.* New York/London: Guilford.

Casper, L., and Bryson, K. 1998. "Co-Resident Grandparents and Their Grandchildren: Grandparent Maintained Families" (Population Division Working Paper #26). Washington, DC: U.S. Bureau of the Census.

Catanzarite, L. 2003. "Race-Gender Composition and Occupational Pay Degradation." *Social Problems* 50(1): 14–37.

Cattagni, A., and Farris, E. 2001. "Internet Access in U.S. Public Schools and Classrooms: 1994–2000" (NCES 2001–071). Washington DC: U.S. Department of Education.

CBS News. 2003. "Sex Crimes Cover-Up by Vatican." CBS Evening News (August 8). (http://www.cbsnews.com/storeis/2003/08/06/eveningnews/main566978.shtml)

Center for the American Woman and Politics. 2003. "Women in Elected Office 2003." Eagleton Institute of Politics, Rutgers University. (http://www.rci.rutgers.edu/~cawp/facts/cawpfs.html)

Center on Budget and Policy Priorities. 1998. "Strengths of the Safety Net: How the EITC, Social Security, and Other Government Programs Affect Poverty." (http://www.cbpp.org/pubs/povinc. htm)

———. 2002. "Census Data Show Increases in Extent and Severity of Poverty and Decline in Household Income." Analysis of Census Bureau's Poverty and Income Data for 2001. (http://www.cbpp.org/9-24-02pov.htm)

Center on Budget and Policy Priorities. 2003. "The New Definitive CBO Data on Income and Tax Trends." Data from Table 2 and Appendix Table 2, Sept 23. (http://www.cbpp.org/9-23-03tax.htm)

Centers for Disease Control and Prevention. 2002. *Web-based Injury Statistics Query and Reporting System (WISQARS).* (www.cdc.gov/ncipc/wisqars)

Cerulo, K. A. 1995. *Identity Designs: The Sights and Sounds of a Nation.* ASA Rose Book Series. New Brunswick, NJ: Rutgers University Press.

_____. 1997. "Re-framing Sociological Concepts for a Brave New (Virtual?) World." *Sociological Inquiry* 67(1): 48–58.

_____. 1998. *Deciphering Violence: The Cognitive Structure of Right and Wrong.* New York: Routledge.

_____. 2002. "Individualism . . . Pro Tem: Reconsidering U.S. Social Relations." Pp. 135–171 in K. A. Cerulo (Ed.), *Culture in Mind: Toward a Sociology of Culture and Cognition.* New York: Routledge.

Cerulo, K. A., and Ruane, J. M. 1997. "Death Comes Alive: Technology and the Re-conception of Death." *Science As Culture* 6(28): 444–466.

_____. 1998. "Coming Together: New Taxonomies for the Analysis of Social Relations." *Sociological Inquiry* 68(3): 398–425.

_____. 2004. "Who Is a Social Actor?" Paper presented at the Annual Meetings of the Eastern Sociological Society, February, New York.

Cerulo, K. A., Ruane, J. M., and Chayko, M. 1992. "Technological Ties That Bind: Media-Centered Primary Groups." *Communication Research* 19(1): 109–129.

Chan, K. B. 2002. "Coping With Work Stress, Work Satisfaction, and Social Support: An Interpretive Study of Life Insurance Agents." *Southeast Asian Journal of Social Science* 30(3): 657–685.

Charles, S., Mather, M., and Carstensen, L. 2003. "Aging and Emotional Memory: The Forgettable Nature of Negative Images for Older Adults." *Journal of Experimental Psychology: General* 132(2).

Chase-Lansdale, P., Cherlin, A., and Kiernan, K. 1995. "The Long-Term Effects of Parental Divorce on the Mental Health of Young Adults: A Developmental Perspective." *Child Development* 66: 1614–1634.

Chayko, M. 2002. *Connecting: How We Form Social Bonds and Community in the Internet Age.* Albany: SUNY Press.

Cherlin, A. 1999. "I'm OK, You're Selfish." *The New York Times* (October 17) A:44–45.

Cherlin, A., Chase-Lansdale, P., and McRae, C. 1998. "Effects of Parental Divorce on Mental Health Throughout the Life Course." *American Sociological Review* 63(2): 239–249.

Chia, R. C., and Alfred, L. J. 1998. "Effects of Attractiveness and Gender on the Perception of Achievement Related Variables." *Journal of Social Psychology* 138(4): 471–478.

Chick, K., Heilman-Houser, R., and Hunter, M. 2002. "The Impact of Child Care on Gender Role Development and Gender Stereotypes." *Early Childhood Education Journal* 29(3): 149–154.

Chideya, F. 1995. *Don't Believe the Hype: Fighting Cultural Misinformation About African-Americans.* New York: Plume.

Children's Defense Fund. 2000. "Child Abuse and Neglect." (http:www.childrensdefense.org/ss_ chabuse_fs.php)

_____. 2001. "A Fragile Foundation: State Child Care Assistance Policies." (http://www.childrens defense.org/pdf/cc_statecc_execsumm.pdf)

_____. 2002. "The State of America's Children Yearbook 2001." (http:www.childrensdefense.org/keyfacts.htm)

_____. 2002a. "The State of Children in America's Union 2002." (http:www.childrensdefense.org)

Children's Defense Fund. 2002b. "Frequently Asked Questions." (December). (http://www.childrensde fense.org/fs_cpfaq_facts.php.)

_____. 2002c. "Child Support." (http://www.childrensdefense.org/fs_chsup.php.)

_____. 2003. "Immunization." (http://www.childrensdefense.org/hs_tp_immuniz.php)

Children's Monitor. 2003. "Hill Highlights: FY 2004 Bush Budget and Children." *Children's Monitor* 16(2): 2–9.

Chiodo, A., and Owyang, M. 2003. "Financial Aid and College Choice." *National Economic Trends*. The Federal Reserve Bank of St. Louis. (http://research.stlouisfed.org/publications/net/20030801/cover.pdf)

Chira, S. 1992. "Bias Against Girls Is Found Rife in Schools, With Lasting Damage." *The New York Times* (February 12): A1.

Christopher, A. N. 1998. "The Psychology of Names: An Empirical Examination." *Journal of Applied Social Psychology* 28(13): 1173–1195.

Church, G. 1993. "Send Back Your Tired, Your Poor . . ." *Time* (June 21): 26–27.

Clarke, E. H. 1873. *Sex in Education: Or a Fair Chance for Girls.* Boston: J.R. Osgood.

Clifford, M. M., and Walster, E. H. 1973. "The Effects of Physical Attractiveness on Teacher Expectation." *Sociology of Education* 46: 245–258.

Cockerham, W. 1997. *This Aging Society.* 2d ed. Englewood Cliffs, NJ: Prentice Hall.

_____. 2003. *Sociology of Mental Disorder.* 6th ed. Upper Saddle River, NJ: Prentice Hall.

_____. 2004. *Medical Sociology.* 9th ed. Upper Saddle River, NJ: Prentice Hall.

Cohen, L., and Gray, C. B. 2003. "The Blaine Game: School Vouchers and State Constitutions." *The Taubman Center Report—Our 15th Anniversary.* John F. Kennedy School of Government, Harvard University, Cambridge, MA.

Coleman, B., and Pandya, S. 2002. "Family Caregiving and Long-Term Care." American Association of Retired Persons. (http://research.aarp.org/il/fs91_ltc.html)

Coleman, R., and Rainwater, L. 1978. *Social Standing in America: New Dimensions of Class.* New York: Basic Books.

Collier, J. L. 1991. *The Rise of Selfishness in America.* New York: Oxford University Press.

Collins, P. H. 1990. *Black Feminist Thought.* New York: Routledge.

Collins, R. 1979. *The Credential Society: An Historical Sociology of Education.* New York: Academic Press.

Coltrane, S., and Messineo, M. 2000. "The Perpetuation of Subtle Prejudice: Race and Gender Imagery in 1990s Television Advertising." *Sex Roles* 42(5–6): 363–389.

Combs, A. (Ed.). 1992. *Cooperation: Beyond the Age of Competition.* Philadelphia: Gordon and Breach.

Commonwealth Fund. 1994. "Health Care Reform: What Is at Stake for Women?" New York: Commonwealth Fund.

_____. 2000. "Women's Health," Tables 1–8. (http://www.cmwf.org/programs/women/sandman_men'ssurvey2000_tabs1_374.asp)

Conner, G., and Smith, D. 1991. "Home Mortgage Disclosure Act: Expanded Data on Residential Lending." *Federal Reserve Bulletin* (November).

Consumer Attorneys of California. 1995. (http:www.caoc.com/)

Cooley, C. H. 1902. *Human Nature and Social Order.* New York: Scribner.

_____. 1909. *Social Organization.* New York: Charles Scribner.

Coontz, S. 1998. *The Way We Really Are: Coming to Terms With America's Changing Families.* New York: Basic Books.

_____. 2000. *The Way We Never Were: American Families and the Nostalgia Trap.* New York: Basic Books.

Cooper, M. 2002. "Poverty Increases in the United States, U.S. Census Bureau Reports." National Council of Churches. (http://www.ncccusa.org/publicwitness/poverty/increases.html)

Coopersmith, S. 1967. *Antecedents of Self-Esteem.* San Francisco: Freeman.

Correll, S. 2001. "Gender and the Career Choice Process: The Role of Biased Self-Assessments." *American Journal of Sociology* 106(6): 1691–1730.

Coser, L. 1956. *The Function of Social Conflict.* Glencoe, IL: Free Press.

_____. 1963. *Sociology Through Literature: An Introductory Reader.* Englewood Cliffs, NJ: Prentice Hall.

Courtney, A., and Whipple, T. 1983. *Sex Stereotyping in Advertising.* Lexington, MA: D.C. Heath.

Cowe, R. 1990. "New Ice Cream Plans to Lick Rivals." *Guardian II* (April 2): 3.

Craver, Matthews, Smith, & Company. 1999. "Socially Engaged Internet Users: Prospects for Online Philanthropy and Activism." (http://www.craveronline.com)

Critser, G. 2003. *Fat Land: How Americans Became the Fattest People in the World.* Boston: Houghton Mifflin.

Crocker, P. 1985. "The Meaning of Equality for Battered Women Who Kill Men in Self-Defense." *Harvard Women's Law Journal* 8: 121–153.

Cross, S., and Bagilhole, B. 2002. "Girls' Jobs for the Boys? Men, Masculinity and Non-Traditional Occupations." *Gender, Work and Organization* 9(2): 204–226.

Cross, S. E., and Vick, N. V. 2001. "The Interdependent Self-Construal and Social Support: The Case of Persistence in Engineering." *Personality and Social Psychology Bulletin* 27(7): 820–832.

Crowder, K. 2001. "Racial Stratification in the Actuation of Mobility Expectations: Microlevel Impacts of Racially Restrictive Housing Markets." *Social Forces* 79(4): 1377–1397.

Cummings, J. 2003. "When Poverty Cripples. *NEA Today* 21(4): 22.

Curry, T., Arriagada, P., and Cornwell, B. 2002. "Images of Sport in Popular Nonsport Magazines: Power and Performance Versus Pleasure and Participation." *Sociological Perspectives* 45(4): 397–413.

Dai, D. 2002. "Incorporating Parent Perceptions: A Replication and Extension Study of the Internal-External Frame of Reference Model of Self-Concept Development." *Journal of Adolescent Research* 17(6): 617–645.

Dalphonse, S. 1997. "Choosing to be Childfree: Broadening the Definition of Family." *The Population Connection Reporter* (May/June). (http://www.populationconnection.org/Reports_Publications/Reports/report213.html)

Daly, K. 2001. "Controlling Time in Families: Patterns That Sustain Gendered Work in the Home." *Contemporary Perspectives in Family Research* 3: 227–249.

Daniels, R. 1990. *A History of Immigration and Ethnicity in American Life.* New York: Harper Perennial.

Danner, D. D., Snowden, D. A., and Friesen, W. V. 2001. "Positive Emotions in Early Life and Longevity: Findings From the Nun Study." *Journal of Personality and Social Psychology* 80: 804–813.

Davis, F. J. 1991. *Who Is Black: One Nation's Definition.* University Park: Pennsylvania State University Press.

Davis, K., and Moore, W. 1945. "Some Principles of Stratification." *American Sociological Review* 27(1): 5–19.

Davison, K. P., Pennebaker, J. W., and Dickerson, S. S. 2000. "The Social Psychology of Illness Support Groups." *American Psychologist* 55: 205–217.

De Cremer, D. 2001. "Relations of Self-Esteem Concerns, Group Identification, and Self-Stereotyping to In-Group Favoritism." *Journal of Social Psychology* 14(3): 389–400.

Dedman, B. 1989. "Blacks Turned Down for Home Loans from S&L's Twice as Often as Whites." *Atlanta Constitution* (January 22): A1.

De Dreu, C. K. W., Weingart, L. R., and Kwon, S. 2000. "Influence of Social Motives on Integrative Negotiation: A Meta-Analytic Review and Test of Two Theories." *Journal of Personality and Social Psychology* 78(5): 889–905.

Degher, D., and Hughes, G. 1992. "The Identity Change Process: A Field Study of Obesity." *Deviant Behavior* 2: 385–401.

deMunck, V., and Korotayev, A. 1999. "Sexuality Equality and Romantic Love: A Reanalysis of Rosenblatt's Study on the Function of Romantic Love." *Cross-Cultural Research: The Journal of Comparative Social Science* 33(3): 265–277.

DeNavas-Walt, C., and Cleveland, R. 2002. "Money Income in the United States: 2001." *Current Population Reports* (P60–218). Washington, DC: U.S. Government Printing Office.

Dent, K. 2003. "Facts for Citizens, 2003." Sarasota, FL: County Supervisor of Elections.

Denton, N., and Massey, D. 1989. "Racial Identity Among Caribbean Hispanics: The Effect of Double Minority Status on Residential Segregation." *American Sociological Review* 54: 790–808.

DePaulo, B. M., Kashy, D. A., and Kirkendol, S. E. 1996. "Lying in Everyday Life." *Journal of Personality and Social Psychology* 70 (May): 979–995.

DeSantis, A., and Kayson, W. 1997. "Defendants' Characteristics of Attractiveness, Race, Sex, and Sentencing Decisions." *Psychological Reports* 81 (October): 679–683.

De Schipper, S., Hirschberg, C., Sinha, G. 2002. "Blame the Name." *Popular Science* 261(1): 36.

Deutsch, M. 2000. "Cooperation and Competition." Pp. 21–40 in M. Deutsch and P. T. Coleman (Eds.), *The Handbook of Conflict Resolution: Theory and Practice.* Jossey-Bass: San Francisco.

Deustch, M., and Krauss, R. M. 1960. "The Effect of Threat on Interpersonal Bargaining." *Journal of Abnormal and Social Psychology* 1: 629–636.

Devine, J., and Wright, J. D. 1993. *The Greatest of Evils.* New York: Aldine de Gruyter.

de Vries, M. 2002. "Can You Afford Honesty? A Comparative Analysis of Ethos and Ethics in Local Government." *Administration & Society* 34(3): 309–334.

Dewar, D. 2000. "Gender Impacts on Health Insurance Coverage: Findings for Unmarried Full-Time Employees." *Women's Health Issues* 10(5): 268–277.

Diamond, L. M., and Dube, E. M. 2002. "Friendship and Attachment Among Heterosexual and Sexual-Minority Youths: Does the Gender of Your Friend Matter?" *Journal of Youth and Adolescence* 31(2): 155–166.

Dickard, N. 2002. "Federal Retrenchment on the Digital Divide: Potential National Impact." *Benton Foundation* (Policy Brief No. 1) (March).

Dickard, N., Honey, M., and Wilhelm, A. 2003. "Introduction: The Challenge of Taking Edtech to the Next Level" *The Sustainability Challenge: Taking Edtech to the Next Level.* Benton Foundation and the Center for Children and Technology. (http://www.benton.org/)

Diefenbach, D. L., and West, M. D. 2001. "Violent Crime and Poisson Regression: A Measure and Method for Cultivation Analysis." *Journal of Broadcasting and Electronic Media* 45(3): 432–445.

Dietz, T. 1998. "An Examination of Violence and Gender Role Portrayals in Video Games: Implications for Gender Socialization and Aggressive Behavior." *Sex Roles* 38(5–6): 425–442.

Dines, G., and Humez, J. (Eds.). 2003. *Gender, Race and Class in Media: A Text-Reader.* Thousand Oaks: Sage.

Dion, K. K. 1979. "Physical Attractiveness and Interpersonal Attraction." In M. Cook and G. Wilson (Eds.), *Love and Attraction.* New York: Pergamon.

Dion, K. K. 2001. "Cultural Perspectives on Facial Attractiveness." Pp. 239–259 in G. Rhodes and L. A. Zebrowitz (Eds.), *Facial Attractiveness: Evolutionary, Cognitive, and Social Perspectives.* Greenwich, CT: Ablex.

Dion, K. K., and Berscheid, E. 1974. "Physical Attractiveness and Peer Perception Among Children." *Sociometry* 37: 1–12.

Dion, K. K., Berscheid, E., and Walster, E. 1972. "What Is Beautiful Is Good." *Journal of Personality and Social Psychology* 24: 285–290.

Dion, K. K., and Dion, K. 1996. "Cultural Perspectives on Romantic Love." *Personal Relationships* 3: 5–17.

Dion, K. L. 1979. "Intergroup Conflict and Intragroup Cohesiveness." In W. G. Austin and S. Worschel (Eds.), *The Social Psychology of Intergroup Relations.* Monterey, CA.: Brooks/Cole.

Diversity Digest. 1998. "How Do Americans View One Another? The Persistence of Racial/Ethnic Stereotypes." (http://www.diversityweb.org/Digest/W98/research2.html)

Dizard, J. E., and Gadlin, H. 1990. *The Minimal Family.* Amherst: University of Massachusetts Press.

Do It Yourself Weight Loss. 2001. (http://www.fforward.com/dan/weightloss/)

Doggett, S., and Haddad, A. 2000. "Global Savvy: Cosmetics Maker Is All Smiles as Sales Blossom in Overseas Markets." *Los Angeles Times* (March 27): C2.

Doherty, W., Kouneski, E., and Erikson, M. 1996. "Responsible Fathering: An Overview and Conceptual Framework." Washington, DC: Administration for Children and Families and the Office of the Assistant Secretary for Planning and Evaluation of the U.S. Department of Health & Human Services. (http://fatherhood.hhs.gov/concept.htm)

Dolgin, K. G., and Minowa, N. 1997. "Gender Differences in Self-Presentation: A Comparison of the Roles of Flatteringness and Intimacy in Self-Disclosure to Friends." *Sex Roles* 36(5–6): 371–380.

Donald, R. R. 2001. "Masculinity and Machismo in Hollywood's War Films." Pp. 170–183 in S. M. Whitehead and F. J. Barrett (Eds.), *The Masculinities Reader.* Cambridge, UK: Polity Press.

Donohue, B. 2002. "Their Own Names Are What They Fear." *The Star Ledger* (March 3): A1.

Doyle, R. 2002. "Calculus of Happiness." *Scientific American* 287(5): 32–33.

Drucker, P. 1993. "The Rise of the Knowledge Society." *Wilson Quarterly* (Spring): 52–71.

Du Bois, W. E. B. [1903] 1982. *The Souls of Black Folks.* New York: Penguin.

Dudley, D. 2003. "Forever Cool." *AARP Magazine.* (http://www.aarpmagazine.org/lifestyle/articles/a2003-0121-eldercool.htm)

Dunne, J. G. 1986. "The War That Won't Go Away." *New York Review of Books* (September 25): 25–29.

Durkheim, E. [1938] 1966. *The Rules of Sociological Method.* 8th ed. S. A. Solovay and J. H. Mueller, Trans. New York: Free Press.

Ebenkamp, B. 2003. "The Amazing Ratings Race." *Brandweek* 44(18): 18.

ECI. 2002. "Cheating and Succeeding: Record Numbers of Top High School Students Take Ethical Shortcuts." *ECI Who's Who 29th Annual Survey.* (http://www.eci-whoswho.com/highschool/annualsurveys/29.shtml)

Economist. 2003. "Take it Block by Block." *Economist* 366(8308): 35.

Eder, D. 1981. "Ability Grouping as a Self-Fulfilling Prophecy: A Micro-Analysis of Teacher Student Interaction." *Sociology of Education* 54(3): 151–162.

Edin, K., and Lein, L. 1997a. "Work, Welfare, and Single Mothers' Economic Strategies." *American Sociological Review* 62(2): 253–266.

_____. 1997b. *Making Ends Meet: How Single Mothers Survive Welfare and Low-Wage Work.* New York: Russell Sage.

Ehrenreich, B. 2001. *Nickel and Dimed: On (Not) Getting By in America.* New York: Owl Books.

Eichenwald, K. 2003. "In String of Corporate Troubles, Critics Focus on Boards' Failings." *The New York Times* (September 21): 1.

Eichenwald, K., and Atlas, R. 2003. "2 Banks Settle Accusations They Aided in Enron Fraud." *The New York Times* (July 29).

Ekman, P. 2001. *Telling Lies: Clues to Deceit in the Marketplace, Politics, and Marriage.* San Francisco: University of California.

Ekman, P., and Frank, M. G. 1993. "Lies That Fail." Pp. 184–200 in M. Lewis and C. Saarni (Eds.), *Lying and Deception in Everyday Life.* New York: Guilford.

Ekman, P., O'Sullivan, M., Friesen, W. V., and Scherer, K. R. 1991. "Face, Voice and Body in Detecting Deceit." *Journal of Nonverbal Behavior* 15(2): 125–135.

Elasmar, M., Hasegawa, K., and Brain, M. 1999. "The Portrayal of Women in U.S. Prime Time Television." *Journal of Broadcasting and Electronic Media* 43(1): 20–34.

Eliasoph, N. 1998. *Avoiding Politics: How Americans Produce Apathy in Everyday Life.* Cambridge, England: Cambridge University Press.

Elles, L. 1993. *Social Stratification and Socioeconomic Inequality.* Westport, CT: Praeger.

Ellis, B., Bates, J., Dodge, K., Fergusson, D. Horwood, L. Pettit, G., and Woodward, L. 2003. "Does Father Absence Place Daughters at Special Risk for Early Sexual Activity and Teenage Pregnancy?" *Child Development* 74(3): 801–821.

Ellis, H. C. 1972. "Motor Skills in Learning." In *Fundamentals of Human Learning and Cognition.* Dubuque, IA: Wm. C. Brown.

Emerson, M., Yancey, G., and Chai, K. 2001. "Does Race Matter in Residential Segregation? Exploring the Preferences of White Americans." *American Sociological Review* 66(6): 922–935.

Employment Policy Foundation. 2001. "Give Yourself the Gift of a Degree." News Release—Work Place Trends (December 19). (http://www.epf.org/media/newsreleases/2003/nr2003template.asp?nrid=51)

———. 2002. "Where Are Tomorrow's Workers?" News Release, August 14. (http://www.epf.org/media/newsreleases/2003/nr2003template.asp?nrid=29)

Epstein, C. F. 1988. *Deceptive Distinctions: Sex, Gender, and the Social Order.* New Haven, CT: Yale University Press.

Equal Employment Opportunity Commission. 2003. "EEOC Reports Discrimination Charge Filings Up." (http://www.eeoc.gov/pres/2-6-03.html)

Erian, M., Lin, C., Patel, N., Neal, A., and Geiselman, R. E. 1998. "Juror Verdicts as a Function of Victim and Defendant Attractiveness in Sexual Assault Cases." *American Journal of Forensic Psychology* 16(3): 25–40.

Eschholz, S. Bufkin, J., and Long, J. 2002. "Symbolic Reality Bites: Women and Racial/Ethnic Minorities in Modern Film." *Sociological Spectrum* 22(3): 299–334.

Espino, R., and Franz, M. M. 2002. "Latino Phenotypic Discrimination Revisited: The Impact of Skin Color on Occupational Status." *Social Science Quarterly* 83(2): 612–623.

Etaugh, C. E., Bridges, J. S., Cummings-Hill, M., and Cohen, J. 1999. "Names Can Never Hurt Me?: The Effects of Surname Use on Perceptions of Married Women." *Psychology of Women Quarterly* 23(4): 819–823.

Etzioni, A. 1994. *The Spirit of Community: The Reinvention of American Society.* New York: Touchstone Books.

Etzioni, A. 1996. *The New Golden Rule.* New York: Basic Books.

———. 2003. *Monochrome Society.* New York: New Forum Books.

Fallows, J. 1983. "Immigration: How It Is Affecting Us." *The Atlantic Monthly* 252(5):45–48.

Family Violence Prevention Fund. 1998. "General Statistics." (http://www.fvpf.org/fund/the_facts/stats.html)

———. 2003. "Prevalence of Domestic Violence." (http://www.endabuse.org/resources/facts/stats.html)

Famous Art Reproductions. 2003. "Interesting Famous Art Facts." (http://www.famousartreproductions. com/factsaboutart.html)

Feagin, J. R. 1975. *Subordinating the Poor.* Englewood Cliffs, NJ: Prentice Hall.

Federal Interagency Forum on Aging-Related Statistics. 2000. *Old Americans 2000: Key Indicators of Well-Being.* Washington, DC: U.S. Government Printing Office.

Feeley, T. H. 2002. "Evidence of Halo Effects in Student Evaluations of Communication Instruction." *Communication Education* 51(3): 225–236.

Feingold, A. 1988. "Cognitive Gender Differences Are Disappearing." *American Psychologist* 43: 95–103.

Feliciano, C. 2001. "The Benefits of Biculturalism: Exposure to Immigrant Culture and Dropping out of School Among Asian and Latino Youths." *Social Science Quarterly* 82(4): 865–879.

Felson, R. B., and Reed, M. 1986. "Reference Groups and Self-Appraisals of Academic Ability and Performance." *Social Psychology Quarterly* 49: 103–109.

_____. 1987. "The Effect of Parents on the Self-Appraisals of Children." *Social Psychology Quarterly* 49: 302–308.

Festinger, L., Schachter, S., and Back, K. 1950. *Social Pressures in Informal Groups: A Study of Human Factors in Housing.* New York: Harper and Brothers.

Fields, J. 2003. "Children's Living Arrangements and Characteristics: March 2002." *Current Population Reports* (P20–547). Washington, DC: U.S. Census Bureau.

Fields, J., and Casper, L. 2001. "America's Families and Living Arrangements: March 2000." *Current Population Reports* (P20–537). Washington, DC: U.S. Census Bureau.

Fiese, B., and Skillman, G. 2000. "Gender Differences in Family Stories: Moderating Influence of Parent Gender Role and Child Gender." *Sex Roles* 43(5–6): 267–283.

Figueroa, C. 2003. "Self-Esteem and Cosmetic Surgery: Is There a Relationship Between the Two?" *Plastic Surgical Nursing* 23(1): 21–25.

Finkelstein, J. 1991. *The Fashioned Self.* Philadelphia: Temple University Press.

Finlinson, A. R., Austin, A. M. B., and Pfister, R. 2000. "Cooperative Games and Children's Positive Behaviors." *Early Child Development and Care* 164: 29–40.

Fischer, C. 1982. *To Dwell Among Friends: Personal Networks in Town and City.* Chicago: University of Chicago Press.

Fischer, D. H. 1977. *Growing Old in America.* New York: Oxford University Press.

Fitzpatrick, J. 2003. "EPA Deception on Ground Zero." *The Patriot Ledger* (August 29). Quincey, MA.

Flashpoints. 2003. "The Patriot Act." PBS Broadcast. July 15. (http://www.pbs.org/flashpointsusa/about/ tvpoll_results.html)

Flippen, C. 2001. "Racial and Ethnic Inequality in Home Ownership and Housing Equity." *Sociological Quarterly* 42(2): 121–150.

Foucault, M. 1971. *The Order of Things: An Archeology of Human Sciences.* New York: Pantheon.

Fox, V., and Quit, M. 1980. *Loving, Parenting, and Dying: The Family Cycle in England and America, Past and Present.* New York: Psychohistory Press.

Frank, J. B. 2002. *The Paradox of Aging in Place in Assisted Living.* Westport, CT: Bergin and Garvey.

Frankenberg, E., and Lee, C. 2002. "Race in American Public Schools: Rapidly Resegregating School Districts." The Civil Rights Project, Harvard University, Cambridge, MA. (http://www.civilrights project.harvard.edu)

Frankenberg, E., Lee, C., and Orfield, G. 2003a. "A Multiracial Society with Segregated Schools: Are We Losing the Dream?" The Civil Rights Project, Harvard University, Cambridge, MA. (http://www.civilrightsproject.harvard.edu)

———. 2003b. "Charter Schools and Race: A Lost Opportunity for Integrated Education." The Civil Rights Project, Harvard University, Cambridge, MA. (http://www.civilrightsproject.harvard.edu)

Frazier, P. A., Tix, A. P., Klein, C. D., and Arikian, N. J. 2000. "Testing Theoretical Models of the Relations Between Social Support, Coping, and Adjustments to Stressful Life Events." *Journal of Social and Clinical Psychology* 19: 314–335.

Freeman, J. 2002. *Media Violence and Its Effects on Aggression: Assessing the Scientific Evidence.* Toronto: University of Toronto Press.

Freeman, M. 2002. "Fewer Series Feature Black-Dominant Casts." *Electronic Media* 21(15): 3–5.

Fremstad, S. 2003. "State Fiscal Relief Funds Do Not Address the Need for Substantial Increases in Child Care Funding." Center on Budget and Policy Priorities. (http://www.cbpp.org/7-25-03 tanf.htm)

French, D., and Rothman, S. 1990. *Structuring Schools for Student Success: A Focus on Ability Grouping.* Quincy, MA: Massachusetts State Department of Education, Bureau of Research, Planning, and Evaluation.

Freudenheim, B. 1988. "Who Lives Here, Go-Getter or Grouch?" *The New York Times* (March 31): 15–16.

Friedman, L. 1975. *The Legal System: A Social Science Perspective.* New York: Russell Sage.

Fry, R. 2002. "Latinos in Higher Education: Many Enroll, Too Few Graduate." Pew Hispanic Center. (http://www.pewhispanic.org)

Fukuoka, Y. 1998. "Japanese Alias vs. Real Ethnic Name: On Naming Practices Among Young Koreans In Japan." Paper Presented at the Annual Meetings of the International Sociological Association.

Fuligni, A., and Pedersen, S. 2002. "Family Obligation and the Transition to Young Adulthood." *Developmental Psychology* 38(5): 856–868.

Funiciello, T. 1990. "The Poverty of Industry." *Ms.* (November/December): 32–40.

Furstenburg, F. Jr. 1979. "Pre-Marital Pregnancy and Marital Instability." In G. Levinger and O. C. Moles (Eds.), *Divorce and Separation.* New York: Basic Books.

Furstenburg, F. F. Jr., and Talvitie, K. G. 1980. "Children's Names and Parental Claims: Bonds Between Unmarried Fathers and Their Children." *Journal of Family Issues* 1: 31–57.

Gallup, G. Jr. 1976–2003. *The Gallup Poll: Public Opinion.* Wilmington, DE: Scholarly Resources.

Gallup Poll. 2001. "Recreation." (December 6–9). Roper Center for Public Opinion Research, University of Connecticut. (http://www.ropercenter.uconn.edu/cgi-bin/hsrun.exe/Roperweb/pom/StateId/SmeliaHcoWtjzAMysYAhVu_VYAqDq-UtL9/HAHTpage/Summary_Link?qstn_id=455723)

———. 2003. "Race Relations." *Race and Ethnicty* (June 12–18). (http://www.pollingreport.com/race.htm)

Gans, H. 1971. "The Uses of Poverty: The Poor Pay for All." *Social Policy* (Summer): 20–24.

Garcia, S. D. 1998. "Appearance Anxiety, Health Practices, Metaperspectives and Self-Perception of Physical Attractiveness." *Journal of Social Behavior and Personality* 13(2): 12–15.

Gardyn, R. 2002. "The Mating Game." *American Demographics* (July/August): 33–37.

Gelles, R., and Straus, M. 1988. *Intimate Violence.* New York: Simon and Schuster.

Gelles, R. J., and Loseke, D. R. (Eds.). 1993. *Current Controversies on Family Violence.* Newbury Park, CA: Sage.

General Social Survey. 1998. (http://www.icpsr.umich.edu:8080/GSS/rnd1998/merged/cdbk/wrkwayup.htm)

General Social Survey. 1999. *Cumulative Codebook. 1972–1998.* Chicago: National Opinion Research Center. (http://www.norc.uchicago.edu/)

———. 2000. (http://www.icpsr.umich.edu:8080/GSS)

Gerbner, G., Gross, L., Morgan, M., Signorielli, N., and Shanahan, J. 2002. "Growing Up With Television: Cultivation Processes." Pp. 43–67 in J. Bryant and D. Zillmann (Eds.), *Media Effects: Advances in Theory and Research.* 2d ed. Mahwah, NJ: Lawrence Erlbaum.

Gergen, K. 1971. *The Concept of Self.* New York: Holt, Rinehart and Winston.

Gergen M. M., Gergen, K. J., March, K., and Ellis, C. 2003. "The Body and the Physical Self." Pp. 301–340 in J. A. Holstein and J. F. Gubrium (Eds.), *Inner Lives and Social Worlds: Readings in Social Psychology.* London: Oxford University Press.

Gerull, F., and Rapee, R. 2002. "Mother Knows Best: The Effects of Maternal Modeling on the Acquisition of Fear and Avoidance Behavior in Toddlers." *Behavior Research and Therapy* 40(3): 279–287.

Gettleman, T. E., and Thompson, J. K. 1993. "Actual Differences and Stereotypical Perceptions in Body Image and Eating Disturbance: A Comparison of Male and Female Heterosexual and Homosexual Sample." *Sex Roles* 29(7/8): 545–562.

Gewertz, C. 2003. "Racial Gaps Found to Persist in Public's Opinion of Schools." *Education Week* 22(37): 9.

Giannerelli, L., Adelman, S., and Schmidt, S. 2003. "Getting Help With Child Care Expenses." *Assessing the New Federalism* (Occasional Paper No. #62). Washington, DC: Urban Institute. (http://www.urban.org/url.cfm?ID=310615)

Giddens, A. 1992. *The Transformation of Intimacy, Sexuality, Love and Eroticism in Modern Societies.* Stanford, CA: Stanford University Press.

Gilbert, D. 2003. *The American Class Structure in an Age of Growing Inequality.* Belmont, CA: Wadsworth/Thompson.

Gilman, S. 1999. *Making the Body Beautiful: A Cultural History of Aesthetic Surgery.* Princeton, NJ: Princeton University Press.

Gimlin, D. 2000. "Cosmetic Surgery: Beauty As Commodity." *Qualitative Sociology* 23(1): 77–98.

———. 2002. *Body Work: Beauty and Self-Image in American Culture.* Berkeley: University of California Press.

Glaberson, W. 1999. "When the Verdict is Just a Fantasy." *The New York Times* (June 6): 1.

Glassman, M. 2000. "Mutual Aid Theory and Human Development: Sociability as Primary." *Journal for the Theory of Social Behavior* 30(4): 391–412.

Glassner, B. 1999. *The Culture of Fear: Why Americans Are Afraid of the Wrong Things.* New York: Basic Books.

Gleick, J. 2003. "Tangled Up in Spam." *The New York Times Magazine* (February 9): 42–47.

Glenn, N. D., and Supancic, M. 1984. "The Social and Demographic Correlates of Divorce and Separation in the United States." *Journal of Marriage and the Family* 46: 563–575.

Glick, P., and Sung-Ling, L. 1986. "Recent Changes in Divorce and Remarriage." *Journal of Marriage and Family* 48: 737–747.

Glovin, G. 2003. "What Lies Beneath." *Rutgers Magazine* (Winter).

Goffman, E. 1959. *The Presentation of Self in Everyday Life.* New York: Anchor.

———. 1963. *Stigma: Notes on the Management of Spoiled Identity.* Englewood Cliffs, NJ: Prentice Hall.

Goffman, E. 1974. *Frame Analysis.* Cambridge: Harvard University Press.

Goldberg, S., and Lewis, M. 1969. "Play Behavior in the Year-Old Infant: Early Sex Differences." *Child Development* 40: 21–31.

Goldiner, D. 2001. "What's In a Name? At Least 500G Couple Hopes" *New York Daily News* (July 27).

Goldstein, J., and Morning, A. 2002. "Back in the Box: The Dilemma of Using Multiple-Race Data for Single-Race Laws. Pp. 119–136 in J. Perlman and M. Waters (Eds.), *The New Race Question: How the Census Counts Multiracial Individuals.* New York: Russell Sage.

Goleman, D. 1985. *Vital Lies, Simple Truths.* New York: Simon and Schuster.

Gonzalez Faraco, J. C., and Murphy, M. D. 1997. "Street Names and Political Regimes in an Andalusian Town (Almonte, Spain)." *Ethnology* 36 (Spring): 123–148.

Goode, E. 1997. *Deviant Behavior.* 5th ed. Upper Saddle River, NJ: Prentice Hall.

Goodlad, J. 1984. *A Place Called School: Prospects for the Future.* New York: McGraw-Hill.

Gouldner, H., and Strong, M. S. 1987. *Speaking of Friendship: Middle-Class Women and Their Friends.* New York: Greenwood.

Gourville, J., and Soman, D. 2002. "Pricing and the Psychology of Consumption." *Harvard Business Review* (September): 91–96.

Graham, R. 2002. "The Science of Gray Hair." InteliHealth. (http://www.intelihealth.com/IH/ihtIH/WSIHW000/22030/23724/348513.html?d=dmtContent)

Grant, M. J., Button, C. M., Hannah, T. E., and Ross, A. S. 2002. "Uncovering the Multidimensional Nature of Stereotype Inferences: A Within-Participants Study of Gender, Age, and Physical Attractiveness." *Current Research in Social Psychology* 8(2): 19–38.

Grassl, W. 1999. "The Reality of Brands: Towards an Ontology of Marketing." *American Journal of Economics and Sociology* 58(2): 313–359.

Greenhouse, S. 2003. "Going for the Look, but Risking Discrimination." *The New York Times* (July 12): A12.

Greenstein, R., and Shapiro, I. 2003. "The New Definitive CBO Data on Income and Tax Trends." Center on Budget and Policy Priorities. (http://www.cbpp.org/9-23-03tax.htm)

Greven, P. J. 1970. *Four Generations: Population, Land, and Family in Colonial Andover.* Ithaca, NY: Cornell University Press.

Griffiths, R. A., Mallia-Blanco, R., Boesenberg, E., Ellis, C., Fischer, K., Taylor, M., and Wyndham, J. 2000. "Restrained Eating and Sociocultural Attitudes to Appearance and General Dissatisfaction." *European Eating Disorders Review* 8(5): 394–402.

Groesz, L. M., Levine, M. P., and Murnen, S. K. 2002. "The Effects of Experimental Presentation of Thin Media Images on Body Satisfaction: A Meta-Analytic Review." *International Journal of Eating Disorders* 31(1): 1–16.

Grover, K. J., Russell, C. S., and Schumm, W. 1985. "Mate Selection Processes and Marital Satisfaction." *Family Relations* 34: 383–386.

Guillen, M. 2001. "Is Globalization Civilizing, Destructive or Feeble? A Critique of Five Key Debates in the Social Science Literature." *Annual Review of Sociology* 27: 235–60.

Guimond, S., Dif, S., and Aupy, A. 2002. "Social Identity, Relative Group Status and Intergroup Attitudes: When Favorable Outcomes Change Intergroup Relations . . . for the Worse." *European Journal of Social Psychology* 32(6): 739–760.

Guimond, S., and Roussel, L. 2001. "Bragging about One's School Grades: Gender Stereotyping and Students' Perceptions of Their Abilities in Science, Mathematics, and Language." *Social Psychology of Education* 4(3–4): 275–293.

Gumbel, A. 2002. "Fast Food Nation: An Appetite for Litigation." *Independent.co.uk.* June 4. (http://news.independent.co.uk/world/americas/story.jsp?story=302005)

Gunnthorsdottir, A. 2001. "Physical Attractiveness of an Animal Species as a Decision Factor for Its Preservation." *Anthrozoos* 14(4): 204–215.

Gupta, S. 1999. "The Effects of Transitions in Marital Status on Men's Performance of Housework." *Journal of Marriage and the Family* 61: 700–711.

Gusdek, E. 1998. "Parental Rights are Fundamental Human Rights." Family Research Council. (http://www.frc.org/get/is98f5.cfm)

Gusfield, J. 1963. *Symbolic Crusade: Status Politics and the American Temperance Movement.* Urbana, IL: University of Illinois Press.

Haaga, J. 2003. "UN Projects Slower Population Growth." Population Reference Bureau. (http://www.prb.org:)

Hacker, A. 2003a. *Mismatch: The Growing Gulf Between Women and Men.* New York: Scribner.

_____. 2003b. *Two Nations: Black and White, Separate, Hostile, Unequal.* New York: Scribner

Hacking, I. 1995. "The Looping Effect of Human Kinds." Pp. 351–394 in D. Sperber, D. Premack, A. J. Premack and J. Premack (Eds.), *Causal Cognition: A Multidisciplinary Debate,* New York: Oxford University Press.

_____. 1999. *The Social Construction of What?* Cambridge, MA: Harvard University Press.

Hagan, J., MacMillan, R., and Wheaton, B. 1996. "New Kid in Town: Social Capital and the Life Course Effects of Family Migration on Children." *American Sociological Review* 61(3): 368–385.

Halbert, D. J. 2002. "Citizenship, Pluralism, and Modern Public Sphere." *Innovation* 15(1): 33–42.

Hall, W. 1986. "Social Class and Survival on the S.S. *Titanic.*" *Social Science and Medicine* 22: 687–690.

Hallinan, M., and Sorensen, A. 1985. "Ability Grouping and Student Friendships." *American Educational Research Journal* 22: 485–499.

Hamilton, K., and Wingert, P. 1998. "Down the Aisle." *Newsweek* (July 20): 54–57.

Hareven, T. 1978. "The Dynamics of Kin in an Industrial Community." In John Demos and Sarane Boocock (Eds.), *Turning Points: Historical and Sociological Essays on the Family.* Chicago: University of Chicago Press.

Hargreaves, D., and Tiggermann, M. 2002. "The Effect of Television Commercials on Mood and Body Dissatisfaction: The Role of Appearance-Schema Activation." *Journal of Social and Clinical Psychology* 21(3): 287–308.

Harris, T. G. 1978. *Introduction to E. H. Walster and G. W. Walster, A New Look at Love.* Reading, MA: Addison-Wesley.

Harrison, K. 2000. "Television Viewing, Fat Stereotyping, Body Shape Standards, and Eating Disorder Symptomatology in Grade School Children." *Communication Research* 27(5) 617–640.

Harrison, K., and Cantor, J. 1997. "The Relationship Between Media Consumption and Eating Disorders." *Journal of Communication* 47(1): 40–67.

Hartman, H. 1976. "Capitalism, Patriarchy, and Job Segregation by Sex." *Signs* 1(3): 137–170.

Hartmann, H., and Yi, H. 2001. "The Rhetoric and Reality of Welfare Reform." In N. Hirschmann and U. Liebert (Eds.), *Women and Welfare: Theory and Practice in the United States and Europe.* New Brunswick, NJ: Rutgers University Press.

Haub, C. 2003. "The U.S. Birth Rate Falls Further." Population Reference Bureau. (http://www.prb.org)

Hausman, C. 2000. *Lies We Live By: Defeating Double-Talk and Deception in Advertising, Politics, and the Media.* New York: Routledge.

Healey, J. F. 2002. *Statistics: A Tool for Social Research.* 6th ed. Belmont, CA: Wadsworth.

Health and Medicine Work. 2002. "Aging: A Dilemma for Parents and Kids" (October 7): 16.

Health, Retirement, and Aging Study. 1998. "Respondent Report: Overview." University of Michigan. (http://www.umich.edu/~hrswww/overview/hrarr.html)

Hebl, M. R., and Heatherton, T. F. 1998. "The Stigma of Obesity in Women: The Difference Is Black and White." *Personality and Social Psychology* 24(4): 417–426.

Hecker, D. 2001. "Occupational Employment Projections to 2010. *Monthly Labor Review* (November): 57–84.

Heeren, J. W. 1999. "Emotional Simultaneity and the Construction of Victim Unity." *Symbolic Interaction* 22(2): 163–179.

Heimann, L. B. 2002. "Social Proximity in Swedish Mother-Daughter and Mother-Son Interactions in Infancy." *Journal of Reproductive and Infant Psychology* 20(1): 37–43.

Heinz, J., Nelson, R., and Laumann, E. 2001. "The Scale of Justice: Observations on the Transformation of Urban Law Practice." *Annual Review of Sociology* 27: 337–62.

Henriques, D. 2000. "New Front Opens in Effort to Fight Race Bias in Loans." *The New York Times* 150 (October 22).

Hensler, D. 2001. "Revisiting the Monster: New Myths and Realities of Class Action and Other Large Scale Litigation." *Duke Journal of Comparative and International Law* 11: 179–213.

Hetherington, E. M., and Kelly, J. 2000. *For Better or for Worse: Divorce Reconsidered.* New York: W.W. Norton.

Hewstone, M., Rubin, M., and Willis, H. 2002. "Intergroup Bias." *Annual Review of Psychology* 53: 575–604.

Ho, D. 2003. "'Do Not Call' Still a Big Hit." Associated Press, CBS News (July 1). (http://www.cbsnews.com/stories/2003/03/11/politics/main543573.shtml)

Hochschild, A. R. (with Machung, A). 1997. *The Time Bind: When Work Becomes Home and Home Becomes Work.* New York: Henry Holt.

———. 2003. *The Second Shift: Working Parents and the Revolution at Home.* New York: Penguin.

Hochschild, J. 2001. "Public Schools and the American Dream." *Dissent* (Fall): 35–40.

Hoffer, T., Greeley, A., and Coleman, J. 1987. "Catholic High School Effects on Achievement Growth." Pp. 67–88 in E. Haertel, T. James, and H. Levin (Eds.), *Comparing Public and Private Schools. Vol 2: Student Achievement.* New York: Falmer.

Holman, T. B., Larson, J. H., and Olsen, J. A. 2001. *Premarital Predictors of Marital Quality or Breakup: Research, Theory and Practice.* New York/London: Kluwer Academic/Plenum.

Holtz, R., and Miller, N. 2001. "Intergroup Competition, Attitudinal Projection, and Opinion Certainty: Capitalizing on Conflict." *Group Processes and Intergroup Relations* 4(1): 61–73.

Hope, S., Rodgers, B., and Power, C. 1999. "Marital Status Transitions and Psychological Distress: Longitudinal Evidence from a National Population Sample." *Psychological Medicine* 29(2): 381–389.

Hope, T. 1995. "Deception and Lying." *Journal of Medical Ethics* 21 (April): 67–68.

Hopkins, N., and Rae, C. 2001. "Intergroup Differentiation: Stereotyping as a Function of Status Hierarchy." *Journal of Social Psychology* 141(3): 323–333.

Horn, L., Chen, X., and Chapman, C. 2003. "Getting Ready to Pay for College" (NCES 2003–0300). Washington, DC: U.S. Department of Education.

Horowitz, L. M., Krasnoperova, E. N., Tatar, D. G., Hansen, M. B., Person, E. A., Galvin, K. L., and Nelson, K. L. 2001. "The Way To Console May Depend on the Goal: Experimental Studies of Social Support." *Journal of Experimental Social Psychology* 37: 49–61.

House, J. S., Strecher, V., Metzner, H. L., and Robbins, C. A. 1986. "Occupational Stress and Health Among Men and Women in the Tecumseh Community Health Study." *Journal of Health and Social Behavior* 31(2): 123–140.

Houston, J. M., Kinnie, J., Lupo, B., Terry, C., and Ho, S. S. 2000. "Competitiveness and Conflict Behavior in Simulation of a Social Dilemma." *Psychological Reports* 86 (3, Pt. 2): 1219–1225.

Hout, M. 1982. "The Association Between Husbands' and Wives' Occupations in Two-Earner Families." *American Journal of Sociology* 88 (September): 397–409.

Howell, M. 1986. "Women, the Family Economy, and Market Production." In B. Hanawalt (Ed.), *Women and Work in Pre-Industrial Europe*. Bloomington: Indiana University Press.

Hoxby, C. 1998. "How Much Does School Spending Depend on Family Income? The Historical Origins of the Current School Finance Dilemma." *The American Economic Review* 88(2): 309–314.

———. 2001. "The Return to Attending a Highly Selective College: 1960 to the Present." In M. Devlin and J. Meyerson (Eds.), *Forum Future: Exploring the Future of Higher Education, 2000 Papers. Forum Strategy Series* (Vol. 3). (http://www.educause.edu/ir/library/pdf/ffp0002.pdf)

Hughes, E. C. 1945. "Dilemmas and Contradictions of Status." *American Journal of Sociology* 50(5): 353–359.

Hull, K., and Nelson, R. 2000. "Assimilation, Choice or Constraint? Testing Theories of Gender Differences in the Careers of Lawyers." *Social Forces* 79(1): 229–64.

Hunt, S. 2000. "'Winning Ways': Globalization and the Impact of the Health and Wealth Gospel." *Journal of Contemporary Religion* 15(3) 331–347.

Hunter, M. L. 2002. "If You're Light You're Alright: Light Skin Color as Social Capital for Women of Color." *Gender and Society* 16(2): 175–193.

Hurd, L. C. 2000. "Older Women's Body Image and Embodied Experience: An Exploration." *Journal of Women and Aging* 12(3–4): 77–97.

Hyde, J. S., Fennema, E., and Lamon, S. J. 1990. "Gender Differences in Mathematics Performance." *Psychological Bulletin* 107: 139–155.

Immerwahr, J. 2002. "Losing Ground: A National Status Report on the Affordability of American Higher Education—The Affordability of Higher Education: A Review of Recent Survey Research." National Center for Public Policy and Higher Education. (http://www.highereducation.org/reports/losing_ground/ar.shtml)

Independent Sector. 2001. "Giving & Volunteering in the United States 2001—Key Findings." (http://IndependentSector.org)

Information Please Almanac. 1997. O. Johnson (Ed.). Boston: Houghton Mifflin.

Insaf, S. 2002. "Not the Same by Any Other Name." *Journal of the American Academy of Psychoanalysis* 31(3): 463–473.

Institute of Medicine. 2001. "Exploring the Biological Contribution to Human Health: Does Sex Matter?" Institute of Medicine of the National Academies (April 24). (http://www.iom.edu/ reports.asp)

Institute on Race & Poverty. 1998. "Examining the Relationship Between Housing, Education, and Persistent Segregation." (http://umn.edu/irp/final5.htm)

———. 2002. "Racism and Metropolitan Dynamics: The Civil Rights Challenge of the 21st Century." (http://www.umn.edu/irp)

Institute for Women's Policy Research. 2001. "Today's Women Workers: Shut Out of Yesterday's Unemployment Insurance System" (IWPR Publication # A127). (http://www.iwpr.org)

Interpol. 2003. "International Crime Statistics." (http://www.interpole.int/Pubic/Statistics/ICS/Default.asp)

Isaacs, H. 1975. *Idols of the Tribe*. Cambridge: Harvard University Press.

Iwata, N., and Suzuki, K. 1997. "Role Stress-Mental Health Relations in Japanese Bank Workers: A Moderating Effect of Social Support." *Applied Psychology: An International Review* 46(2): 207–218.

Jackman, M. R. 2002. "Violence in Social Life." *Annual Review of Sociology* 28: 387–415.

Jackson, L. A. 1992. *Physical Appearance and Gender: A Sociobiological and Sociocultural Perspective.* Albany: SUNY Press.

Jackson, L. A., Hunter, J. E., and Hodge, C. N. 1995. "Physical Attractiveness and Intellectual Competence: A Meta-Analytic Review." *Social Psychology Quarterly* 58(2): 108–122.

Jackson, L. A., and McGill, O. D. 1996. "Body Type Preferences and Body Type Characteristics Associated With Attractive and Unattractive Bodies by African Americans and Anglo Americans." *Sex Roles* 35 (September): 295–307.

Jacobs, P. 1988. "Keeping the Poor, Poor." In J. H. Skolnick and E. Currie (Eds.), *Crisis in American Institutions.* Glenview, IL: Scott, Foresman.

Jacobson, D. 1989. "Context and the Sociological Study of Stress." *Journal of Health and Social Behavior* 30(3): 257–260.

Jacquet, S., and Surra, C. 2001. "Parental Divorce and Premarital Couples: Commitment and other Relationship Characteristics." *Journal of Marriage and the Family* 63(3): 627–638.

Jankowiak, W., and Fischer, E. 1992. "A Crosscultural Perspective on Romantic Love." *Journal of Ethnology* 31: 149–156.

Jefferson, A., and Hughes, A. 2003. "An American Dilemma." *Black Enterprise* 34(1): 24.

Jeffries, V., and Ransford, E. 1980. *Social Stratification: A Multiple Hierarchy Approach.* Boston: Allyn & Bacon.

Jehn, K. A., and Shah, P. P. 1997. "Interpersonal Relationships and Task Performance: An Examination of Mediating Processes in Friendship and Acquaintance Groups." *Journal of Personality and Social Psychology* 72 (April): 775–790.

Jenny Craig. 2003. "Success Stories." (http://www.jennycraig.com/success/teri_c.asp)

Jensen, M., Johnson, D. W., and Johnson, R. T. 2002. "Impact of Positive Interdependence During Electronic Quizzes on Discourse and Achievement." *Journal of Educational Research* 95(3): 161–166.

Johnson, C. 2000. "Perspective on American Kinship in the Later 1990s." *Journal of Marriage and the Family* 62(November): 623–39.

Johnson, D., and Wu, J. 2002. "An Empirical Test of Crisis, Social Selection, and Role Explanations of the Relationship between Marital Disruption and Psychological Distress: A Pooled Time-Series Analysis of Four-Wave Panel Data." *Journal of Marriage & the Family* 64(1): 211–224.

Johnson, D. R., and Scheuble, L. K. 2002. "What Should We Call Our Kids? Choosing Children's Surnames When Parents' Last Names Differ." *Social Science Journal* 39(3): 419–429.

Johnson, D. W., and Johnson, R. T. 1989. *Cooperation and Competition: Theory and Research.* Edina, MN: Interaction Books.

_____. 2000. "The Three Cs of Reducing Prejudice and Discrimination." Pp. 239–268 in S. Oskamp (Ed.), *Reducing Prejudice and Discrimination: The Claremont Symposium on Applied Social Psychology.* Mahwah, NJ: Lawrence Erlbaum.

Johnson, D. W., and Johnson, R. T. 2002. "Social Interdependence Theory and University Instruction: Theory Into Practice." *Swiss Journal of Psychology* 61(3): 119–129.

Johnson, J. L., McAndrew, F. T., and Harris, P. B. 1991. "Sociobiology and the Naming of Adopted and Natural Children." *Etiology and Sociobiology* 12: 365–375.

Jones, L. 1980. *Great Expectations.* New York: Ballantine Books.

Jones, W., Hansson, R. O., and Phillips A. L. 1978. "Physical Attractiveness and Judgements of Psychopathology." *Journal of Social Psychology* 105: 79–84.

Jones-DeWeever, A., Peterson, J., and Song, X. 2003. "Before and After Welfare Reform: The Work and Well-Being of Low-Income Single Parent Families." Institute for Women's Policy Research. (http://www.iwpr.org.)

Joubert, C. E. 1994. "Relation of Name Frequency to the Perception of Social Class in Given Names." *Perceptuual and Motor Skills* 79(2): 623–626.

Judicial Council of California. 2002. "Improving Justice: The Business of the Courts." *Annual Report 2002.* Administrative Office of the Courts. (http://www.courtinfo.ca.gov/reference/1_annualreports.htm)

Kahane, H., and Cavender, N. 2002. *The Use of Reason in Everyday Life.* 9th ed. Belmont, CA: Wadsworth.

Kalick, S. M., and Hamilton, T. E. 1986. "The Matching Hypothesis Re-Examined." *Journal of Personality and Social Psychology* 51(4): 673–682.

Kalisch, P. A., and Kalisch, B. J. 1984. "Sex-Role Stereotyping of Nurses and Physicians on Prime-Time Television: A Dichotomy of Occupational Portrayals." *Sex Roles* 10: 533–553.

Kalmijn, M. 1991. "Shifting Boundaries: Trends in Religious and Educational Homogamy." *American Sociological Review* 56(6): 786–800.

———. 1994. "Assortive Mating by Cultural and Economic Occupational Status." *American Journal of Sociology* 100(2): 422–452.

———. 1998. "Intermarriage and Homogamy." *Annual Review of Sociology* 24: 395–421.

Kalmijn, M., and Flap, H. 2001. "Assortive Meeting and Mating: Unintended Consequences of Organized Settings for Partner Choices." *Social Forces* 79(4): 1289–1312.

Karen, D. 1990. "Toward a Political Organizational Model of Gatekeeping: The Case of Elite Colleges." *Sociology of Education* 63: 227–240.

Karraker, K., Vogel, D., and Lake, M. 1995. "Parents' Gender-Stereotyped Perceptions of Newborns: The Eye of the Beholder Revisited." *Sex Roles* 33(9–10): 687–701.

Karylowski, J. J., Motes, M. A., Wallace H. M., Harckom, H. A., Hewlett E. M., Maclean, S. L., Paretta, J. L., and Vaswani, C. L. 2001. "Spontaneous Gender-Stereotypical Categorization of Trait Labels and Job Labels." *Current Research in Social Psychology* 6(6): 77–90.

Katz, J. E., and Rice, T. E. 2002. *Social Consequences of Internet Use: Access, Involvement, and Interaction.* Cambridge, MA: MIT Press.

Katz, M. (Ed.). 1971. *School Reform Past and Present.* Boston: Little, Brown.

———. 1986. *In the Shadow of the Poorhouse: A Social History of Welfare in America.* New York: Basic Books.

Kaufman, P., Alt, N., and Chapman, C. 2001. "Dropout Rates in the U.S.: 2000." *Education Statistics Quarterly* (NCES 2002–114). (http://nces.ed.gov/pubs2002/dropout_2001/)

Kaufman, P., Chen, X., Choy, S. P., Peter, K., Ruddy, S. A., Miller, A. K., Fleury, J. K., Chandler, K. A., Planty, M. G., and Rand, M. R. 2001. *Indicators of School Crime and Safety: 2001* (NCES 2002–113/NCJ 190075). Washington, DC: U.S. Departments of Education and Justice.

Kay, F., and Hagan, J. 1998. "Raising the Bar: The Gender Stratification of Law-Firm Capital." *American Sociological Review* 63(5): 728–743.

———. 1999. "Cultivating Clients in the Competition for Partnership: Gender and the Organizational Restructuring of Law Firms in the 1990s." *Law and Society Review* 33(3): 517–555.

Kay, J. 2003. "9.11.01: Two Years Later: Ground Zero Air Quality was 'Brutal' for Months; UC Davis Scientist Concurs That EPA Reports Misled the Public." *San Francisco Chronicle* (September 10): A1.

Keefe, K., and Berndt, T. 1996. "Relations of Friendship Quality to Self-Esteem in Early Adolescence." *Journal of Early Adolescence* 16(1): 110–129.

Keller, J. 2002. "Blatant Stereotype Threat and Women's Math Performance: Self-Handicapping as a Strategic Means to Cope with Obtrusive Negative Performance Expectations." *Sex Roles* 47(3–4): 193–198.

Keller, M. C., and Young, R. K. 1996. "Mate Assortment in Dating and Married Couples." *Personality and Individual Differences* 21(2): 217–221.

Kelley, H. H., and Stahelski, A. J. 1970. "Errors in Perception of Intentions in a Mixed-Motive Game." *Journal of Experimental Social Psychology* 6: 379–400.

Kenealy, P., Frude, N., and Shaw, W. 1988. "Influences of Children's Physical Attractiveness on Teacher Expectations." *Journal of Social Psychology* 128(3): 373–383.

Kent, G. 2000. "Understanding the Experiences of People With Disfigurements: An Integration of Four Models of Social and Psychological Functioning." *Psychology, Health, and Medicine* 5(2): 117–129.

Kent, M., and Mather, M. 2002. "What Drives U.S. Population Growth?" *Population Bulletin* 57: 4.

Kessler, R. C., Price, R. H., and Wortman, C. B. 1985. "Social Factors in Psychopathology: Stress, Social Support, and Coping Processes." *Annual Review of Psychology* 36: 531–572.

Kessler-Harris, A. 2003. *Out to Work: A History of Wage-Earning Women in the United States.* New York: Oxford University Press.

Kids Count. 2003. "The High Cost of Being Poor." (http://www.kidscount.org)

Kifner, J. 1994. "Pollster Finds Error on Holocaust Doubts." *The New York Times* (May 20): A12.

Kilker, E. 1993. "Black and White in America: The Culture and Politics of Racial Classification." *International Journal of Politics, Culture, and Society* 7: 229–258.

Kingsley, T., and Pettit, K. 2003. "Concentrated Poverty: A Change in Course" (Pub ID# 310790). *Urban Institute* 2 (May). (http://www.urban.org/nnip)

Kitson, G. C., Babri, K. B., and Roach, M. J. 1985. "Who Divorces and Why?" *Journal of Family Issues* 6: 285–293.

Klein, H., Shiffman, K., and Welka, D. 2000. "Gender-Related Content of Animated Cartoons, 1930 to the Present." *Advances in Gender Research* 4: 291–317.

Knauer, K. (Ed.). 1998. *Time 75th Anniversary Celebration.* New York: Time, Inc.

Koernig, S. K., and Page, A. L. 2001. "What If Your Dentist Looks Like Tom Cruise? Applying the Match-Up Hypothesis to a Service Encounter." *Psychology and Marketing* 19(1): 91–110.

Kohn, A. 1986. *No Contest: The Case Against Competition.* Boston: Houghton Mifflin.

Kollock, P. 1998. "Social Dilemmas: The Anatomy of Cooperation." *Annual Review of Sociology* 24: 183–214.

Komarovsky, M. 1962. *Blue-Collar Marriage.* New Haven, CT: Vintage.

Kostanski, M., and Gullone, E. 1998. "Adolescent Body Image Dissatisfaction: Relationships With Self-Esteem, Anxiety, Depression Controlling for Body Mass." *Journal of Child Psychology and Psychiatry and Allied Disciplines* 39 (February): 255–262.

Kovaleski, S. F. 1999. "In Jamaica, Shades of an Identity Crisis: Ignoring Health Risks, Blacks Increase Use of Skin Lighteners." *Washington Post* (August 5): A15.

Kowalski, R. 2003. *Complaining, Teasing and Other Annoying Behaviors.* New Haven, CT: Yale University Press.

Kowner, R., and Ogawa, T. 1995. "The Role of Raters' Sex, Personality, and Appearance in Judgements of Facial Beauty." *Perceptual and Motor Skills* 81(1): 339–349.

Kozol, J. 1991. *Savage Inequalities.* New York: Crown.

———. 1995. *Amazing Grace: The Lives of Children and the Conscience of a Nation.* New York: Crown.

———. 2001. *Ordinary Resurrections: Children in the Years of Hope.* New York: HarperCollins.

Kramer, L. 2001. *The Sociology of Gender A Brief Introduction.* Los Angeles: Roxbury.

Kraut, R. E., Kiesler, S. Boneva, B., Cummings, J., Helgeson, V., and Crawford, A. 2002. "Internet Paradox Revisited." *Journal of Social Issues* 58(1): 49–74.

Kreider, R., and Fields, J. 2002. "Number, Timing and Duration of Marriages and Divorces: 1996." *Household Economic Studies Current Population Reports* (P70–80). Washington DC: U.S. Census Bureau.

Kristof, N. 2003. "Is Race Real?" *The New York Times* (July 11): A17.

Kritzer, H. 1997. "Holding Back the Floodtide: The Role of Contingent Fee Lawyers." *Wisconsin Lawyer* 70: 3.

Krugman, P. 2002. "For Richer." *The New York Times* Magazine Section (October 20): 62–67.

Krysan, M. 2002. "Community Undesirability in Black and White: Examining Racial Residential Preferences through Community Perceptions." *Social Problems* 49(4): 521–543.

Krysan, M., and Farley, R. 2002. "The Residential Preferences of Blacks: Do They Explain Persistent Segregation?" *Social Forces* 80(3): 937–980.

Kulik, J. A., and Mahler, H. I. 1990. "Stress and Affiliation Research: On Taking the Laboratory to Health Field Settings." *Annals of Behavioral Medicine* 12(3): 106–111.

Kulik, J. A., Mahler, H. I. M., and Moore, P. J. 1996. "Social Comparison and Affiliation Under Threat: Effects on Recovery from Major Surgery." *Journal of Personality and Social Psychology* 71: 967–979.

Lafky, S., Duffy, M., Steinmaus, M., and Berkowitz, D. 1996. "Looking Through Gendered Lenses: Female Stereotyping in Advertisements and Gender Role Expectations." *Journalism and Mass Communication Quarterly* 73(2): 379–388.

Lake, A. 1975. "Are We Born Into Our Sex Roles or Programmed Into Them?" *Woman's Day* (January): 25–35.

Landers, M., and Fine, G. A. 2001. "Learning Life's Lessons in Tee-Ball: The Reinforcement of Gender and Status in Kindergarten Sport." Pp. 73–77 in Andrew Yiannakis and Merrill Melnick (Eds.), *Contemporary Issues in Sociology of Sport.* Champaign, IL: Human Kinetics.

Langlois, J. H., Kalakanis, L., Rubenstein, A. J., Larson, A., Hallam, M., and Smoot, M. 2000. "Maxims or Myths of Beauty? A Meta-Analytic and Theoretical Review." *Psychological Bulletin* 126(3): 390–423.

Langlois, J. H., and Stephan, C. W. 1981. "Beauty and the Beast: The Role of Physical Attractiveness in the Development of Peer Relations and Social Behavior." In S. S. Brehm, S. M. Kassin, and F. X. Gibbons (Eds.), *Developmental Social Psychology.* New York: Oxford University Press.

Lanzetta, J. T. 1955. "Group Behavior Under Stress." *Human Relations* 8: 29–53.

Larkin, M. 1999. "Ways to Win at Weight Loss." *FDA Consumer.* (http://www.cfsan.fda.gov/~dms/fdweight.html)

Larose, M., and N. Wallace. 2003. "Online Giving Rose at Many Big Charities." *The Chronicle of Philanthropy* (June 12).

Lasch, C. 1979. *The Culture of Narcissism: American Life in an Age of Diminishing Expectations.* New York: W.W. Norton.

Laslett, B., and Warren, C. B. 1975. "Losing Weight: The Organizational Promotion of Behavior Change." *Social Problems* 23(1): 69–80.

Latané, B., and Glass, D. C. 1968. "Social and Nonsocial Attraction in Rats." *Journal of Personality and Social Psychology* 9: 142–146.

Lauer, R., and Lauer, J. 1991. "The Long-Term Relational Consequences of Problematic Family Backgrounds." *Family Relations* 40: 286–290.

Lauzen, M., and Dozier, D. 2002. "You Look Mahvelous: An Examination of Gender and Appearance Comments in the 1999–2000 Prime-Time Season. *Sex Roles* 46 (11–12): 429–437.

Lavelle, M. 2003. "Scandal Redux?" *U.S. News & World Report* 135(4): 30.

Lawson, T. 2000. "Are Kind Lies Better than Unkind Truths? Effects of Perspective and Closeness of Relationship." *Representative Research in Social Psychology* 24: 11–19.

Lawton, L. Silverstein, M., and Bengtson, V. L. 1994. "Solidarity Between Generations in Families. In V. L. Bengtson and R. A. Harootyan (Eds.), *Intergenerational Linkages: Hidden Connections in American Society.* New York: Springer.

Layman, R. (Ed.). 1995. *American Decades 1950–59.* Detroit, MI: Gale.

Lazarsfeld, P. 1949. "The American Soldier: An Expository Review." *Public Opinion Quarterly* 13(3): 376–404.

Leahey, E., and Guo, G. 2001. "Gender Differences in Mathematical Trajectories." *Social Forces* 80(2): 713–732.

Leaper, C., Breed, L., Hoffman, L., and Perlman, C. 2002. "Variations in the Gender-Stereotyped Content of Children's Television Cartoons Across Genres." *Journal of Applied Social Psychology* 32(8): 1653–1662.

Lee, J. 2002. "Some States Track Parolees by Satellite." *The New York Times On the Web* (January 31). (http://www.innovationlaw.org/pages/innovationlaw_nytimes.htm)

Lee, S. 2003. "The Genetics of Differences: What Genetic Discovery and the Modern Biology of 'Race' Mean for Communities of Color Fighting Health Inequities." *ColorLines* 6(2): 25–27.

Lee, V., and Burkam, D. 2002. "Inequality at the Starting Gate: Social Background Differences in Achievement as Children Begin School." Economic Policy Institute. (http://www.epinet.org/content.cfm/books_starting_gate.)

Lehrman, S. 2003. "The Reality of Race." *Scientific American* 288(2): 32–34.

Leigh, J. P., Markowitz, S. B., Fahs, C. S., and Landrigan, P. J. 1997. "Occupational Injury and Illness in the United States: Estimates of Costs, and Morbidity, and Mortality." *Archives of Internal Medicine* 157(14): 1557–1568.

Leinbach, M. D., and Fagot, B. I. 1991. "Attractiveness in Young Children: Sex-Differentiated Reactions of Adults." *Sex Roles* 25(5–6): 269–284.

Leite, R., and McKenry, P. 2002. "Aspects of Father Status and Postdivorce Father Involvement with Children." *Journal of Family Issues* 23(5): 601–623.

Lemert, E. 1951. *Social Pathology: A Systematic Approach to the Theory of Sociopathic Behavior.* New York: McGraw-Hill.

Lennon, M. C. 1989. "The Structural Contexts of Stress." *Journal of Health and Social Behavior* 30(3): 261–268.

Leonard, S. 1996. "Feeling Appealing." *Psychology Today* 29(1): 18.

Leone, R. 1994. "What's Trust Got to Do with It?" *The American Prospect* 17: 78–83.

Levin, S., VanLaar, C., and Sidanius, J. 2003. "The Effects of Ingroup and Outgroup Friendships on Ethnic Attitudes in College: A Longitudinal Study." *Group Processes & Intergroup Relations* 6(1): 76–92.

LeVine, R. A., and White, M. 1992. "The Social Transformation of Childhood." In A. S. Skolnick and J. H. Skolnick (Eds.), *Family in Transition.* New York: HarperCollins.

Levine, R. V. 1993. "Is Love A Luxury?" *American Demographics* 15(2): 27–28.

Levi-Strauss, C. 1964. *The Raw and the Cooked: Introduction to a Science of Mythology.* New York: Harper & Row.

Levy, B. R., Slade, M. D., Kunkel, S. R., and Kasl, S. V. 2002. "Longevity Increased by Positive Self-Perceptions of Aging." *Journal of Personality and Social Psychology.* 832(2): 261–270.

Levy, G., Sadovsky, A., and Troseth, G. "Aspects of Young Children's Perceptions of Gender-Typed Occupations." *Sex Roles* 42(11–12): 993–1006.

Lewis, A. 2003. "Marbury v. Madison v. Ashcroft." *The New York Times* (February 24): Op-Ed.

Lewis, M. 1978. *The Culture of Inequality.* New York: New American Library.

Lichter, D., Graefe, D., and Brown, B. 2003. "Is Marriage a Panacea? Union Formation Among Economically Disadvantaged Unwed Mothers." *Social Problems* 50(1): 60–86.

Liddell, C., and Lycett, J. 1998. "Simon or Sipho: South African Children's Names and Their Academic Achievement in Grade One." *Applied Psychology* 47(3): 421–437.

Lieberson, S. 2000. *A Matter of Taste.* New Haven: Yale University Press.

Liebler, C. A., and Sandefur, G. D. 2002. "Gender Differences in the Exchange of Social Support With Friends, Neighbors, and Co-Workers at Midlife." *Social Science Research* 31(3): 364–391.

Lillard, L., and Waite, J. 1995. "'Til Death Do Us Part: Marital Disruption and Mortality." *American Journal of Sociology* 100 (March): 1131–1156.

Lin, N., Ye, X., and Ensel, W. W. 1999. "Social Support and Depressed Mood: A Structural Analysis." *Journal of Health and Social Behavior* 40: 344–359.

Lindsey, E., and Mize, J. 2001. "Contextual Differences in Parent-Child Play: Implications for Children's Gender Role Development." *Sex Roles* 44(3–4): 155–176.

Lino, M. 2002. *Expenditures on Children by Families, 2001 Annual Report.* U.S. Department of Agriculture, Center for Nutrition Policy and Promotion (Misc. Publ. No. 1528–2001). (http://www.cnpp.usda.gov.)

Lips, H. 1993. *Sex and Gender: An Introduction.* Mountain View, CA: Mayfield.

Liptak. 2002. "In the Name of Security, Privacy for Me, Not Thee." *The New York Times* (November 24): Week in Review.

Livingston, R. W. 2001. "What You See Is What You Get: Systematic Variability in Perceptual-Based Social Judgment." *Personality and Social Psychology Bulletin* 27(9): 1086–1096.

Lord, W. 1981. *A Night to Remember.* New York: Penguin.

Lovejoy, M. 2001. "Disturbances in the Social Body: Differences in Body Image and Eating Problems Among African American and White Women." *Gender & Society* 15(2): 239–261.

Lucas, S.R. 1999. *Tracking Inequality: Stratification and Mobility in American High Schools.* New York: Teachers College Press.

Lumsden, L. 1997. "Expectations for Students." *Emergency Librarian* 25(2).

Lupart, J., and Cannon, E. 2002. "Computers and Career Choices: Gender Differences in Grades 7 and 10 Students." *Gender, Technology & Development* 6(2): 233–248.

Luscri, G., and Mohr, P. B. 1998. "Surname Effects in Judgments of Mock Jurors." *Psychological Reports* 82(3): 1023–1026.

Lye, D. 1996. "Adult Child-Parent Relationships." *Annual Review of Sociology* 22: 79–102.

Lynn, J., and Adamson, D. 2003. "Living Well at the End of Life: Adapting Health Care to Serious Chronic Illness in Old Age." Santa Monica, CA: RAND.

Lynn, M., and Simons, T. 2000. "Predictors of Male and Female Servers' Average Tip Earnings." *Journal of Applied Social Psychology* 30(2): 241–252.

Lytton, H., and Romny, D. 1991. "Parents Differential Socialization of Boys and Girls: A Meta-Analysis." *Psychological Bulletin* 109: 267–296.

Macmillan, R. 2001. "Violence and the Life Course: The Consequences of Victimization for Personal and Social Development." *Annual Review of Sociology* 27: 1–22.

Madrick, J. 2002. "A Rise in Child Poverty Rates is at Risk in U.S." *The New York Times* (June 13): C2.

Malley, J., Beck, M., and Adorno, D. 2001. "Building an Ecology for Non-Violence in Schools." *International Journal of Reality Therapy* 21(1): 22–26.

Mandel, M. 1992. "Who'll Get the Lion's Share of Wealth in the 90's? The Lion." *Business Week* (June): 86–88.

Manning, P. 1974. "Police Lying." *Urban Life* 3: 283–306.

––––––. 1984. "Lying, Secrecy, and Social Control." Pp. 268–279 in J. Douglas Newton (Ed.), *The Sociology of Deviance*. Newton, MA: Allyn & Bacon.

Marcus, A. 2002. "When Janie Came Marching Home: Women Fought in the Civil War." *The New York Times* (March 25).

Marks, G., Miller, N., and Maruyama, G. 1981. "Effects of Targets' Physical Attractiveness on Assumptions of Similarity." *Journal of Personality and Social Psychology* 41: 198–206.

Marlar, M. R., and Joubert, C. E. 2002. "Liking of Personal Names, Self-Esteem, and the Big Five Inventory." *Psychological Reports* 91(2): 407–410.

Marlowe, C. M., Schneider, S. L., and Nelson, C. E. 1996. "Gender and Attractiveness Biases in Hiring Decisions: Are More Experienced Managers Less Biased?" *Journal of Applied Psychology* 81(1): 11–21.

Martin, P., and Midgley, E. 1999. "Immigration to the United States." *Population Bulletin* 54(2).

Martin, R. A., and Svebak, S. 2001. "Stress." In M. J. Apter (Ed.), *Motivational Styles in Everyday Life*. Washington, DC: American Psychological Association.

Martin, T. C., and Bumpass, L. L. 1989. "Recent Trends in Marital Disruption." *Demography* 26: 41.

Marx, G. T. 1999. "What's In A Name?: Some Reflections on the Sociology of Anonymity." *Information Society* 15(2): 99–112.

Mather, M. 2002. "Patterns of Poverty in America." (http://www.AmeriStat.org)

Mathisen, J. A. 1989. "A Further Look At 'Common Sense' in Introductory Sociology." *Teaching Sociology* 17(3): 307–315.

May, E. 1988. *Homeward Bound: American Families in the Cold War Era*. New York: Basic Books.

Mazzeo, C., Rab, S., and Eachus, S. 2003. "Work-First or Work-Only: Welfare Reform, State Policy, and Access to Postsecondary Education." *Annals of the American Academy of Political and Social Science* 586 (March): 144–171.

McCabe, M. P., and Ricciardelli, L. A. 2003. "Sociocultural Influences on Body Image and Body Changes Among Adolescent Boys and Girls." *Journal of Social Psychology* 143(1): 5–26.

McConahay, J. B. 1981. "Reducing Racial Prejudice in Desegregated Schools." In W. D. Hawley (Ed.), *Effective School Desegregation*. Beverly Hills, CA: Sage.

McDonald, P. 2001. "Low Fertility Not Politically Sustainable." *Population Today* (August/September): 3–8.

McDonald, W. F. 2003. "Immigrant Criminality: In the Eye of the Beholder?" (http://www.stranieriinitalia. com/briguglio/immigrazione-e-asilo/2003/maggio/mcdonald-criminalita.'html#_ftn1)

McEwen, B. S., and Seeman, T. 1999. "Protecting and Damaging Effects of Mediators of Stress: Elaborating and Testing the Concepts of Allostasis and Allostatic Load." *Annals of the New York Academy of Sciences* 896: 30–47.

McFalls, J. 1992. "Delayed Childbearing, Reproductive Impairment, and Frustrated Fertility in the United States." *Sociological Viewpoints* 8 (Fall): 67–91.

McLanahan, S. 2002. "Life Without Father: What Happens to the Children?" *Contexts* 1(1): 35–44.

McLean, C. 1998. "Name Your Baby Carefully." *Alberta Report* 25(23): 34–36.

McLeod, J. D., and Nonnemaker, J. M. 2000. "Poverty and Child Emotional Behavioral Problems: Racial and Ethnic Differences in Processes and Effects." *Journal of Health and Social Behavior* 41: 137–161.

McPherson, M., Smith-Lovin, L., and Cook, J. M. 2001. "Birds of a Feather: Homophily in Social Networks." *Annual Review of Sociology* 27: 415–444.

MDRC. 2003. "Fast Fact: Welfare Policies and Adolescent School Performances." (http://www.mdrc.org/area_fact_10.html)

Mehan, H., Hubbard, L., Lintz, A., and Villanueva, I. 1994. "Tracking Untracking: The Consequences of Placing Low Track Students in High Track Classes" (Research Report 10). Santa Cruz, CA: National Center for Research on Cultural Diversity and Second Language Learning.

Mehrabian, A. 2000. "Beyond IQ: Broad-Based Measurement of Individual Success Potential or 'Emotional Intelligence.'" *Genetic, Social, and General Psychology Monographs* 126(2): 133–239.

———. 2001. "Characteristics Attributed to Individuals on the Basis of Their First Names." *Genetic, Social and General Psychology Monographs* 127(1): 59–89.

Memorial Hospital. 2000. "Good Stress/Bad Stress." (http://www.memorialhospital.org/Library/general/stress-GOOD.html)

Mencimer, S. 2002. "You Call This a Vacation?" *The New York Times Magazine* (June 12).

Merton, R. K. 1938. "Social Structure and Anomie." *American Sociological Review* 3: 672–682.

———. 1957. *Social Theory and Social Structure.* Glencoe, IL: Free Press.

Meyers, P. M., and Crull, S. R. 1994. "Question Order Effect: A Preliminary Analysis." Paper Presented at the Annual Meetings of the Association of Applied Sociology, Detroit, MI.

Miceli, T. J. 1992. "The Welfare Effects of Non-Price Competition Among Real Estate Brokers." *Journal of the American Real Estate and Urban Economics Association* 20(4): 519–532.

Mignon, S., Larson, C., and Holmes, W. 2002. *Family Abuse: Consequences, Theories, and Responses.* Boston: Allyn & Bacon.

Milkie, M. A. 1999. "Social Comparisons, Reflected Appraisals, and Mass Media: The Impact of Pervasive Beauty Images on Black and White Girls' Self-Concepts." *Social Psychology Quarterly* 62(2): 190–210.

Miller, C. 2002. *Leavers, Stayers, and Cyclers: An Analysis of the Welfare Caseload.* Manpower Demonstration Research Corporation. Office of the Assistant Secretary for Planning and Evaluation, U.S. Department of Health and Human Services: Washington, DC.

Miller, J. 2004. *Writing About Numbers: Effective Presentation of Quantitative Information.* Chicago: University of Chicago Press.

Miller, L. 2002. "Charities Hope 9/11 Inspires 'e-philanthropy.'" *USA Today* (March 18).

Millman, M. 1980. *Such a Pretty Face: Being Fat in America.* New York: W.W. Norton.

Mills, C. 1992. "The War on Drugs: Is It Time to Surrender?" In K. Finsterbusch and G. McKenna (Eds.), *Taking Sides: Clashing Views on Controversial Social Issues.* 7th ed. Guilford, CT: Dushkin Publishing.

Mills, C. W. 1959. *The Sociological Imagination.* London: Oxford University Press.

Mills, R. 2001. "Health Insurance Coverage: 2000." *Current Population Reports.* Washington, DC: U.S. Government Printing Office.

Mills, R., and Mills, R. 1996. "Adolescents' Attitude Toward Gender Roles: Implications for Education." *Adolescence* 31: 742–745.

Minas, J. S., Scodel, A., Marlowe, D., and Rawson, H. 1960. "Some Descriptive Aspects of Two-Person, Zero-Sum Games." *Journal of Conflict Resolution* 4: 193–197.

Mintz, S., and Kellogg, S. 1988. *Domestic Revolutions: A Social History of American Family Life.* New York: Free Press.

Miron, L. 1997. *Resisting Discrimination. Affirmative Strategies for Principals and Teachers.* Thousand Oaks, CA: Corwin.

Mirowsky, J., and Ross, C. E. 1989. *Social Causes of Psychological Stress.* New York: Aldine de Gruyter.

Mirowsky, J., Ross, C. E., and Reynolds, J. 2000. "Links Between Social Status and Health Status." Pp. 47–67 in C. Bird, P. Conrad, and A. Fremont (Eds.), *Handbook of Medical Sociology.* 5th ed. Upper Saddle River, NJ: Prentice Hall.

Mirsky, S. 2000. "What's In A Name?" *Scientific American* 283(3): 112.

Mitchell, G., Obradovich, S., Harring, F., Tromborg, C., and Burns, A. 1992. "Reproducing Gender in Public Places: Adults' Attention to Toddlers in Three Public Locals." *Sex Roles* 26(7/8): 323–330.

Mitra, A. 2002. "Mathematics Skill and Male-Female Wages." *Journal of Socio-Economics* 31(5): 443–456.

Mok, T. A. 1998; "Asian Americans and Standards of Attractiveness: What's In the Eye of the Beholder?" *Cultural Diversity and Mental Health* 4(1): 1–18.

Moller, E. 1996. *Trends in Civil Jury Verdicts Since 1985.* Santa Monica, CA: Rand.

Molnar, S. 1991. *Human Variation: Races, Types and Ethnic Groups.* 3d ed. Englewood Cliffs, NJ: Prentice Hall.

Mondschein, E., Adolph, K., and Tamis-LeMonda, C. 2000. "Gender Bias in Mothers' Expectations about Infanct Crawling." *Journal of Experimental Child Psychology* 77(4): 304–316.

Monge, P. T., and Kirste, K. K. 1980. "Measuring Proximity in Human Organizations." *Social Psychology Quarterly* 43: 110–115.

Monthly Labor Review. 2003. June. (http://www.bls.gov/opub/ted/2003/jun/wk5/art02.htm)

Moore, J. F. 1997. *The Death of Competition: Leadership and Strategy in the Age of Business Ecosystems."* New York: Harper Business.

Morrongiello, B., and Dawber, T. 1999. "Parental Influences on Toddlers' Injury-Risk Behaviors: Are Sons and Daughters Socialized Differently?" *Journal of Applied Developmental Psychology* 20(2): 227–251.

Mortimer, J. T., and Simmons, R. G. 1978. "Adult Socialization." *Annual Review of Sociology* 4: 421–454.

Moss, N. 2002. "Gender Equity and Socioeconomic Inequality: A Framework for the Patterning of Women's Health." *Social Science and Medicine* 54(5): 649–661.

Moss, P., and Tilly, C. 2001. *Stories Employers Tell: Race, Skill, and Hiring in America.* New York: Russell Sage.

Mruk, C. 1999. *Self-Esteem: Research, Theory, and Practice.* 2d ed. New York: Springer.

Mughal, S., Walsh, J., and Wilding, J. 1996. "Stress and Work Performance: The Role of Trait Anxiety." *Personality and Individual Differences* 20(6): 685–691.

Mui, A. C. 2001. "Coping and Depression Among Elderly Korean Immigrants." *Journal of Human Behavior in the Social Environment* 3(3–4): 281–299.

Mulford, M. Orbell, J., Shatto, C., and Stockard, J. 1998. "Physical Attractiveness, Opportunity, and Success in Everyday Exchange." *American Journal of Sociology* 103(6): 1565–1592.

Murphy, D. 2002. "As Security Cameras Sprout, Someone's Always Watching." *The New York Times* (September 29).

Murstein, B. I. 1999. "The Relationship of Exchange and Commitment." Pp. 205–219 in J. M. Adams and W. H. Jones (Eds.), *Handbook of Interpersonal Commitment and Relationship Stability.* New York: Plenum.

Myers, D., and Cranford, C. 1998. "Temporal Differentiation in the Occupational Mobility of Immigrant and Native-Born Latina Workers." *American Sociological Review* 63(1): 68–93.

Myers, P. N. Jr., and Biocca, F. A. 1992. "The Elastic Body Image: The Effect of Television Advertising and Programming on Body Image Distortions in Young Women." *Journal of Communication* 42(3): 108–134.

Myers, P. N. Jr., Biocca, F. A., Wilson, G., Nias, D., Kaiser, S. B., Frank, M. G., Gilovich, T., Furlow, F. B., and Aune, R. K. 1999. "Appearance and Adornment Cues." In L. K. Guerro, J. A. DeVito, and M. Hecht (Eds.), *The Nonverbal Communication Reader: Classic and Contemporary Readings.* 2d ed. Prospect Heights, IL: Waveland.

Nagata, M. L. 1999. "Why Did You Change Your Name? Name Changing Patterns and the Life Course in Early Modern Japan." *History of the Family* 4(3): 315–338.

Nardi, P. M. 2003. *Doing Survey Research.* Boston: Allyn & Bacon.

Nass, C., and Moon, Y. (2000). Machines and Mindlessness: Social Responses to Computers. *Journal of Social Issues,* 56(1), 81–103.

Nass, C., Moon, Y., & Carney, P. (1999). "Are Respondents Polite to Computers? Social Desirability and Direct Responses to Computers." *Journal of Applied Social Psychology* 29(5), 1093–1110.

National Center for Education Statistics. 2003a. "International Comparisons of Education." *Digest of Education Statistics, 2002.* (http://nces.ed.gov/)

———. 2003. "Fast Facts Tool." (http://nces.ed.gov/fastfacts/faqtopics.asp?type=2)

National Center for Health Statistics. 1998. *Health, United States, 1998.* Hyattsville, MD: Author.

———. 2001. "43% of First Marriages Break Up Within 15 Years." 2001 News Releases. (http://www. cdc.gov/nchs/releases/01news/firstmarr.htm)

———. 2002a. *Health, United States, 2002, With Chartbook on Trends in the Health of America.* Hyattsville, MD: Author.

———. 2002b. "New Reports Sheds Light on Trends and Patterns in Marriage, Divorce, and Cohabitation." *2002 Fact Sheet.* (http://www.cdc.gov/nchs/releases/02news/div_mar_cohab.htm)

National Center for Injury Prevention and Control. 2002. "Suicide in the United States." (http://www.cdc.gov/ncipc/factsheets/suifacts.htm.)

National Center for Public Policy and Higher Education. 2003. "College Affordability in Jeopardy" (http://www.highereducation.org/reports/affordability/)

National Clearinghouse on Child Abuse and Neglect Information. 2003. "Child Maltreatment 2001: Summary of Key Findings." (http://nccanch.acf.hhs.gov/pubs/factsheets/canstats.cfm)

National Coalition for the Homeless. 2002. *Fact Sheet #3: Who is Homeless?* (http://www.nationalhome less.org/who.html)

National Committee on Pay Equity. 2002. "Fact Sheets." (http://www.feminist.com/fairpay/factsheets. htm)

National Council of Churches. 2003. "Status of Child Care Legislation." (http://www.ncccusa.org/ publicwitness/tanf-may2003report.html)

National Institute for Literacy. 2002. "National Adult Literacy Survey." (http://www.nifl.gov/nifl/ facts/NALS.html)

National Institute of Mental Health. 2001. "The Numbers Count: Mental Disorders in America" (NIH Publication # 01-4584). (http://www.nimh.nih.gov/publicat/numbers.cfm)

———. 2003. "In Harm's Way: Suicide in America." (http://www.nimh.nih.gov/publicat/ harmaway.cfm)

National Marriage Project. 2003. *The State of Our Unions.* New Brunswick, NJ: Rutgers University.

National Mental Health Association. 2003. "Elderly—Alzheimer's Disease." *Factsheet.* (http://www. nmha.org/infoctr/factsheets/101.cfm)

National Park Service. 1998. "Peak Immigration Years." Ellis Island Exhibit, New York.

National Public Radio. 1999. "Americans Distrust Government, But Want It To Do More." (http://www.npr.org/programs/special/poll/government/summary.html)

National Television Violence Study. 1996–1998. (Vols. 1–3). Center for Communication and Social Policy, University of California at Santa Barbara (Ed.). Thousand Oaks, CA: Sage.

Nationmaster. 2003. "Murder, Rape, and Assault Per Capita." (http://www.nationmaster.com)

Nelson, T. 2001. "Tracking, Parental Education and Child Literacy Development: How Ability Grouping Perpetuates Poor Education Attainment Within Minority Communities." *Georgetown Journal on Poverty Law and Policy* VIII(2): 363–375.

Nelson, T. (Ed.). 2002. *Ageism: Stereotyping and Prejudice Against Older Persons.* Cambridge, MA: MIT Press.

Netreach.com. 2003. "Physicians." (http://www.netreach.net/~bhohlfeld/career_project/shal/8s_medical.htm#Salary/Conclusion)

Neumark-Sztainer, D., Faulkner, N., Story, M., Perry, C., Hannan, P. J., and Mulert, S. 2002. "Weight-Teasing Among Adolescents: Correlations With Weight Status and Disordered Eating Behaviors." *International Journal of Obesity and Related Metabolic Disorders* 26(1): 123–131.

The New York Times. 2003a. "Suits Accuse Toyota of Bias in Lending." (April 10).

———. 2003b. "The Terrorism Link that Wasn't." (September 19) Editorial/Op-Ed.

Nichter, M. 2000. *Fat Talk: What Girls and Their Parents Say About Dieting.* Cambridge, MA/London: Harvard University Press.

Nie, N., and Erbring, L. 2000. *Internet and Society.* (http://www.stanford.edu/group/siqss/Press_Release/Preliminary_Report.pdf)

Nielsen Media Research. 2003. "Highest-Rated Primetime Programs." (http://www.nielsenmedia.com/top_frame.html)

Nippert-Eng, C. 1996. *Home and Work.* Chicago: University of Chicago Press.

Nock, S. 1993. *The Costs of Privacy: Surveillance and Reputation in America* New York: Aldine de Gruyter.

Nord, C., and Zill, N. 1996. *Non-Custodial Parents' Participation in Their Children's Lives: Evidence from the Survey of Income and Program Participation. Vol II.* Washington, DC: U.S. Department of Health and Human Services.

Olbrich, R. 1986. "Attribution Psychology: An Approach to Explaining Productive Psychotic Symptoms." *Fortschritte der Neorologie-Psychiatre* 54(12): 402–407.

Oliker. S. 2000. "Examining Care at Welfare's End." Pp. 167–185 in M. Meyer (Ed.), *Care Work: Gender, Class and the Welfare State.* New York: Routledge.

Orbuch, T. Thornton, A., and Cancio, J. 2000. "The Impact of Marital Quality, Divorce, and Remarriage on the Relationships Between Parents and Their Children." *Marriage & Family Review* 29(4) 221–246.

Orfield, G., and Eaton, S. 2003. "Back to Segregation." *Nation* 276(8): 5–8.

Orfield, G., Eaton, S., and the Harvard Project on Desegregation. 1996. *Dismantling Desegregation: The Quiet Reversal of Brown v. Board of Education.* New York: New Press.

Ottati, V. C., and Deiger, M. 2002. "Visual Cues and the Candidate Evaluation Process." In V. C. Ottati and R. S. Tindale (Eds.), *The Social Psychology of Politics: Social Psychological Applications to Social Issues* (pp. 75–87). New York: Kluwer Academic/Plenum.

Owsley, H. 1977. "The Marriage of Rachel Donelson." *Tennessee Historical Quarterly* 36 (Winter): 479–492.

Pace, T. M., Mullins, L. L., Beesley, D., Hill, J. S., and Carson, K. 1999. "The Relationship Between Children's Emotional and Behavioral Problems and the Social Responses of Elementary School Teachers." *Contemporary Educational Psychology* 24(2): 140–155.

Padavic, I., and Reskin, B. 2002. *Women and Men at Work*. 2d ed. Thousand Oaks, CA: Pine Forge.

Pampel, F. 2002. "Cigarette Use and the Narrowing Sex Differential in Mortality." *Population and Development Review* 28(1): 77–104.

Parker-Pope, T. 1997. "Avon Is Calling, With New Way to Make a Sale." *Wall Street Journal* (October 27): B1.

Parrott, S. 2002. *The TANF-Related Provisions in the President's Budget*. Washington, DC: Center on Budget and Policy Priorities.

Parrott, S., and Mezey, J. 2003. "New Child Care Resources Are Needed to Prevent the Loss of Child Care Assistance for Hundreds of Thousands of Children in Working Families." Center for Law and Social Policy. Center on Budget and Policy Priorities. (http://www.cbpp.org/7-15-03tanf.htm)

Parsons, T. [1951] 1964. *The Social System*. Glencoe, IL: Free Press.

Passas. N. 1990. "Anomie and Corporate Deviance." *Contemporary Crises* 14: 157–178.

Pearce, D. 1983. "The Feminization of Ghetto Poverty." *Society* 21(1): 70–74.

Pearlin, L. I. 1989. "The Sociological Study of Stress." *Journal of Health and Social Behavior* 30(3): 242–256.

Pearlin, L. I., Menaghan, E. G., Lieberman, M. A., and Mullan, J. T. 1981. "The Stress Process." *Journal of Health and Social Behavior* 22(4): 337–356.

Pearlin, L. I., and Skaff, M. M. 1996. "Stress and the Life Course: A Paradigmatic Alliance." *Gerontologist* 36(2): 239–247.

Pearson, D. E. 1993. "Post Mass Culture." *Society* 30(5): 17–22.

Peirce, K., and McBride, M. 1999. "Aunt Jemima Isn't Keeping Up With the Energizer Bunny: Stereotyping of Animated Spokescharacters in Advertising." *Sex Roles* 40(11–12): 959–968.

Peiss, K. 1999. *Hope in a Jar: The Making of America's Beauty Culture*. New York: Owl Books.

Perlini, A. H., Marcello, A., Hansen, S. D., and Pudney, W. 2001. "The Effects of Male Age and Physical Appearance on Evaluations of Attractiveness, Social Desirability, and Resourcefulness." *Social Behavior and Personality* 29(3): 277–287.

Persell, C., and Cookson, P. 1990. "Chartering and Bartering: Elite Education and Social Class." In P. Kingston and L. Lewis (Eds.), *The High Status Track*. Albany: SUNY Press.

Pescosolido, B., Grauerholz, E., and Milkie, M. 1997. "Culture and Conflict: The Portrayal of Blacks in U.S. Children's Picture Books Through the Mid and Late Twentieth Century." *American Sociological Review* 62(3): 443–464.

Peterson, K. 1992. "The Maquilladora Revolution in Guatemala" (Occasional Paper Series 2). New Haven, CT: Yale Law School, Orville H. Schell Jr. Center for International Human Rights.

Peterson, R. 1996. "A Re-Evaluation of the Economic Consequences of Divorce." *American Sociological Review* 61: 528–536.

Pew Foundation. 2000. "Internet and American Life Project." (http://www.pewinternet.org)

Pfohl, S. 1977. "The Discovery of Child Abuse." *Social Problems* 24(3): 310–323.

Pham, L. B., Taylor, S. E., and Seeman, T. E. 2001. "Effects of Environmental Predictability and Personal Mastery on Self-Regulatory and Physiological Processes." *Personality and Social Psychology Bulletin* 27: 611–620.

Philipson, I. 2002. *Married to the Job: Why We Live to Work and What We can Do About It*. New York: Free Press.

Phillips, R. G., and Hill, A. J. 1998. "Fat, Plain, but Not Friendless: Self-Esteem and Peer Acceptance of Obese Adolescent Girls." *International Journal of Obesity* 22(4): 287–295.

Philogene, G. 1999. *From Black to African American: A New Social Representation*. Westport, CT: Praeger.

Pienta, A., Hayward, M., and Jenkins, K. 2000. "Health Consequences of Marriage for the Retirement Years." *Journal of Family Issues* 21(5): 559–586.

Pierce, J. W., and Wardle, J. 1997. "Cause and Effect Beliefs and Self-Esteem of Overweight Children." *Journal of Child Psychology and Psychiatry and Allied Disciplines* 38 (September): 645–650.

Poblete, P. 2000. "The Price to Pay for an 'American' Nose and Eyes Is More Than $2,500." *San Francisco Chronicle* (February 24): E1.

_____. 2001. "Beauty Ideals Still In the Dark Ages." *San Francisco Chronicle* (June 24): B4.

Polakow, V. 1993. *Lives on the Edge.* Chicago: University of Chicago Press.

Pollack, A. 2000. "Is Everything for Sale?: Patenting a Human Gene As If It Were An Invention." *The New York Times* (June 28): C2.

Population Reference Bureau. 2000. "The Aging of the United States, 1999–2025." (http://www.prb.org/ AmeristatTemplate.cfm?Section=Estimates__Projections&template=/ContentManagement/ ContentDisplay.cfm&ContentID=7859)

Population Reference Bureau. 2003. "World Population Data Sheet." (http://www.prb.org)

Population Reference Bureau. 2003a. "Traditional Families Account for Only 7% of U.S. Households." (http://www.ameristat.org/Content/NavigationMenu/Ameristat/Topics1/MarriageandFamily/ Traditional_Families_Account_for_Only_7_Percent_of_U_S__Households.htm)

Portes, A. 2002. "English-Only Triumphs, But the Costs are High." *Contexts* 1(1): 10–15.

Portes, A., and Rumbaut, R. 1996. *Immigrant America: A Portrait.* Berkeley, CA: University of California Press.

Posner, R. 1995. *Aging and Old Age.* Chicago: University of Chicago Press.

Poulin-Dubois, D., Serbin, L., Eichstedt, J., Sen, M., and Beissel, C. 2002. "Men Don't Put on Make-Up: Toddlers' Knowledge of the Gender Stereotyping of Household Activities." *Social Development* 11(2): 166–181.

Powell, K., and Abels, L. 2002. "Sex-Role Stereotypes in TV Programs Aimed at the Preschool Audience: An Analysis of Teletubbies and Barney and Friends." *Women and Language* 25(1): 14–22.

The President's Commission on Law Enforcement and Administration of Justice. 1968. *The Challenge of Crime in a Free Society.* Washington, DC: U.S. Government Printing Office.

Prabhakaran, V. 1999. "A Sociolinguistic Analysis of South African Teluga Surnames." *South African Journal of Linguistics* 17(2/3): 149–161.

Proctor, B., and Dalaker, J. 2002. "Poverty in the United States: 2001." *Current Population Reports* (P60–219). U.S. Census Bureau. Washington, DC: U.S. Government Printing Office.

_____. 2003. "Poverty in the United States: 2002." *Current Population Reports* (P60–222). U.S. Census Bureau. Washington, DC: U.S. Government Printing Office.

Progressive. 2000. "The Housing Crunch." *Progressive* 64(5): 8–10.

Public Interest Research Group (PIRG). 2002. "The Burden of Borrowing." (http://www.pirg.org/ highered/burdenofborrowing.html.)

Public Perspective. 2001. "Differences and Differential Treatment" (May/June): 24.

Putnam, R. 1995. "Bowling Alone: America's Declining Social Capital." *Journal of Democracy* (January): 65–78.

_____. 1998. "The Strange Disappearance of Civic America." *New Prospect Inc.* (http://epn.org/ prospect/24/24putn.html)

_____. 2000. *Bowling Alone: The Collapse and Revival of American Community.* New York: Simon and Schuster.

_____. 2003. *Better Together: Restoring American Community.* New York: Simon and Schuster.

Quigley, S. J. 2003. "That's My Name, Don't Wear It Out." *American Journalism Review* 25(3): 49–52.

Quint, J., Widom, R. and Moore, L. 2001. "Post-TANF Food Stamp and Medicaid Receipt." Project on Devolution and Urban Change. Manpower Demonstration Research Corporation.

Rabois, D., and Haaga, D. A. F. 2002. "Facilitating Police-Minority Youth Attitude Change: The Effects of Cooperation Within a Competitive Context and Exposure to Typical Exemplars." *Journal of Community Psychology* 30(2): 189–195. Mahwah, NJ: Lawrence Erlbaum.

"Race: The Power of an Illusion." 2003. PBS. (http://www.pbs.org/race/000_General/000_00-Home.htm)

Ramsey, J. L., and Langlois, J. H. 2002. "Effects of the 'Beauty Is Good' Stereotype on Children's Information Processing." *Journal of Experimental Child Psychology* 81(3): 320–340.

Rangarajan, A. 1998. "Keeping Welfare Recipients Employed: A Guide for States Designing Job Retention Services." *Mathematica Policy Research Inc.* (June).

Rapoport, A. 1960. *Fights, Games, and Debates.* Ann Arbor: University of Michigan Press.

Rawlins, W. 1992. *Friendship Matters: Communication, Dialectics, and the Life Course.* New York: Aldine de Gruyter.

Reardon, S., and Yun, J. 2002. "Private School Racial Enrollments and Segregation." The Civil Rights Project, Harvard University, Cambridge, MA. (http://www.law.harvard.edu/civilrights)

Reeves, B., and Nass, C. (1996). *The Media Equation: How People Treat Computers, Television, and New Media Like Real People and Places.* New York: Cambridge University Press.

Regan, P. C. 2002. *The Mating Game: A Primer on Love, Sex, and Marriage.* Thousand Oaks, CA: Sage.

Reifman, A., Villa, L. Amans, J., Rethinam, V., and Relesca, T. 2001. "Children of Divorce in the 1990s: A Meta-Analysis." *Journal of Divorce and Remarriage* 36(1–2): 27–36.

Reiman, J. 2004. *The Rich Get Richer and the Poor Get Prison.* 7th ed. Boston: Allyn & Bacon

Reis, H. T., Nezlek, J., and Wheeler, L. 1980. "Physical Attractiveness in Social Interaction." *Journal of Personality and Social Psychology* 38: 604–617.

Rensberger, B. 1981. "Racial Odyssey." *Science Digest* (January/February).

Rentner, D., Chadowsky, N., Fagan, T., Gayles, K., Hamilton, M., Jennings, J., and Kober, N. 2003. "From the Capital to the Classroom: State and Federal Efforts to Implement the No Child Left Behind Act." Center on Educational Policy and American Youth Policy Forum. (http://wwwaypf.org)

Renzetti, C. M., and Curran, D. J. 1989. *Women, Men and Society: The Sociology of Gender.* Boston: Allyn & Bacon.

Reskin, B. 2000. "Getting It Right: Sex and Race Inequality in Work Organizations." *Annual Review of Sociology* 26: 707–709.

Reskin, B., and McBrier, D., and Kmec, J. 1999. "The Determinants and Consequences of Workplace Sex and Race Composition." *Annual Review of Sociology* 25: 335–361.

Rhodes, G., Geddes, K., Jeffrey, L., Dziurawiec, S., and Clark, A. 2002. "Are Average and Symmetric Faces Attractive To Infants? Discrimination and Looking Preferences." *Perception* 31(3): 315–321.

Richard, J. F., Fonzi, A., Tani, F., Tassi, F., Tomada, G., and Scneider, B. H. 2002. "Cooperation and Competition," Pp. 515–532 in P. K. Smith and C. H. Hart (Eds.), *Blackwell Handbook of Child Social Development.* Malden, MA: Blackwell.

Richardson, L. W. 1988. *The Dynamics of Sex and Gender: A Sociological Perspective.* New York: Harper and Row.

Riley, D. 1988. *Am I That Name?* Minneapolis: University of Minnesota Press.

Riley, G. [1991] 1997. *Divorce: An American Tradition*. University of Nebraska Press, Lincoln.

Rimer, S. 2003. "A Campus Fad That's Being Copied: Internet Plagiarism." *The New York Times* (September 3).

Ritzer, G. 1995. *Expressing America: A Critique of the Global Credit Card Society*. Thousand Oaks, CA: Pine Forge.

———. 2001. *Explorations in the Sociology of Consumption: Fast Food, Credit Cards, and Casinos*. Thousand Oaks, CA: Sage.

Rivera, C. 2003. "Study Says Welfare-to-Work Reforms Leave Recipients Below Poverty Line." *Los Angeles Times* (July 23): B3.

Robert, S. A., and House, J. S. 2000. "Socioeconomic Inequalities in Health: An Enduring Sociological Problem." Pp. 79–97 in C. Bird, P. Conrad, and A. Fremont (Eds.), *Handbook of Medical Sociology*. 5th ed. Upper Saddle River, NJ: Prentice Hall.

Roberts, D. F. 1975. "The Dynamics of Racial Intermixture in the American Negro: Some Anthropological Considerations." *American Journal of Human Genetics* 7: 361–367.

Robinson, J. 2003. *Work To Live*. New York: Perogee.

Robinson, J., and Godbey, G. 1997. *Time for Life*. Philadelphia: Pennsylvania State University Press.

Roper Center. 2003. "Public Opinion on Race Relations." (January 19–21). (http://www.ropercenter. uconn.edu/cgi-bin/hsrun.exe/roperweb/pom/pom.htx;start=Hs_special_topics?Topic=race)

Rosen, J. 2001. *The Unwanted Gaze: The Destruction of Privacy in America*. New York: Knopf.

Rosenbush, S., and Haddad, C. 2003. "MCI is Under a New Cloud, But It Can Weather the Storm." *Business Week* (August 11): 31.

Rosenhan, D. L. 1973. "On Being Sane in Insane Places." *Science* 179: 250–258.

Rosenthal, R., and Jacobson, L. 1968. *Pygmalion in the Classroom*. New York: Holt, Rinehart and Winston.

Ross, C. E., and Broh, B. A. 2000. "The Roles of Self-Esteem and the Sense of Personal Control in the Academic Achievement Process." *Sociology of Education* 73(4): 270–284.

Ross, C. E., and Huber, J. 1985. "Hardship and Depression." *Journal of Health and Social Behavior* 26(4): 312–327.

Ross, C., and Mirowsky, J. 2002. "Family Relationships, Social Support and Subjective Life Expectancy." *Journal of Health and Social Behavior* 43(4): 469–489.

Ross, H., and Taylor, H. 1989. "Do Boys Prefer Daddy or His Physical Style of Play?" *Sex Roles* 20 (January): 23–33.

Rossi, A. S., and Rossi, P. 1990. *Of Human Bonding: Parent-Child Relations Across the Life Course*. New York: Aldine de Gruyter.

Roth, L. 1999. "Selling Women Short: Gender Differences in Compensation on Wall Street." American Sociological Association Annual Meetings.

Ruane, J. 1993. "Tolerance Revisited: The Case of Spousal Force." *Sociological Focus* 26(4): 333–343.

Ruane, J. 2004. *Essentials of Research Methods*. Malden, MA: Blackwell.

Ruane, J., Cerulo, K., and Gerson, J. 1994. "Professional Deceit: Normal Lying in an Occupational Setting." *Sociological Focus* 27(2): 91–109.

Rubenstein, A. J., Kalakanis, L., and Langlois, J. H. 1999. "Infant Preferences for Attractive Faces: A Cognitive Explanation." *Developmental Psychology* 35(3): 848–855.

Rubinstein, S., and Cabellero, B. 2000. "Is Miss America an Undernourished Role Model." *Journal of the American Medical Association* 283(2): 1569.

Rubin, B. 1996. *Shifts in the Social Contract: Understanding Change in American Society.* Thousand Oaks, CA: Pine Forge.

Rubin, J. Z., Provenzano, F. J., and Luria, Z. 1974. "The Eye of the Beholder: Parents' Views on Sex of Newborns." *American Journal of Orthopsychiatry* 44: 512–519.

Rubin, L. B. 1993. *Just Friends: The Role of Friendship in Our Lives.* New York: Harper and Row.

Rubin, N., Shmilovitz, C., and Weiss, M. 1993. "From Fat to Thin: Informal Rites Affirming Identity Change." *Symbolic Interaction* 16(1): 1–17.

_____. 1994. "The Obese and the Slim: Personal Definition Rites of Identity Change in a Group of Obese People Who Became Slim After Gastric Reduction Surgery," *Megamot* 36(1): 5–19.

Rudd, N. A., and Lennon, S. J. 1999. "Social Power and Appearance Management Among Women." Pp. 153–172 in K. K. P. Johnson and S. J. Lennon (Eds.), *Appearance and Power: Dress, Body, Culture.* New York: Oxford University Press.

Rudman, L., Feinberg, J., and Fairchild, K. 2003. "Minority Members' Implicit Attitudes: Automatic Ingroup Bias as a Function of Group Status." *Social Cognition* 20(4): 294–320.

Rust, J., Golombok, S., Himes, M., Johnston, K., and Golding, J. 2000. "The Role of Brothers and Sisters in the Gender Development of Preschool Children." *Journal of Experimental Child Psychology* 77(4): 292–303.

Ryan, A. 1996. "Professional Liars." *Social Research* 63 (Fall): 619–641.

Sacks, H. 1975. "Everyone Has to Lie." Pp. 57–79 in M. Sanches and B. Blount (Eds.), *Sociocultural Dimensions of Language Use.* New York: Academic Press.

Sadker, M., and Sadker, D. 1985. "Sexism in the Schoolroom of the '80s." *Psychology Today* 19:54–57.

_____. 1998. "Failing at Fairness: How America's Schools Cheat Girls." Pp. 503–509 in P. Rothenberg (Ed.), *Race, Class, and Gender in the United States.* 4th ed. New York: St. Martin's.

Salmon, M. 1986. *Women and the Law of Property in Early America.* Chapel Hill: University of North Carolina Press.

Sanabria, H. 2001. "Exploring Kinship in Anthropology and History: Surnames and Social Transformation in the Bolivian Andes." *Latin American Research Review* 36(2): 137–155.

Sanderson, C. A., Darley, J. M., and Messinger, C. S. 2002. "I'm Not As Thin As You Think I Am: The Development and Consequences of Feeling Discrepant From the Thinness Norm." *Personality and Social Psychology Bulletin* 28(2): 172–183.

Sands, E. R., and Wardle, J. 2003. "Internalization of Ideal Body Shapes in 9–12 Year-Old Girls." *International Journal of Eating Disorders* 33(2): 193–204.

Sangmpam, S. N. 1999. "American Civilization, Name Change, and African-American Politics." *National Political Science Review* 7: 221–248.

Sapkidis, O. 1998. "To Whom Do You Belong?: Catholic and Orthodox Names at Syros (Greece)." In P. H. Stahl (Ed.), *Naming and Social Structure: Example From Southeast Europe.* New York: Columbia University Press.

Saporta, I, and Halpern, J. J. 2002. "Being Different Can Hurt: Effects of Deviation From Physical Norms on Lawyers' Salaries." *Industrial Relations* 41(3): 442–466.

Satran, O. R., and Rosenkrantz, L. 2003. *Cool Names for Babies.* New York: St Martin's Griffin.

Scassa, T. 1996. "National Identity, Ethnic Surnames and the State." *Canadian Journal of Law and Society* 11(2): 167–191.

Schachter, S. 1959. *The Psychology of Affiliation.* Stanford, CA: Stanford University Press.

Schaefer, N. C., and Presser, S. 2003. "The Science of Asking Questions." *Annual Review of Sociology* 29: 65–88.

Schmidley, D. 2001. "Profile of the Foreign-Born Population of the Untied States: 2000." *Current Population Reports* (P23–206). Washington, DC: U.S. Census Bureau.

_____. 2003. "The Foreign-Born Population in the U.S.: March 2002." *Current Population Reports* (P20–539). Washington, DC: U.S. Census Bureau.

Schneiderman, R. 1967. *All for One.* New York: P.S. Eriksson.

Schopler, J., Insko, C. A., Drigotas, S., and Graetz, K. A. 1993. "Individual/Group Discontinuity: Further Evidence for Mediation by Fear and Greed." *Personality and Social Psychology Bulletin* 19(4): 419–431.

Schott, L. 2000. "Ways that States can Serve Families that Reach Welfare Time Limits." Center on Budget and Policy Priorities. (http://www.cbpp.org)

Schroeder, K., and Ledger, J. 1998. *Life and Death on the Internet.* Menasha, WI: Supple.

Schul, Y., and Vinokur, A. 2000. "Projection in Person Perception Among Spouses as a Function of the Similarity in Their Shared Experiences." *Personality and Social Psychology Bulletin* 26: 987–1001.

Schulman, D. 2004. "Labeling Theory." In G. Ritzer (Ed.), *Handbook of Social Theory.* Thousand Oaks, CA: Sage.

Schulman, K. 2000. *The High Cost of Child Care Puts Quality Care Out of Reach for Many Families.* Washington, DC: Children's Defense Fund. (http//www.childrensdefense.org)

Schultz, J. W., and Pruitt, D. G. 1978. "The Effect of Mutual Concern on Joint Welfare." *Journal of Experimental Social Psychology* 14: 480–492.

Schuman, D., and Olufs, R. 1995. *Diversity on Campus.* Boston: Allyn & Bacon.

Schur, E. 1984. *Labeling Women Deviant.* Philadelphia: Temple University Press.

Schutt, R. K., Medchede, T., and Rierdan, J. 1994. "Distress, Suicidal Thoughts and Social Support Among Homeless Adults." *Journal of Health and Social Behavior* 35: 134–142.

Scott, D., and Church, T. 2001. "Separation/Attachment Theory and Career Decidedness and Commitment: Effects of Parental Divorce." *Journal of Vocational Behavior* 58(3): 328–347.

Segrin, C., and Nabi, R. 2002. "Does Television Viewing Cultivate Unrealistic Expectations About Marriage?" *Journal of Communication* 52(2): 247–263.

Seidman, S. 1992. "An Investigation of Sex-Role Stereotyping in Music Videos." *Journal of Broadcasting and Electronic Media* (Spring): 210–216.

Seiter, J, Bruschke, J and Bai, C. 2002. "The Acceptability of Deception as a Function of Perceivers' Culture, Deceiver's Intention, and Deceiver-Deceived Relationship." *Western Journal of Communication* 66(2): 158–180.

Sennett, R. 1977. *The Fall of Public Man.* New York: Knopf.

Sennett, R., and Cobb, J. 1972. *The Hidden Injuries of Class.* New York: Vintage.

Shaffer, D. R., Crepaz, N., and Sun, C. 2000. "Physical Attractiveness Stereotyping in Cross-Cultural Perspective: Similarities and Differences Between Americans and Taiwanese." *Journal of Cross-Cultural Psychology* 31(5): 557–582.

Shalala, D. 2003. "Older Americans: Living Longer, Living Better." *The World Almanac and Book of Facts 2003.* New York: World Almanac Books.

Shapiro, A., and Leone, R. 1999. *The Control Revolution: How the Internet Is Putting Individuals in Charge and Changing the World We Know.* New York: Public Affairs/Century Foundation.

Sharma, U., and Black, P. 2001. "Look Good, Feel Better: Beauty Therapy As Emotional Labor." *Sociology* 35(4): 913–931.

Sharpe, R. 1994. "The Waiting Game." *Wall Street Journal* (March 29): A1, A8.

Shavit, Y., and Featherman, D. 1988. "Schooling, Tracking, and Teenage Intelligence." *Sociology of Education* 61: 5.

Sherif, M. 1966. *In Common Predicament: Social Psychology of Intergroup Conflict and Cooperation.* Boston: Houghton Mifflin.

Sherif, M., Harvey, O. J., White, B. J., Hood, W. R., and Sherif, C. W. 1961. *Intergroup Conflict and Cooperation: The Robbers' Cave Experiment.* Norman, OK: University Book Exchange.

Shipman, P. 1994. *The Evolution of Racism: Human Differences and the Use and Abuse of Science.* New York: Simon and Schuster.

Sidel, R. 1991. *On Her Own: Growing Up in the Shadows of the American Dream.* New York: Viking.

Sigelman, L., Sigelman, C. K., and Fowler, C. 1987. "A Bird of a Different Feather? An Investigation of Physical Attractiveness and the Electability of Female Candidates." *Social Psychology Quarterly* 50(1): 32–43.

Signorielli, N., and Bacue, A. 1999. "Recognition and Respect: A Content Analysis of Prime-Time Television Characters Across Three Decades. *Sex Roles* 40(7–8): 527–544.

Signorielli, N., Gerbner, G., and Morgan, M. 1995. "Violence on Television: The Cultural Indicators Project." *Journal of Broadcasting and Electronic Media* 39 (Spring): 278–283.

Signorielli, N., and Morgan, N. 1988. *Cultivation Analysis.* Newbury Park, CA: Sage.

Silverstein, M. J., and Fiske, N. 2003. "Luxury for the Masses." *Harvard Business Review* (April): 48–54.

Simendinger, A. 2003. "Week in Review" Transcript. PBS. (September 19).

Simmel, G. 1950a. "The Lie." Pp. 312–316 in K. Wolff (Ed.), *The Sociology of Georg Simmel.* New York: Free Press.

————. 1950b. "The Stranger." Pp. 402–408 in K. Wolff (Ed.), *The Sociology of Georg Simmel.* New York: Free Press.

Simmons, J. L. 1966. "Public Stereotypes of Deviants." *Social Problems* 13: 223–232.

Simmons, T., and O'Neill, G. 2001. "Households and Families" (C2KBR/01–8 Census 2000 Brief). Washington, DC: U.S. Census Bureau.

Simon, B. L. 1987. *Never Married Women.* Philadelphia: Temple University Press.

Simon, R. 2002. "Revisiting the Relationship Among Gender, Marital Status, and Mental Health." *American Journal of Sociology* 107(4): 1065–1096.

Simon, R., and Marcussen, K. 1999. "Marital Transitions, Marital Beliefs, and Mental Health." *Journal of Health and Social Behavior* 40(2): 111–125.

Simon, R. W. 1997. "The Meanings Individuals Attach to Role Identities and Their Implications for Mental Health." *Journal of Health and Social Behavior* 38(3): 256–274.

Simpson, J., Campbell, B., and Berscheid, E. 1986. "The Association Between Romantic Love and Marriage: Kephart (1967) Twice Revisited." *Personality and Social Psychology Bulletin* 12: 363–372.

Skolnick, A. 1991. *Embattled Paradise: The American Family in an Age of Uncertainty.* New York: Basic Books.

Slater, A., Bremner, G., Johnson, S. P., Sherwood, P., Hayes, R., and Brown, E. 2000. "Newborn Infants' Preference for Attractive Faces: The Role of Internal and External Facial Features." *Infancy* 1(2): 265–274.

Slater, P. 1970. *The Pursuit of Loneliness: American Culture at the Breaking Point.* Boston: Beacon.

Slavin, R. E., and Madden, N. A. 1979. "School Practices That Improve Race Relations." *American Educational Research Journal* 16: 169–180.

Smith, A. 1991. *National Identity.* Reno: University of Nevada Press.

Smith, K. 2000. "Who's Minding the Kids? Child Care Arrangements: Fall 1995." *Current Population Reports* (P70–70). Washington DC: U.S. Census Bureau.

Smith, T. W. 1997. *Changes in Family and Family Values.* Chicago: National Opinion Research Center.

Snyder, M. 2001. "Self-Fulfilling Stereotypes." Pp. 30–35 in A. Branaman (Ed.), *Self and Society.* Malden, MA: Blackwell.

Sobal, J., and Maurer, D. (Eds.). 1999. *Interpreting Weight: The Social Management of Fatness and Thinness.* New York: Aldine de Gruyter.

Social Security Online. 2003. *The 2003 Annual Report of the Board of Trustees of the Federal Old-Age and Survivors Insurance and Disability Insurance Trust Funds.* Fast Facts and Figures About Social Security. (http://www.socialsecurity.gov/policy/docs/chartbooks/fast_facts/2003/ff2003. html#generalinfo)

Solomon, D., Battistich, V., and Hom, A. 1996. "Teacher Beliefs and Practices in Schools Serving Communities That Differ in Socioeconomic Level." *Journal of Experimental Education* 64(4): 327–347.

Sorenson, A. 1990. "Estimating the Economic Consequences of Separation and Divorce: A Cautionary Tale from the U.S." In L. Weitzman and M. Maclean (Eds.), *Economic Consequences of Divorce: The International Perspective.* Oxford, England: Clarendon.

South, S. 2001. "Time-Dependent Effects of Wives' Employment on Marital Dissolution." *American Sociological Review* 66(2): 226–245.

South, S., and Lloyd, K. 1995. "Spousal Alternatives and Marital Dissolution." *American Sociological Review* 60(1): 21–35.

South, S., and Spitze, G. 1994. "Housework in Marital and Nonmarital Households." *American Sociological Review* 59: 327–347.

Spain, D. 1999. "America's Diversity: On the Edge of Two Centuries." *PBR Reports on America* 1(2).

Spivey, A. 2002. "How is Work First Working?" *Endeavors.* University of North Caroline at Chapel Hill. (http://research.unc.edu/endeavors/spr2002/work_first.html)

Sprecher, S., and Regan, P. C. 2002. "Liking Some Things (in Some People) More Than Others: Partner Preferences in Romantic Relationships and Friendships." *Journal of Social and Personal Relationships* 19(4): 463–481.

Stack, S., and Eshleman, J. 1998. "Marital Status and Happiness: A 17-Nation Study." *Journal of Marriage & Family* 60(2): 527–537.

Stearns. M. 2003. "Bill to Limit Awards in Malpractice Lawsuits Fails in Senate." *The Kansas City Star* (July 10).

Steinke, J., and Long, M. 1996. "A Lab of Her Own? Portrayals of Female Characters on Children's Educational Science Program." *Science Communication* 18(2): 91–115.

Stenson, J. 2003. "Extra Stress Stresses Immune System Too." (http://www.nim.nih.gov/medlineplus/ news/fullstory_13213.html)

Stern, P., and Carstensen, L. (Eds.). 2000. *The Aging Mind: Opportunities in Cognition Research.* Washington, DC: National Academy Press.

St-Hilaire, A. 2002. "The Social Adaptation of Children of Mexican Immigrants: Educational Aspirations beyond Junior High School." *Social Science Quarterly* 83(4): 1026–1043.

Stice, E., Spangler, D., and Agras, W. S. 2001. "Exposure to Media-Portrayed Thin-Ideal Images Adversely Affects Vulnerable Girls: A Longitudinal Experiment." *Journal of Social and Clinical Psychology* 20(3): 270–288.

Stinchcombe, A. 1963. "Some Empirical Consequences of the Davis-Moore Theory of Stratification." *American Sociological Review* 28(5): 805–808.

_____. 1997. "On the Virtues of the Old Institutionalism." *Annual Review of Sociology* 23: 1–18.

Stock, P. 1978. *Better Than Rubies: A History of Women's Education.* New York: G.P. Putnam.

Stodder, J. 1998. "Double Surnames and Gender Equality: A Proposition and the Spanish Case." *Journal of Comparative Family Studies* 29(3): 585–593.

Stolberg, S. 2003a. "Senate Refused to Consider Cap on Medical Malpractice Awards." *The New York Times* (July 10).

_____. 2003b. "Senate Becomes OK Corral for a Surgeon and a Lawyer." *The New York Times* (July 11).

Stone, L. 1989. "The Road to Polygamy." *New York Review of Books* (March): 13.

Strand, K., and Mayfield, E. 2000. "The Effects of 'Female Friendly' Teaching Strategies on College Women's Persistence in Mathematics." Presentation at Southern Sociological Society.

Straughan, R., and Lynn, M. 2002. "The Effects of Salesperson Compensation on Perceptions of Salesperson Honesty." *Journal of Applied Social Psychology* 32(4): 719–731.

Straus, M. (with Donnelly, D.). 2001. *Beating the Devil Out of Them: Corporal Punishment in American Families and its Effects on Children.* New Brunswick, NJ: Transaction.

Straus, M., and Gelles, R. 1990. *Physical Violence in American Families: Risk Factors and Adaptations to Violence Families.* New Brunswick, NJ: Transaction.

Straus, M., Gelles, R., and Steinmetz, S. 1980. *Behind Closed Doors: Violence in American Families.* New York: Doubleday.

Strobino, D., Grason, H., and Mikovitz, C. 2002. "Charting a Course for the Future of Women's Health in the United States: Concepts, Findings and Recommendations." *Social Science and Medicine* 54(5): 839–848.

Strum, C. 1993. "School Tracking: Efficiency or Elitism?" *The New York Times* (April 1): B5.

Stuart, G. 2003. "Suburbanization Without Integration in Chicago: Land Use, Development & Infrastructure." *The Taubman Center Report.* John F. Kennedy School of Government, Harvard University, Cambridge, MA.

Suarez, E. 1997. "A Woman's Freedom To Choose Her Surname: Is It Really A Matter Of Choice?" *Women's Right Law Reporter* 18(2): 233–242.

Suinn, R. M. 2001. "The Terrible Twos—Anger and Anxiety: Hazardous To Your Health." *American Psychologist* 56(1): 27–36.

Suitor, J., Mecom, D., and Feld, I. 2001. "Gender, Household Labor, and Scholarly Productivity Among University Professors." *Gender Issues* 19(4): 50–67.

Sullins, P. 2000. "The Stained Glass Ceiling: Career Attainment for Women Clergy." *Sociology of Religion* 61(3): 243–266.

Sum, A., Kirsch, I., and Taggart, R. 2002. "The Twin Challenges of Mediocrity and Inequality: Literacy in the U.S. from an International Perspective 2002." Educational Testing Service. (http://www.ets.org/research/pic)

Sumner, W. G. 1963. "Sociology." Pp. 9–29 in *Social Darwinism: Selected Essays of William Graham Sumner.* Englewood Cliffs, NJ: Prentice Hall.

Swartz, D. 2003. "From Correspondence to Contradiction and Change: Schooling in Capitalist America Revisited." *Sociological Forum* 18(1): 167–186.

Sweeney, J., and Bradbard, M. R. 1988. "Mothers' and Fathers' Changing Perceptions of their Male and Female Infants Over the Course of Pregnancy." *Journal of Genetic Psychology* 149: 393–404.

Swidler, A. 2001. *Talk of Love: How Culture Matters.* Chicago: University of Chicago Press.

Sykes, G., and Matza, D. 1957. "Techniques of Neutralization: A Theory of Delinquency." *American Sociological Review* 22: 664–670.

Tajfel, H. 1982. "Social Psychology of Intergroup Relations." *Annual Review of Psychology* 33: 1–39. Palo Alto, CA: Annual Reviews.

Taleporos, G., and McCabe, M. P. 2002. "The Impact of Sexual Esteem, Body Esteem and Sexual Satisfaction on Psychological Well-Being in People with Physical Disability." *Sexuality and Disability* 20(3): 177–183.

Tanur, J. 1992. *Questions About Questions.* New York: Russell Sage Foundation.

Taubman Center for State and Local Governments. 1999. "The Resegregation of American Schools." (http://www.harvard.edu/taubman/edu/deseg1.htm)

Teachout, T. 2002. "Is Tony Soprano Today's Ward Cleaver?" *The New York Times* (September 15).

Teichner, G., Ames, E., and Kerig, P. 1997. "The Relation of Infant Crying and the Sex of the Infant to Parents' Perceptions of the Infant and Themselves." *Psychology—A Quarterly Journal of Human Behavior* 34(3–4): 59–60.

Teigen, K. H. 1986. "Old Truths or Fresh Insights? A Study of Students' Evaluations of Proverbs." *Journal of British Social Psychology* 25(1): 43–50.

TenBensel, R., Rheinberger, M., and Radbill, S. 1997. "Children in a World of Violence: The Roots of Child Maltreatment." In M. Helfer, R. Kempe, and R. Krugman (Eds.), *The Battered Child.* Chicago: University of Chicago Press.

Tennen, H., and Affleck, G. 1999. "Finding Benefits in Adversity." In C. R. Snyder (Ed.), *Coping: The Psychology of What Works.* New York: Oxford University Press.

Thoits, P. 1983. "Dimensions of Life Events That Influence Psychological Distress: An Evaluation and Synthesis of the Literature." Pp. 33–103 in H. Kaplan (Ed.), *Psychosocial Stress: Trends in Theory and Research.* New York: Academic Press.

_____. 1994. "Stressors and Problem-Solving: The Individual as Psychological Activist." *Journal of Health and Social Behavior* 35(1): 143–160.

_____. 1995. "Stress, Coping, and Social Support Processes: Where Are We? What Next?" *Journal of Health and Social Behavior* 36 (extra issue): 53–79.

Thomas, B., and Reskin, B. 1990. "A Woman's Place Is Selling Homes: Occupational Change and the Feminization of Real Estate Sales." In B. Reskin and P. Roos (Eds.), *Job Queues, Gender Queues. Explaining Women's Inroads Into Male Occupations.* Philadelphia: Temple University Press.

Thompson, J. K., and Stice, E. 2001. "Thin-Ideal Internalization: Mounting Evidence for a New Risk Factor for Body-Image Disturbance and Eating Pathology." *Current Directions in Psychological Science* 10(5): 181–183.

Thompson, S. H., Sargent, R. G., and Kemper, K. A. 1996. "Black and White Adolescent Males' Perceptions of Ideal Body Type." *Sex Roles* 34 (March): 391–406.

Thomsen, S. R., Weber, M. M., and Beth-Brown, L. 2002. "The Relationship Between Reading Beauty and Fashion Magazines and the Use of Pathogenic Dieting Methods Among Adolescent Females." *Adolescence* 37(145): 1–18.

Thorne, B. 1995. "Girls and Boys Together . . . But Mostly Apart: Gender Arrangements in Elementary School." Pp. 93–102 in D. M. Newman (Ed.), *Sociology: Exploring the Architecture of Everyday Life.* Thousand Oaks, CA: Pine Forge.

Time-Life Books. 1988. *This Fabulous Century 1920–1930.* New York: Time-Life Books.

Tippet, S. 1993. "I've Got the Family I Always Wanted." *Ladies Home Journal* (April): 150.

Tjaden, P., and Thoennes, N. 2000. "Extent, Nature, and Consequences of Intimate Partner Violence." *Findings from the National Violence Against Women Survey.* Washington, DC: National Institute of Justice.

Trebay, G. 2003. "From Woof to Warp." *The New York Times* (April 6) sec. 9: 1.

Treharne, G. J., Lyons, A. C., and Tupling, R. E. 2001. "The Effects of Optimism, Pessimism, Social Support, and Mood on Lagged Relationship Between Daily Stress and Symptoms." *Current Research in Social Psychology* 7(5): 60–81.

Trehub, S., Hill, D., and Kamenetsky, S. 1997. "Parents' Sung Performances for Infants." *Canadian Journal of Experimental Psychology* 51(4): 385–396.

Trombley, W. 2003. "The Rising Price of Higher Education." *College Affordability in Jeopardy.* National Center for Public Policy and Higher Education. (http://www.highereducation.org/)

Tropp, L. 2003. "The Psychological Impact of Prejudice: Implications for Intergroup Contact." *Group Processes & Intergroup Relations* 6(2): 131–149.

Tuggle, J., and Holmes, M. 1997. "Blowing Smoke Status Politics and the Smoking Ban." *Deviant Behavior* 18, 1.

Tumin, M. 1967. *Social Stratification: The Forms and Functions of Inequality.* Englewood Cliffs, NJ: Prentice Hall.

Turkel, G. 2002. "Sudden Solidarity and the Rush to Normalization: Toward an Alternative Approach." *Sociological Focus* 35(1): 73–79.

Turkle, S. 1996. *Life on the Screen.* New York: Simon and Schuster.

_____. 1997. "Multiple Subjectivity and Virtual Community in the End of the Freudian Century." *Sociological Inquiry* 67(1): 72–84.

Twenge, J. M., and Manis, M. 1998. "First-Name Desirability and Adjustment: Self-Satisfaction, Others' Ratings, and Family Background." *Journal of Applied Social Psychology* 28(1): 41–51.

UCLA Internet Project. 2002. "Surveying the Digital Future." UCLA Center for Communication Policy. (http://www.ccp.ucla.edu)

Umberson, D. 1996. "Relations Between Adult Children and Their Parents: Psychological Well-Being." *Journal of Marriage and the Family* 51: 999–1012.

UNICEF. 2000. "Child Mortality Statistics." (http://www.childinfo.org/cmr/revis/dbl.htm)

_____. 2002. *The State of the World's Children 2002 Leadership.* New York: UNICEF Headquarters.

United Nations. 2002. *2000 Demographic Yearbook.* New York: Author.

University of Michigan. 2002. "U.S. Husbands are Doing More Housework While Wives are Doing Less." News and Information Services. (http:www.umich.edu/~newsinfo/Releases/2002/Mar02/r031202a.html)

Urban Institute. 1999. "Do We Need a National Report Card on Discrimination?" (http://www.urban.org/url.cfm?ID=900310)

U.S. Bureau of Labor Statistics. 2002. *Current Population Survey 2000.* (http://stats.bls.gov.oco)

_____. 2003. "Foreign Labor Statistics." (ftp://ftp.bls.gov/pub/special.requests/ForeignLabor/ind2000.txt)

U.S. Census Bureau. 1993. "Money Income of Households, Families and Persons in the United States: 1992." *Current Population Reports* (Series P-60, no. 184). Washington, DC: U.S. Government Printing Office.

_____. 2000. "Keeping Up with Older Adults: Older Adults, 2000." *Population Profile of the United States: 2000.* (http://www.census.gov/population/www/pop-profile/profile2000.htm)

_____. 2000a. "America's Families and Living Arrangements: March 2000." (http://www.census.gov/population/www/socdemo/hh-fam/p20–537_00.html)

_____. 2000b. "Our Diverse Population: Race and Hispanic Origin, 2000." *Population Profile of the United States: 2000* (chap. 16). (http://www.census.gov/population/www/pop-profile/profile2000.htm)

_____. 2000c. Table 1: "Nativity of the Population and Place of Birth of the Native Population: 1850–1990." (http://www.census.gov/population/www/documentation/twps0029/tab02.html)

_____. 2000d. Table 2: "Region of Birth of the Foreign Born Populations: 1850–1930; 1960–1990." (http://www.census.gov/population/www/documentation/twps0029/tab02.html)

_____. 2000e. *Current Population Survey, March 2000.* Washington, DC: U.S. Census Bureau, Population Division, Ethnic & Hispanic Statistics.

_____. 2000f. "From Birth to Seventeen: The Living Arrangements of Children, 2000." Population Profile of the United States: 2000. (http://www.census.gov/population/www/pop-profile/profile2000.htm)

_____. 2002. *Statistical Abstract of the United States: 2002.* 122d ed. Washington, DC: U.S. Census Bureau.

_____. 2002a. "Single Years of Age—Poverty Status of People in 2001." Annual Demographic Supplement, Table 23. *Current Population Survey, 2002.* (http://ferret.bls.census.gov/macro/032002/pov/new23_001.htm)

_____. 2002b. "Poverty Rate Rises, Household Income Declines, Census Bureau Reports." (http://www.census.gov/Press-Release/www/2002/cb02–124.html)

_____. 2002c. Table 10: "Work Experience During Year by Selected Characteristics and Poverty Status in 2001 of People 16 Years Old and Over." *Current Population Survey.* (http://ferret.bls.census.gov/macro/032002/pov/new10_001.htm)

_____. 2003. "Poverty Thresholds—Poverty 2002." (http://www.census.gov/hhes/poverty/threshold/thresh-2.html)

_____. 2003b. "Women Edge Men in High School Diplomas, Breaking 13-Year Deadlock." (http://www.census.gov/Press-Release/www/2003/cb03–51.html)

U.S. Conference of Mayors. 2002. "A Status Report on Hunger and Homelessness in America's Cities: 2001." (http://usmayors.org)

U.S. Department of the Army. 2003. "Stress and Combat Performance." *Leader's Manual for Combat Stress Control* (chap. 2). Washington, DC: Headquarters, Department of the Army.

U.S. Department of Education. 1988/1994. National Center for Education Statistics. *National Education Longitudinal Study of 1988, "Third Follow-Up"* (NELS: 1988/1994).

_____. 1997. *The Condition of Education 1997* (NCES 97–388). T. Smith, B. Aronstamm, B. Young, Y. Bae, S. Choy, and N. Alsalam. Washington, DC: U.S. Government Printing Office.

_____. 2000. *National Household Education Surveys Program (NHES) 1999 Data Files: Adult Education and Life-Long Learning Survey* (NCES 2000–079). Washington, DC: U.S. Government Printing Office.

U.S. Department of Education. 2001. *The Condition of Education 2001* (NCES 2001-072). Washington, DC: U.S. Government Printing Office.

U.S. Department of Education. 2002. *The Condition of Education 2002* (NCES 2002–025). Washington, DC: U.S. Government Printing Office.

_____. 2003. *The Condition of Education 2003* (NCES 2003–067). Washington, DC: U.S. Government Printing Office.

U.S. Department of Health and Human Services. 2002. "Trends in the Well-Being of America's Children and Youth." Office of the Assistant Secretary for Planning and Evaluation. (http://aspe.os.dhhs.gov/hsp/hspinddb.htm)

_____. 2002a. "A Profile of Older Americans: 2002." Administration on Aging. (http://www.hhs.gov/prof/statistics/profile/profiles2002.asp)

_____. 2002b. *Indicators of Welfare Dependence Annual Report to the Congress 2002.* (http://aspe.hhs.gov/hsp/indicators02/)

_____. 2003. *Child Maltreatment 2001.* Administration on Children, Youth and Families. Washington, DC: U.S. Government Printing Office.

_____. 2003a. "The 2003 HHS Poverty Guidelines." (http://aspe.hhs.gov/poverty/03poverty.htm)

_____. 2003b. "Improving the Health and Safety of Our Nation." FY 2004 Budget in Brief, Medicare, Medicaid #17. (http://www.hhs.gov)

U.S. Department of Justice. 1995. "Civil Jury Cases and Verdicts in Large Counties" (Special Report NCJ 154346). Bureau of Justice Statistics. Washington, DC: Author.

_____. 2000. "Crimes Against Persons Age 65 or Older, 1992–97." Bureau of Justice Statistics (NCJ 176352). Washington, DC: Author.

_____. 2001a. *Uniform Crime Reports: Crime in the United States—2000.* (http://www.fbi.gov/ucr/01cius.htm)

_____. 2001b. "National Crime Victimization Survey Violent Crime Trends, 1973–2001." (http://www.ojp.usdoj.gov/bjs/glance/tables/viotrdtab.htm)

_____. 2002. *Uniform Crime Reports: Crime in the United States—2001.* (http://www.fbi.gov/ucr/01cius.htm)

U.S. Department of Labor. 1998. "About Welfare—Myths, Facts, Challenges and Solutions." (http://wtw.doleta.gov/ resources/myths.htm)

_____. 2002. "Highlights of Women's Earnings in 2001" (Report 960). Washington, DC: Bureau of Labor Statistics.

_____. 2002b. "A Profile of the Working Poor, 2000." Bureau of Labor Statistics. (http://www.bls.gov/cps/cpswp2000.htm)

_____. 2003. "Rate of Working Poor Rises in 2001." *Monthly Labor Review: The Editor's Desk.* (http://www.bls.gov/opub/ted/2003/jun/wk4/art03.htm)

_____. 2003b. "Working Poor and Education in 2001. *Monthly Labor Review: The Editor's Desk.* (http://www.bls.gov/opub/ted/2003/jun/wk5/art02.htm)

U.S. Immigration and Naturalization Service. 2002. *2002 Yearbook of Immigration Statistics.* (http://www. immigration.gov/graphics/shared/aboutus/statistics/IMM02yrbk/IMM2002.pdf)

U.S. Surgeon General. 2001. "Women and Smoking—A Report of the Surgeon General—2001." Centers for Disease Control and Prevention, Office on Smoking and Health. (http://www.cdc.gov/tobacco/sgr_forwomen.htm.)

USA Today. 2002. "Donations, Volunteers: Giving Till it Helps." *USA Today* (March 18).

Useem, M., and Karabel, J. 1986. "Pathways to Top Corporate Management." *American Sociological Review* 51.

Vago, S. 1997. *Law and Society.* 5th ed. Englewood Cliffs, NJ: Prentice Hall.

Vago, S. 2003. *Law and Society.* 7th ed. Englewood Cliffs, NJ: Prentice Hall.

Van Avermaet, E., Buelens, H., Vanbeselaere, N., and Van Vaerenbergh, G. 1999. "Intragroup Social Influence Processes in Intergroup Behavior." *European Journal of Social Psychology* 29(5–6): 815–823.

Vande Berg, L., and Streckfuss, D. 1992. "Prime-Time Television's Portrayal of Women and the World of Work: A Demographic Profile." *Journal of Broadcasting and Electronic Media* (Spring): 195–208.

Van den Buick, J. 2000. "Is Television Bad for Your Health? Behavior and Body Image of the Adolescent 'Couch Potato.'" *Journal of Youth and Adolescence* 29(3): 273–288

van der Lippe, T., and van Dijk, L. 2002. "Comparative Research on Women's Employment." *Annual Review of Sociology* 28: 221–241.

Vanfossen, B., Jones, J., and Spade, J. 1987. "Curriculum Tracking and Status Maintenance." *Sociology of Education* 60: 104–122.

Vanman, E. J., Paul, B. Y., and Ito, T. A. 1997. "The Modern Face of Prejudice and the Structural Features That Moderate the Effect of Cooperation on Affect." *Journal of Personality and Social Psychology* 73 (November) 941–959.

Van Overwalle, F. 1997. "Dispositional Attributions Require the Joint Applications of the Methods of Difference and Agreement." *Personality and Social Psychology Bulletin* 23: 974–980.

Vartanian, L. R., Giant, C. L., and Passino, R. M. 2001. "Ally McBeal vs. Arnold Schwarzeneggar: Comparing Mass Media, Interpersonal Feedback and Gender as Predictors of Personal Satisfaction With Body Thinness and Muscularity." *Social Behavior and Personality* 29(7): 2001.

Vernez, G., and Abrahamse, A. 1996. *How Immigrants Fare in U.S. Education.* Santa Monica, CA: RAND.

Veroff, J., Douvan, E., and Kulka, R. 1981. *The Inner American: A Self-Portrait from 1957 to 1976.* New York: Basic Books.

Vinorskis, M. 1992. "Schooling and Poor Children in 19th Century America." *American Behavioral Scientist* 35(3): 313–331.

Visher, E., Visher, J., and Pasley, K. 2003. "Remarriage Familes and Stepparenting." Pp. 153–175 in F. Walsh (Ed.), *Normal Family Processes: Growing Diversity and Complexity.* 3d ed. New York: Guilford.

Vogel, C. 1998. "Sale of Homer Seascape Sets Record." *The New York Times* (May 5): A18.

Volunteer Match. 2002. *Annual Report.* (VM2002AR.pdf)

Voss, K., Markiewicz, D., and Doyle, A. B. 1999. "Friendship, Marriage, and Self-Esteem." *Journal of Social and Personal Relationships* 16(1): 103–122.

Vrij, A., and Firmin, H. R. 2002. "Beautiful Thus Innocent? The Impact of Defendants' and Victims' Physical Attractiveness and Participants Rape Beliefs on Impression Formation in Alleged Rape Cases." *International Review of Victimology* 8(3): 245–255.

Waite, L. 2000. "Trends in Men's and Women's Well-Being in Marriage." Pp. 368–392 in L. Waite, C. Bachrach, M. Hindlin, E. Thomson and A. Thornton (Eds.), *The Ties That Bind: Perspectives on Marriage and Cohabitation.* New York: Aldine de Gruyter.

Waldfogel, J. 2003. "Welfare Reform and the Child Welfare System." Paper prepared for the Joint Center for Poverty Research Conference on Child Welfare Services Research and Its Policy Implications, March 20–21, Washington, DC.

Walker, K. 1995. "Always There for Me: Friendship Patterns and Expectations Among Middle and Working Class Men and Women." *Sociological Forum* 10(2): 273–296.

Wallerstein, J., and Blakeslee, S. 1990. *Second Chances: Men, Women, and Children a Decade After Divorce.* New York: Ticknor and Fields.

Wall Street Journal. 1993. "Civil Rights: The Next Generation" (August 31): A10.

Wang, M. K. 2002. "The Ancient Foundations of Modern Nation-Building in China: The Case of the Offspring of Yan and Yellow Emperors." *Bulletin of the Institute of History and Philology Academia Sinica* 73(3): 583–624.

Wapnick, J., Mazza, J. K., and Darrow, A. A. 2000. "Effects of Performer Attractiveness, Stage Behavior, and Dress on Evaluation of Children's Piano Peformances." *Journal of Research in Music Education* 48(4): 323–336.

Wartik, N. 2002. "Hurting More, Helped Less?" *The New York Times* (June 23).

Waskul, D. D., and van der Riet, P. 2002. "The Abject Embodiment of Cancer Patients: Dignity, Selfhood, and the Grotesque Body." *Symbolic Interaction* 25(4): 487–513.

Watkins, L. M., and Johnston, L. 2000. "Screening Job Applicants: The Impact of Physical Attractiveness and Application Quality." *International Journal of Selection and Assessment* 8(2): 76–84.

Watson, D., Hubbard, B., and Wiese, D. 2000. "Self-Other Agreement in Personality and Affectivity: The Role of Acquaintanceship, Trait Visibility, and Assumed Similarity." *Journal of Personality and Social Psychology* 78: 546–558.

Watson, W. H., and Maxwell, R. J. (Eds.). 1977. *Human Aging and Dying: A Study in Sociocultural Gerontology.* New York: St. Martin's.

Weber, M. [1922] 1968. *Economy and Society.* New York: Bedminster.

Weinberg, D. 2001. "Press Briefing on 2000 Income and Poverty Estimates." *Income and Poverty 2000.* U.S. Census Bureau. (http://www.census.gov/hhes/income/income00/prs01asc.html)

Weis, L. (Ed.). 1988. *Class, Race, and Gender in American Education.* Albany: SUNY Press.

Weisberg, K. 1975. "'Under Great Temptations Here': Women and Divorce in Puritan Massachusetts." *Feminist Studies* 2(2/3): 183–193.

Weiss, M. 1998. "Parents' Rejection of Their Appearance-Impaired Newborns: Some Critical Observations Regarding the Social Myth of Bonding." *Marriage and Family Review* 27(3–4): 191–209.

Wellman, B., Haase, A. Q., Witte, J., and Hampton, K. 2001. "Does the Internet Increase, Decrease, or Supplement Social Capital? Social Networks, Participation, and Community Commitment." *American Behavioral Scientist* 45(3): 436–455.

Wellman, B., and Haythornethwaite, C. 2002. *The Internet in Everyday Life.* Oxford, UK: Blackwell.

Wells, R. 1982. *Revolutions in Americans' Lives: A Demographic Perspective on the History of Americans, Their Families and Their Society.* Westport, CT: Greenwood.

Wertheimer, B. 1977. *We Were There: The Story of Working Women in America.* New York: Pantheon.

West, C. 1994. *Race Matters.* Boston: Beacon.

Wheaton, B. 1982. "A Comparison of the Moderating Effects of Personal Coping Resources on the Impact of the Exposure to Stress in Two Groups." *Journal of Community Psychology* 10: 293–311.

———. 1983. "Stress, Personal Coping, Resources, and Psychiatric Symptoms: An Investigation of Interactive Models." *Journal of Health and Social Behavior* 24(3): 208–229.

———. 1990. "Life Transitions, Role Histories, and Mental Health." *American Sociological Review* 55(2): 209–223.

Whitehead, B. 1993. "Dan Quayle Was Right." *The Atlantic Monthly* (April): 47–84.

Wichman, H. 1970. "Effects of Isolation and Communication on Cooperation in a Two-Person Game." *Journal of Personality and Social Psychology* 16: 114–120.

Wilder, D. A., and Shapiro, P. N. 1984. "Role of Outgroup Cues in Determining Social Identity." *Journal of Personality and Social Psychology* 47: 342–348.

Wilkinson, I., and Young, L. 2002. "On Cooperating: Firms, Relations, and Networks." *Journal of Business Research* 55(2): 123–132.

Will, J. A., Self, P. A., and Dalton, N. 1976. "Maternal Behavior and Perceived Sex of Infant." *American Journal of Orthopsychiatry* 49: 135–139.

Williams, P. 2002. "Test, Tracking and Derailment." *Nation* 274(15): 9.

Williams, S. 2001. "Sexual Lying Among College Students in Close and Casual Relationships." *Journal of Applied Social Psychology* 31 (November): 2322–2338.

Williamson, D. A., Zucker, N. L., Martin, C. K., and Smeets, M. A. M. 2001. "Etiology and Management of Eating Disorders." In P. B. Sutker and H. E. Adams (Eds.), *Comprehensive Handbook of Psychopathology.* New York: Kluwer Academic/Plenum.

Willis, F. N., Willis, L. A., and Grier, J. A. 1982. "Given Names, Social Class, and Professional Achievement." *Psychological Reports* 54: 543–549.

Wilson, G., and Nias, D. 1999. "Beauty Can't Be Beat." Pp. 133–163 in L. K. Guerrero, J. A. DeVito, and M. L. Hecht (Eds.), *The Nonverbal Communication Reader: Classic and Contemporary Readings.* 2d ed. Prospect Heights, IL: Waveland.

Wilson, J. 2000. "Volunteering." *Annual Review of Sociology* 26: 215–240.

Wilson, W. J. 1980. *The Declining Significance of Race: Blacks and Changing American Institutions.* 2d ed. Chicago: University of Chicago Press.

_____. 1990. *The Truly Disadvantaged: The Inner City, the Underclass, and Public Policy.* Chicago: University of Chicago Press.

Winter, G. 2003. "Tens of Thousands Will Lose College Aid, Report Says." *The New York Times* (July 18): A13.

The Wirthlin Report. 2001. "Americans' Attitudes Toward Crime and Prevention." McLean, VA: Wirthlin Worldwide.

Wiseman, C. V., Gray, J. J., Mosimann, J. E., and Ahrens, A. H. 1992. "Cultural Expectations of Thinness in Women: An Update." *International Journal of Eating Disorders* 11(1): 85–89.

Wisman, J. D. 2000. "Competition, Cooperation, and the Future of Work." *Peace Review* 12(2): 197–203.

Witkin-Lanoil, G. 1984. *The Female Stress Syndrome: How to Recognize and Live With It.* New York: Newmarket.

Witt, S. 1997. "Parental Influence on Children's Socialization to Gender Roles." *Adolescence* 32: 253–259.

Wolf, N. 1991. *The Beauty Myth: How Images of Beauty Are Used Against Women.* New York: W. Morrow.

Wolfe, T. 1976. "The Me Decade and the Third Great Awakening." Pp. 126–167 in *Mauve Gloves and Madmen Clutter and Vine.* New York: Farrar, Straus and Giroux.

Wong, F. Y., McCreary, D. R., Bowden, C. C., and Jenner, S. M. 1991. "The Matching Hypothesis: Factors Influencing Dating Preferences." *Psychology* 28(3–4): 27–31.

Wong, J. 2002. "What's In A Name?: An Examination of Social Identities." *Journal for the Theory of Social Behavior* 32(4): 451–464.

Wood, N. T., Solomon, M. R., and Englis, B. G. 2003. "No One Looks That Good in Real Life!: Projections of the Real Versus Ideal Self in the Online Visual Space." Pp. 383–395 in L. M. Scott and R. Batra (Eds.), *Persuasive Imagery: A Consumer Response Perspective.* Mahwah, NJ: Lawrence Erlbaum.

The World Almanac and Book of Facts 1998. 1998. R. Farmighetti (Ed.). Mahwah, NJ: Funk and Wagnall.

The World Almanac and Book of Facts 2003. 2003. R. Farmighetti (Ed.). Mahwah, NJ: Funk and Wagnall.

World Health Organization. 1998. "WHO Estimates of Health Personnel." (http://www3.who.int/whosis/health_personnel/health_personnel.cfm)

World Health Organization. 1999. "Poverty and Health." (http://216.239.39.104/cobrand_univ? q=cache:OvatDdRam_0J:www.who.int/gb/EB_WHA/PDF/EB105/ee5.pdf+%22poverty%22&hl= en&ie=UTF-8)

———. 2000. "Gender, Health, and Poverty." (www.who.int/inf-fs/en/fact251.html)

———. 2003. "Child Health Research." (www.who.int/consultation-child-adolescent/Documents/ HealthyChild.pdf)

Wu, Z., and MacNeill, L. 2002. "Education, Work, and Childbearing after Age 30. *Journal of Comparative Family Studies* 33(2): 191–213.

Wuthnow, R. 1998. *Loose Connections: Civic Involvement in America's Fragmented Communities.* Cambridge, MA: Harvard University Press.

Yahoo News. 2003. "Majority in US Believes Bush 'Stretched Truth' About Iraq: Poll." (http://story.news.yahoo.com/news?tmpl=story&u=/afp/20030702/)

Zagorin, P. 1996. "The Historical Significance of Lying and Dissimulation." *Social Research* 63 (Fall): 863–912.

Zaidel, D. W., Bava, S., and Reis, V. A. 2003. "Relationship Between Facial Asymmetry and Judging Trustworthiness in Faces." *Laterality* 8(3): 225–232.

Zebrowitz, L. A., Collins, M. A., and Dutta, R. 1998. "The Relationship Between Appearance and Personality Across the Life Span." *Personality and Social Psychology Bulletin* 24(7): 736–749.

Zebrowitz, L. A., Hall, J., Murphy, N. A., and Rhodes, G. 2002. "Looking Smart and Looking Good: Facial Cues to Intelligence and Their Origins." *Personality and Social Psychology Bulletin* 28(2): 238–249.

Zeitlin, M., Lutterman, K. G., and Russell, J. W. 1977. "Death in Vietnam: Class, Poverty, and the Risks of War." Pp. 143–155 in M. Zeitlin (Ed.), *American Society Incorporated.* 2d ed. Chicago: Rand McNally.

Zelizer, V. 1985. *Pricing the Priceless Child.* New York: Basic Books.

Zimmerman, M. 2000. "Women's Health and Gender Bias in Medical Education." *Research in the Sociology of Health Care* 17: 121–138.

Zimmerman, T., Haddock, S., Ziemba, S., and Rust, A. 2001. "Family Organizational Labor: Who's Calling the Plays?" *Journal of Feminist Family Therapy* 13(2–3): 65–90.

Zitner, A. 2003. "Nation's Birthrate Drops to its Lowest Level Since 1909." *Los Angeles Times* (June 26): 1.

Zuckerman, M., Miyake, K., and Elkin, C. S. 1995. "Effects of Attractiveness and Maturity of Face and Voice on Interpersonal Impressions." *Journal of Research in Personality* 29(2): 253–272.

Glossary / Index

AARP (American Association of Retired Persons), 55, 56, 62

Achieved status: status earned or gained through personal effort, 132

Administration of Children and Families, 141

AFDC (Aid to Families with Dependent Children), 187, 192

Affirmative action, 125, 126

Age Discrimination in Employment Act, 55

Age structure: the distribution that results from dividing a population according to socially defined, age-based categories: childhood, adolescence, young adulthood, middle age, and old age, 62

Aging. *See* Geriatric population

AIDS Memorial Quilt, 84

Alzheimer's disease, 59, 87

Amber Alert system, 30

American Association of Retired Persons (AARP), 55, 56, 62

American Civil Liberties Union, 154

American Dream, 194, 195

American Immigrant Wall of Honor, 84

American Jewish Committee, 16

American Society for Aesthetic Plastic Surgery, 91-92

Andersen Worldwide, 158

Annenberg School of Communication, 144

Anonymity, 87

Anorexia nervosa, 94

Anthropology, 18, 131

Anticipatory socialization: socialization that prepares a person to assume a role in the future, 60

Appearance norms: society's generally accepted standards of appropriate body height, body weight, distribution or shape, bone structure, skin color, etc., 4, 93

attractiveness quotient, identity and, 92

body-transition rituals, 93-94

body weight/body image, 92-93

conformity/deviance and, 93

cosmetics industry and, 92

cultural capital and, 91

cultural inconsistency and, 89

definition of, 94-95

life cycle stages and, 90

looking-glass self and, 95

objects, evaluation of, 95

plastic surgery and, 91-92, 94

positive characteristics and, 90-91

self-fulfilling prophecy and, 91

socialization process and, 92-93

valuation/rewards and, 90

Ascribed status: status assigned or given without regard to person's efforts or desires, 132

Assimilation: the process by which immigrant groups come to adopt the dominant culture of their new homeland as their own, 203, 206